the
politics
of
power

A CRITICAL INTRODUCTION
TO AMERICAN GOVERNMENT

the politics of power

A CRITICAL INTRODUCTION TO AMERICAN GOVERNMENT

Ira Katznelson
University of Chicago

Mark Kesselman
Columbia University

HARCOURT BRACE JOVANOVICH, INC.

New York   Chicago   San Francisco   Atlanta

ISBN: 0-15-570744-2

Library of Congress Catalog Card Number: 74-20319

Printed in the United States of America

To the memory of Paul Kesselman,
to Anne Kesselman
and to
Ephraim and Sylvia Katznelson

preface

Our aim in this book is to introduce students to American government and to explore how the interplay of politics and power influences their lives. We examine the country's political institutions and practices, how they evolved and changed over the years, and how they function today. However, rather than presenting what exists as natural and desirable, we attempt to describe the politics of American power from a coherent, critical perspective.

We do not assume that American politics is working successfully, or that piecemeal reform is sufficient to make it work successfully. Nor do we accept the prevailing American creed that defines democracy in procedural terms and confines it to the selection of government officials. It is our view that to achieve genuine democracy, we must be equally concerned with the way in which goods, services, and culture are produced and distributed as well as with the way formal governmental institutions affect the lives of Americans.

For these reasons, we discuss the workings of the entire socioeconomic structure with particular attention to the relationship between American capitalism and politics. We also stress the fundamental inequalities—educational, political, economic, and social—that exist among groups, what these inequalities mean in terms of a group's ability to understand and defend its interests, and the need to question whether what exists is freely chosen by the majority.

Many people contributed generously to the writing of this book. Deborah Socolow Katznelson's and Wendy Kesselman's enthusiastic encouragement, critical assistance, and love helped in the most important ways. Irwin Gertzog, Allegheny College, and J. David Greenstone and Benjamin I. Page, University of Chicago, read the manuscript in its entirety; the book has benefited from their sympathetic yet telling criticism. For their careful help on various chapters, we wish to thank James David Barber, Duke University; Anne H. Bedlington, Smith College; Shawn Bernstein; Philip Brenner, Trinity College; Lief Carter, University of Georgia; François D'Arcy, University of Grenoble; Murray Edelman, University of Wisconsin; Francis H. Heller,

University of Kansas; Thomas Lewis; Peter Lupsha, University of New Mexico; William Marvin; Grant McConnell, University of California at Santa Cruz; Seymour Melman, Columbia University; Richard M. Pious, Barnard College; and David Vogel, University of California at Berkeley.

We are the fortunate beneficiaries of the superb craftsmanship and professionalism of the editorial and production staff at Harcourt Brace Jovanovich. In particular we wish to thank Elizabeth Holland, Lee Shenkman, and Thomas Williamson, whose efforts are reflected on every page. Our thanks also to Nancy Demmon and Ann MacCauley Frankel, who typed most of the manuscript, and to research assistants Arie Bucheister, Ralph Perez, and Cyrus Veeser.

IRA KATZNELSON
MARK KESSELMAN

contents

9

formal representation: congress 284

10

the quality of justice 315

managing political struggle 353

11

ideology and the creation of consciousness 355

12

urban politics and social control 402

13

the welfare state   429

conclusion   459

14

capitalism, socialism, and democracy   461

capitalism
and
democracy

1

the politics
of power

On Wednesday, September 18, 1971, during the recreation period at New York's Attica State Prison, a white inmate who coached the prison football team was demonstrating some plays to a young black prisoner. A prison guard noticed the two and mistakenly thought they were fighting. He approached the black man from the rear, placing a hand on his shoulder. The prisoner whirled around and, to the amazement of the other inmates, hit the guard. When the guard tried to summon the two prisoners, they protested and refused to come.

Two months earlier, Attica prisoners had sent a petition to State Corrections Commissioner Russell Oswald, requesting that they "get more than one shower a week, that our food be covered to keep the flies off, that the bugs be washed off the lettuce, and that they improve the medical treatment."[1] State officials had promised to consider instituting reforms in the future, but no further action had been taken by the time of the incident.

Later that evening, guards removed the two prisoners from their cells. A rumor quickly spread that they had been beaten. The next morning, a large number of prisoners seized one of the

[1] Nat Hentoff, "Rockefeller's Bullets and the Press," *Village Voice,* Sept. 23, 1971.

3

four cell blocks, holding thirty-nine guards as hostages. The prisoners swiftly organized a rough system of government and drew up demands for releasing the hostages and ending the uprising. The demands included the right to telephone relatives at the prisoners' own expense, an end to political censorship of mail, and the establishment of procedures to deal with inmate grievances. After two days of negotiations between Commissioner Oswald and a prisoner negotiating committee (attended by a group of invited outside observers), the commissioner agreed to all of the thirty demands but two: the replacement of Attica's warden and immunity from possible criminal charges arising from participation in the uprising. (Prisoners never asked for a reduction of their original sentences.) Since many of the demands that Oswald now granted had been accepted in principle by prison authorities for months but not implemented, prisoners were skeptical about his verbal assurances. Another reason for their skepticism was that some of the prisoners had been at Auburn State Prison the previous year when, following a one-day uprising, prisoners released hostages on a promise of "no reprisals" that prison authorities later repudiated. A critical turning point feeding distrust occurred when Commissioner Oswald delivered an impassioned address to prisoners requesting that they free the hostages. At the climax of his speech, he was interrupted by a television crewman who said, "We had a bad angle. Could you repeat that?" And he did.

When negotiations on the final two demands were deadlocked, the observer committee called on Governor Nelson Rockefeller to intervene personally by coming to Attica. Rockefeller refused, replying that no useful purpose could be served by his presence. Instead, he ordered an assault on the prison by New York State troopers equipped with tear gas and heavy arms. New York State Assemblyman Clark Wemple, chairman of the legislature's prisons subcommittee, who had been with Commissioner Oswald at the final strategy sessions, stated, "There was absolutely no doubt in anyone's mind that if we went in there, the guards would be killed."[2] Nevertheless, the action had to be taken, according to Commissioner Oswald, since the uprising "threatened the security of the entire correctional facility of the state," and even "the destruction of our free society."[3]

[2] *New York Times,* October 4, 1971.
[3] *New Republic,* September 25, 1971.

During the several-hour assault on the prison by state troopers, forty persons died: nine of the thirty-eight hostages and thirty-one prisoners. The *New York Times'* front-page account reported, "In this worst of recent American prison revolts, several of the hostages—prison guards and civilian workers—died when convicts slashed their throats with knives."[4] The *Times'* editorial accounted for the widespread violence and brutality of prison guards and state troopers by explaining, "Prisoners slashed the throats of utterly helpless, unarmed guards. . . . Police officers storming the prison to rescue the hostages and restore order were stirred to savage retaliation by the horror within."[5] That day's *New York Daily News* account was entitled "I Saw Seven Throats Cut," and another story in the newspaper stated, "Eight of the dead hostages died of slashed throats. The ninth was stabbed to death." The *Wall Street Journal* reported, "A task force of 1,700 New York State troopers and militiamen were ordered to storm the prison walls after the convicts 'Callously herded eight hostages within our view with weapons at their throats,' state officials said. The eight hostages' throats were slit as the assault began."[6]

Governor Rockefeller justified the assault by saying that prisoners "had carried out cold-blooded killings they had threatened from the start of their takeover." Rockefeller also praised the troopers' "skill," "courage," and "restraint." President Nixon sent Rockefeller a telegram praising his courage. New York Senator James Buckley echoed the sentiment of many when he stated, "Retribution must be swift and merciless for those responsible for killings."

Several hours after the prison had been retaken, Deputy Commissioner of Corrections Walter B. Dunbar led a tour of legislators through the prison and pointed to a naked black man seated on a table. Dunbar said the man was guilty of castrating one of the dead prison guards and described the mutilation "in lurid detail. He then described the slashing of the throats of the slain hostages."[7]

The next day, however, after official autopsies had been performed on the dead guards by the local coroner, the original account of their deaths, which newspapers had unquestioningly

[4]*New York Times,* September 24, 1971.
[5]*New York Times,* September 24, 1971.
[6]*Wall Street Journal,* September 24, 1971.
[7]*New York Times,* October 4, 1971.

accepted as accurate, was proved completely false. No hostages had been mutilated or had had their throats slashed. In every case, death was the result of bullet wounds from guns fired by state troopers. Although it had been known by authorities that the prisoners did not have guns, state troopers had used shotguns that fired shells containing lethal .32-caliber slugs that dispersed in a random pattern.

After they were captured, the inmates were stripped naked and forced to run through a gauntlet "of club-wielding troopers . . . who shouted epithets." Then they were forced to crawl on their elbows and knees into the cell block with their faces in the dirt. "Keep your nigger nose down," some troopers shouted. "Don't you know state troopers don't like niggers."[8] (Eighty-five percent of the prisoners were black or Puerto Rican, virtually all guards and state troopers white.)

Governor Rockefeller described his own feelings two days after the uprising had been suppressed. "I want to tell you I just was absolutely overwhelmed," he said. "I just didn't see how it [putting down the uprising] was possible, with 1,200 men in there armed, with electrified barricades, with trenches, with a pledge which said they would all go right down to the last man, how it was going to be possible."

He was then asked: "What does this tell you about the prisoners, Governor, the fact that so many men did emerge unharmed?"

"I think," he replied, "what it tells is that the use of gas is a fantastic instrument in a situation of this kind."[9]

* * *

After Robert Kennedy's assassination in 1968, Congress authorized the Secret Service to take all steps necessary to protect the safety of presidents and presidential candidates. The Secret Service was granted additional funds for security measures to make it easier to guard the president. Five years later, Congress repealed this open-ended authorization. The measure had proved more costly than anticipated.

At the time he was elected president in 1968, Richard Nixon purchased two houses, one in Key Biscayne, Florida, the other in San Clemente, California. In 1973, at the time of the Watergate

[8]*New York Times,* October 4, 1971.
[9]*New York Times,* October 4, 1971.

investigation by Congress, a San Diego newspaper charged that Nixon had used large sums of government money to improve his homes. The White House angrily retorted that a total of only $38,000 of federal funds had been spent on the two homes—for security measures authorized by Congress. However, not long afterward, the General Services Administration (GSA—the government agency responsible for overseeing government expenditures) reported that the expenses on the San Clemente home alone exceeded $1 million, that a similar sum had been spent on Nixon's Key Biscayne property, that additional government funds had been used to improve a home for Julie Nixon Eisenhower (Nixon's daughter), and that the final total might run higher. Several months later, the GSA was forced to revise its estimates again: the final figure released exceeded $17 million.[10]

Among the "security improvements" that taxpayers had provided for their president were: a silver service and a new kitchen for Mrs. Nixon, a $12,000 redwood fence, five brass lanterns costing $2,000 used at the president's pool, furniture for Mr. Nixon's private den, interior lighting, flower gardens, a lawn sprinkler system, a beach hut, and roof repairs. Many local residents could not understand why, despite the value added to the San Clemente property, Mr. Nixon's local property taxes were still assessed at the preimprovement rate, a tax saving for the president of approximately $65,000 between 1969 and 1973.[11]

In repealing its authorization for unlimited improvements to protect presidential security, Congress specified that future presidential requests would have to be justified on an item-by-item basis.

* * *

The United States is not among the ninety-six countries that have ratified the 1925 Geneva Protocol banning chemical and biological warfare. At the time the treaty was originally debated in the Senate, a coalition of the Army and the American chemical industry was instrumental in preventing its ratification. In December 1969, the United Nations General Assembly, by a vote of eighty to three, with twenty-six abstentions, declared that the use of all chemicals in war violates the protocol. The three countries that voted against the resolution were Portugal, which has used

[10]*New York Times*, March 22, 1974.
[11]*New York Times*, October 13, 1973.

gas and herbicides against guerrillas in its colony Angola; and Australia and the United States, which were using them against civilian and military targets in Indochina.

Secretary of State William Rogers, testifying before the Senate Foreign Relations Committee, disingenuously defended the use of tear gas, "We think it is more humane than napalm or other methods of warfare." Others who appeared before the committee, however, testified that the major purpose of the gas was to flush out those in hiding so that they could be killed by other means including napalm and cluster bombs. When pressed, Rogers retorted, "If you do not use the tear gas, you would be using two lethal weapons, say napalm and something else." Later an assistant secretary of defense stated that this policy "has been a very important factor in avoiding unnecessary suffering."[12]

* * *

In 1966, General Motors opened a new Chevrolet plant at Lordstown, Ohio, that turned out 60 cars per hour, the company's usual production rate. In late summer 1971, the company brought in a new management team that introduced production methods aimed at increasing the number of cars produced to 110 per hour. The pace of work, which traditionally had been rapid, became maddening. A worker whose assembly-line job was the installation of front seats was now expected to perform eight different operations—walking about twenty feet to a conveyor belt that transported the seats, lifting the seat and hauling it to the car, lifting the car's carpet, bending to fasten the bolts by hand, fastening them with an air gun, replacing the carpet, and putting a sticker on the hood signifying that the job had been properly done—in a total period of thirty-six seconds.

In the winter and spring of 1971–72, plant workers, mainly high-school graduates in their twenties, began to sabotage the work process. The workers began to pass many cars down the production line with bolts and parts missing. Unassembled engines were passed along, covered by their outer shells. More than half the cars that came off the production line had to be returned for major repairs.

This situation was threatening both to General Motors and to the leadership of the workers' union, the United Automobile Workers (UAW). The company's production and profits were

---

[12]Robert C. Bazell, "CBW Ban: Nixon Would Exclude Tear Gas and Herbicides," *Science*, vol. 172, no. 3980, April 16, 1971, pp. 246–48.

jeopardized; even more importantly, the command authority of the plant's management to regulate the work process was directly challenged by the workers' in-plant protests. Similarly, the UAW had much to lose, since the workers' sabotage bypassed the union completely and implicitly raised issues of worker control that transcended the routine pattern of wage bargaining between the company and the union.

Thus, it was in the interests of both the company and the union officials to regain control over the workers. When 350 workers were dismissed for "efficiency" reasons in February, the UAW stepped in and called for a strike vote. In March, Lordstown's workers walked off the job. The strike did not revolve around the issue of the debilitating work process, but concentrated instead on wages, layoffs, and back pay for those who had been fired. The spring strike ended with a proclaimed victory by the union. The real victory belonged not to the strikers but to company and union officials who had succeeded in restoring normal patterns of bargaining and in cooling the workers' discontent by channeling it in traditional directions. The union had gained *for* wages and job security; control of the work process was bargained away in return. Working conditions were unchanged.

Although the union leadership claimed "total victory" at the end of the strike, some workers were not so sure. One bitterly complained, "Before the strike the union was in favor of not working faster than you could. Now people are afraid not to work. The company and the union say everything is settled, we had a strike. But what did we achieve for it?"[13]

PRODUCTION AND POLITICS

These cases illustrate what we mean by the politics of power. In each case, power, which is the essence of politics, was distributed unequally. Those with power were able to defend their interests, protect their positions, and achieve their goals, and they did so at the expense of those without power. Attica prison officials emerged from the rebellion with their authority intact; the

[13]Stanley Aronowitz, *False Promises* (New York, 1973), p. 43.

prisoners were shot, flogged, and brutalized. United States government officials were able to implement their ideas about how to protect American interests in Southeast Asia; many Vietnamese died as a result. President Nixon lavished $17 million on improving his private properties; the public paid the bill. Lordstown workers attempted to gain some control over their work environment; company and union management successfully thwarted their efforts.

Like wealth, power can be used for a variety of ends, according to the possessor's interests and goals. But unlike wealth, power is not measured by material goods alone; it is composed of many resources: social background, education, wealth, position, access to others in positions of authority, and the ability to exercise control through institutions such as the justice system and the media. As we shall see in this book, the possession of these resources is related to one's position in the class structure.

As with any resource, the use of power may involve costs and sacrifices. A's attempts to carry out his goals may be resisted by B. For A to succeed, he may have to expend some of his resources to overcome B's resistance. Although power-holders try to minimize the costs of achieving goals and may even renounce the goals when the costs are too high, in extreme cases they may be willing to make sacrifices to achieve their ends. Governor Rockefeller's image as a humane politician was tarnished at Attica—and hence he lost a measure of his political power—but he was prepared to pay the price to crush the rebellion.

To understand the politics of power—and powerlessness—we need to begin at the most fundamental level: the basis on which society is organized. As we shall argue throughout this book, the way people organize the production and distribution of necessities and other goods is the most critical factor shaping organized human life. According to Karl Marx:

> Men can be distinguished from animals by consciousness, by religion or anything else you like. They themselves begin to distinguish themselves from animals as soon as they begin to *produce* their means of subsistence. . . . By producing their means of subsistence men are indirectly producing their actual material life.[14]

[14]Karl Marx, *The German Ideology* (New York, 1947), p. 7.

The particular form that production takes divides members of a society into different groups depending on their relationship to the means of production. The process of producing goods thus involves more than producing material articles; it also involves producing and reproducing through time relationships connected with production. In a feudal order, for example, the process of production created anew in each generation the relationship of serf to feudal lord.

In the United States, production is organized within a capitalist framework. The central relationship in a capitalist order is "the relation of capital and labor itself, of capitalist and worker."[15] Most members of the community contribute their labor to producing goods and services. But the tools of production—the factories, machines, and raw materials—are privately owned and controlled by a small minority.

Structure and Interests

The relationship between these classes is systematic and relatively stable and constitutes a social *structure*. The most important feature of this structure is the fundamental contradiction between the interests of the dominant minority who own and control the production apparatus and the interests of workers who must sell their labor for a wage. Those in control make decisions that shape the lives of all Americans. They are also the principal beneficiaries of capitalist production and receive substantially more of the material rewards and social benefits from the process. Those who work for wages have little say over the broad shape of the society or over major decisions affecting their lives, and they receive a lesser share of capitalism's rewards and benefits.

This basic structure underpins the complexity of everyday life in the United States. Although Americans have diverse ethnic and racial backgrounds, work in different kinds of jobs, live in different places, and hold widely different political opinions, all are part of the class structure and are affected by it. Capitalist production interpenetrates virtually every aspect of American society, including the place of racial minorities and women, the quality of city neighborhoods, and the political choices made by government officials and citizens.

[15]Karl Marx, *Grundrisse,* translated by Martin Nicolaus (New York, 1974), p. 458.

Thus we can say that it is in the *interest* of members of the capitalist class to use their resources to maintain their position, protect existing arrangements, and thereby freeze inequality. We can also say that, logically, it is in the interest of the subordinate majority to direct their limited resources to the overthrow of the capitalist system.

From this perspective, widespread challenges against the basic contours of the social structure should dominate American politics. Such challenges do occur (as at Attica) and political life is marked by incessant conflict and struggle (as at Lordstown). Yet much of the everyday political life we observe— speechmaking, elections, congressional debate—does not appear to be a playing out of the fundamental antagonisms of interest. We are thus confronted by the paradox of apparent political stability despite structural class inequality.

Mediations

There are two ways to analyze the paradox. The first sees the absence of structural challenge as implying support for existing arrangements, and therefore it denies the political relevance of the class structure. This view sees people's political behavior merely as the product of everyday political life, including party activity, interest-group competition, and electioneering. We reject this view since it misses the essential link between structure and behavior.

Our preferred explanation of apparent stability begins with the concept that people's behavior results most fundamentally from the acting out of structurally rooted interests. Diagramatically, this relationship between structure and behavior can be understood as follows:

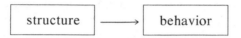

In this view the social structure is like a coiled spring whose natural thrust is to uncoil.

Though this is the point of departure for the analysis of political behavior, it is a starting point only, since structural antagonisms are not translated directly into behavior. People do not experience the social structure abstractly or analytically, but concretely in their daily lives. These arenas of experience and action may be called *mediations* since they intervene, or mediate, between the social structure and people's behavior:

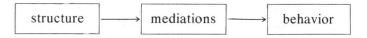

Adapting the German sociologist Max Weber's analysis of social life, we can distinguish three arenas of mediation: work, culture, and politics.[16] Each captures an important segment of people's lives. Each incorporates the basic capital-labor relationship. But each does so in different ways. The nature of these three mediations may foster the expression of the capital-labor antagonism or may suppress it.

The mediation *work* refers to the occupational world, the places where most people sell their labor for a wage. There is an incredible diversity to the ways people experience work: dishwashers, computer technicians, engineers, baseball players, housewives, and the unemployed. The character of the work experience is probably the most important factor in the way people develop a conception of themselves and of the world in which they live. As in the other two arenas—culture and politics—underlying the immense variety of work experiences is the distinction between the majority of wage earners and those who own and control the means of production.

However, the conflict of interest between labor and capital may or may not be expressed in work-place struggles. Some jobs facilitate class-related organization and action, while others do not. Work places such as automobile factories—where large numbers of workers are brought together in a common situation, communicate easily, and are clearly subject to direct hierarchical orders of factory managers—are likely to be the scene of organized worker activity. At Lordstown, for example, workers collectively challenged the authority of corporate management to define the organization and pace of work. Other work situations may be similar to the factory in terms of the capital-labor

[16]Max Weber, *The Theory of Social and Economic Organizations* (New York, 1947); and Hans Gerth and C. Wright Mills, eds., *From Max Weber* (New York, 1946).

relationship but different in the way that relationship is experienced. Some workers, like doormen, work alone and therefore cannot communicate easily and combine with other workers. Work situations may also decrease the likelihood of working-class organization because workers are given the trappings of status (typists and other clerical employees) compared to manual workers or because the labor market is so harsh that organization would bring swift reprisal (sharecroppers, dishwashers). Within the mediation of the work place, therefore, the antagonism of capital and labor may be expressed in different ways.

This book concentrates on politics as mediation. The place to begin analyzing this mediation is government or the state. The vastly increased role of the state in the twentieth century is one of the most important and widely noted features of American politics. The national government reaches into every area of American life: through welfare programs, military spending, education from the preschool level to postgraduate training and research, management of the economy, taxation, the legal system, and surveillance of political dissidents. The government's power is indeed enormous. But what needs to be asked is, to what ends is this power directed? Does the state facilitate or restrain structurally rooted antagonisms?

THE STATE

The state has two broad functions. The first is to contribute to the stable operation of the system of production. In a capitalist order, successful production means making capitalism work, which in turn means insuring that the productive apparatus generates a surplus that can be invested for growth. We come here to one of the main features of capitalism. Unlike any other system of production, capitalism requires constant growth in order to make profits possible for those who own and control capital. Companies cannot maintain high profits simply by meeting the existing demand for their products; they must continually seek ways to increase the demand—through advertising, new packaging and design, planned obsolescence, and by expanding into foreign markets. To achieve continuous economic growth in the United

States and abroad, the government has been forced to intervene in the productive process to an ever greater extent. The interlocking alliance of government and corporate producers in the United States, discussed in Part Three, may be considered the single most significant feature of American political life in the twentieth century. The usual explanation for this development emphasizes collusion between business leaders and political officials. This explanation suggests that, as a result of shared social background, illicit deals, outright corruption, or pressure applied by business groups, some form of conspiracy is at work in the state's involvement with capitalism. This interpretation is inadequate. Although it is true that political officials and business leaders are often recruited from similar backgrounds, that backroom deals and outright corruption occur (as the Watergate events amply documented), and that business groups use their resources to lobby for preferred outcomes, these do not constitute the most important links between capitalism and the state.

What is omitted from the conspiracy explanation is the fact that the state in a capitalist order has no choice but to support the successful functioning of capitalism. The state depends on the productive apparatus to generate a surplus that provides the revenue for state activities. As Richard Goodwin, former White House adviser to Presidents Kennedy and Johnson, observes, "One can no more expect government to attack the sources of economic power than one can anticipate that rock and roll groups will espouse the dissolution of the record industry."[17] A state that limited or disrupted capitalist production would thereby be risking its own existence. To put it another way, it is not so much that the state as a separate entity supports capitalism as that the state is an integral part of the capitalist order.

The government's attempt to contribute to successful capitalist production sharpens the contradiction between capital and labor. This dichotomy is expressed in struggles in diverse arenas of everyday life, in which subordinates attempt to overcome structural inequality: at Attica, the struggle took the form of a prisoners' revolt; at Lordstown, of a wildcat strike. These struggles are a constant feature of American politics. Focusing on

[17]Richard N. Goodwin, "The Structure Itself Must Change," *Rolling Stone* (June 6, 1974), p. 38.

political struggle brings us to the state's second function—social control. In the clash between capital and labor (the structurally dominant and the structurally subordinate), the state is not a neutral arbiter of conflict; the state's power is directed to maintaining the dominance of capital.

State actions can thus be understood as an attempt to *manage but not overcome* the tensions and contradictions of capitalism. This attempt to contain the conflicts created by a capitalist order sets the broad limits of American politics. The state does not seek to end all conflict, nor could it: the basic capitalist contradiction is expressed in so many ways that the suppression of all conflict is a hopeless task. Rather, the state acts to prevent conflict from eliminating the capital-labor relationship and transforming the boundaries of the social order.

This task of controlling and managing behavior may take physical, symbolic, and institutional forms.

Physical control—outright coercion and intimidation— comes to mind first. Coercion involves the actual use of force to prevent the emergence of organized opposition (Attica). Coercion is the most vivid, open, and brutal means of control. Intimidation by the state involves the threat rather than the actual use of force. The threat may be symbolic, implying the use of force in the future, or it may be direct and immediate, in which case it is nearly indistinguishable from coercion. Examples include surveillance of private citizens (wiretapping, infiltration of dissident groups, secret compilation of unconfirmed complaints), threats by authorities to use force against those who provoke them (warning passively resisting hippies that they will be run over), and the massive deployment of police conspicuously equipped with clubs, helmets, guns, gas masks, and disabling chemicals at the scene of a possible confrontation.

The second form of social control is symbolic and seeks to control people's minds rather than their bodies. Like physical control, the purpose of symbolic control is to prevent the emergence of resistance. From the perspective of authorities, it is much more advantageous to prevent the development of opposition in the first place than to use force to suppress opposition that has already arisen. Control through symbols attempts to distort people's awareness of their structural position.

One example of control by symbols is the use of patriotic images such as the flag, pictures of the White House, and references to historic events (often inaccurately presented) to foster a diffuse pride and support for existing arrangements. Symbolic control also takes the form of persuasion, such as the use of arguments and evidence by political leaders to defend and legitimize their policies. Persuasion, however, can be carried out by the appearance, but not the substance, of rational discourse. A prime example of this involves presidential rhetoric and power. After major decisions are made, the president may preempt prime time on television to present his views to the American people. The address takes the form of a rational, nonpartisan presentation of the arguments "in the national interest." There is no dialogue, no question-and-answer period. Even when the president's views are subsequently challenged, the terms of the discussion are set by his address. Moreover, no one can command the authority, expertise, or access to the mass audience that the president can.

The third form of social control is institutional. According to sociologists Peter Berger and Thomas Luckmann, institutions

> by the very fact of their existence, control human conduct by setting up predefined patterns of conduct, which channel [conduct] in one direction as against the many other directions what would theoretically be possible.[18]

By formalizing power relations between participants, institutions such as the courts and political party organizations inherently freeze structural contradictions and confirm the hierarchy of existing power relationships.

Paradoxically, political participation can be a form of institutional control. Obviously, authentic participation in the classic democratic manner permits participants to shape conditions that affect their lives. Participation, however, is not always authentic. Subordinates may participate in political activities in ways that do not challenge the distribution of power and that in fact may reinforce structural inequality. Under conditions of inauthentic participation, there is no meaningful opportunity for participants to bring about changes that would be in their interest. An example might be an election in which candidates basically agree on existing structural arrangements. For the structurally subordi-

---

[18]Peter Berger and Thomas Luckmann, *The Social Construction of Reality* (New York, 1967), p. 55.

nate, such an election represents a case of inauthentic participation because it cannot possibly overcome patterns of structural inequality. Inauthentic participation thus serves an important political function. By diverting energies of subordinates into system-supporting activity, inauthentic participation can be used by authorities as evidence of the legitimate, democratic, open, and responsive nature of the political system.

We said earlier that political struggles reflect the antagonism of interest between capital and labor. However, that antagonism is managed by authorities' application of the three forms of control. Within the mediation of politics, their use of control techniques, in such diverse sites as Congress, the party system, the judiciary, and urban affairs, aims to contain the potential explosion of structural contradictions.

The *Politics of Power* addresses three central questions. How does the system of corporate-capitalist production structure American political life? How does the contradiction between capital and labor get expressed in political conflict? And conversely, how, in a country with democratic procedures, is politics used to maintain a class division that is contrary to the interests of the majority?

The issues discussed in this chapter provide a framework for the analysis of American politics. The primacy of production and the concepts of structure, interest, power, and mediation are the scaffolding of this framework. This introductory discussion, however, is not yet complete. The United States, by most current definitions, is a political democracy. Before proceeding to our view of the politics of power in the United States, we must first ask, what is the place of democracy within the American political system?

2

standards of democracy

In 1961, political scientist Robert Dahl published an influential study of politics in New Haven, Connecticut. By commonly accepted standards, he argued, the city was a democracy, since virtually all its adult citizens were legally entitled to vote, their votes were honestly counted, and "two political parties contest elections, offer rival slates of candidates, and thus present the voters with at least some outward show of choice." Although the city's residents were legally equal at the ballot box, they were substantively unequal. Economic inequality in New Haven contrasted sharply with its formal political equality. Fewer than one-sixteenth of the taxpayers owned one-third of the city's property. In the wealthiest ward, one family out of four had an income three times the city average; the majority of the families in the poorest ward earned under $2000 per year. Only one out of thirty adults in the poorest ward had attended college, as contrasted to nearly half of those in the richest ward.[1]

This contrast between legal equality and substantive inequality is characteristic of the United States as a whole. Today, no American over the age of eighteen faces legal barriers (except residency requirements) to voting. But, as in New Haven, the

[1]Robert Dahl, *Who Governs?: Democracy and Power in an American City (New Haven, Conn., 1961), pp. 3–4.*

Table 2-1

Percentage of money income received by each fifth of families and individuals and by top 5 percent

Families and individuals ranked from lowest to highest income	1947	1957	1962	1967	1968
Total	100%	100%	100%	100%	100%
Lowest fifth	4	4	3	4	4
Second fifth	11	11	11	11	11
Middle fifth	17	18	17	17	17
Fourth fifth	24	25	25	24	25
Highest fifth	46	43	44	44	44
Top 5 percent	19	17	17	16	15

Source: From *Rich Man, Poor Man* (p. 50) by Herman P. Miller. Copyright © 1971 by Thomas Y. Crowell Company, Inc., with permission of the publisher.

disparities in material resources among Americans are very wide. The chief executives of the country's major corporations earn astounding salaries. In 1972, Richard Gerstenberg of General Motors took home $875,000 ($16,450 per week); J. Paul Austin of Coca-Cola, $300,000; and Harold Geneen of International Telephone and Telegraph, $813,000.[2] At the opposite and more crowded end of the income spectrum are the very poor. According to the federal government, approximately twenty-five million Americans are poverty stricken; with a family income of under $4,000 per year, they earn less in one year than Richard Gerstenberg does in two days.

In a capitalist system, there are two related areas of economic inequality: income and wealth. In the United States, the pattern of income distribution has remained virtually unchanged in this century. In 1910, the top fifth of income earners received 46 percent of the national income; today, the richest fifth's share is still over 40 percent. The share of the bottom fifth has actually declined from over 8 percent in 1910 to just over 5 percent today.[3]

This pattern of inequality in income is tied directly to even

[2]*Forbes,* May 15, 1973, pp. 225–26.
[3]Charles Anderson, *The Political Economy of Social Class* (Englewood Cliffs, N. J., 1974), chapter four; Douglas Dowd, *The Twisted Dream: Capitalist Development in the United States Since 1776* (Cambridge, Mass., 1974), pp. 117–21.

Table 2–2
Percentage share of wealth held by fifths, top 5 percent and top 1 percent, 1962

Consumer units ranked from lowest to highest wealth	Total wealth	Corporate stock
Poorest fifth	(–)*	(–)
Second through fourth fifth	23%	3%
Richest fifth	77	97
Top 5 percent	53	86
Top 1 percent	33	62

*(–) means less than ½ of 1 percent.
Source: Letitia Upton and Nancy Lyons, "Basic Facts: Distribution of Personal Income and Wealth in the United States," in Douglas Dowd, *The Twisted Dream*. Copyright © 1974 by Winthrop Publishers, Inc. Cambridge, Massachusetts.

greater disparities in the distribution of wealth—ownership of corporate stock, businesses, homes and property, cash reserves, government bonds, and retirement funds. Roughly 20 percent of personal wealth in the United States is owned by one-third of 1 percent of the population; the richest 1 percent own over 28 percent of the wealth; and the top 10 percent of Americans own over half (56 percent). The bottom 10 percent actually owe more than they own.[4]

Is the combination of legal equality and class inequality democratic? Dahl put the question this way, "In a system where nearly every adult may vote but where knowledge, wealth, social position, access to officials, and other resources are unequally distributed, who actually governs? . . . How does a 'democratic' system work amid inequality of resources?"[5] He placed quotation marks around the term *democratic* because its meaning in this situation is unclear. Should a democratic system be measured only by legal standards of equality, such as fair and open election procedures, or should it be measured by substantive standards, according to the distribution of resources? What, in short, is the relationship of capitalism and democracy?

[4]Frank Ackerman, Howard Birnbaum, James Wetzler, and Andrew Zimbalist, "Income Distribution in the United States," *Review of Radical Political Economics* 3 (Summer 1971): 24–26; Thomas E. Weisskopf, "Capitalism and Inequality," in Richard Edwards, Michael Reich, and Thomas Weisskopf, eds., *The Capitalist System*, (Englewood Cliffs, N. J., 1972), pp. 125–32.
[5]Dahl, pp. 1, 3.

PROCEDURAL DEMOCRACY: STRUCTURE IGNORED

In his study of New Haven, Dahl argued that, rather than one elite group making political decisions, different elite groups determined policy in different issue areas, such as urban renewal, public education, and the nomination of candidates for office. In each area, however, there was a wide disparity between the ability of politically and economically powerful people and average citizens to make decisions. As a result of such disparities, Dahl noted, New Haven was "a long way from achieving the goal of political equality advocated by the philosophers of democracy and incorporated into the creed of democracy and equality practically every American professes to uphold."[6]

Nevertheless, he concluded that "New Haven is an example of a democratic system, warts and all."[7] Dahl never resolved the problem of capitalist inequalities in a "democratic" system. Rather, he reached his conclusion by assessing democracy only according to the procedural test (Can citizens vote? Do they have a choice between candidates? Are elections honest and conducted freely?). The structure of society and class inequalities are ignored.

This approach has dominated much recent thinking about democracy. The most influential twentieth-century discussion of the relationship of capitalism and democracy is by economist Joseph Schumpeter. In his book *Capitalism, Socialism, and Democracy,* Schumpeter defines democracy wholly in procedural terms. Even though we reject his proposed standard of democracy, it is important to review his arguments here because his work underpins the way that most American social scientists think about democracy and because the issues he raises are basic to the elaboration of the approach to democracy we propose in this chapter.

Schumpeter began his discussion by rejecting the "classical view of democracy," which held that democracy exists when the people decide issues in the interest of the common good of all. This view assumed that there exists a "common good"—that all

[6]*Ibid.*, p. 86.
[7]*Ibid.*, p. 311.

the members of the political system share basic interests. Since all members of the polity share these interests, it is possible to talk of "the people" who actually make decisions—either directly by themselves or indirectly through representatives whose job it is to accurately reflect the "common good".

Schumpeter powerfully questioned the existence of these assumed entities in a capitalist society. He wrote, "There is . . . no such thing as a uniquely determined common good that all people could agree on or be made to agree on by the force of rational argument."[8] A "common good" does not exist in societies characterized by basic structural inequalities because of the absence of shared interests. So long as patterns of inequality persist, it is impossible to speak of a "common good," since the good of some depends on the subordination of others.

Hence it is also impossible to speak of "the people," for when members of a society have different interests, there is no single, natural direction their will can take. Rather, "the people" are divided into groups that reflect the unequal distribution of power. Schumpeter thus concluded that "both the pillars of the classical doctrine inevitably crumble into dust."

Because he found the classical approach to democracy out of touch with reality Schumpeter proposed that we accept "another theory which is much truer to life and at the same time salvages much of what sponsors of the democratic method really mean by this term."

Whereas the classical doctrine saw democracy as a set of institutional arrangements for reaching decisions to realize the people's common good, Schumpeter viewed democracy as "that institutional arrangement for arriving at political decisions in which individuals acquire the power to decide by means of a competitive struggle for the people's vote." Democracy thus becomes a set of rules for choosing, by election, among competing political leaders; the substance of what is decided by those selected is only secondary. Schumpeter's alternative to the classical doctrine of democracy is also rooted in a profound distrust of the governed. Indeed, for Schumpeter, it is best that political elites, not "the people," make decisions, because the people are incompetent:

[8]Joseph Schumpeter, *Capitalism, Socialism, and Democracy* (New York, 1962), p. 251.

The typical citizen drops down to a lower level of mental performance as soon as he enters the political field. He argues and analyzes
in a way which he would readily recognize as infantile within the
sphere of his real interests. He becomes a primitive again.[9]

For Schumpeter, and for the vast majority of American
social scientists who have accepted his approach, a political
system is democratic when citizens are provided with an opportunity to vote either for the political leaders in office or for a set of
competing leaders who wish to get into office. Democracy is seen
as a method, a set of formal procedures by which citizens can
select among a limited number of alternative sets of leaders.

The role of voters in this conception resembles the role of
consumers in a market economy. Much as consumers choose
among competing products packaged by businessmen, so voters
choose among competing candidates packaged by political parties. "The psycho-technics of party management and party
advertising," Schumpeter wrote, "slogans and marching tunes,
are not accessories. They are of the essence of politics."[10] Since
neither major party challenges the basic structure of capitalist
inequality, the act of choice, a legal right, replaces the substance
of choice at the heart of democratic theory.

This purely procedural definition of democracy has become
an ideological tool of social control. Those who benefit most from
the capitalist social structure may maintain, since citizens can
choose their leaders, that they have little cause for grievance. The
system, by definition, is open and democratic. Those with complaints can express them in the next election. In this way, the
procedural approach to democracy requires and promotes a
relatively passive citizenry.

"Democracy" emerges from Schumpeter's discussion without its cutting edge. The classical view of democracy, however
flawed by its reliance on the concepts of "common good" and
"the people," was concerned fundamentally with the substance
of political decision making and the rule of the many against the
powerful few. For this reason, democracy commanded far from
universal acceptance. The emasculation of the term by Schumpeter has made it far more acceptable to dominant interests.

[9]*Ibid.*, p. 262.
[10]*Ibid.*, p. 283.

Democracy is not a standard against which existing practice can be measured critically but is a rather uncritical, incomplete description of present electoral arrangements. Not surprisingly, almost all those who define democracy in wholly procedural terms find that there is no clash between democracy and capitalist inequality.

In rejecting the classical definition of democracy, Schumpeter had three alternatives. The first was to abandon the term *democracy* altogether as hopelessly utopian. The second, which he opted for, was to retain the term but redefine it to conform to existing realities. The third alternative, which we support, was to maintain the term *democracy* as a yardstick against which to measure and test reality. Thus, in a preliminary way, we define *democracy* as *a situation in which all citizens have relatively equal chances to influence and control the making of decisions that affect them.*

This alternative recognizes that although formal democratic procedures are essential to democracy, they do not guarantee it. For democracy approached this way does not depend simply on a set of rules, important though rules may be, but on the nature of the social structure within which the rules of procedural democracy operate.

Broadly, we may distinguish three different, though related, approaches to our definition of democracy. The first stresses popular participation in decision making; the second, the representation of interests; and the third, the transformation of the social structure itself. Let us examine each of these approaches in turn.

THE IMPORTANCE AND LIMITS
OF DIRECT PARTICIPATION

Citizen participation in decision making has traditionally been regarded as the centerpiece of democracy. Convincing arguments for a participatory form of democracy were put forward by Jean Jacques Rousseau, an eighteenth-century French philosopher. His influential political theory hinged on the *direct* experience of political participation. For Rousseau, participation has objective and subjective components. The objective component is that citizens exercise control by participating in decision making; the subjective component is that, because they feel they have been able to participate authentically in the making of decisions that affect them, citizens come to identify with the decisions taken and develop feelings of loyalty to the society. In addition, citizens learn to participate effectively. As social theorist Carole Pateman put it in her interpretation of Rousseau's *The Social Contract,* "the more the individual citizen participates, the better he is able to do so. . . . He learns to be a public as well as a private citizen."[11]

One of the byproducts of authentic participation is that citizens learn to identify and interpret their own interests accurately and need not depend on the interpretations of others. Conversely, if participation is inauthentic, if individuals are given the feeling of participating in decision making but are not accorded the power to actually control the decision-making process, the inevitable short-term result is that they are prevented from arriving at an accurate perception of their interests. Though eighteenth-century New England town meetings were examples of direct democracy, many were dominated by a small elite who controlled the agenda and often successfully manipulated the group discussions. The key issue is thus not whether people participate in the political system but what the *terms* of their participation are.

In the past fifteen years, many organizations—including communes, antiwar protest groups, and women's-rights groups—have been founded on classical, Rousseauian democratic principles. They reject the formal procedural approach to democracy and run themselves, instead, as participatory democracies. Their members have self-consciously sought to create open, democratic communities in which all members participate directly in decision making. For many political activists, this kind of direct democracy provides a model for how democracy should be practiced in American society as a whole.

The leap from the small group to the society, however, is impossible to make. The program of participatory groups, including face-to-face unanimous decision making and absolute equali-

[11]Carole Pateman, *Participation and Democratic Theory* (Cambridge, Mass., 1970), p. 25.

ty of status and power, is actually based on principles of friendship. As political scientist Jane Mansbridge notes

> friendship is an equal relation, it does not grow or maintain itself well at a distance, and its expression is in unanimity. . . . As participatory democracies grow from groups of fairly close acquaintances to associations of strangers, friendship can no longer serve as the basis of organization. Distrust replaces trust, and the natural equality, directness, and unanimity of friendship are transformed into rigid rules whose major purpose becomes the prevention of coercion and the protection of the individual.[12]

In small groups where people know each other intimately and are present voluntarily, the principles of direct, unanimous democracy may work to produce a natural, organic consensus of the group's will. Beyond such small groups, however, consensus is likely to be the result of manipulation, since shared values and mutual respect can develop only in situations where group members share interests. Small groups may constitute a "people" with a "common good," but as Schumpeter demonstrated, these entities in a capitalist society are fictions on a larger scale.

If democracy is to be used as a yardstick to assess both what exists and what is possible, the direct-participation approach is ruled out, because society as a whole does not provide the "friendship" basis that direct democracy requires. Hence a second approach to our definition of democracy argues that the crucial issue is not whether people participate directly, but whether all groups of the capitalist social structure and their interests achieve political *representation.*

REPRESENTATIVE DEMOCRACY

There are four dimensions of representative democracy that provide us with an immediately useful yardstick against which to test present realities. The first is *procedures.* It is essential in a democracy that individuals and groups be able to make their views known and fairly select their leaders and public officials. Hence civil liberties are essential. Free speech, free assembly, and freedom of the press are basic aspects of procedural repre-

---

[12]Jane Mansbridge, "The Limits of Friendship," unpublished manuscript, pp. 1–2.

sentation. When these procedural guarantees are suppressed, it is extraordinarily difficult for people to formulate and express their interests.

The electoral mechanisms available to citizens for selecting their representatives are also an important factor in procedural representation. How wide is the electorate? How is party competition organized? What, in short, are the rules of the electoral process? As we have seen, electoral choice is at the heart of the formal procedural standard of democracy developed by Schumpeter.

But, unlike those who advocate procedural democracy, we believe that it is a mistake to limit the discussion of procedures of representation to elections. Rather, we must consider the nature of all of the rules that determine whether an individual or group has access to the political system and whether that access is likely to have an effect on decision making. Thus the traditionally narrow focus of issues raised about the procedures of representation must be widened. Are workers permitted to join unions? How are congressional committee chairmen selected? How does an elected mayor exercise control over nonelected city bureaucrats? To whom and how is a school system's personnel formally accountable? How are key foreign-policy decision makers chosen? How, if at all, are they formally held accountable? What are the procedures for representation in areas such as the space program, where expertise is available only to a few? Who selects the experts and to whom are they accountable? What are the procedures of leadership selection in interest groups (unions, farmers' organizations, professional associations)?

The list could easily be extended. The procedural dimension of representative democracy depends not only on equitable electoral procedures but more broadly on the mechanisms of access, influence, and accountability in government and in organizations that claim to represent the interests of their constituents. It is essential that the "rules of the game" ensure that the line that divides representatives and represented not harden and that access to ruling positions be open to all and not limited by racial, class, sexual, or other forms of discrimination.

Let us briefly consider an historical example. In the early 1900s, the Democratic party Tammany Hall machine dominated politics in New York City. During this period, most of the city's population consisted of European immigrants and their children.

Because the populations of ethnic neighborhoods were relatively homogeneous, the ethnic groups gained control over the Tammany political clubs in their area. Blacks, however, were excluded from these organizations. They participated in party affairs through a citywide organization called the United Colored Democracy, whose leaders were selected by the white leaders of Tammany Hall, not by other blacks. Not surprisingly, studies of political patronage in the period indicate that blacks did the least well of all the groups in the city in securing political jobs; and the jobs they did get were the least desirable.[13]

Thus both the blacks from the South and the white ethnics from Europe joined the Democratic party, but on very different procedural terms. Although both groups could vote, the differences blacks experienced in the rules of access to the Democratic party severely limited their chances of reaping the rewards of municipal patronage.

The second dimension of representation is *personnel*. Irrespective of the way in which representatives have been selected, those who govern may or may not accurately reflect the demographic characteristics of class, race, ethnicity, sex, and geography of those they formally represent. During the Cuban missile crisis of 1962, for example, which was resolved when the Soviet Union removed its offensive missiles from Cuba after an American blockade of the island had been imposed, fewer than twenty individuals made the decisions that, by their own account, might have resulted in 150,000,000 casualties. The executive committee of the National Security Council met regularly in the two-week period of crisis to recommend courses of action to President Kennedy. Almost all of the council's members were Protestant, all were white, male, and wealthy. They included an investment banker, four corporation lawyers, a former automobile company president, and a number of multimillionaires.

In this instance, a very small group of men, hardly representative of the population as a whole, had the power to make decisions of the highest consequences. Judged by the personnel dimension of representation, the absence of democracy in this case is beyond doubt. The demographic representativeness of those who make political decisions is not important just in order to fulfill abstract numerical quotas of representation. Rather, the

[13]Ira Katznelson, *Black Men, White Cities* (New York, 1973), chapter 5.

personnel dimension of representation is important because the more demographically representative a political system is, the more likely it is that the interests of the basic groups of the social structure will be adequately and substantively represented. It is highly unlikely, for example, that a group of businessmen will accurately represent the interests of workers or that the interests of blacks will be best represented by whites. This might occasionally be the case, but group members are much more likely to represent their own interests than those of their structural antagonists. It is not surprising, therefore, that workers in unions earn better wages than those whose wage levels are entrusted to the discretion of their employers; nor is it surprising that Southern blacks have been treated more equitably by police since the passage of the Voting Rights Act of 1965 than they had been when they had to depend on the goodwill of the white community.

To represent group interests adequately, representatives must also fulfill the dimension of *consciousness*—they must be aware of and responsive to their constituents' concerns. In this respect, subordinates often find it much more difficult than the privileged to achieve representation of their interests, since those with more resources tend to perceive their interests more accurately than subordinates who are subject to the arsenal of control techniques discussed in Chapter 1. The privileged are also in a better position to put pressure on their representatives than those who are politically powerless. Thus representation concerns not only *who* rules but also the *uses* to which power is put by those who rule. The first two dimensions of representation—procedures and personnel—refer to the first of these two issues. But the dimension of *consciousness* asks how representatives see the interests of their constituents and how they act on behalf of these interests. To satisfy the requirements of representative democracy, those who formally represent the population must use the power conferred by their positions to promote the interests of the represented.

But even where the first three dimensions of representation are satisfied, political democracy cannot be said to exist. The last dimension that must be realized is effectiveness—the ability of representatives to produce the results they desire. A system cannot be democratically representative if effectiveness is distributed very unequally among representatives. For example, given the fact that most congressional legislation is decided by the various committees, it would be difficult to argue that Polish working-class citizens who select a Polish working-class congressman will be democratically represented if the congressman is placed on committees irrelevant to their concerns.

Thus representative democracy is achieved only when all four dimensions are satisified: when leaders are selected by regular procedures that are open to all people and all groups have relatively equal access to the political system; when representatives reflect the demographic composition of the population as a whole; when they are conscious of and responsive to their constituents' interests; and when they can effectively act on behalf of those interests.

SUBSTANTIVE DEMOCRACY:
STRUCTURE TRANSFORMED

Unlike the purely procedural approach to democracy, the standard of representative democracy does not simply endorse present practices as democratic. Rather, it allows us to measure the degree of representative democracy that exists and, conversely, shows us how much needs to be done to achieve a fully representative democracy. As such, this standard is the best available to test the democratic content of existing political institutions and processes.

Nevertheless, it is limited. It leaves us with the basic dilemma posed at the beginning of the chapter: in Dahl's words, "How does a 'democratic' system work amid inequality of resources?" What is the relationship between a political system based on equality of representation and an economic system based on the inequality of capital and labor?

The answer to this question is that the two systems are incompatible. The full achievement of representative democracy is impossible to imagine in a social structure that embodies systematic inequalities in the distribution of resources. Indeed, the realization of the one presages the demise of the other. Once subordinate groups succeed in placing personnel in key decision-making positions, once their interests are accurately perceived and effectively represented, the privileged position of the minority will be increasingly recognized and challenged. The contradiction between capitalism and democracy can be finally resolved only by the transformation of the social structure.

Thus the most demanding, complete, critical standard of democracy—a standard of substantive democracy—is based not only on the dimensions of representation but on the criterion of structural change. The goal of substantive democracy is a situation in which all citizens have relatively equal chances to influence and control the making of decisions that affect them, which as we shall see requires that the economy be socialized and the distribution of resources equalized.

The rest of this book is organized so that we can explore the implications of applying the two standards of democracy—representation and structural transformation—to the United States. Part II analyzes the organization of production and the social relationships that link corporate capitalism and American workers. Part III examines how the national government, democratic in procedural terms, has come to be an essential partner of corporate capitalism, thus reinforcing existing structural inequalities. Part IV discusses national political institutions in terms of the standard of democratic representation, and Part V looks at three arenas of political struggle between structurally unequal political participants. Finally, Part VI suggests possible alternative courses of political development and argues that only a socialist outcome can create a substantive democracy.

the organization of production

3

corporate capitalism

Suppose it was learned that a small group had obtained critical power in the United States. Imagine that, in a country with a population of 210,000,000, several thousand Americans—unrepresentative, not democratically chosen nor even known to most people—had control over some of the most important aspects of American life. This small group decided what kinds of products Americans would manufacture. It owned and controlled the factories in which production occurred. It not only employed but could also promote or fire a large proportion of Americans. This group produced dangerous and expensive weapons for the military. It controlled radio and television networks and deeply influenced Americans' values and attitudes. It dominated the companies that produce the automobiles, television sets, and electric appliances found in many American homes.

Because this group controlled much of the country's productive capacity, its decisions affected all Americans. Yet members of the group based their decisions not on what the country needed but on what would be profitable for the small controlling group. As a result, some Americans were saturated with a profusion of possessions, while many others could barely obtain basic necessities, such as food, housing, and medical care.

Further, this group was also able to influence political decisions. Its contributions to political parties were vital for a candidate to be nominated and elected to office. It developed close ties to Congress, the president, and government agencies. Most government policies were designed to help this group retain its favored position.

One can imagine the outcry that would greet the announcement that such a group existed. After all, its existence would not only make democratic government an illusion but would also prevent many Americans from achieving the benefits America promises. And yet, such a group does exist. All that has been described is fact, not fiction. A convenient shorthand label for the process of production, distribution, and consumption, over which this group exerts control, is corporate capitalism. What makes it such a powerful force in America?

There are approximately twelve million economic enterprises in the United States, from small family farms and shoe repair shops to the United States Steel Corporation and Gulf Oil Corporation. In terms of value, their individual net worth ranges from several hundred dollars to the $60 billion in assets controlled by American Telephone and Telegraph.

One can distinguish between two sectors of private production: corporate capital, which includes the largest mining and manufacturing corporations, banks, retail chain stores, insurance companies, utilities, television networks, and law firms; and small-scale capital, which includes restaurants, local newspapers, clothing stores, small construction companies, and small manufacturers (such as garment factories). In terms of the number of workers employed, the two sectors are nearly equal. However, that is about all they have in common. Productive resources are owned, organized, and managed very differently in the two sectors: the sphere of corporate capital is far more productive, centralized, and powerful than the sphere of small-scale capital. Measured by the ability to shape the major decisions regarding the organization of society and the distribution of benefits, corporate capital far outdistances small-scale capital.

Some idea of the power concentrated within the corporate sector can be conveyed by the following figures. Among the over 400,000 manufacturing concerns in the United States, a fortunate few—about 100—have assets worth over $1 billion. They are the

Table 3-1
The 20 largest industrial corporations 1973 (ranked by sales)

Rank '73	'72	Company (Headquarter in parentheses)	Sales ($000)	Rank	Assets ($000)	Rank	Net Income ($000)	Rank	Employees Number	Rank
1	1	General Motors (Detroit)	35,798,289	2	20,296,861	2	2,398,103	2	810,920†	1
2	2	Exxon (New York)	25,724,319*	1	25,079,494	1	2,443,286	1	137,000†	12
3	3	Ford Motor (Dearborn, Mich.)	23,015,100	4	12,954,000	4	906,500	5	474,318†	2
4	5	Chrysler (Detroit)	11,774,372	14	6,104,898	14	255,445	26	273,254†	6
5	4	General Electric (New York)	11,575,300	11	8,324,200	11	585,100	11	388,000†	4
6	8	Texaco (New York)	11,406,876	3	13,595,413	3	1,292,403	4	74,918	33
7	7	Mobil Oil (New York)	11,390,113*	7	10,690,431	7	849,312	6	73,900	37
8	6	International Business Machines (Armonk, N. Y.)	10,993,242	5	12,289,489	5	1,575,467	3	274,108	5
9	9	International Tel. & Tel. (New York)	10,183,055	8	10,132,571	8	527,837	12	438,000	3
10	11	Gulf Oil (Pittsburgh)	8,417,000*	9	10,074,000	9	800,000	8	51,600	59
11	12	Standard Oil of California (San Francisco)	7,761,835*	10	9,082,248	10	843,577	7	39,269	98
12	10	Western Electric (New York)	7,037,290	19	4,828,143	19	315,305	18	206,608	7
13	13	U. S. Steel (New York)	6,951,905	13	6,918,535	13	325,758	17	184,794	10
14	14	Westinghouse Electric (Pittsburgh)	5,702,300	20	4,407,665	20	161,928	44	194,100†	9
15	15	Standard Oil (Ind.) (Chicago)	5,415,975*	12	7,018,013	12	511,249	13	46,589	81
16	16	E. I. Du Pont de Nemours (Wilmington, Del.)	5,275,600	18	4,832,200	18	585,600	10	118,423	16
17	•	General Telephone & Electronics (Stamford, Conn.)	5,105,296	6	10,749,370	6	352,076	14	196,000	8
18	17	Shell Oil (Houston)	4,883,805*	16	5,381,164	16	332,694	16	32,080	127
19	18	Goodyear Tire & Rubber (Akron, Ohio)	4,675,265	25	3,871,043	25	184,756	37	152,929†	11
20	19	RCA (New York)	4,246,800	29	3,300,800	29	183,700	38	126,000	13
Total			**217,333,731**		**189,930,538**		**15,430,106**		**4,292,810**	
Total, 500 largest Industrial Corporations			**667,105,712**		**555,462,284**		**38,680,461**		**15,531,683**	

•Indicates that a corporation was not among the 500 or the Second 500 in 1972.   *Does not include excise taxes.   †Average for the year.
Source: *Fortune*, May 1974, pp. 232–33. Reprinted by special permission from the 1974 Fortune Directory; © 1974 Time Inc.

industrial giants of America, whose names are household words: Ford, General Electric, Exxon, International Business Machines (IBM), Chrysler. These corporations are immense individually; their combined worth and power are staggering. The top 500 corporations control three-quarters of all industrial assets in the United States—leaving the remaining one-quarter to the other 400,000 firms. The same 500 corporations had $667 billion in sales in 1973—over half the total sales of the entire American economy.

Yet, even within the top group of 500 there are further inequalities between the biggest and smallest corporations: the largest (General Motors) had sales in 1973 more than one hundred times greater than the smallest corporation (Avery Products). The 200 largest corporations control nearly two-thirds of all manufacturing assets in the United States, and the top 10 alone account for about one-tenth of America's total manufactured output.[1]

The lives of all Americans are extensively affected by these colossal firms. Most of the products Americans buy, from toothpaste to automobiles, are produced by corporate capitalism. The top 500 corporations employ fifteen million workers—about two-thirds of the industrial workers and one-third of all workers in the United States.[2] Many Americans who are not directly dependent on giant corporations for their livelihood are indirectly dependent. Small manufacturers produce parts and other supplies that they sell to these corporations. Retail dealers sell and repairmen service what corporate capitalism produces. Many local retail stores, gasoline stations, bus companies, and banks would not exist were it not for the economic activity of the corporate giants. Newspapers and television stations also would not survive without the advertising revenue they receive from corporate capitalism.

A typical mammoth corporation constitutes a powerful force in American politics. Together, the few hundred largest corporations control most of the country's productive resources. The requirements of corporate capitalism are a first priority on the American political agenda.

---

[1]John Kenneth Galbraith, *Economics and the Public Purpose* (Boston, 1973), pp. 43, 105.
[2]James O'Connor, *The Fiscal Crisis of the State* (New York, 1973), p. 34, footnote 7.

CHARACTERISTICS OF CORPORATE CAPITALISM

Much can be learned about corporate capitalism by examining one giant corporation in detail. We have chosen to study General Motors (GM) for two reasons. First, its main activity, automobile production, is aimed at the individual consumer and thus its effect on Americans is quite visible and direct. Second, the automobile industry is a keystone of the American economy, affecting the fortunes of many other giant corporations, and GM is the leading automobile producer.

Size   GM is the largest industrial corporation in the world. Its assets are worth $20 billion, its annual sales are more than $35 billion, and its annual income (profits) after taxes exceeds $2 billion. GM's total production makes it the twelfth largest economic unit in the world, with an output larger than productively hefty countries like Yugoslavia, Austria, or Denmark. GM employs over 800,000 workers throughout the world, most of whom are in the United States. If all of GM's workers and their families lived in one city, it would rank among the top ten cities in the United States.

But GM is not located in one city. It is a national enterprise, with 112 manufacturing plants scattered in 67 American cities (and other facilities located in many foreign countries). The GM empire extends to 45,000 additional firms located in every state who, while not formally part of GM, sell it raw materials and parts.[3] GM's decision to open a factory in Fairfax, Kansas, means an economic boom in that city; its decision to reduce production at Janesville, Wisconsin, spells hard times in Janesville. So dependent is the country on GM's prosperity that economists scan the corporation's monthly automobile sales for clues about the general direction of the American economy. Judged by the worth of its annual output, GM's power is greater than that of any city or state government.

Like most giant corporations, GM continues to grow: in many years, its sales set a record. Growth by individual corporations at the top produces great stability and continuity in the

[3]William Serrin, *The Company and the Union: The Civilized Relationship of the General Motors Corporation and the United Automobile Workers* (New York, 1973), chapter 3; *New York Times*, March 24, 1974.

relative position of the largest firms. Every one of the top 20 firms in 1955 ranked among the top 35 in 1967.[4] Notice in Table 3–1 that most companies in the top 20 hardly changed rank from one year to the next.

Concentration   Economists call an industry *concentrated* if a few large firms dominate production and sales. Automobile production is one such industry. Four companies—GM, Ford, Chrysler, and American Motors—produce 95 percent of the nine million automobiles made in the United States each year. More than half of these—about five million—are produced by GM. Thus GM is the powerful leader in a concentrated industry.

Firms in a concentrated industry behave differently than firms in a competitive industry. In the latter, many small companies compete with each other and none get a large share of the market—the typical situation for what we have labelled small-scale capital. In a concentrated industry, firms enter into long-term arrangements with other firms to stabilize their supplies and sales. They informally cooperate to set prices high enough to assure profits even when demand for their products may lag. (One study found that the average rate of profit before taxes was 20 percent in concentrated industries, but only 13 percent in nonconcentrated industries.[5])

Corporate capitalism has emerged as a stable powerful force in large part because in many major industries production is concentrated in the hands of a few large corporations. For example, four firms account for over half the total sales in the aluminum industry; other concentrated industries are steel, copper, aircraft, glass, computers, electrical equipment, and tires. Alcoa in aluminum, U.S. Steel in steel, Anaconda in copper, and Boeing in aircraft are leaders in their respective industries.

The trend toward high concentration in the American economy has been rapid. In the period from 1948 to 1968, the 200 largest corporations increased their share of total manufacturing assets in the United States by 14 percent (from 46 to 60 percent).[6] The same proportion of sales that the top 200 firms controlled in 1950 was controlled by only half as many firms twenty years later.

[4]Richard J. Barber, *The American Corporation: Its Power, Its Money, Its Politics* (New York, 1970), p. 25.
[5]Howard Sherman, *Radical Political Economy: Capitalism and Socialism from a Marxist Humanist Perspective* (New York, 1972), p. 108.
[6]John Blair, *Economic Concentration* (New York, 1972), p. 64.

Table 3–2
Concentration in manufacturing industries

Percentage of sales, total assets,
net capital assets, and profits after taxes accounted for by the
4 largest firms in each industry for 28 selected industry groups,
4th quarter, 1962

		Percent of total		
Industry	Sales	Total assets	Net capital assets	Profits
Motor vehicles	80.8	79.7	83.1	89.1
Aircraft	47.3	41.9	32.6	46.6
Other transportation equipment	30.3	44.2	59.9	51.6
Electrical machinery	34.4	35.6	41.5	44.4
Metalworking machinery	14.5	16.3	18.5	19.1
Other machinery	20.6	24.3	31.5	39.6
Primary iron and steel	40.2	48.0	48.8	44.3
Primary nonferrous metals	27.3	41.1	47.7	37.1
Other fabricated metal products	14.7	19.9	30.3	17.7
Stone, clay, and glass products	18.1	19.9	19.8	23.4
Furniture and fixtures	5.2	8.4	9.6	5.3
Lumber and wood products	21.2	31.0	41.5	48.6
Instruments	37.9	41.2	50.2	56.6
Miscellaneous manufacturing	16.3	33.1	34.3	25.2
Dairy products	42.9	48.8	47.4	73.9
Bakery products	33.6	39.6	38.2	52.8
Other food	12.5	13.2	14.9	20.1
Textile mill products	22.0	26.1	25.7	30.5
Apparel	4.9	7.7	11.4	7.4
Paper	20.7	23.2	22.3	35.0
Basic industrial chemicals	42.0	45.5	44.6	64.6
Drugs and medicines	31.0	29.2	33.3	32.6
Other chemicals	28.5	30.0	33.6	35.8
Petroleum refining	50.3	50.1	47.7	54.3
Rubber	48.1	55.0	56.4	51.6
Leather	26.7	32.1	35.4	28.8
Alcoholic beverages	41.4	47.2	30.8	58.3
Tobacco	70.9	72.7	69.8	72.5

Source: Bureau of Economics, Federal Trade Commission.

Concentration occurs not only *within* given industries but *across* industries, and in the economy as a whole. The American economy has become nationalized, integrated, concentrated, and centralized around a cluster of privately owned industries and firms. Thus, in describing the contours of concentrated industries, we are also describing the results of private decisions about the allocation of resources in the United States and how these decisions affect people's lives. For example, during the past half century, the automobile industry has dominated and interconnected major areas of the economy. About $100 billion is spent each year for automobiles, spare parts and accessories, gasoline, automobile insurance, and highway construction and maintenance. About one-sixth of the total American labor force is directly or indirectly part of the auto industry. (This figure includes auto workers, suppliers of automobile parts, and many workers in the steel, rubber, aluminum, and insurance industries.) The three largest industrial corporations (GM, Exxon, and Ford) are centrally involved in the automobile industry. The top twenty corporations include ten automobile and petroleum companies as well as other giants whose fortunes are closely linked to the automobile, including U.S. Steel and Goodyear Tire and Rubber. (One-fifth of annual steel production and two-thirds of rubber goes to automobiles.) Automobiles may get better care than people: the ratio of auto mechanics to cars is greater than that of physicians to people in the United States.[7]

Integrated production GM, like other large corporations, centralizes numerous operations involving all phases of manufacturing. The process starts long before and extends beyond the assembling of automobiles. As we noted earlier, GM enters into long-term agreements with independent suppliers to obtain a guaranteed supply of steel, glass, and other raw materials; it contracts out the manufacturing of parts it does not produce, thus partially integrating suppliers of parts into its own production process. GM itself produces many of the parts it needs in assembling automobiles. GM's Fisher Body Division manufactures automobile bodies; its AC Spark Plug Division makes spark plugs, oil filters, and fuel pumps; and its Delco Division produces radios, air conditioners, heaters, and batteries.

GM's integration of automobile production does not end when the finished automobile rolls off the assembly line. It integrates the sales operation by franchising 12,000 dealers to sell its automobiles—and has begun to buy up and operate for itself the most profitable dealerships. GM is also in the automobile credit business: it owns the General Motors Acceptance Corporation (GMAC), which provides credit to GM customers. GM

---

[7]Barry Weisberg, *Beyond Repair: The Ecology of Capitalism* (Boston, 1971), pp. 98, 102.

integrates the maintenance of its automobiles by training mechanics at thirty GM training centers and licensing GM service centers. Through integration, GM has developed an automobile empire—providing benefits for itself at every step of the operation. For example, the GMAC is a lucrative financial institution, the largest short-term credit agency in the United States. Integration increases GM's control, profits, and success.

Diversification   When one thinks of GM, one thinks first of automobiles. But GM does not only produce Chevrolets, Pontiacs, Buicks, Oldsmobiles, and Cadillacs. It has diversified its operations by entering other lines of production. GM is the country's largest producer of trucks and locomotives. Further afield, GM's Frigidaire Division is the world's leading producer of refrigerators, and among the largest manufacturers of freezers, washers, and other home appliances. And GM also produces jet and diesel engines, gas turbines, tanks, rifles, and missiles. (Many giant corporations produce weapons in addition to civilian products. This topic will be studied in Chapter 6.)

In contrast to GM, whose main activity (despite diversification) continues to be automobile production, some corporations are so diversified that they have no major recognizable activity. This new breed of corporation, called the conglomerate—since it is a collection of unrelated firms—became prominent during the past decade.

International Telephone and Telegraph (ITT), America's ninth largest corporation, is the best-known conglomerate. Since the 1960s it has grown from $1 billion in assets to $10 billion by buying up new firms at a dizzying pace—and using the assets of the new firms to pay back stockholders of firms it had bought in the past. In this fashion, ITT was able to purchase large and successful companies in a bewildering variety of fields. It currently controls Continental Baking Company (the world's largest baking company), Sheraton Corporation of America (the world's largest operator of hotels and motels), a steel company, a fire insurance company, a publishing company, and a mutual investment fund.

Multinational activities   GM's manufacturing and sales operations span the globe—from Japan, New Zealand, and Australia to Canada, Italy, and Portugal; and from Norway and Sweden to Argentina and South Africa. Altogether, GM has factories in thirty-one foreign countries; in 1973 its overseas sales came to $5.8 billion, one-sixth of its total sales.[8] In the quest to expand sales, most large American corporations have begun to look abroad. While the American market is becoming saturated with products, foreign markets represent new opportunities. As a result, foreign sales occupy a large and growing place in corporate capitalism.

Control by a few   GM and other corporate Goliaths are controlled by a very few people: a handful of directors, officers, wealthy stockholders, and top management personnel. The total number of directors and top management personnel of the few hundred most powerful corporations is several thousand. To this group should be added the several thousand men (and several women) who control the largest banks, insurance companies, utilities, transportation companies, law firms, and retail chains. These fields are also highly concentrated. (For example, fifty commercial banks control half the country's total commercial deposits.)[9] By owning and controlling corporate capitalism, this small private group dominates America's productive apparatus.

STABILITY, PLANNING, AND CONTROL

Huge corporations produce for both nationwide and international markets. Immense resources are at stake. All phases of production and distribution must be coordinated; if one step fails, much is lost. Such an elaborate production process requires stability—a high degree of certainty and predictability.

Difficulties are multiplied because success depends not only on correct decisions made within the corporation but also on the decisions of others, for example, suppliers and customers. Corporations try to foresee the risks that might arise to endanger growth and profits—and they then try to take steps to eliminate these risks.

Corporate planning anticipates every step of the production process long in advance in an attempt to maximize control. The

[8]*New York Times,* March 24, 1974.
[9]Barber, p. 64.

initial design of a product may require much scientific research—sometimes by a variety of specialists. The product must have a design that allows it to be manufactured at a reasonable cost. The necessary raw materials must be readily available. Some materials may require modification to perform adequately under special conditions. (For example, new types of steel or plastics may have to be developed to hold up under conditions of high operating temperature or stress.) The manufacturing process must be planned in detail: machine tools designed, a work force trained, production facilities built. Provision must be made for packaging and transporting the new product to retail outlets. Advertising campaigns must be developed to assure demand for the new product.

Much of what has been described previously in this chapter can be considered part of the planning and control process. Entering into long-term supply arrangements enables large firms to avoid competing for supplies in the open market. Thus, during the fuel shortage in the winter of 1973, they were assured of a steady supply of petroleum through previous agreements with suppliers. Integrating production frees big corporations even further from dependence on suppliers. Naturally, all business firms would prefer to engage in planning and establish control. Yet only the fortunate few powerful corporations that comprise corporate capitalism are able to do so. Three areas of prime concern are price, labor supply, and consumption.

Setting prices In a concentrated industry, the giant corporation is able to bring the setting of price for its products under its control. GM, Ford, and Chrysler have nothing to gain by trying to maintain the lowest possible price. The price to be charged is usually set by the largest firm in an industry, informally known as the price leader, and it is set high enough so that all producers can obtain a profit. In this way, the chances of gaining a profit year after year are excellent. In the bleak recession years of 1970 and 1971, only 7 of the top 100 corporations did not enjoy a profit each year.[10] As a result, however, consumers pay a higher price for many manufactured goods so that firms can achieve their targeted rate of profit. GM, for example, sets prices for automobiles at a level high enough to enable it to achieve and usually exceed its annual after-tax profit target of 20 percent of investment.

[10]Galbraith, p. 16. Only two firms lost money two years in a row.

Manual labor supply   Large firms need a stable supply of unskilled and skilled labor. Although technological advances have enabled machines to perform many tasks more cheaply than men, manual workers are still needed for much of the manufacturing process. As the result of labor struggles in the 1930s, corporations were forced to accept the principle of labor unions, in which workers organized to bargain with corporate management over the setting of wages and working conditions. Although corporate management initially opposed unions as constituting unwarranted interference with management control, unions have provided management with unanticipated benefits. By taking responsibility for organizing and disciplining workers, unions help reduce the uncertainty that might result from a large unstable work force. As William Serrin notes, "What the companies desire—and receive—from the union is predictability in labor relations."[11] The benefits provided by unions are twofold. Within the factory, unions deliver "labor peace": they discipline their workers to accept the existing hierarchy and management control and to carry out the job according to management wishes. (In Chapter 1, we saw that at Lordstown young workers opposed both management and their own union leadership on the issue of management control.) Second, on the political front, unions organize workers to accept corporate capitalism as legitimate. Working-class movements in other countries frequently oppose private ownership and control of the means of production; instead, they advocate other alternatives, such as socialism. However, the leadership of American labor unions fully supports the corporate capitalist form of production.

Labor unions demand a price for their support: relatively high wages for their members. As a result, large corporations generally pay well. GM workers, for example, make six dollars per hour, nearly three times the federal minimum hourly wage; their weekly wages are 56 percent higher than the average for American manufacturing employees. Firms in concentrated industries can afford to pay workers above-average wages because they are able to set prices high enough to meet unions' demands. Thus, the cost of good wages for corporate workers is passed along to consumers and need not endanger corporate profits.

White collar and skilled labor supply   The increasing use of

---

[11]Serrin, p. 156.

technology means that white collar and skilled workers are replacing manual workers. Large corporations need engineers, keypunchers, typists, and programmers to run the intricate industrial machine. The importance of education in modern industry can be seen from two facts: in some advanced industries, like aerospace, there are as many skilled supervisory, scientific, and engineering personnel as manual workers. Second, a study has found that over half the increased output per worker in the United States from 1929 to 1957 resulted from the higher educational skills of workers.[12]

Hence the large corporation must make sure that workers trained in the necessary skills will be available. One way is for industry to support government programs for job training, which means that the whole community pays the costs. Another way is for corporations to establish close ties to colleges and universities. Businessmen are heavily represented on college and university boards of trustees.

Control over the consumer market   Large corporations do not take the risk of leaving the final step of the process to chance. All previous efforts will be useless if they cannot sell their products. Therefore, just as they try to plan and establish control over early phases of the production process, so they attempt to control consumer behavior.

There are two kinds of consumers: the large firm that buys in bulk and the individual who buys in small quantities. In some industries, most of the output is purchased by a few giant consumers. The steel industry, for example, sells one-fifth of its output to the four largest automobile manufacturers. The most extreme case is military production—where giant firms like Lockheed sell virtually all their billion-dollar-yearly output to the Department of Defense. With large producers and large consumers, the result is very much like what occurs between corporate management and labor unions—a generous arrangement benefiting both sides, and the costs are passed along to small consumers (who ultimately buy what is produced) or, in the case of military hardware, the taxpayers (who thereby subsidize large military producers). GM, on the other hand, does not sell most of its output to a few large consumers but to millions of households.

[12]Edward F. Denison, *The Sources of Economic Growth in the United States and the Alternatives Before Us* (New York, 1962), p. 148.

Producing for a mass market would seem to prevent corporate control. After all, are not customers free to buy what they want? To a large extent they are not. Corporations that sell to mass markets plan their marketing operations to manipulate consumer demand and assure that their products will be sold. Two important ways are product research and design, and advertising.

Much of what is called product research and design is geared to sales. Rather than making the best possible product, the aim is to make the product that will have the best chance of being sold at a profit. Intensive efforts are devoted to making the packaging of the product more attractive. Most changes in automobile models, for example, do not improve the automobile's performance. New upholstery, swing-around seats, and fancy chrome trim are all designed to increase consumer appeal and thus to boost sales.

At the extreme, products may be intentionally designed to wear out fast. This practice is called planned obsolescence and means that a product is engineered to need costly repairs after a while—and thus will probably be discarded in favor of a new purchase. Planned obsolescence assures that there will be a constantly renewed demand for goods. It accounts for the fact that automobiles have a shorter life span now than they did before the Second World War, when technology was far less advanced. Designed-in failures are a dramatic example of the misuse of technology to boost sales.

Advertising is another means corporations use to control consumer behavior. Through massive campaigns, people are warned they will be unattractive if they do not use certain soaps, lotions, deodorants, and hair sprays; housewives are branded as failures unless they use the latest laundry detergents, floor waxes, and disinfectants; and children are manipulated to believe that popularity and happiness come from having the newest toys. The free enterprise system is based on consumers expressing preferences for goods through their purchasing decisions. Advertising reverses the sequence by shaping consumer preferences. Advertising plays on people's fears, hopes, and desires in order to sell the products poured out by corporate production. The pharmaceutical industry spends $1 billion yearly—one-quarter of its total revenue—on advertising campaigns that exploit Americans' unhappiness, anxiety, and illness and overdose them with drugs.[13] Advertising also increases corporate concentration and

---

[13] *The Progressive* (January 1973), p. 9.

the power of large companies by influencing consumers to purchase brand names. One study found that the degree of concentration in a group of industries was directly related to the amounts spent on advertising. Industries that do not advertise are often less concentrated.[14] In addition to creating a demand for specific products, advertising helps sustain the notion that corporate capitalism is desirable and that it is normal for a society to allocate its resources as they are allocated in the United States. Thus, advertising serves a political purpose that goes far beyond sales promotion.

The process of planning and control is an interrelated system. By setting a high price for their products, large corporations in a concentrated industry can obtain the funds needed for higher wages, advertising, and expansion of production. The result is to assure continued control.

WHO OWNS AMERICA?

In a highly industrialized, technological society, the means of production—the enormously complex and expensive machines and manufacturing plants—make it possible for man's power to multiply beyond measure. Compare copying a book by hand and using a printing press; or moving earth with a hand shovel and a steam shovel. However, the highly technological means of production required by modern industry are costly. Research and technical ingenuity are needed to design machines that produce with ease and efficiency. Large sums of capital are needed to make possible cheap mass production.

In the United States, the means of production are primarily private, organized within the framework of corporate capitalism. The corporate form facilitates the pooling of large amounts of capital. In the corporate form, each person who invests money receives shares in the assets or stock of the corporation. In return for the use of their money, stockholders receive certain benefits. They share in the corporation's profits in proportion to the amount of stock they own. Stockholders also are entitled to vote

[14]Blair, pp. 321–31.

for the board of directors of the corporation. As with profits, the number of votes a stockholder has is proportional to the amount of stock he owns. The board of directors chooses the corporation's top management and reviews management decisions. Only those who own stock in the corporation are able to share in the corporation's profits and to participate in choosing the board of directors. (Note that, except for the firm's management, those who work for the corporation do not have a share in the firm's profits or a voice in its decisions.) Thus, it is important to establish who owns stock in the major American corporations. Since corporations control most of America's productive assets (means of production), those who own stock and control corporations are those who decide what America will produce and consume.

To begin with, relatively few Americans own stock: only one family in six. Most Americans use their income for necessities and luxuries; few families have money left over to invest. In fact, through the lure of installment buying, a majority of Americans spend more than they earn. Rather than having savings to invest, they have debts to pay. Only the rich have the surplus necessary to purchase stock. In fact, over half of all savings in the United States is supplied by those in the top 5 percent income bracket. Those in the lowest 50 percent income bracket have no net savings at all.[15]

If only one-sixth of American families own stock, it indicates that the means of production in the United States are controlled by a minority of the whole community. Yet even this figure is misleading, for it implies that, at least within the small group of stockholders, ownership of stock is relatively equal. But ownership of stock is highly unequal. Two-thirds of all stockholders own less than $10,000 in stock, a negligible investment compared to what is needed to gain a voice in a large corporation. For participation in the corporation depends not only on owning stock in the corporation but on how *much* one owns: a person owning one share has one vote at the annual stockholder's meeting, while a person with one hundred shares has one hundred votes, and a person with ten thousand shares has ten thousand votes. Small stockholders are lavishly praised at annual meetings, but they are

[15]John Kenneth Galbraith, *The New Industrial State* (New York, 1972), rev. ed., pp. 48, 53; and Galbraith, *Economics and the Public Purpose*, p. 306.

Figure 3-1
The distribution of common stock in publicly held corporations in 1951

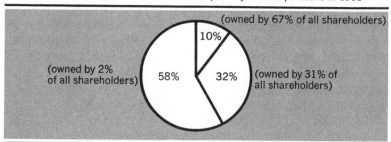

Source: From *Wealth and Power in America: An Analysis of Social Distribution* (p. 52) by Gabriel Kolko. © 1962 by Frederick A. Praeger, Inc. Excerpted and reprinted by permission.

"owners" of a corporation only in legal appearance. In reality, it requires a block of many thousands of shares of stock in a corporation to have an *effective* voice.

Most stock is held by a tiny proportion of the one-sixth of American families who own stock. An examination of the upper range of the stock-owning pyramid indicates that less than one-tenth of all stockholders own 80 percent of all stock. Thus, the upper one-tenth owns four times more capital than all other stockholders combined. Even within the extremely privileged small group of wealthy stockholders there is substantial inequality between the top and the bottom. Less than .3 percent of the population, about 200,000 out of 58 million families, own two-thirds of all stock.

Controlling Interest

Much stock in a corporation is dispersed among small and medium stockholders. Such stockholders usually do not have the time, motivation, or resources to participate actively in corporate affairs. For these small investors, owning stock is like putting money in the bank; there is no desire for real participation. Very few investors in a corporation own large blocks of stock. (For example, only 10 percent of the 4.7 million shares of GM stock are held by those who own over 200 shares of stock.)

A block of shares large enough to give its owner a powerful voice in the corporation is called a *controlling interest*. A block of shares representing 10 percent of a corporation's total stock is usually sufficient to exercise control. When many shares of stock are owned by a large stockholder or a family group, a controlling interest can be achieved by voting the shares as a block. Unlike the small stockholder, large stockholders have the resources and motivation to gain a leading voice in the corporation. Moreover, since it is in the firm's interest to avoid a fight for control, large stockholders and management usually act together.

A small group of Americans, probably numbering in the tens of thousands, collectively owns blocks of stock large enough to control many large corporations. In a nation of 210,000,000 people, the means of production are controlled by a group no larger than the population of a small town.

The Superwealthy

Who are the extraordinarily privileged Americans (one family in several thousand) with fortunes in excess of $100 million, who own a controlling interest in corporate capitalism? How were they able to enter the ranks of the superwealthy? Must they not have superior qualities to amass such enormous capital? On the contrary: the essential characteristic of the superwealthy is not ambition, merit, wit, talent, or intelligence—but wealthy parents. Most of the superwealthy were millionaires at birth, thanks to trust funds established by their parents or grandparents. If not superwealthy, their families have nearly all been at least close to the magic circle. Even those cited as examples of self-made men are generally not from humble circumstances. There are few new superwealthy, and the number would be even smaller if it were not for Texas oil, which is responsible for the fortunes of Paul Getty, H. L. Hunt, and Sid Murchison. (Among the few fabulously rich self-made men who created an industrial enterprise not based on oil was Dr. Edwin Land, inventor of the Polaroid camera.) Big wealth is usually inherited wealth in the United States of the 1970s. Bright young men and women may seek their fortunes, but if they were not born rich, they are unlikely to join the ranks of the very wealthy.

Many of those at the top are from families with legendary names: Ford, Firestone, Rockefeller, du Pont, Vanderbilt, and Mellon. The superwealthy are likely to be listed in the *Social Register* and belong to exclusive private clubs. Most are Anglo-Saxon Protestants. Jews and Catholics have earned large fortunes, but only a few have made it to the very top of the social and corporate pyramid. Blacks and other minorities are even less represented. (In 1970, there were three blacks among the 3,182 senior officers and directors of the top 50 corporations).[16]

The fortunes of the very wealthy come from owning and managing the means of production. Some idea of the immense benefits they derive can be gleaned from the following information: In 1961, four hundred Americans filed federal income tax returns reporting incomes over $1 million. (Although many more than four hundred Americans have incomes exceeding $1 million a year, the very wealthy can under-report their income through a variety of tax loopholes.) The four hundred reported receiving a total of $30 million in salaries, an average of less than $80,000 apiece. The rest of their million-dollar incomes came from stock dividends or capital gains, which represent a rise in the value of their stocks.[17] Thus, most of the income the very rich receive comes not from the work they perform but from the benefits they derive from owning the means of production.

If the very rich were only to ride to hounds or sail expensive yachts, supporting themselves by clipping the coupons from stock certificates and living off their inherited and invested wealth, they might not have a decisive voice within corporate capitalism. But these same investors use their wealth to attain positions of corporate power. The present power of the tiny group at the top probably derives as much from their *current* economic activity as from their *inherited* wealth and upper-class social trappings. For the group being described not only *owns* many large corporations but it also *controls* them in a close, day-to-day fashion—in fact, many of its members are directors and officers of the largest corporations and financial institutions and are intimately involved in their management.

Some of the largest American corporations continue to be partly family-controlled, including A&P, Du Pont, Ford, Westinghouse, Gulf Oil, Alcoa, and Firestone Tire and Rubber. William Domhoff found that more than half the directors of the top 20 industrial corporations, 15 banks, and 15 insurance companies were members of the social elite (as defined by member-

---

[16]*New York Times,* October 1, 1970.
[17]Much of the above section is based on Ferdinand Lundberg, *The Rich and the Super-rich: A Study in the Power of America Today* (New York, 1969), p. 43.

ship in the *Social Register,* exclusive private clubs, or graduation
from exclusive preparatory schools).[18]

Corporate Managers

Despite their strategic position, the fabulously wealthy upper
class does not rule corporate capitalism by itself. (For one thing,
there just are not enough members to do so.) An essential element
in the continued success of the superwealthy has been their
ability to recruit a loyal corps of professional managers, usually
from comfortable but not wealthy backgrounds, who have risen
through the corporate ranks to leading positions in modern
corporations.

Although the largest stockowners and the top management
of many corporations are not the same, the two groups share
common interests. In order to rise in the business world, the
junior executive must demonstrate both competence and loyalty
to prevailing values of corporate capitalism. The key to success is
the willingness to perform well as a loyal member of the
corporate management "team." The rise of corporate managers
has strengthened corporate capitalism. The new breed of managers are often business school graduates trained to apply modern
methods of statistical and economic analysis to furthering corporate aims. Relatively anonymous bureaucrats, the new managers are quite different from the colorful magnates of an earlier
era. And because they are out of the public eye, they are less
likely than old-time tycoons like J. P. Morgan or John D.
Rockefeller to provide a target for popular discontent. (Has
anybody heard of Elliot M. Estes? He is president of GM.)

A second common interest of the two groups derives from
the fact that most corporate executives, even those not in the
ranks of the superwealthy, own large blocks of shares in the
corporations they manage. About one-half of an executive's pay
is in the form of stock bonuses and options, deferred compensation, and profit sharing rather than straight salary. (This is not to
say that corporate executives do not receive handsome salaries:
the presidents of GM and ITT, the country's highest-paid executives, have an annual salary of about $1 million.) A study of
ninety-three top executives in the country's largest corporations

[18]G. William Domhoff, *Who Rules America?* (Englewood Cliffs, N.J., 1967), p. 51.

found that nearly half owned $1 million apiece in stocks in their corporation.[19] Although this amount is not sufficient to provide a controlling interest in the corporation, it does mean that top management has similar interests to the corporation's other large stockholders.

A final piece of evidence suggests that it makes little difference for corporate performance whether a corporation is controlled by a family group or other large stockholders, as was typical for corporations in the past, or whether, as is becoming more common, professional managers play a dominant role without one family or large stockholder group in active control. A study conducted by economist Robert J. Larner compared the performance of two such groups of corporations and found little difference between the two.[20] Contrary to the view of those who have asserted that manager-controlled corporations in the modern era are more "mature," less aggressive, less interested in profits, and more interested in stability than were owner-controlled corporations in the past, Larner finds that both types of corporations act about the same.

What emerges from this examination is the intertwining and convergence of wealth, position, and status. Each element helps explain the overall dominance exercised by those who own and control the means of production in America. Those with great wealth have been able to obtain controlling positions in the corporate sector and to recruit others to help manage corporate capitalism. Thus they have been able to insure that decisions will be made that protect the interests of invested wealth. Social status plays its part through the opportunities provided by being born into the "right" families, attending superior schools, marrying within the proper circles. Social status makes it possible to get useful introductions, call on influential friends for help, and exercise power with ease and flair. The way in which wealth, position, and status interact and reinforce each other serves to separate the group at the top of corporate capitalism from other Americans and to maintain a basic structural cleavage in American society.

---

[19]Robert J. Larner, "The Effect of Management-Control on the Profits of Large Corporations," in Maurice Zeitlin, ed., *American Society, Inc.* (Chicago, 1970), pp. 251–62.

[20]*Ibid.* For a similar view see Edward S. Mason, "Corporation," in *International Encyclopedia of the Social Sciences* vol. 3 (New York, 1968): 396–403.

NEW CONTENDERS FOR POWER?

The Technostructure

Production today is highly technical. Complex machines have replaced much manual labor. The corporation needs trained specialists to maintain machinery, control employees, process the huge volume of information on which the firm relies, and develop new products, methods of distribution, packaging, and advertising. The corporate recruiting advertisements in college newspapers give some hint of the new specialities: operations research, system engineers, modulation and signal processing, digital transmission, computer processor monitoring equipment, industrial psychology, and production engineering. As a result, a new group has arisen that, some say, has challenged the dominance of large stockholders and top management. These technical specialists (along with clerical, sales, and other white-collar workers) now outnumber manual workers in industry.

Harvard economist John Kenneth Galbraith has been so impressed by the importance of the new specialists that he believes they have come to control the corporation. He says, "Effective power of decision is lodged deeply in the technical, planning and other specialized staff."[21] Galbraith calls this new group the technostructure; its power stems from the fact that the corporation could not exist without its scientific and technical expertise. Galbraith holds that scientific and technical talent have replaced capital as the vital force within industry. Although top management continues to retain formal authority within the corporation, technical ignorance has eroded its real power.

Galbraith is right to stress the dependence of modern industry on science and technology. But the fact that the technostructure is *essential* to the corporation's survival does not necessarily mean that the technostructure has obtained the *power to control* the corporation—any more than unskilled workers controlled the corporation when they constituted the majority of its employees, or than a ship's maintenance crew, rather than its captain, runs the ship. Corporate management utilizes the technostructure to

[21]Galbraith, *New Industrial State*, p. 82.

advance the interests of those who own and manage the corporation. But control of corporate capitalism remains firmly lodged in owners and managers, and the growth of the technostructure has not fundamentally altered corporate goals of profits, growth, and control.

New Sources of Capital

Savings by individuals have not kept pace with corporations' need for new capital. In 1969, individuals saved $38 billion; however, more than twice as much new capital—$99 billion—came from savings by business firms.[22] More and more, new capital to fuel corporate expansion has been coming from organizations.

Retained earnings Giant corporations in concentrated industries have found a more reliable source of new capital than individual investors: themselves. A common corporate practice, called retained earnings, is for the corporation to save some of its profits rather than distributing them all to stockholders. Since one would expect stockholders to want to receive all the profits earned by the corporation, the practice of retained earnings does not seem consistent with our earlier observation that large stockholders are in general agreement with corporate policies. Yet large stockholders do in fact support the practice. By retaining earnings, a corporation can grow and produce even greater profits in the future, clearly in stockholders' interests. In addition, earnings that are retained increase the total worth of the corporation and thus the value of its stock. As a result, stockholders benefit indirectly, since the worth of their stock increases. Indeed, wealthy stockholders benefit even more because this increased value—called capital gains—is taxed at a lower rate than dividends and other income.

Corporate management can use retained earnings at its discretion and thus increase the corporation's autonomy. In general, only large firms in a concentrated industry can charge high enough prices to make retained earnings possible. Retained earnings derive from the high prices large corporations charge. In this manner, they represent "forced savings" corporations extract from consumers. (Several estimates place the yearly cost of

[22]*Ibid.*, p. 53.

higher prices to consumers from corporate concentration at over $40 billion.[23]) In 1973, about half of the $70 billion after-tax corporate profits was retained; the rest was distributed as dividends to stockholders.[24] In the past decade, the nation's largest corporations obtained over 60 percent of their new capital from retained earnings.[25]

Financial Institutions Banks, insurance companies, investment bankers, trust funds, pension funds, and mutual investment funds have come to constitute an additional source of corporate capital. Banks are the largest institutional suppliers. With the deposits from checking and saving accounts, banks make investments, using the dividends to pay interest to their own depositors. A growing part of banking business comes from managing pension funds for corporate workers and trust funds, a device used by wealthy individuals to minimize inheritance taxes. It was estimated in 1973 that banks controlled $170 billion in corporate stock, making them an enormously influential force in corporate affairs. Insurance companies and mutual funds are estimated to control an additional $95 billion in corporate stock.[26]

Financial institutions now manage investment funds worth more than individual investments. As in the case of a very large stockholder, a bank that invests in a corporation or makes a large loan to the corporation expects a share in the corporation's management in return. A common practice is for one of the bank's officers to be made a member of the corporation's board of directors. This is called an interlocking directorate, and it gives the bank a direct voice in the corporation's affairs. One study found that the largest banks have interlocks with 286 of the 500 largest corporations.[27] For example, there are five bank executives on GM's twenty-eight-member board of directors. Economist Robert Sheehan has estimated that one-fifth of the 500 largest corporations are controlled by banks and other financial institutions.[28]

[23]Mark J. Green, with Beverly C. Moore, Jr., and Bruce Wasserstein, *The Closed Enterprise System: Ralph Nader's Study Group Report on Antitrust Enforcement* (New York, 1972), p. 14.
[24]*New York Times,* January 2, 1974.
[25]Daniel Bell, *The Coming of Post-Industrial Society* (New York, 1973), p. 294.
[26]*Business Week* (June 2, 1973) p. 58.
[27]U.S., Congress, House, Committee on Banking and Finance, Subcommittee for Domestic Finance, Staff Report, *Commercial Banks and Their Trust Activities,* 90th Cong., 2d sess., 1968, in Zeitlin, p. 75.
[28]Robert Sheehan, "Proprietors in the World of Big Business," in Zeitlin, p. 79.

Yet the fact that banks have been gaining a greater role in the running of large corporations probably does not much affect the performance of these corporations. Both the bank and the corporation prosper together. While the corporation suffers a loss of autonomy, it also enjoys advantages in having a close relationship with a bank: when capital is scarce, the corporation stands a better chance than a small firm of getting a bank loan.

Government subsidy A final source of capital for the corporation is government subsidy. (This subject will be discussed more fully in Chapters 5 and 6.) The largest capital grants by government have gone to military contractors. The government has provided billions of dollars for research and development, for building and equipping factories, and (in the case of Lockheed) for a loan guarantee to keep a firm in business. Particularly in the case of military contractors, the government has become closely involved in corporate management.

COORDINATION WITHIN CORPORATE CAPITALISM

Several broad patterns of corporate control can thus be distinguished. Some of the largest corporations are still controlled either by a family or by a group of large wealthy stockholders. A second group (to which GM belongs) is management-controlled, with large stockholders having less direct say in company affairs. A third group is controlled by a bank or other financial institution. And, in the case of military and aerospace firms, the government plays a leading role in corporate decision-making. Yet the differences among corporations in terms of how they are controlled are less important than what they have in common: all are privately owned by a wealthy powerful few, all strive to achieve the goals of profits, growth, stability, and control. And they cooperate with each other to succeed in their aims.

The structure of relationships *among* corporations is partly a result of how control is exercised *within* corporations. In both cases, the "rules of the game" and loyalty to corporate capitalism prevail. In a concentrated industry, as we have seen, firms reach agreements that avoid bitter price wars and other forms of competition. Antitrust laws prohibit formal agreements to fix prices. But, although numerous cases exist of conspiracies to violate antitrust laws, price-setting is usually done on an informal basis.

Banks and other financial institutions further reduce competition by linking giant corporations through control of stock in competing corporations. Banks, insurance companies, and law firms serve as the hub of a wheel connecting many giant corporations. For example, the Morgan Guaranty Trust (a leading investment bank) controls more than 7 percent of the stock in American Airlines, United Airlines, and TWA, the three largest domestic airlines. As one of the largest stockholders in all three, Morgan Guaranty Trust obviously stands to gain if price competition among the three airlines is limited. A Senate committee found that banks often conceal the extent of their stock control. It was found that the Chase Manhattan Bank, for example, holds over 5 percent of all stock in four competing airlines, six railroads, and seventeen industrial companies.[29]

Another mechanism for coordinating corporate activity and reducing competition is interlocking directorates. It is common for corporations to have interlocking directorates with large suppliers of parts and raw materials, with favored customers, and even (although this is illegal) with competitors. As mentioned earlier, banks also interlock competing corporations. Interlocking directorates create a tight network reaching throughout corporate capitalism. One study notes, "Less than 4,000 managers of large corporations hold the directorships that interconnect the elite classes of officers and managers of the major corporations that employ most of the workers and do most of the business in American life."[30] Economist Peter Dooley found that in 1935 all but 25 of the top 250 corporations had interlocks with each other. By 1965, the number without interlocks had fallen to 17.[31] Dooley notes that one-eighth of these interlocks were with competitors and therefore probably illegal. The power of corporate capitalism partly derives from outright violations of law. Some of the largest corporations were convicted of election-campaign illegalities in

[29]U.S., Congress, Senate, Committee on Government Operations, *Disclosure of Corporate Ownership,* 93rd Cong., 1st sess., December 27, 1973, p. 22.
[30]L. Lloyd Warner, *The Emergent American Society* (New Haven, 1967), p. 157.
[31]Peter C. Dooley, "The Interlocking Directorate," *American Economic Review* 59 (June 1969): 315.

connection with the Watergate affair, and, each year, corporations break laws concerning antitrust, safety conditions, taxes and advertising. But even more important than criminal activity in explaining corporate power are the routine activities described here that are not prohibited by law. Yet this is not surprising, for the political system is decisively shaped by the *requirements* of corporate capitalism.

Trade associations also reduce competition within corporate capitalism. A trade association brings together the major firms in an industry (for example, the American Petroleum Institute for oil companies). It provides a neutral meeting ground where common policy, whose purpose is to benefit member firms, is developed. Thousands of trade associations exist, often gaining a voice within the government in an attempt to obtain favorable treatment for their members.

"Umbrella" business organizations, like the National Association of Manufacturers, the National Industrial Conference Board, the United States Chamber of Commerce, and the Committee for Economic Development, also act as spokesmen for broad sectors of business and attempt to defend their interests. Business publications like *Fortune* and *Business Week* help to coordinate and integrate corporate capitalism by developing a common viewpoint, and defending the basic interests and desirability of corporate capitalism.

The government also plays a central part in coordinating corporate capitalism. Its role as an agent promoting the interests of corporate capitalism will be described in Chapter 5.

Nevertheless, a degree of competition does exist among corporations and between industries. For example, the glass container industry competes with paperboard and plastic; railroads compete with the trucking industry. Although corporations in a given industry do not compete to lower prices, each corporation attempts to increase its share of the market through product design, advertising, and sales promotion. Competition continues to divide corporate capitalism. The mechanisms described above do not assure that all companies and industries benefit equally when circumstances change. The fuel shortage benefited petroleum companies, whose profits soared to all-time highs, and harmed automobile manufacturers, whose sales plummeted. Yet corporate capitalism is united on the most fundamental level, defined by David Rockefeller, chairman of the

Chase Manhattan Bank, as "a community of interests and search for stability in which business can thrive and capital be protected."[32] Whatever differences exist within corporate capitalism, there is agreement on perpetuating a business-oriented economy based on private ownership and control of the means of production organized within large corporate units.

The sector of large-scale capital reaches far afield to play a leading role in the wider society. A study by political scientist Thomas Dye and his associates traced recruitment patterns among the leading social, political, and economic sectors in the United States: industry, higher education, law, civic and cultural associations, foundations, government, military, large personal wealthholders, and large political campaign contributors. Using various criteria to locate the top positions in each field, Dye selected 5,400 such positions in the United States. About 40 percent of these positions were interlocked—held by someone who was currently holding at least one other similar position. (Some individuals held more than two positions; twenty-one Americans, including two Rockefellers and one Ford, held at least six positions simultaneously.) Dye's finding indicates a substantial degree of overlap among those in top positions both inside and outside the corporate-capital sector.

> *Richard King Mellon*: chairman of the board of Mellon National Bank and Trust Company; president, Mellon and Sons; member of the board of directors of Aluminum Company of America, of General Motors Corporation, of Gulf Oil Corporation, of the Koppers Company, of the Pennsylvania Company, and of the Pennsylvania Railroad. *Fortune* magazine lists Mellon's personal wealth in excess of one-half billion dollars. He is a lieutenant general in the Reserves, a member of the board of trustees of the Carnegie Institute of Technology, of the Mellon Institute, and of the University of Pittsburgh.

> *David Rockefeller*: chairman of the board of directors of the Chase Manhattan Bank; member of the board of directors of the B. F. Goodrich Company, of the Rockefeller Brothers, Inc., and of the Equitable Life Insurance Society; a trustee of the Rockefeller Institute for Medical Research, of the Council on Foreign Relations, of the Museum of Modern Art, of Rockefeller Center, and of the Board of Overseers of Harvard College.

[32]*New York Times,* November 7, 1973.

Paul C. Cabot: partner, State Street Research and Management Company (investment firm); member of the board of directors of J. P. Morgan and Company, of the Continental Can Company, of the Ford Motor Company, of the National Dairy Products Corporation, of the B. F. Goodrich Company, and of the M. A. Hanna Company; former treasurer of Harvard University, and a trustee of the Eastern Gas and Fuel Association.

Crawford H. Greenewalt: chairman of the board of directors of E. I. du Pont de Nemours; member of the board of the Equitable Trust Company, of the Christiana Securities Company, and of the Morgan Guaranty Trust Company; a trustee of Massachusetts Institute of Technology, of Wilmington General Hospital, of the Philadelphia Academy of Natural Sciences, of the Philadelphia Orchestra Association, of the American Museum of Natural History, of the Carnegie Institute of Technology, and of the Smithsonian Institute.[33]

Additional data reported by Dye suggest that, among the various sectors, the industrial sphere is critical. Dye found that industry and large law firms provided the largest number of people in top positions for most sectors. The only sector remaining outside the embrace of industry and law is the military—whose officers are usually recruited from sons of former military officers.[34] And even in the military sector, top civilian chiefs—the Secretary of Defense, Deputy Secretary, and Assistant Secretaries—are usually corporate executives or bankers.

Corporate control extends far beyond what one might consider the traditional domain of industrial and mining activity. Corporations have moved into the entertainment and leisure fields, including motion picture companies, hotels, travel and tour companies, and restaurants (Howard Johnson's and McDonald's, rather than the corner drugstore, now supply Americans with hamburgers). In the field of agriculture, "agricorporations" are fast replacing the family farm, centralizing the production, processing, and distribution of food. (By 1966, the 100 largest food manufacturers accounted for nearly half of all food commercially

[33]Thomas R. Dye and L. Harmon Zeigler, *The Irony of Democracy: An Uncommon Introduction to American Politics* (North Scituate, Mass., 1971), p. 103.
[34]Thomas Dye, Eugene R. De Clercq, and John W. Pickering, "Concentration, Specialization, and Interlocking among Institutional Elites," *Social Science Quarterly* 54 (June 1973): 8–28.

marketed.[35]) The field of professional sports is another example of corporate domination. Syndicates have bought up many major professional sports clubs. The New York Yankees were sold in 1973 by CBS to a national syndicate that included a vice president of GM, a law partner in Richard Nixon's former law firm, a Texas oilman, and a Cleveland shipping magnate.[36] The Montreal Expos are owned by a distillery, and the California Angels and Detroit Tigers by radio and television interests. Professional sports is a booming $2.5-billion-a-year business, comfortably integrated into the domain of corporate capitalism.[37]

SOCIAL COSTS OF CORPORATE PRODUCTION

Science and technology make possible material comforts and the reduction of disease and suffering. But the organization of modern production by corporate capitalism has produced systematic costs.

The logic of capitalism is profit, not need. In the early days of capitalism, economists like Adam Smith argued that free enterprise, where thousands of firms competed with each other for the customer's favor, served public needs indirectly. Through the search for private profits, producers would attempt to gauge consumer demand and produce what was wanted at the lowest possible price. Producers who produced what was not wanted or could not produce desired goods at a low price would be forced out of business. Given free competition, easy mobility of producers in and out of the market, and consumer sovereignty, an "invisible hand" (in Adam Smith's words) utilized the profit motive to allocate society's resources efficiently and to satisfy consumer needs. As long as consumers remained sovereign individually—and the other conditions for free competition were met—the theory had merit, although from the beginning it was

---

[35]James Hightower, "The Case for the Family Farmer," *Washington Monthly* (September 1973), p. 28.
[36]*New York Times,* January 11, 1973.
[37]Paul Hoch, *Rip Off the Big Game: The Exploitation of Sports by the Power Elite* (Garden City, N.Y., 1972), p. 47.

based on a view of human nature as acquisitive, materialistic, competitive, private, and selfish.

However, the initial conditions no longer hold true. Corporate production has replaced the individual entrepreneur, free competition no longer exists, entry into the world of corporate concentration is nearly impossible, and the consumer is no longer sovereign. The minority who own and control corporate capitalism decide what will be produced by and for the majority of Americans. Although production is still carried out for profit, the invisible hand insuring that the quest for private profits will serve society's needs is nowhere in evidence.

Even the meaning of profit has changed in a situation of corporate concentration. Profit is no longer a reward for taking the risk of entering into production. The risks and costs of production are likely to be borne by the whole community, not the individual firm. (This has been brought about in part by government measures, which will be discussed in Chapter 5.) To the contrary, a large firm in a concentrated industry is nearly assured of making profits. Indeed, the chances are better than nine in ten that a firm in the top 100 corporations will return a profit every year.

The needs of society as a whole are not served by corporate capitalism. First, it has misallocated society's resources. Corporate production involves the indiscriminate consumption of energy and raw materials; the result has been to shower the country with automobiles, electrical appliances, cosmetics, drugs, convenience foods, soft drinks, and color TV sets—while millions of Americans lack adequate housing, mass transit, recreational, and health facilities. Conspicuous consumption has become a way of life, fostered by corporate capitalism as a means to increase demand for its products. But it is an irrational way for people to live and it neglects social values in favor of material acquisitions. It is especially irrational in an age of shrinking resources.

Second, corporate capitalism produces systematic inequalities. It has overindulged the private needs of the relatively affluent at the expense of the less well-off. It has created a transportation system based on private automobile ownership, which discriminates against those unable to afford the costs of purchasing, insuring, repairing, and maintaining automobiles. Through price-fixing, planned obsolescence, and massive advertising, it has maintained high prices. The greatest benefits of corporate production go to a small minority, the harshest costs are borne by millions of other American families.

Third, the logic of corporate production places the interests of those who own and control capital ahead of even the most basic human needs. A depressing example is provided by the attitude of automobile manufacturers toward the issue of auto safety. For many years, automobile producers ignored the problem. When carnage on the road mounted (reaching fifty thousand deaths annually from traffic accidents—as many Americans as were killed in the Vietnam war), the issue gained public salience. But this did not come about through the efforts of GM and other automobile companies. GM's response to Ralph Nader's campaign for safety improvements in automobile design was to assign a detective to uncover any damaging information in Nader's private life that could be used to discredit him. Daniel Moynihan, a social scientist and public official, suggests an explanation for the automobile companies' resistance to safety features designed to reduce traffic accidents: auto sales are inflated by highway accidents (in which one out of every three automobiles is involved at one time or another). "To a perhaps surprising degree, the profits of the [automobile] industry are related to these accidents. . . . I believe it can no longer be doubted that within the higher executive levels of the industry there has been the conviction that an excessive concern for safety is bad for business."[38]

Those who make the major decisions shaping corporate behavior may not consciously intend these results; nevertheless, they are the product of a system geared to maximizing profits deriving from private ownership and control of the means of production.

Despite the considerable success enjoyed by corporate capitalism, it is facing fundamental difficulties. Here, too, GM can serve as a good example. For years, GM continued to produce large, fuel-hungry, expensive automobiles, rather than small automobiles without frills that cost less to produce and repair. Why? Because GM made far larger profits by selling large automobiles and the optional features (air conditioning, power steering and brakes, cassette systems, and so on) designed to go

[38]Daniel P. Moynihan, *Coping: Essays on the Practice of Government* (New York, 1973), p. 83.

with them. Yet, as a result, GM was particularly vulnerable in 1973 and 1974 when the fuel shortage sent gasoline prices soaring—for most of GM's cars get considerably less gas mileage than smaller, more efficient compacts. A system of production geared to maximum social need, not to what was most profitable for GM, would have emphasized compact automobile production long ago. The mistake was not stupid planning on GM's part: since GM made twice as much profit on a large automobile as on a compact, it made good sense (from GM's point of view) to push such an economically wasteful package.

More generally, a contradiction exists in the fact that what is most profitable for large corporate producers may not be most needed from the point of view of the whole community. The socially wasteful consequences of a transportation system based on automobiles have already been described. Despite the efforts of the automobile lobby, economic changes may be impossible to resist. Social critic Emma Rothschild has suggested that the whole American automobile industry may be a declining industry, in which the possibilities for continued expansion and high profits are limited. It may thus suffer the same fate as railroads and the steel industry, which were once pillars of the economy but slowly became less central.[39] If it were not for powerful groups organized to protect automobile interests, cheaper and more efficient means of public transportation might have been developed long ago. But while corporate interests may resist economic and technological changes up to a point, they cannot hold out forever.

THE CRISIS OF CAPITALISM

Corporate capitalism is capable of great adaptation. Among the changes that it has partially accepted—despite their apparent violation of capitalist principles—have been the rise of trade unions, corporate expenditures for environmental protection, improved safety conditions for workers, and increased product safety and reliability.

[39]Emma Rothschild, *Paradise Lost: The Decline of the Auto-Industrial Age* (New York, 1972).

Nonetheless, there are certain bedrock principles that set limits to how much change corporate capitalism can accept. Foremost among these is the principle of profit for the private owners of capital. It is this necessity that poses the basic dilemma of capitalism. Continued profits require continued expansion, which in turn depends on a never-ending supply of resources. But the world's resources are not unlimited; in fact, they are diminishing. While economic growth may not be necessary to society as a whole, the capitalist system must grow or stagnate. Lack of growth means a loss of rewards to those owning and controlling capital. Herein lies the basic contradiction between what can be called the logic of profit central to capitalism and the logic of social need. The growing split between the two has produced a fundamental crisis of capitalism. As possibilities for growth through expanding production and sales in the domestic American market slacken, the whole American economy may be running down.

Additional outlets for corporate capitalism, notably government-stimulated demand (through military purchases) and overseas expansion, have been of vital help since the 1950s in assuring corporate success, but they are proving less effective in the present. To understand the current crisis of American corporate capitalism, it is necessary to examine the role of government. This will be studied in Part Three. However, we must first complete the analysis of the organization of production by looking at the workers who make corporate production possible.

4

workers
and work

Alexis de Tocqueville arrived in the United States from France in 1831. Like other travellers to pre-Civil War America when the country was mostly agrarian and the cities were unindustrialized, he was impressed most by the absence of class divisions. "Among the novel objects that attracted my attention during my stay in the United States," he wrote, "nothing struck me more forcibly than the general equality of condition among the people."[1]

Similarly, on his trip to the United States in 1842, the English novelist Charles Dickens discovered that even in the newly established textile mills of New England, conditions contrasted sharply with those in factories in Great Britain. Describing factory life in Lowell, Massachusetts, where virtually all the employees were teenage farmgirls, he wrote:

> The girls, as I have said, were all well dressed; and that phrase necessarily includes extreme cleanliness. They had serviceable bonnets, good warm cloaks, and shawls; and were not above clogs and patterns. . . . They were healthy in appearance, many of them remarkably so, and had the manners and deportment of young women; not of degraded brutes of burden. . . . The rooms in which they worked were as well ordered as themselves. In the windows

[1] Alexis de Tocqueville, *Democracy in America* (New York, 1945), p. 3.

of some there were green plants, which were trained to shade the glass; in all, there was as much fresh air, cleanliness, and comfort as the nature of the occupation could possible admit of.[2]

Dickens, like Tocqueville, devoted much of his account to a discussion of the consequences of relative economic and social equality. The analyses of both chroniclers (especially of Tocqueville) have been influential in shaping the popular view of America's social structure. But their accounts documented an era that was coming to a close. In the 1840s and 1850s, the country's social structure began to undergo fundamental change. The development of early industrial capitalism created new class divisions that were soon to supplant the more egalitarian, individualistic democracy Tocqueville and Dickens observed.

THE DECLINE OF THE INDEPENDENT MIDDLE CLASS

By the late 1840s, the paternalism of the Lowell factories was a quaint memory. Had Dickens returned to Massachusetts in 1850, he would have had to confront a very different industrial reality. During the decade, the wages of the mill workers became severely depressed. Historian Norman Ware has found:

> In 1846 the wages of weavers in Newburyport were reduced 10 percent and in Lowell it was said that never since the beginning of the industry had the operatives received lower wages, though "they are compelled to do all of one-third more work and, in some cases, double." Whereas in 1840 weekly time wages were from 75 cents to $2 per week and board, in 1846 they ran from 55 cents to $1.50, making a 25 percent reduction in spite of the fact that they were doing 33 percent more work.[3]

There were sporadic strikes throughout the decade, in opposition both to more work at lower wages and to the length of the work day, which averaged twelve hours. Without exception, all the strikes, including one that lasted six months in the winter of 1850–51, were broken by the employers. When Dickens had visited Lowell, it was possible "for the New England women who

[2]Charles Dickens, *American Notes* (London, 1972), p. 115.
[3]Norman Ware, *The Industrial Worker, 1840–1860* (Chicago, 1924), p. 113–14.

lived isolated lives in farming communities to feel, when they
went to Lowell, as if they were going to boarding-school, in spite
of the long hours." But, according to Ware, as the logic of profit
replaced this genteel paternal tradition

> the older amenities had to go . . . the boarding-school dream
> faded. The girls were no longer able to relieve one another at their
> work, to snatch a rest of fifteen minutes, to read a book propped up
> on the frame. They ceased the cultivation of window flowers—in
> fact, they left the mills altogether and were replaced by new
> workers.[4]

By the end of the 1840s, the deterioration of working conditions
drove the women out. They were replaced by immigrants
escaping the Irish famine of 1848.

By the outbreak of the Civil War, the basis for conflict
between workers and industrialists was developing rapidly. In
community after community, the events that occurred in Lowell
in the 1840s were replicated. By the end of the nineteenth
century, as the Western frontier closed, capitalist class divisions
overtook an older America of self-employed merchants, artisans,
farmers, professionals, and traders.

The impact of these changes on everyday life was overwhelming. In their study of Muncie, Indiana, between 1890 and
1924, sociologists Helen and Robert Lynd documented the massive shift in social relationships that resulted from the development of industrial capitalism. Traditional craft patterns broke
down under the impact of machines and assembly-line techniques
in the local factories; skilled labor was now unnecessary for most
jobs. As self-employed craftsmen and local entrepreneurs were
forced out of business, workers' traditional neighborhoods lost
their cohesiveness and autonomy. The city as a whole lost its
sense of autonomy as well, since most of the urban economic
changes were the result of national forces outside the city's
control. The businessman, not the independent craftsman, was
now at the top of the town's wealth, status, and power hier-
archies.[5] In short, the division between the capitalist class and the
working class came into being.

People became divided by class not only at the work place
but also in their daily lives in the community and in politics. New

[4]*Ibid.,* p. 120–21.
[5]Robert S. Lynd and Helen Merrell Lynd, *Middletown* (New York, 1929).

institutions, including unions and businessmen's associations, developed that became vehicles for the expression and containment of the new structural antagonisms of interest. Unlike regional or religious distinctions, class distinctions underpinned the experience of living in a total, inescapable way.

Tocqueville and Dickens visited an America of *independent* workers; after the Revolution, four out of five workers (excluding slaves) were farmers, artisans, merchants, doctors, traders, small businessmen, lawyers, and craftsmen. Property was a liberating force. Because property, especially land, was distributed relatively equally, it provided a basis for a more substantive level of democracy than any country had known before. In this respect, the United States was truly a revolutionary society. Thomas Jefferson's dream of a dynamic agrarian democracy had been put into practice for white American men (excluding, however, a politically invisible majority of the population, made up of blacks, women, and Indians).

By 1900, however, the independent middle class had declined in size and was replaced by a growing percentage of Americans who did not own their tools of production but sold their labor for a wage. Whereas in 1780, only 20 percent of the work force were paid employees, in 1900, 68 percent were wage earners; the independent middle class had shrunk to less than one-third of all workers.[6]

Today, the demise of the independent property-owning middle class is virtually complete. Fewer than 3 percent of Americans are farm owners, and fewer than 7 percent are self-employed. Thus, with the development of industrial capitalism, ownership of the tools of production has come to divide Americans rather than unite them. As a result of the dual trend of the decline of the independent middle class and the development of a working-class majority, almost all Americans belong to one of two basic classes: those who own and control the means of production and workers—from dishwashers to skilled engineers—who sell their labor for a wage.

We have defined workers as those who sell their labor for a

---

[6]Michael Reich, "The Evolution of the United States Labor Force," in Richard C. Edwards, Michael Reich, Thomas E. Weisskopf, eds., *The Capitalist System: A Radical Analysis of American Society* (Englewood Cliffs, N.J., 1972), p. 175.

Table 4-1
The proletarianization of the U.S. labor force [a]

Year	Percent wage and salaried employees [b]	Percent self-employed entrepreneurs [c]	Percent salaried managers and officials	Total
1780 [d]	20.0	80.0	—	100.0
1880	62.0	36.9	1.1	100.0
1890	65.0	33.8	1.2	100.0
1900	67.9	30.8	1.3	100.0
1910	71.9	26.3	1.8	100.0
1920	73.9	23.5	2.6	100.0
1930	76.8	20.3	2.9	100.0
1939	78.2	18.8	3.0	100.0
1950	77.7	17.9	4.4	100.0
1960	80.6	14.1	5.3	100.0
1969	83.6	9.2	7.2	100.0

[a] Defined as all income recipients who participate directly in economic activity; unpaid family workers have been excluded.
[b] Excluding salaried managers and officials.
[c] Business entrepreneurs, professional practicioners, farmers and other property owners.
[d] Figures for 1780 are rough estimates. Slaves, who comprised one fifth of the population, are excluded; white indentured servants are included in the wage and salaried employees category.
Source: Michael Reich, "The Evolution of the United States Labor Force," in Richard C. Edwards, Michael Reich, and Thomas E. Weisskopf, eds., *The Capitalist System: A Radical Analysis of American Society,* © 1972, p. 175. By permission of Prentice-Hall, Inc., Englewood Cliffs, N.J.

wage. Technically, those who make salaries in the upper income brackets are workers, but they will be excluded from our discussion of the working class for two reasons: first, high-income wage earners such as those in middle- and top-management positions in powerful corporations receive benefits from corporate capitalism that are overwhelmingly disproportionate to those received by the majority of workers, and, as we saw in Chapter 3, they strongly identify their interests with the success of corporate capitalism; and, second, as we saw in Chapter 2, they comprise but a small privileged minority of all United States wage earners.

By contrast, the majority of American workers live on the margin. One useful measure of living standards is the federal government's Moderate But Adequate City Worker's Budget (MBA). In 1967, this budget was set at $9,100 for a family of four. It provided for the minimum housing standards of the Federal

Housing Administration, moderate food costs, no legal assistance, and no savings of any kind. Fully 59 percent of all American families earned incomes below the MBA budget.[7]

The decline of the independent middle class was no accident. Rather, it was required by the development of industrial capitalism. Mass production had two effects: one was to force independent craftsmen and entrepreneurs out of business; the second was to standardize the labor force. As factories grew rapidly in size at the turn of the century, working conditions became more uniform and impersonal. Technological innovations mechanized work and undermined the need for skilled craftsmen. In the automobile industry, for example, skilled mechanics and work gangs were replaced by semiskilled assembly-line workers. The skills needed in one industry became similar to those needed in others. As a result, "workers became members of an increasingly faceless mass of indistinguishable factory labor."[8]

Although the development of American capitalism has made workers more and more alike as wage laborers, workers today differ significantly from each other in terms of their sexual, ethnic, and racial backgrounds, the kind of work places they work in, and the kind of work they do. These differences, we argue, are not as fundamental as the distinction between capital and labor. But to comprehend the politics of class relations in the United States, it is essential to grasp the intricate web of social relationships imposed on the basic two-class division.

THREE HISTORIES

Americans are not a homogeneous lot. In particular, today's working class of wage earners consists of three broad groups, each with its own distinct history, each having entered the industrial work force at different periods of American economic development, and each of which today plays an economic role

---

[7]Robert Cherry, "Class Struggle and the Nature of the Working Class," *The Review of Radical Political Economics* 5 (Summer 1973): 51.

[8]David M. Gordon, Richard Edwards, and Michael Reich, "Labor Segmentation in American Capitalism," unpublished manuscript.

different from the others. These three groups are women, white Europeans, and blacks and other non-European minorities.

Women

In his report on manufacturers in 1796, Alexander Hamilton proposed that women and children be put to work in developing industries to save them from the "curse of idleness." In Lowell, Massachusetts, and in other New England mill towns, unmarried women were recruited to meet the labor needs of the new factories. But it was assumed that married women would stay in the home. As the country industrialized in the middle and late nineteenth century and the economic world of the independent middle class was shattered, an increasing number of men began to work in impersonal factory surroundings beyond the immediate embrace of home and community. Ideas about women conformed to this new reality:

> With men removed from contact with children during the lengthy and exhausting day, women had to fill the breach. Simultaneously, [capitalist] economic policies which emphasized individualism, success and competition replaced the old puritan ethic which emphasized morality, hard work and community. Men who worked hard and strove for success required wives who could competently supervise the household and exercise supportive roles as well. . . . In what Bernard Wishy calls a reappraisal of family life that took place after 1830, motherhood rose to new heights, and children became the focus of womanly activity.[9]

But this new ethos applied almost exclusively to white, native-born American women. Immigrant and black women were driven into the labor force by need and, from 1850 on, took jobs in the burgeoning industries. The prevailing feminine ideal of domesticity, however, "provided employers with a docile labor force of women who, for the most part, were convinced that their real calling lay in marriage and child-rearing, and had only a transient interest in their jobs."[10] In complementary fashion, since women "really" belonged at home, employers were permitted to treat them as if their earnings were not necessary for family

[9]Alice Kessler Harris, "Women, Work, and the Social Order," unpublished manuscript.
[10]*Ibid.*

survival. Thus, from the very entry of women into the main-stream work force to the present, women's wages have been considerably lower than men's (a tendency that has been rein-forced by consistently lower rates of union membership by women).

During the last decades of the nineteenth century, the place of women in the labor force began to undergo considerable change. Before then, most clerical workers were men. But with the growing concentration of American industry and the expansion of corporate capitalism, the demand for clerical workers rose rapidly, and the number of available literate men was inadequate. A large pool of educated women was tapped.

In this century, the entry of women into office work has increased at such a rate that clerical labor has become feminized: many jobs are labeled "women's work" and entail services of a sex-stereotyped nature. Indeed, as sociologist Margery Davies points out, the work of a secretary came to be compared functionally with the role of a wife.

> Secretaries began to be expected to remind their bosses of birthdays and other social occasions, go out to buy sandwiches or coffee, and even run such personal errands as buying Christmas presents. All clerical workers were expected to dress nicely and be personable to visitors to the office; in other words, to be conscious and careful of their female roles as decorative sex objects and practitioners of the social graces.[11]

Women have thus come to occupy low-wage white- and blue-collar jobs. Collectively, they make up a marginal, exploited labor force. Only just over one-third of women work full time; the many women who work on a part-time or temporary basis never achieve seniority or fringe benefits. Women are readily fired in periods of economic recession and rehired when employers need them. Because many must stop working to look after their families, they have high turnover rates in the work force and are more exposed than men to the risks of unemployment. They are discriminated against in being promoted to supervisory jobs. And they are paid significantly less than men. In 1939, the median income of men was $1,419, as compared to $863 for women, or 60.8 percent of men's wages. Twenty-five years

[11]Margery Davies, "Woman's Place Is at the Typewriter: The Feminization of the Clerical Labor Force," *Radical America* 8 (July–August 1974): 19.

later, the relative position of women not only had not improved but had slightly declined: in 1964, men earned a median income of $6,497, while women earned $3,859, or 59.4 percent of men's wages.[12] This systematic pattern of discrimination is exacerbated because married women who work usually hold two jobs, one of which—housework—is unpaid labor.

White Europeans

The United States is a nation of immigrants, most of whom have come from Europe. With the exception of American Indians (the country's real native Americans), virtually all Americans came from overseas, or their ancestors did, no earlier than the seventeenth century. Colonial America was largely settled by Protestant English, French, and Dutch settlers. Their descendants today (sometimes referred to as WASPs, for White-Anglo-Saxon Protestants) do not often think of themselves as immigrants or as an ethnic group. Yet, they too have been an integral part of the massive migration of European ethnics to the United States during the past four centuries. Hence they are included in this discussion of white European workers.

Factory capitalism, however, did not develop during a period of mass Protestant European immigration, but during a period of Catholic and Jewish immigration. Thus, while many white Protestants joined the industrial labor force from the farms and smaller cities of rural America, the newer, late nineteenth and early twentieth century, European immigrants entered the industrial work force directly. In 1850, 11.5 percent of the population was foreign-born; in 1890, 16.6 percent, a figure that remained roughly constant until the passage of restrictive immigration legislation in the early 1920s. Major industrial centers were mosaics of numerous distinct ethnic communities.

In late nineteenth-century America, class and ethnicity interpenetrated each other. Before 1880, when the large-scale migration from Southern and Eastern Europe began, the members of the newly developing working class consisted of the following basic ethnic elements: (1) native-born white Protestant artisans who continued to work in handicraft industries that

---

[12]Marilyn Power Goldberg, "The Economic Exploitation of Women," *The Review of Radical Political Economics* 2 (Spring 1970): 41.

predated the American revolution; (2) a small number of white native-born farmers who came to the cities and factories of the Northeast instead of joining the larger migration westward to new agricultural lands; (3) skilled Northern European immigrants— German, French, English, Welsh, and Scotch-Irish—who had craft occupations in the new factories; and (4) Irish and Chinese peasants who "were propertyless in the historical sense of possessing neither capital nor land, as well as in the modern sense of possessing no skills that would give them status within the industrial system."[13] Most were employed in railway construction, which required large numbers of unskilled laborers.

As the economy developed in the late nineteenth century, work that had been done by skilled mining, textile, and steel workers could now be done by unskilled workers tending machines. The massive migration from Southern and Eastern Europe brought the millions of unskilled workers needed to staff the developing corporate industries. In 1880, only 4 percent of the miners in the coal fields of eastern Pennsylvania were from Southern or Eastern Europe; but as the coal industry was mechanized and skill levels were reduced, immigrant workers poured into the mines from Italy, Poland, Russia, Czechoslovakia, Austria, Hungary, and Lithuania. Similar changes in the work force occurred in textile, iron, and steel plants. By 1900, the new ethnic immigrants provided the core of productive factory labor.

As more and more factory jobs became unskilled and were filled by the white-ethnic immigrants from Southern and Eastern Europe, native-born and Northern European skilled workers established formidable craft-union barriers to protect their jobs from incursion by the rest of the labor force. Especially by the use of separate seniority lists, unskilled workers were barred from skilled jobs even when they accumulated company seniority. Until the 1930s, in many industries only the skilled workers were represented by trade unions; the unskilled remained without union protection.

Hence, at least until the late 1930s, there was little occupational mobility available to the newer ethnic immigrants who had joined the industrial work force at the bottom rungs. There were exceptions—mainly Jewish and Greek—who had arrived with experience as artisans and proprietors that facilitated their entry

[13]Stanley Aronowitz, *False Promises* (New York, 1973), p. 146.

into small business as owners. The great bulk of Catholic immigrants, on the other hand, had no such entrepreneurial preparation.

Most of the newer ethnic immigrants were peasants from societies that were sharply stratified along hierarchical, semifeudal lines. The inheritance of semifeudal social relations was a major factor in fragmenting the developing industrial working class and in dividing workers from each other. As sociologist Stanley Aronowitz has noted:

> Contrary to the commonly held belief that the success of our economic development has been due, in large measure, to the absence of a feudal past, it is evident that the genius of American capital consisted in its ability to incorporate the institutions of rank and obligation, the separation of mental and physical labor, the distinction between town and country, and the authority relations that marked feudalism. Feudalism was not denied, but transformed and used by employers in the development of capitalism.[14]

Today, children and grandchildren of the newer European immigrants provide the bulk of the work force for the country's largest industrial corporations. Indeed, with the development of industrial unionism in the 1930s and the relative prosperity of the corporate sector of the economy, these white ethnics as a group are better off economically than women workers and racial minorities. Although ethnic categories are an important basis for the organization of the daily lives of many Americans (ethnic schools, churches, neighborhoods, and shops continue to provide a sense of solidarity and identity), the distinctions between old and new ethnics no longer differentiate workers from each other in terms of either their wages or their occupations. With minor exceptions, the Southern and Eastern European ethnics have achieved an occupational profile remarkably like that of the society as a whole. Proportionately, roughly as many ethnics are managers, white-collar workers, blue-collar workers, and farmers as the American population as a whole.

Blacks and Other Non-European Minorities

The experience of America's non-European minorities—blacks, Indians, Chicanos, Asians, and Caribbean Hispanics—has been

[14]*Ibid.*, p. 183.

considerably different from that of other Americans, including European immigrants. With the notable exceptions of Indians and some Chicanos, minorities came to the United States for the same reason as European immigrants: to work. But the answers to where and under what circumstances they worked were quite different for the two groups.

The history of minority groups in the United States can best be understood as an example of internal colonialism. The conquest of the Indian population and the introduction of plantation slavery in the South were important events in the establishment of a worldwide colonial order. These events, sociologist Robert Blauner notes

> established the pattern for labor practices in the colonial regimes of Asia, Africa and Oceania during the centuries that followed. The key equation was the association of free labor with people of white European stock and the association of unfree labor with non-western people of color.[15]

The native North American Indian tribes, many of whom were mobile hunters, withstood the attempts made by the New World colonists to force them into dependent labor relationships, including slavery. They resisted agricultural peonage and fought for their lands. South of the Rio Grande, where Indian settlements were dense, the Spanish succeeded in subjugating the Indians economically and in capturing their labor. By contrast, in the territories that eventually became the United States, Indian settlements were sparse and thus difficult to colonize for labor. Instead, a process of genocide drove Indians off their lands to make room for European settlements.

Today, the surviving remnant live on reservations and, increasingly, in middle-size and large cities. Their living conditions are more depressed than those of any other American minority group. Indian unemployment is over 40 percent, and an overwhelming number of those who work have low-paid menial jobs.

In the American South, neither Indian nor white labor was sufficient to meet the demands of large-scale plantation agriculture. Slaves were imported to meet that need. There, as in other parts of the continent, property ownership was largely restricted to whites. "White men, even if from lowly origins and serf-like

<hr>

[15]Robert Blauner, *Racial Oppression in America* (New York, 1972), p. 55.

pasts, were able to own land, property and sell their labor in the free market."[16] Even the most degrading "free labor" jobs of the developing capitalist sectors of the economy were for whites only. Blacks and the other racial minorities were channelled into a secondary labor market that was both noncapitalist and unfree. The correlation between color and "free" work was nearly exact.

After the Civil War, as America rapidly industrialized, the manpower needs of the factories were not filled by newly freed blacks but by white ethnics from Europe.

> American captains of industry *and* the native white proletariat preferred the employment of despised, unlettered European peasants to that of the emancipated Negro population of the South. Low as was the condition and income of the factory laborer, his status was that of a free worker.[17]

Black Americans became sharecroppers and tenant farmers on Southern plantations, little removed from their former conditions of slavery.

Similarly, a colonial pattern of work relations was created in the Southwest in the nineteenth century. After the Mexican defeats in the Texas war of independence in 1836 and the Mexican War of 1846 to 1848, a new pool of dependent Mexican labor was available to the colonizers. This work force was usually bound to contractors and landowners in a status little above peonage. Asians, too, especially the Chinese, were contract rather than "free" laborers in the Southwest, where they were used in work gangs to build railroads and mines.

In our discussion of class relations, we emphasized the basic distinction between those who own and control capital and those who sell their labor for a wage. The colonized minorities, however, at least until well into the twentieth century, were outside of this class dynamic. Workers in capitalist enterprises, including the European immigrants, worked within the wage system, whereas the minorities filled jobs in the least advanced, most industrially backward sectors of the economy. As a result, Blauner notes:

> In a historical sense, people of color provided much of the hard labor (and also technical skills) that built up the agricultural base and mineral-transport-communication "infrastructure" necessary

[16]*Ibid.,* p. 58.
[17]*Ibid.,* p. 59.

for industrialization and modernization, whereas the Europeans worked primarily within the industrialized modern sectors. The initial position of European ethnics while low, was therefore strategic for movement up the economic and social pyramid. The placement of nonwhite groups, however, imposed barrier upon barrier on such mobility, freezing them for long periods of time in the least favorable segments of the economy.[18]

A dual labor market, in which whites are distinguished from nonwhites, continues to exist in the United States at present. Although the following discussion examines the particularities of the black experience, the same general trends hold for Indians, Chicanos, Asians, and Caribbean Hispanics.

A wide disparity between the incomes of whites and blacks is the most obvious indicator of the continuing existence of racial inequality at the work place. The most exhaustive study published on the subject in the past decade reported that "median family income for nonwhites in 1966 was $4,628 and for white families $7,722, giving a nonwhite to white median income ratio of 59.9 percent." Since then, the gap in income between blacks and whites has widened. Although black families now earn $7,269 a year, white family income has increased even more rapidly to $12,595; hence the average black American earns roughly $6 for every $10 earned by his white counterpart.[19]

Moreover, the higher the wage and prestige of an occupation, the lower the percentage of black workers in that occupation. Blacks represent about 12 percent of the labor force, yet only 5 percent of professionals, 3 percent of managers, 6 percent of clerks, and 3 percent of salespeople. By contrast, blacks make up half the country's domestic household workers, and one-quarter of the unskilled laborers.[20]

The majority of blacks work for small business firms, not the big corporations, or are unemployed (in 1974 the unemployment rate for blacks was 9.4 percent, more than double the rate of 4.6 percent for whites). And within the relatively depressed sector of the economy in which most blacks work, a significant amount of discrimination limits blacks to the meanest, lowest-paid, most

[18]*Ibid.*, p. 62.
[19]Albert Wohlstetter and Sinclair Coleman, "Race Differences in Income," Report Prepared for the Office of Economic Opportunity, October 1970, mimeographed manuscript.
[20]*New York Times*, July 24, 1974.

transient work, or to black service firms that sell goods and services to the ghettoes. A recent study of Chicago's labor market found that 70 percent of small firms did not employ any blacks; of the 30 percent that did, virtually all had a majority of black workers.

This bleak economic picture was relieved somewhat in the 1960s as a result of the gains of the civil-rights movement. Barriers to black employment in many corporate jobs were broken. By 1972, 26 percent of black families had incomes above the federal government's intermediate-level family budget of $11,446 a year (compared to 56 percent of white families). Yet one ironic result of black gains has been a widening of the gap between the quarter of the black population that works for the large corporations and government, and the vast majority who are confined to small-firm jobs, unemployment, and welfare. As a recent *New York Times* survey concluded:

> The decade produced the most extensive gains for the most favored segments of black America—the middle class and working class blacks. Blacks who entered the decade with educational and marketable skills were in a better position generally to exploit the newly created opportunities. . . . Those mired in rural poverty and the urban welfare system derived peripheral benefits of food stamps, improved health care and larger dependency payments, but on the whole remained poor, unskilled, and disaffected.
> These deepening divisions created a new generation of haves and have-nots in black America. . . . If middle class blacks complained about the widening gap with whites, lower income blacks bitterly pointed to the widening gap between them and the black middle class.[21]

Half of all the black poor, as defined by federal government standards, are under eighteen, and—given their skill levels and the patterns of discrimination—they are likely to remain poor for a long time. The nearly eight million poor blacks live either in the rural South where colonial-like labor conditions still prevail or in the urban ghettoes whose economic, cultural, and political organization has taken on the form of colonial patterns of dominance.

Like classic colonies, the ghettoes live off what they export. In classic colonies, exports are usually raw materials; in the

[21]*New York Times*, August 26, 1973.

ghettoes, the cheap labor of the colonized. Politically, the ghettoes are administered from the outside. Stokely Carmichael and Charles Hamilton have argued that black America is subject to the political decisions made for them by colonial masters:

> The black community perceives the "white power structure" in very concrete terms. The man in the ghetto sees his white landlord come only to collect exorbitant rents and fail to make the necessary repairs, while both know that the white-dominated city building inspection department will wink at violations or impose only slight fines. The man in the ghetto sees the white policeman on the corner brutally manhandle a black drunkard in a doorway, and at the same time accept a payoff from one of the agents of the white-controlled rackets. . . . He is not about to listen to intellectual discourses on the pluralistic and fragmented nature of political power. He is faced with a "white power structure" as monolithic as Europe's colonial offices have been to African and Asian colonies.[22]

Finally, there is a cultural component to American internal colonialism. Because the European immigrants came to America voluntarily, they were able to move freely within their adopted society. They did face profound discrimination, but they had the advantage of white skins and were free to travel about the country in search of jobs and improved living conditions in a way that was impossible for the early generations of blacks, Chicanos, and Asians. This wider range of choice for the ethnics made it possible for them to reestablish their social relationships and cultural forms in the United States and create cohesive neighborhood institutions that could preserve and develop indigenous cultures.

By contrast, America's racial minorities were workers in circumstances that tended to weaken, and sometimes completely destroy, traditional communal and cultural ties. More than any other colonial labor system, American slavery shattered indigenous cultural forms, including patterns of family life, language, and religion. Whereas the Catholic and Jewish religions were mocked and scorned by native Protestants, black religious patterns were obliterated by the colonizers.

This pattern of cultural oppression has been legitimized by an ideology of racism, which denies the essential adult humanity

---

[22]Stokely Carmichael and Charles Hamilton, "Institutional Racism and the Colonial Status of Blacks," in Edwards, Reich, and Weisskopf, p. 292.

of the colonized and assumes the innate superiority of whites and their culture. The cultural heritages of black, Indian, Chicano, Caribbean, and Asian groups have been systematically violated by the dominant white society.

WORK PLACES

Thus far we have examined two basic features of the work force: the emergence in the late nineteenth century of a two-class economic structure and the histories of the groups that compose the working class. A third distinctive feature is the division of the work force into different labor markets that correspond to the basic division of the economy into three sectors: relatively small capitalist firms, large-scale corporate enterprises, and government employment.[23] As we shall see in later chapters, it is impossible to understand the process of American politics without grasping the significance of these divisions.

The *small-capital sector* is the oldest sector of the American economy. It combines traditional, even precapitalist, businesses (such as neighborhood shops and family farms), small-scale, usually local, industrial factories (such as furniture and printing plants), and locally based real estate and insurance firms. Though firms in this sector can be very prosperous—at least for their owners—both production and markets of these firms are small and often precarious. Their productive output depends much less on technology and capital investment than on low-paid labor. One-third of American workers work in this sector; most receive wages just above or below the minimum wage. Wages, as well as profits and prices, depend on market competition. Because it is relatively easy to establish a small business firm, there are usually many more small-capital businesses than are needed, and competition is keen between those who provide equivalent products or services. This competition is largely unregulated by the government. The "fittest" survive, usually because they are able to keep their labor costs low. The small businessmen, who must depress wages to survive, are assisted by the almost total lack of

[23]The analysis that follows is based on the discussion in James O'Connor, *The Fiscal Crisis of the State* (New York, 1973), chapter one.

unionization of workers in the small-capital sector. Because these workers are usually without union protection, have few marketable skills, and are more numerous at any given time than the number of jobs available, they are America's most exploited workers.

Employment in this sector is not only low paid but without security. Many jobs are temporary, seasonal, or casual. Unemployment and underemployment tend to be high; but these workers are ill prepared to be out of work or sick. In addition to the lack of union protection, there are few company retirement and health plans in this sector. As a result of job insecurities, low pay, and scant protection against unemployment and sickness, workers in the small-capital sector are heavily dependent on government programs, including welfare, food stamps, subsidized housing, and public hospital clinic services.

The *corporate sector,* which employs another third of the work force, dominates the American economy. Production and markets are large and national or international in scope. Once, corporations in this sector were organized along competitive lines; today, wages, prices, and profits are not determined by the operation of a traditional capitalist market but are planned by the corporations and government. As economist James O'Conner notes:

> Monopolistic corporations have substantial market power. Prices are administered, and in comparative terms price movements are sealed off from market forces. Most corporations operate on the basis of an after-tax profit target (normally between 10 and 15 percent). If labor costs rise, monopolistic corporations will attempt to protect planned profit targets by increasing prices. Assuming that labor productivity remains unchanged, money wages are thus the main determinants of monopoly sector prices.[24]

Corporate-sector workers (blue-collar, white-collar, and technical workers) are much more likely to belong to unions than small-capital–sector workers, their wages are higher, and employment is relatively more secure on a year-round basis. Nevertheless, most corporate-sector workers find it difficult to meet the rising costs of everyday life. In 1970, the median weekly gross earnings of all full-time workers was $130, or an annual income of

[24]*Ibid.,* pp. 19–20.

$6,760, a figure more than $2,000 below the federal government's moderate living standard.

The organization of business firms in the corporate sector is relatively stable. While small businesses are established easily and have a high casualty rate, the barriers to entry in the corporate sector are formidable. The complexity of modern technology, high capital start-up costs, requirements of government regulatory agencies, and the head start of existing corporations with billions of dollars of assets make it virtually impossible for new major corporations to be created. The only recent exceptions to this rule have been corporations that developed new technological breakthroughs in electronics and computers

The *state sector* is the third major source of employment. One-sixth of American workers work directly for the federal, state, and local governments; another sixth work for industries that produce goods and services under contract with the state, including highway construction, other forms of building, and, most importantly, arms and military hardware production.

Government in this century has grown rapidly and has become an integral part of American capitalism. In 1890, 8 percent of the Gross National Product was made up of government spending; in 1960, 30 percent. Since 1965, there have been massive increases in government spending for defense, education, welfare, health care, police, and corrections. The two major federal budgetary priorities have been military and welfare spending. State and local expenditures have risen even more rapidly than federal spending; from the turn of the century to 1960, there was a seventy-fold increase in state and local budgets.

This massive increase in the scope of government at all levels has produced a more rapid employment growth in the state sector than in any other. In 1929, 3 million Americans worked for the state, or just over 6 percent of the labor force. Today, there are 12 million workers on the government payroll, or just over 16 percent of the labor force. Local government employment alone rose from 3.2 million to 7.1 million between 1950 and 1970.[25]

Most state-sector workers are protected by civil service regulations, and, as a result, have good job security. Nevertheless, the size of the work force in different agencies and localities

[25]Daniel Bell, *The Coming of Post-Industrial Society* (New York, 1973), pp. 132–33; O'Connor, p. 99.

depends on political decisions affecting budgetary priorities. In recent years, many public employees, such as teachers, welfare workers, and police, have formed unions and have secured higher wages and shorter working hours. This sector has become better organized than the small-capital sector but more poorly organized than the corporate sector. Since the government must compete with private corporations for skilled labor, wages of those who work for the state generally tend to be close to corporate-sector wages.

UNEVEN DEVELOPMENT AND A DUAL ECONOMY

In each of the three sectors of the American economy, there is a basic antagonism between workers and those who purchase their labor for a wage. It is in the interest of workers to maximize their wages and reduce the amount of work they have to do; conversely, it is in the interest of their employers to minimize the wages paid and maximize the amount of work their workers do. Moreover, employers seek to control the nature and terms of the work relationship, while the opposite situation is in the interests of workers.

Though all workers share these broad interests, the development of American capitalism in this century has been uneven. The relatively wealthy corporate sector, with the aid of the state, has grown richer; and the small-capital sector, poorer. How does uneven development operate? What are its consequences?

Over time, those who control the investment of capital will tend to reinvest in those product lines, machinery, geographic areas, and workers that promise the highest profit return on their investment. "Conversely," economist Barry Bluestone notes, "investment will tend to decline in segments of the economy where potential profit is relatively low. The outcome is continuous growth and relative prosperity in the former sector and relative stagnation and impoverishment in the latter."[26] In this way, private investors put their money in investments that perpetuate the basic pattern of inequality from which they

[26]Barry Bluestone, "Economic Crisis and the Law of Uneven Development," *Politics and Society* 3 (Fall 1972): 66.

benefit. Hence, corporate-sector monies are plowed back into the corporate sector, leaving the small-capital sector starved for funds for development and expansion:

> Private individuals will thus tend to invest in their "own" rather than contribute to the economic viability (and thus the political viability) of competing individuals or groups. There are many instances where this occurs. Banks often refuse loans—even government guaranteed loans—to minority groups. . . . Alternative transportation modes are rejected as long as they are competitive with traditional automobile and petroleum interests. And conglomerates gobble up hundreds of capital-starved smaller firms rather than extend lines of credit. The outcome in all cases is uneven development where the rich become wealthier and the poor relatively more impoverished. *It is important to remember that this is not an aberration in the private sector of the American economy, but precisely its normal and necessary nature.*[27]

Government expenditures have reinforced this private-investment pattern. State economic policies in this century, discussed more fully in Part III of this book, have enhanced the economic position of the most privileged members of the capitalist class. Government tax policies, for example, have consistently aided the wealthier corporations, who have been granted depreciation and depletion allowances, investment tax credits, and other tax write-offs that make the effective tax base for some industries as little as one-third the rate paid by other industries. Government aid to the small-capital sector, by contrast, has been meager.

Those industries that are in the state sector because they produce for government contracts have also been disproportionately assisted by government policies. In 1970, for example, the federal government purchased $106 billion worth of goods from privately-owned industry, of which $82 billion represented Pentagon spending. These large sums were heavily concentrated in a small number of highly specialized electronics, aerospace, weapons, and transportation industries. "To a great extent, these industries have higher profits and pay higher wages precisely because of government intervention in the marketplace on their behalf."[28]

The combination of private and government investment

[27]*Ibid.*, p. 67. Emphasis added.
[28]*Ibid.*, p. 72.

decisions that has systematically created a process of uneven development has had five major consequences: (1) It has created a *dual economy,* divided between the relatively depressed small-capital sector and a large-capital corporate sector that is allied with the state in a powerful, relatively prosperous embrace. (2) It has fostered the growing concentration of American industry within the corporate sector, with the result that a larger share of the industrial wealth has been concentrated in fewer and fewer hands. (3) It has largely frozen the way in which wealth and income are distributed, in spite of the massive growth in the society's total economic resources. (4) It has produced a growing disparity between wages in the small-capital sector and wages in the corporate and state sectors. In 1947, wages in the small-capital sector were approximately 75 percent of the wages paid to corporate-sector workers. In 1966, according to Department of Labor statistics, small-capital–sector wages were only 60 percent of corporate-sector wages. (5) Perhaps most importantly, it has shaped the way in which class conflicts have achieved expression. In the small-capital sector, casual, low-paid labor stands in an antagonistic relationship with small businessmen. Although this sector of the working class is the most depressed, it is also the most disorganized. In Chapter 1 we compared structural inequalities to a coiled spring; in the small-capital sector the spring remains locked by the organizational impotence of the sector's workers. In the corporate sector, relatively well-paid workers (who like small-capital–sector workers have virtually no control over the work process) confront behemoth corporations. Here class antagonisms are institutionalized by a well-established pattern of union-management industrial relations. The sectoral divisions of American capitalism have fragmented the ways in which class antagonisms are structurally rooted and expressed.

WORK

American workers are not only divided by social background and the dual economy but by a differentiated occupational structure as well. Two major trends characterize the nature of work: the

Table 4–2
The changing occupational structure of the labor force

Occupational group	1910	1920	1930	1940	1950	1960	1967[a]	1975[a,b]
Managers, Officials and Proprietors (except farm)	*6.6%*	*6.6%*	*7.4%*	*7.3%*	*8.8%*	*8.5%*	*10.1%*	*10.4%*
White-Collar Workers	*47.7*	*18.3*	*22.0*	*23.8*	*27.7*	*33.8*	*36.0*	*38.1*
Professional and Technical	4.7	5.4	6.8	7.5	8.5	11.4	13.3	14.8
Clerical	5.3	8.0	8.9	9.6	12.3	15.0	16.6	16.9
Sales	4.7	4.9	6.3	6.7	6.9	7.4	6.1	6.4
Blue-Collar Workers	*38.2*	*40.2*	*39.6*	*39.8*	*41.2*	*39.5*	*36.7*	*34.0*
Craftsmen and Foremen	11.6	13.0	12.8	12.0	14.5	14.3	13.2	13.0
Semi-skilled	14.6	15.6	15.8	18.4	20.9	19.7	18.7	16.9
Unskilled	12.0	11.6	11.0	9.4	6.8	5.5	4.8	4.1
Service Workers	*9.6*	*7.8*	*9.8*	*11.8*	*10.3*	*11.7*	*12.5*	*13.8*
Private Household (e.g., Maids)	5.0	3.3	4.1	4.7	2.5	2.8	2.4	
Other service	4.6	4.5	5.7	7.1	7.8	8.9	10.1	
Agricultural Workers	*30.9*	*27.0*	*21.2*	*17.4*	*11.8*	*6.3*	*4.7*	*3.6*
Farmers and Farm Managers	16.5	15.3	12.4	10.4	7.5	3.9	2.6	
Farm Laborers	14.4	11.7	8.8	7.0	4.3	2.4	2.1	
Total[c]	100.0	100.0	100.0	100.0	100.0	100.0	100.0	100.0

[a] Data for 1967 and 1975 refer to employed persons only.
[b] Projected figures.
[c] Individual items are rounded independently and therefore may not add up to totals.
Source: Michael Reich, "The Evolution of the United States Labor Force," in Richard C. Edwards, Michael Reich, and Thomas E. Weisskopf, eds., *The Capitalist System: A Radical Analysis of American Society* © 1972, p. 178. By permission of Prentice-Hall, Inc. Englewood Cliffs, N.J.

growth of white-collar (professional, clerical, and sales) employment and the transition to a situation in which most workers produce services rather than goods.

As American industry has continued to mechanize and automate, fewer workers are needed to produce increasing amounts of goods. In 1965, coal production was up 38 percent over 1950, yet employment in the mines fell by 10 percent. In the same period, total manufacturing output went up 79 percent with only a 7 percent increase in production workers. By contrast, white-collar employment increased more than 60 percent in the mining industry, and 70 percent in manufacturing as a whole.

This trend is caused by the growing organizational complexity of contemporary corporations and the government. As economist Michael Reich notes:

> With the development of far-flung corporate sales and distribution networks and corporate divisions specializing in research and development and overall corporate coordination, more white collar workers—managerial, professional, technical, clerical and sales— are needed.[29]

In high-technology industries—particularly in electronics— scientists, technicians, and engineers comprise the majority of employees. Indeed, two very different fields of white-collar jobs have developed since the Second World War: clerical jobs (two-thirds of which are held by women) and technical and professional jobs. The increase in both types of white-collar employment is linked to the shift in the economy from manufacturing to service occupations.

The word *services* applies to a number of distinct kinds of employment all of which are expanding. As sociologist Daniel Bell notes, "in the very development of industry there is a necessary expansion of transportation and of public utilities as auxiliary services in the movement of goods and the increasing use of energy, and an increase in the non-manufacturing but still blue collar force."[30] Thus the first kind of service employment is an integral part of the industrial process. This is not a new service sector.

With the growth of the population and mass consumption of goods, more and more people are involved in the distribution of goods and in the fields of insurance, real estate, and finance. This cluster of activities provides the supportive services needed to keep goods circulating and to provide capital for industrial expansion.

Personal services have also expanded numerically, but their organization has changed. Chains of restaurants, hotels, and automobile garages as well as the entertainment and sports

[29]Reich, in Edwards, Reich, and Weisskopf, p. 178.
[30]Bell, p. 127.

industries carry out functions that were once fulfilled by independent entrepreneurs. Today, the production and distribution of personal services is increasingly in impersonal corporate hands.

The fourth major area of services are those provided by government, including education, health care, and welfare. Government service employment has grown enormously; for example, there were 1,254,000 teachers in the United States in 1950; in 1966 the number had risen to 2,353,000.

Stratification and Class

Given the differentiation in the work force, it has become fashionable in academic circles to argue that the class division between capital and labor has been superseded by a more complex, stratified, occupational order in which there are numerous gradings of material rewards, status, and power. A related proposition is that the shift in employment from the production of goods to the production of services has fundamentally transformed American capitalism. Daniel Bell, for one, has suggested that we have entered a new age in which the basic antagonism is not between capitalist and worker in the context of the factory but between the white-collar professional expert and the rest of the population. These views are only partial truths at best. Perhaps most importantly, they overstate the distinctiveness of white-collar and service occupations.

In 1870, there were only 82,200 clerical workers in the whole country (less than 1 percent of the work force). These bookkeepers, secretaries, bank tellers, payroll and postal clerks, and stenographers more often than not had the status of craftsmen and were very well paid. In 1900, economist Harry Braverman reports, "clerical employees of steam railroads and in manufacturing had average annual earnings of $1,011; in the same year the average annual earnings of [blue-collar] workers in these industries was $435 for manufacturing and $548 for steam railroads."[31] The division between the large mass of blue-collar workers and the tiny number of white-collar workers was great. If this gap had

[31]Harry Braverman, "Labor and Monopoly Capital," *Monthly Review* 26 (July–August 1974): 51.

continued, the rapid expansion of white-collar clerical work would have been significant indeed.

But the very process of clerical expansion has made office work more and more like blue-collar work. Indeed, according to the Bureau of Labor Statistics, weekly clerical wages today are lower than those for every type of blue-collar work, including unskilled labor. Moreover, clerical work is now depersonalized. It has been stripped of its craft status, routinized, and systematized. The tasks of most clerical workers have come to resemble those of shopfloor workers. Common office tasks have been precisely quantified so that corporate offices may be run as large, efficient machines. The Systems and Procedures Association of America, for example, has published a guide based on information provided by General Electric, the General Tire and Rubber Company, and other enterprises, which presents a standard for office performance: "File drawer, open and close; no selection, .04 minutes; . . . desk drawer, open side drawer of standard desk, .014 minutes," and so on.[32] As sociologist C. Wright Mills concluded in his study of office work, except for hard physical labor, there are few characteristics of blue-collar work that are not also true for at least some white-collar work. "For here, too, the human traits of the individual, from his physique to his psychic disposition, become units in the functionally rational calculations of managers."[33]

Even skilled and professional white-collar work has changed. Engineers, scientists, and technicians have lost their traditional independent craft status. Like manual laborers, they work for others who control the aims and conditions of their labor. Lawyers and doctors—the best-paid and most respected white-collar workers—have also lost a significant amount of their traditional independence. Year after year, a diminishing proportion of lawyers are engaged in their own practices, as a larger number work for big law firms or are employed directly by government or corporations on a salary basis. Similarly, an increasing proportion of doctors work for a salary in large urban research centers, clinics, and hospitals.

Undeniably, the rapid growth in the production and distribution of services has changed American capitalism. But it has not

[32]*Ibid.*, p. 74.
[33]C. Wright Mills, *White Collar* (New York, 1954), pp. 226–27.

eliminated or transformed the most fundamental distinction between capital and labor. Although the content of production has changed, its class character has not. Like factory workers, service workers (both blue and white collar) remain wage earners without control over the means of production or the work process.

Discontent, Division, and Struggle

The majority of American workers are profoundly discontented with their work. A recent task force report to the secretary of the Department of Health, Education and Welfare found that only 40 percent of white-collar workers and 20 percent of blue-collar workers would choose to do the same work if they had a choice.[34] After having spent three years interviewing people in depth about their work, Studs Terkel wrote of the "scars, psychic as well as physical, brought home to the supper table and the TV set":

> There are, of course, the happy few who find a savor in their daily job. . . . For the many, there is hardly a concealed discontent. The blue-collar blues is no more bitterly sung than the white collar moan. "I'm a machine," says the spot-welder. "I'm caged," says the bank teller, and echoes the hotel clerk. "I'm a mule," says the steel-worker. "A monkey can do what I do," says the receptionist. "I'm less than an implement," says the migrant worker. "I'm an object," says the high fashion model. Blue collar and white call upon the identical phrase: "I'm a robot."[35]

Such discontent, which includes dissatisfaction over the diminishing buying power of the pay packet, poses a threat to the stability of the current order since it is the raw material of political struggle. But the discontent of most workers often does not achieve political expression beyond individualistic solutions (such as high absenteeism) and a low level of craftsmanship. Essentially this is so because the characteristics that divide workers from each other have prevented collective action and because the trade union movement has been integrated into the economic system in the past four decades on terms that do not challenge the hegemony of the American capitalist system.

[34]Special Task Force to the Secretary of Health, Education, and Welfare, *Work in America* (Cambridge, Mass., 1973), pp. 15–16.
[35]Studs Terkel, *Working* (New York, 1974), pp. xi–xii.

EARLY UNION STRUGGLES AND REPRESSION

July 16, 1877 is a landmark date in American labor history. On that date, the Baltimore and Ohio railroad cut wages by 10 percent. In protest of the move, the crew of a cattle train in Martinsberg, West Virginia, abandoned the train, and other trainmen refused to replace them. By the end of the month, the first mass strike in America had spread across the country. "Strikers stopped and seized the nation's most important industry, the railroads, and crowds defeated or won over first the police, then the state militias, and in some cases even the Federal troops" who were called out to deal with the class insurrection. In a dozen major cities, all industrial activity was stopped by general strikes. The strikes were eventually put down by employers with the help of police and military authorities, but the Great Upheaval, as the event came to be known, was profoundly important in two respects. First, it reflected the workers' sense of their new structural position in American society in face of the decline of the independent middle class. ("There was no concert of action at the start," the *Labor Standard* wrote. "It spread because the workmen of Pittsburgh felt the same oppression that was felt by the workmen of West Virginia and so with the workmen of Chicago and St. Louis.") Second, the strikes highlighted the need for workers to organize if they were to successfully resist the repression of workers' movements by employers and the government.[36]

By the middle 1880s, the Knights of Labor, the most important national union organization of the period, was growing at a phenomenal rate. In July 1884, it had just over 71,000 members; two years later it had over 729,000. The Knights sought to link all workers, skilled and unskilled, black and white, men and women. But the Knights' leadership was opposed to the strike weapon and to the wage system as a whole. Instead, they developed a fundamentalist religious perspective that eschewed wage struggles and promoted a cooperative fellowship among workers. The Knights' opposition to strikes proved to be the cause of their undoing, because strikes were the only weapon

[36]Jeremy Brecher, *Strike!* (San Francisco, 1972), pp. 1–21.

workers had to resist collectively the hardships inflicted by the developing factory economy. Hence, by the turn of the century, much strike action was spontaneously organized, outside of the formal structure of unions.

By the First World War, two very different kinds of unions had emerged. The American Federation of Labor (AFL), which had been founded in 1881 and was led by Samuel Gompers, organized skilled craft workers, the most well paid of the new proletariat. The AFL was a conservative union force. It did not challenge the developing distribution of resources or the basic structure of industrial capitalism. Rather, the AFL sought to defend the relatively privileged position of the craftsmen it represented and limited its demands to higher wages and shorter working hours. By contrast, the Industrial Workers of the World (IWW), which was founded in 1905, appealed to the interests of all workers, especially those who were most exploited. By the end of the First World War, the IWW had been smashed, and the AFL was gaining in strength. What accounts for the difference in their relative success?

The key factor was the response of management and government authorities to the two unions. The AFL was tolerated and even welcomed by some employers because, by representing only skilled craft workers, it divided workers from one another. But the IWW, which sought to articulate the interests of all workers as a class and which posed socialist alternatives to prevailing economic arrangements, presented a far greater threat both to capitalist industry and the social order as a whole. Thus, between 1905 and the outbreak of the First World War, IWW activities were systematically countered by government action:

> In Pennsylvania, the state police, which had been originally created by reformers "anxious to abolish the use of private police forces during industrial conflicts" constantly worked for the employers, not for the strikers. In San Diego, Washington State, and Arizona vigilante mobs . . . took direct repressive action against the IWW. Contacts between the mobs and leading state figures made such actions official government policy. . . . Vigilante action was frowned on, however, by some state officials who felt that there were "cleaner" ways to repress the organization. A public safety committee in Minnesota, a council of defense in Washington State, and a Commission on Immigration and Housing

in California became official bodies seeking official solutions for the elimination of the IWW.[37]

Many of these local organizations urged the Wilson administration to take federal action to repress the IWW. There followed a campaign of federal action that included the deportation of many IWW leaders who were aliens and the trial of hundreds on conspiracy charges (conspiracy against industrial production). In one instance, after deliberating less than an hour, a Chicago jury found more than one hundred defendants guilty of four counts of conspiracy each.[38]

The demise of the IWW was also closely linked to the legitimization of the AFL. In particular, Gompers, Felix Frankfurter (who was later to become a justice of the Supreme Court), and Ralph Easley of the National Civic Federation campaigned actively for recognition of the AFL as a "safe" alternative to more threatening workers' organizations. One manufacturer urged that workers should be granted the "shadow of industrial democracy without the substance" to keep them "contented and productive."[39]

The repression of the IWW, of course, was not the only response of capitalists and the government to the militancy of the new industrial working class. Ideological propaganda, the reliance on state militias to protect strike-breakers, and the fostering of antiunion violence were among the common techniques of the day. And among these strategies were the manipulation of existing ethnic, racial, and sexual divisions in the work force and the creation of new divisions between kinds of workers (clerical versus managerial, white collar versus blue collar). Indeed, these strategies were related, since the antagonisms based on personal characteristics were exacerbated in order to legitimize new divisions between levels of work in the firm. As two historians have noted:

> Within the shop immigrants and Negroes did almost all unskilled and some semiskilled work, whereas the skilled jobs and minor administrative positions were reserved for native white Americans. "That job is not a hunky's job, and you can't have it," was the answer given to intelligent foreigners who aspired to rise above

[37]Alan Wolfe, *The Seamy Side of Democracy* (New York, 1973), pp. 26–27.
[38]*Ibid.*, p. 29.
[39]*Ibid.*

the ranks of common labor. Thus a wedge of racial discrimination was driven into the labor force.[40]

And as white-collar work increased, discrimination against women was used to solidify emerging lines of division within the office between jobs with and without managerial career potential. "In the office as well as the plant, organizing internal segments around externally sanctioned divisions—white over black, men over women, native American over immigrant—apparently reinforced the emergent lines of authority within the industrial hierarchy."[41]

UNIONS JOIN THE CORPORATE ECONOMY

Until the 1930s, as a result of the divisions in the work force and in the union movement, the vast majority of American workers were without union protection or representation. Between 1930 and 1940, however, the number of unionized workers more than doubled from 3.1 million to 7 million. In that decade, unions affiliated with the Congress of Industrial Organizations (CIO), founded in 1935, succeeded in unionizing the most important mass-production industries in the country, including steel and automobiles.

But their success came only after bitter, protracted struggles, in which class antagonisms were raw and palpable. "Four men were killed and eighty-four persons went to hospitals with gunshot wounds, cracked heads, broken limbs or other injuries received in a battle late this afternoon between police and steel strikers at the gates of the Republic Steel Corporation plant in South Chicago" as the United Steel Workers of America successfully sought recognition, the *New York Times* reported in May 1937.[42] In January 1936, automobile workers demanding recognition of the United Automobile Workers (UAW) staged sit-ins and took control of General Motors automobile plants in

---

[40]Thomas Cochran and William Miller, *The Age of Enterprise: A Social History of Industrial America* (New York, 1961), pp. 230–31.

[41]Gordon, Edwards, and Reich, "Labor Segmentation in American Capitalism."

[42]Melvyn Dubofsky, ed., *American Labor Since the New Deal* (Chicago, 1971), p. 113.

Flint, Michigan; Atlanta, Georgia; Anderson, Indiana; Norwood, Ohio; and Kansas City, Missouri. On the forty-fourth day of the sit-in and strike at Flint, General Motors gave in and recognized the UAW, but only after massive police violence and cooperative attempts between the governor and the company had failed to dislodge the workers.

Thus in the late 1930s, workers, through union-led mass actions, seemed to be moving rapidly to achieve a significant amount of substantive representation and fundamental structural change.

In 1973, however, thirty-six years after the Flint sit-in, *Business Week* editorialized:

> The unions have become an established institution, well financed and run by highly professional managers. These officers are paid on much the same basis as businessmen. . . . And they deal with many of the same problems—budgets, investments, taxes, even bargaining with staff and office worker unions.[43]

The editorial also noted that the unions were "acting responsibly" and that strike figures had reached "the lowest level in years." In the same year, the steelworkers (led by a president who earned an annual salary of $70,000) signed a contract that pledged the union to fight wildcat strikes by its members. They also agreed—in advance of a wage settlement—not to strike, but to settle all wage disputes by arbitration. A major study of the UAW concluded:

> The relationship between the General Motors corporation and the United Automobile Workers has altered—they are not enemies, nor, in any large sense, adversaries. It is true . . . that the two, General Motors and the UAW, have *a greater community of interest than of conflict.*[44]

What had happened to produce the shift in less than four decades from militant class organization and confrontation to "responsible" routinized cooperation?

The development of a relatively conservative AFL-CIO (they merged in 1954) was made possible by the growing divisions between the corporate and small-capital sectors of the American economy. Unlike small-capital industries whose major costs are wages and who have to absorb wage increases at the expense of profits, the corporate-sector industries are largely able to pass

---

[43]*Business Week,* August 18, 1973, p. 88.
[44]William Serrin, *The Company and the Union* (New York, 1972), pp. 305–06.

along wage increases in the form of higher prices. In the corporate sector, wages, prices, and profits are not determined by the operation of a traditional competitive market but are planned by the corporations and government. Hence corporate-sector companies, whose major expenses relate to technology, not men and women, have been able to accept the emergence of mass industrial unionism as one more element among many to be planned for in advance. Indeed, corporate-sector firms gain tangible benefits from the existence of a unionized work force because the unions guarantee that, outside of strike periods, the companies will have a predictably available work force at predictable wages.

By the end of the Second World War, most industrial unions had entered into permanent collective bargaining agreements with the largest corporations in the corporate sector. The unions succeeded in obtaining higher wages for their members, but not without relinquishing much in return. In addition to agreeing to increased productivity, union leaders began to collaborate with company managements to introduce technologically advanced production methods, which usually are resisted by the rank and file. Overall, from the standpoint of those who own and control corporate capital, "the main function of unions was (and is) to inhibit disruptive spontaneous rank and file activity (e.g., wildcat strikes, and slowdowns) and to maintain labor discipline in general. In other words, *unions were (and are) the guarantors of managerial prerogatives.*"[45]

The restriction of union activity to wage bargaining has been an important feature of union-management relationships. The "right" of company managements to control the conditions and pace of work has not only not been challenged, but has actually been buttressed by union-activity patterns. Thus, when in 1973 the United Automobile Workers were given the contractual right for the first time to monitor factories for work hazards and filth, the union hailed the contract as a "terrific breakthrough." But, as journalist Robert Sherrill noted, this pitifully meager advance "was brought about not by wise negotiations so much as by chaotic pressures: turnover at some plants is so great that to maintain a work force of 100,000 Chrysler had to hire 44,000 new hands in one recent year."[46]

[45]O'Connor, p. 23. Emphasis added.
[46]*New York Times,* October 28, 1973.

The union movement, to be sure, has supported "progressive" welfare-state legislation; in particular, unions have vigorously promoted the expansion of the social security system, unemployment and disability insurance, and other protections against economic insecurity (national health insurance is a present important target). But as we will see in Chapter 13, none of these programs threaten major corporate firms; indeed, to the extent that they make workers more secure and provide them with state, rather than corporate, benefits, the corporations stand to gain a more contented, productive work force. For this reason most major advances in social insurance since the New Deal have been supported by large industrial employers.

Thus, in terms of their economic welfare, the growth of industrial unionism has made a very real difference to corporate-sector workers. But the costs of these gains have been high. In particular, the union movement has left workers without the ability to control decisions that affect them at the workplace. Political scientist David Greenstone notes, "the crucial fact is that the workers neither own nor control—*that they exercise no substantial economic authority over*—the firms in which they work."[47] In fact, the growth of industrial unionization, by conceding management prerogatives, has often made the conditions of work much more difficult. As companies introduce new technological innovations, individual workers have to bear the brunt of the speed-up of the work process.

Because the unions have not been prepared to substantively represent workers' interests, workers have begun to express their discontents in actions that bypass union-management collective bargaining structures. Every available indicator shows that wildcat strikes, plant sabotage, absenteeism rates, and plant-turnover rates are increasing.

The growth of industrial unionism has been achieved at a high cost for nonunionized workers as well. Although unions are seen as the representatives of workers, most workers are not represented by unions and do not receive the benefits of collective bargaining. Yet they have to pay the higher prices companies charge to offset wage increases. Nonunionized labor literally pay the price of unionized workers' gains. Thus, by representing only a portion of the working class, unions splinter workers into

[47]J. David Greenstone, in *The Nation,* September 8, 1969, p. 214.

opposing groups, who are more conscious of antagonisms that divide them than of long-range interests that bind them together. The development and functioning of American unions provide an example both of the mediations discussed in Chapter 1 and of an arena of action where the criteria of representative, substantive democracy developed in Chapter 2 can be applied. The discontents of workers, which are the product of their place in the social structure, are not expressed directly, in unmediated fashion. Rather, they are channelled through the institution of unions. The substantive consequence has been a fragmented working class in which some workers have made limited gains at the expense of others—and in the overall interest of employers concerned with maintaining the present social order. The union experience is an example of what political scientist Harold Laswell called "resistance by partial incorporation" whereby some of the subordinates are incorporated into the economic and political system on favored terms, but the group as a whole remains subordinate.

The situation of American workers described here does meet the procedural criterion of representative democracy; workers can vote and organize unions. To that extent the system is open to them and has enabled workers to alter the distribution of resources slightly in the direction of the unionized corporate-sector work force. But for workers as a whole, the other three tests of representativeness—personnel, consciousness, and effectiveness—are not met. For American workers, the distance between procedural and substantive democracy remains wide.

the
corporate
complex

5

the corporate
complex at home:
the role of government

In a corporate-capitalist society, the smooth functioning of corporate production is essential in maintaining stability. If disruptions occur, the interdependence of the various elements in the economy causes difficulties to ripple throughout the society. When the United Automobile Workers strike General Motors, 500,000 workers and their families as well as hundreds of thousands of workers in companies supplying GM are affected. A long strike at GM can spell a recession for the United States. Similarly, when the whole country is dependent on a dozen large petroleum companies for fuel oil, gasoline, and petroleum by-products (used in plastics, synthetic fibers, and a multitude of other products), any interruption of supply or depletion of oil resources can prove disastrous.

Powerful as they are, giant corporations are particularly vulnerable because, as we saw in Chapter 3, their operations require stable, predictable conditions. Powerful as it is, corporate capitalism cannot provide the overall framework that it needs for survival. The expanded role of American government is a logical outgrowth of the trend toward concentration, coordination, and planning within the corporate sector. Indeed, the history of the federal government is closely bound up with the rise of corporate capitalism. The role of government is complex and cannot be reduced to a simple formula. Countless activities of government at all levels help or harm countless groups. Yet, the broadest significance of government in the United States lies in the fact that it stimulates corporate expansion, harmonizes conflicts within the corporate sphere, and works to reduce challenges to corporate capitalism from within the United States and abroad. Government can be considered the overall guardian of the corporate-capitalist system.

Nor is this a matter of choice in a country where most industrial activity is carried on by several hundred corporations. Whether they want to or not, government officials must place corporate survival and profitability among the top priorities of government policy. Doing otherwise risks economic, political and social disruption. "Giant corporations now are so important that government must preserve them in order to keep the economy functioning."[1] That corporate capitalism is in crisis despite government efforts is a measure of its structural contradictions.

Government is often portrayed as standing above the conflict of particular groups, intervening only to protect the interests of the broad majority. Yet government is never a neutral instrument, and, in present-day America, it has become one of the major participants in every aspect of American life. The government's enormous power and vast resources are not used to help all groups equally. Governmental power benefits some segments of society and penalizes others.

Even if government did no more than maintain law and order, this would mean protecting the existing arrangement of power—which, as we described earlier, involves fundamental inequalities between class and racial groups. Yet as we shall see, government does far more than keep the peace. It is part and parcel of a corporate-capitalist system. Among the vital benefits government provides to corporate capitalism are political protection and ideological support, capital, and activities designed to stabilize economic conditions and assure corporate growth and profits.

Although the federal government has existed for nearly two hundred years, during much of that time the government was

---

[1]Daniel R. Fusfeld, *The Rise of the Corporate State in America* (Andover, Mass., 1973), p. 10.

small, remote from most people, and powerless. The total federal budget was $6 million in 1800. It now exceeds $300 billion. In 1802, there was one federal government official for every two thousand citizens; today the ratio is 1 to 60.[2] Big government in the United States dates only from the early twentieth century. In fact, the rise of big business and big government occurred at the same time, and their fates have been intertwined ever since. To a considerable extent, the federal government has interpreted the national interest of the United States as identical to the interest of large-scale capital. To understand why, it is necessary to study the early development of corporate capitalism.

THE RISE OF CORPORATE CAPITALISM

Until the early twentieth century, the United States was a nation of farmers, merchants, shopkeepers, and manufacturers. Whatever manufacturing was carried on occurred in small units, each of which employed only a few workers. The subsequent rise and consolidation of large corporations was not an automatic result of technological and economic factors. Rather, it was made possible by the active cooperation of the federal government.

Ever since the revision of the Articles of Confederation and the adoption of the Constitution, the government has actively fostered business activity. In the early years, the government (national, state, and municipal) distributed public land, maintained tariff barriers to protect American industry from foreign competition, provided capital grants to business, and sponsored internal improvements (such as canals, irrigation projects, and highways) helpful to private enterprise. These varied activities placed all levels of government—first state and municipal governments, later the national government—squarely in the middle of the economy rather than on the sidelines.[3] Nonetheless, it was not until the late nineteenth century that the United States shifted from an agricultural to an industrial society.

[2]James Sterling Young, *The Washington Community: 1800–1828* (New York, 1966), pp. 28–29.
[3]Robert A. Lively, "The American System: A Review Article," *The Business History Review* 29 (1955): 81.

Economic Changes in America

Until the late nineteenth century, most Americans lived in rural areas and engaged in farming. The United States was an immense, underpopulated area. As a result of the government-sponsored subjugation and confinement of Indians, cheap land was readily available and farming was an easy way to make an independent living.

Toward the end of the century, several changes occurred that produced both a shift of resources to manufacturing and an acceleration of the trend toward large-scale production. The result was a crisis in capitalism that was eventually resolved by the rise of big government in alliance with corporate capitalism. The following changes took place:

The end of the frontier   In 1890, the Bureau of the Census reported that the frontier was closed. Although there were still vast areas of unoccupied land, the most attractive had already come under cultivation. The closing of the frontier meant that growth would henceforth have to come from technological innovation rather than geographic expansion.

A rise in population   Waves of immigration from Europe in the period following the Civil War expanded the population, which provided cheap labor and further increased the need for land, food, and more efficient methods of manufacture. Between 1860 and 1920, the population trebled, from 31 million to 92 million.

Technological innovations   Foremost among major technological developments were shifts in power sources—from water-driven devices to the steam engine to the high-speed compound turbine and the electric motor. In addition, new transportation facilities—canals, roadways, and railroads—made it economically feasible to produce on a large scale for regional and even national markets.

Innovations in finance and organization   Alongside technological advances, new forms of organization developed, notably, the corporation, or limited-liability stock company. Investors were encouraged to pool large amounts of capital, since, if the corporation failed, they would lose no more than the amount they invested, and, if it succeeded, they shared the profits. The rise of the corporate form was as influential as technological advances in transforming the American economy. The links between business and government can be seen from the fact that the corporate form was dependent on government protection. Without government help, in the legal rights accorded of limited liability, the right to sign contracts, and sue in court, the corporate form would have been a shell.

Another advantage to investors was that the corporations could be used to reduce the risks of competition. The classical capitalist doctrine, as developed by Adam Smith, argued that the free market (in which many producers competed for the customer's favor) could allocate resources efficiently. Yet, if the free market was a useful servant for society, it was a cruel master for producers. Competition fostered efficiency by forcing producers to sell at the lowest possible price, and producers who could not match their competitors' low prices were quickly driven out of business. Manufacturers did all they could to control the market—and thereby free themselves from its harsh commands.

As long as there were many manufacturers in a given industry, they had no choice but to compete; it was impossible for all of them to agree to set high prices. But the corporate form offered a means of thwarting the mechanisms of the free market. A large company could profit from its power over the market to undercut its competitors, monopolize sources of supply, and coerce or buy out smaller competitors. A further extension of the trend was the creation of trusts, in which many producers within a given industry were merged into a single large firm. The result was a monopoly in which, unrestrained by competition, the trust could raise prices and achieve huge financial gains. The decisive years were the few decades before and after the turn of the twentieth century. This period in American history has been called the era of the robber barons: men like Andrew Carnegie in steel, John D. Rockefeller in oil, and Edward Harriman and James Hill in railroads, who had large financial backing and exploited America's vast resources to open new markets.

Small businessmen and farmers tried to unite in the face of the corporate threat to their survival. The Greenback, Granger, and Populist parties, created in an attempt to check the power of the emerging giants, were moderately successful. Many state governments passed laws that regulated the new monopolies. For example, Wisconsin, New York, and other states prohibited railroad freight carriers from giving rebates (lower rates) to large shippers. Nationally, the Sherman Antitrust Act of 1887 prohibited "combinations in restraint of trade." The law empowered the federal government to break up conspiracies among competitors. Yet a pattern originated with the Sherman Act that was to be repeated often in the future. When public opposition was strong, the government stepped in to curb the worst excesses of business and to provide the appearance of regulation—without mortal damage to business interests. As described by historian Richard Hofstadter, the Sherman Act was "recognized by most of the astute politicians of that hour as a gesture, a ceremonial concession to an overwhelming public demand for some kind of reassuring action against the trusts."[4]

The Sherman Act did not prevent big units from arising. It was aimed against *monopoly*, not against bigness per se. It did prohibit price-fixing and agreements among competitors to divide a market among themselves. It did not prohibit the consolidation of competitors into a new, larger company by *merger*, nor did it prevent several large firms from informally dominating an industry—that is, *concentration*.

The Critical Period: 1897 to 1912

That the Sherman Act failed to prevent combinations in restraint of trade can be seen from the fact that the largest merger movement in American history (to that time) began in 1897, ten years *after* its passage.

By 1900, however, the merger movement began to slow. Moreover, the giant corporations that developed from the merger movement do not appear to have outperformed their smaller rivals. The point of diminishing returns in achieving efficiency through large size seems to have been reached in the early 1900s; the best example was the United States Steel Corporation. U.S. Steel was organized in 1901 under the leadership of J. P. Morgan, leading financier of the period. It was the largest industrial corporation formed until then. Its assets of over $1 billion made it bigger than other leviathans organized during this period, such as Standard Oil of New Jersey, American Smelting and Refining Company, and Consolidated Tobacco Company. J. P. Morgan created U.S. Steel not to achieve greater efficiency but to eliminate competition. There were already a number of large, efficient steel companies. The most notable of these was Andrew Carnegie's, which Morgan was successful in buying out and

[4]Richard Hofstadter, *The Age of Reform* (New York, 1960), p. 245.

Figure 5-1
Annual firm disappearance by merger, 1895-1968

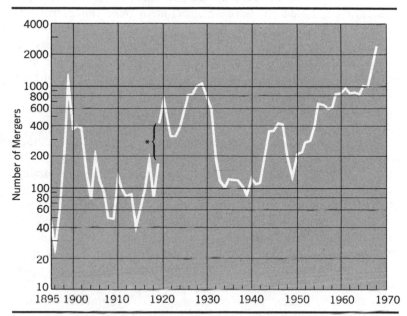

[1]The two series on merger disappearance are not directly comparable. The coverage for the series for 1895-1918 is less complete than that of the series for later years and thus understates the level, though not the trend, within the period. Source: From *Economic Concentration* (p. 258) by John M. Blair, © 1972 by Harcourt Brace Jovanovich, Inc. and reproduced with their permission.

merging with the other companies he had captured to form the new industrial monolith. When it was formed, U.S. Steel had eight hundred plants and controlled 60 percent of American steel production. It was a gigantic test of whether bigness and near-monopoly conditions could prevent competition.

In fact, however, U.S. Steel was neither more efficient nor more profitable than its remaining competitors; and it was not even able to prevent new competition from arising in the steel industry. In the years following its creation, the price of U.S. Steel's stock declined, and its share of total steel output fell from over 60 percent to 40 percent. Its failure was due mainly to its large size, which made it inflexible and slow to innovate compared to its smaller competitors. Moreover, U.S. Steel was unable to persuade other steel companies to abide by price-fixing agreements.[5]

[5]This account draws on Gabriel Kolko, *The Triumph of Conservatism: A Reinterpretation of American History, 1900–1916* (New York, 1963).

What happened in the steel industry occurred in other industries in which there were huge new trusts. After its creation, Standard Oil failed to increase its control over the petroleum industry. In the automobile, copper, telephone, and meat industries, trusts were unable to outperform their competitors or dominate the industry. They, too, were unable to prevent new firms from entering the industry and to enforce price-fixing agreements among competitors. If it had not been for government intervention, the new breed of industrial giant might have continued to decline.

However, such experiences should not obscure the fact that it is more efficient to carry on manufacturing in large plants. The more goods produced, the less each item costs. Mass production permits savings because a large labor force can work more efficiently, supplies can be purchased in volume, and items produced can be standardized. Yet, although *large* units may be more efficient than small ones, *mammoth* size is counterproductive. Beyond a certain size, it may be downright inefficient to grow as administrative costs and red tape pile up. (Today, giant corporations decentralize their operations for this reason.) But what the very largest firms of the early 1900s obtained was not *efficiency* but *power.* Power permitted them to influence suppliers, workers, consumers, and above all, government. Because of their superior political power, large corporations were able to enlist government support to achieve the goal of limited competition that they could not achieve on their own.

From Competition to Cooperation: A New View of Capitalism

At the same time that the industrial giants were unsuccessfully trying to achieve domination in their separate fields, there was a new public outcry about their methods—small entrepreneurs being forced out of business, higher prices often following the creation of big units, and coercive tactics. Furthermore, public opposition was increased by the disclosures of muckraking journalists, who described dangerous and unsanitary conditions in the meatpacking industry, illegal discounts by railroads, and other unsavory practices. There was also political opposition: the Socialist party, the Populist movement, and some elements in the Progressive movement directly opposed business dominance and were successful in getting some state governments to curb business.

Big business was in trouble because of its unsuccessful economic record and political unpopularity. Moreover, despite their informal agreements, big businessmen proved unable to cooperate with each other fully. There was always the danger that some of them would refuse to honor agreements restricting competition and setting prices and would thereby capture a handsome share of the market to the detriment of other firms. Government help eventually solved the problem. Yet, in order to justify government support, a new doctrine was needed, for big business appeared to be in opposition to traditional American belief in the desirability of smallness, competition, and a limited role for the federal government. In a revised view of capitalism (worked out by progressive members of the new corporate elite and sympathetic intellectuals), cooperation was to replace competition. Further, while the federal government was called in apparently to regulate, in reality it was to protect the new corporate giants. Thus, the security and stability of government-guaranteed concentration was to replace the insecurity and instability of the free market. And bigness, rather than being feared as a threat to the independence of small producers, was to be welcomed as a sign of evolution and progress.

The new view turned capitalist doctrine and traditional American values on their heads: it made a virtue of bigness, regarding it as inevitable, and opposed competition as outmoded and harmful. The new ideal was embodied in the image of the "responsible" leaders of the large corporations, whose actions helped to secure a system of corporate dominance.

Perhaps the most important of the new organizations that sponsored the shift—and a key to understanding the strange new development—was the National Civic Federation (NCF), founded in 1900. The NCF was the forerunner of other organizations that, today, play a comparable role in proposing "forward looking" government policies to help business. The NCF brought together business leaders, conservative members of the labor movement, and academic leaders. To indicate the importance of the organization in the big-business community, one-third of the 300 largest corporations were represented among its membership.

The NCF's approach to political and economic affairs was to

try to develop consensus among its members on government policies that favored big business. NCF policies appeared new and progressive and contrasted with the antigovernment stand of traditional spokesmen for business—above all, the National Association of Manufacturers (NAM), which was dominated by small-business interests. The NAM was against government involvement in economic affairs and opposed labor unions as well as trusts and monopoly. The National Civic Federation, on the other hand, groped for a new answer.

Whereas liberalism in Adam Smith's time meant the movement to limit state control over private enterprise, liberalism came to be defined by corporate leaders and others in the NCF as state intervention to supervise corporate activity—a complete reversal of the former definition. The NCF's acceptance of labor unions as having a legitimate place in industrial organization was also an apparent about-face by business. In reality, the NCF favored the conservative labor movement led by Samuel Gompers (the American Federation of Labor) only as a preferable alternative to more radical labor movements, for example, the International Workers of the World (IWW), or the Socialist party. The NCF recognized that if big business would renounce the right to engage in the most outrageous and greedy activity, it might obtain unprecedented and undisturbed power and privilege. It was a good exchange, especially because of the danger big business faced of losing out altogether as a result of popular discontent. Among the NCF's accomplishments was its influence in shaping the Federal Trade Commission Act (1913), which combined weak provisions against monopoly with government authorization of "reasonable" combinations by manufacturers to reduce competition.

Gabriel Kolko, the first historian to describe the role of business in fostering this crucial transition in American history, notes: "The dominant fact of American politics at the beginning of this century was that big business led the struggle for the federal regulation of the economy. . . . Federal economic regulation was generally designed by the regulated industry to meet its own ends, and not those of the public." Kolko adds that the method used by big business to secure dominance over small business, agrarian interests, and labor was "the utilization of political outlets to attain conditions of stability, predictability, and security."[6] To cite one example, the Interstate Commerce Commission, created in 1887, has often been perceived as a move to curb and regulate the railroads. Yet "the intervention of the federal government not only failed to damage the interests of the railroads but was positively welcomed by them."[7] As in other comparable cases of government "regulation" of industry, the railroads used the government to control competition, calm an outraged public, and limit competition—ends that they could not achieve by themselves. The assurance given by Attorney General Richard Olney (himself a former railroad company executive) in a letter in 1892 to a disturbed railroad president suggests the value of regulation to railroad interests:

> The [Interstate Commerce] Commission, as its functions have now been limited by the courts, is, or can be made, of great use to the railroads. It satisfies the popular clamor for a government supervision of railroads, at the same time that the supervision is almost entirely nominal. Further, the older such a Commission gets to be, the more inclined it will be found to take the business and railroad view of things. It thus becomes a sort of barrier between the railroad corporations and the people and a sort of protection against hasty and crude legislation hostile to railroad interests.[8]

Thus, the turmoil of the opening years of the twentieth century ended in the triumph of big business and conservatism—under the guise of reform: "By 1918 the leaders of the large corporations and banks emerged secure in their loose hegemony over the political structure."[9] The contrast with the earlier period could not have been greater. Manufacturers had never constituted a cohesive group in America, instead, they had consisted of many competing small producers, split by regional and economic rivalry. Moreover, business had been only one economic interest in the United States, no more powerful—probably less powerful—than farmers and merchants. The shift to corporate capitalism signified a fundamental transformation of the political and economic structure. A centralized economy (particularly following the New Deal in the 1930s), controlled by large corporate

[6]*Ibid.*, pp. 3, 57–58.
[7]Gabriel Kolko, *Railroads and Regulation, 1877–1916* (Princeton, 1965), p. 3.
[8]Marver H. Bernstein, *Regulating Business by Independent Commission* (Princeton, 1955), p. 265.
[9]James Weinstein, *The Corporate Ideal in the Liberal State, 1900–1918* (Boston, 1968), p. 3.

producers with the help of big government, replaced an economy divided by conflicting interests and controlled by none.

Government Regulation: The Answer to Competition

In industry after industry during the period prior to the First World War, federal government "regulation" began. The major result was to eliminate small competitors, reduce public opposition to large firms, and stabilize corporate production. In the meatpacking industry, the passage of the Pure Food and Drug Act helped reduce competition and drove many small firms out of business. In the railroad industry, the Hepburn Act regulated railroad rates, and the Interstate Commerce Commission licensing procedures reduced competition among railroads and stabilized conditions. The Federal Reserve Act served bankers and gave them direct representation on regional and the national Federal Reserve boards. In manufacturing, the Federal Trade Commission Act was dominated by businessmen.

The new regulatory machinery developed by government functioned in the following manner:

A federal government agency (usually a commission) was created to set and enforce industrywide standards of conduct, usually geared to the interests of large firms. The commission was given broad powers over firms in an industry, wide discretion, and independence from the rest of the executive branch of government.

From the very beginning, businessmen in the affected industry had a leading role in the new agencies. The rules of procedure adopted by the regulatory agencies were often written with the cooperation of business organizations in the affected industry. Since leading businessmen were appointed to the commissions that regulated their industries, the rules were enforced by those in full sympathy with the business firms. Penalties for firms who violated the agency's rules were slight and rarely enforced. The agency had little financial support or staff help and had to rely for information and cooperation on the business firms being regulated.

The regulatory machinery provided important benefits to big business. It brought legitimacy to big business by creating the illusion of regulation, and thereby reduced public opposition to large firms. It forestalled stiffer regulation by state governments (who were more often responsive to farmers, small businessmen, and consumers than to big business). And it provided direct services to corporate capitalism by bringing members of an industry together under government auspices, by increasing stability and predictability (thus facilitating corporate planning), and by acting as defender and spokesman for the industry. The regulatory agencies thus fostered corporate concentration, helped corporations increase profits, and provided corporate capitalism with the protection it needed to achieve a commanding economic position.

Dominant political officials during the first two decades of the century were all probusiness, and most were especially favorable to big business. Theodore Roosevelt, president from 1901 to 1908, was a great admirer of big business, despite his trust-busting reputation; most of his friends were big business-men, and he never opposed the basic drive toward corporate concentration and expansion. Roosevelt distinguished between "good" and "bad" trusts. For example, he often delivered fiery speeches against businessmen who acted wrongly—but he had many good things to say for the "responsible" big businessman. "It is not true," he argued, "that as the rich have grown richer the poor have grown poorer. . . . The captains of industry who have driven the railway systems across this continent, who have built up our commerce, who have developed our manufactures, have on the whole done great good to our people." Roosevelt often warned against reckless tampering with big business: "The mechanism of modern business is so delicate that extreme care must be taken not to interfere with it in a spirit of rashness or ignorance."[10]

According to Woodrow Wilson, president from 1912 to 1920, "Business underlies everything in our national life, including our spiritual life." Although he was in favor of curbing corporate excesses, Wilson regarded corporations as the inevitable and desirable instrument for organizing industrial production. "Modern business is no doubt best conducted upon a grand scale, for which the resources of the single individual are manifestly insufficient." Wilson further suggested that "we cannot go back

[10]Kolko, *Triumph of Conservatism*, pp. 66, 67.

to the old competitive system."[11] Many businessmen supported Wilson's election in 1912, realizing that his liberal "New Freedom" program did not threaten corporate capitalism.[12]

The social background, personal friendships, and ideological convictions of America's political leaders in the early twentieth century helped big business obtain the federal government's help. Federal regulation also appealed to those in government because it signified an expansion of government's role. The new government agencies needed to deal with corporations would result in a larger and more powerful federal government. Big business also meant big government.

Moreover, the federal government was not entirely free to ignore the call of big business. If large corporations were far from dominant at the turn of the century, they did control more resources and could use them more effectively than other groups in America. Whereas corporations carried on less than one-tenth of manufacturing in the mid-nineteenth century, they carried on two-thirds of manufacturing by 1900.[13] Those who opposed big business and who offered alternative programs for organizing production, such as the Populists and Socialists, were far weaker. Big-business leaders and the large corporations they controlled represented great wealth. They were well organized, powerful, and determined. They were well placed to control nominations to public office, finance election campaigns, weaken their opponents, and pressure the federal government. (As described in Chapter 8, no major challenge to business was mounted within the party system.) Through their control of newspapers and respected business organizations (like the National Civic Federation), big-business leaders persuaded many that the new corporate empires represented an evolution of private enterprise that was natural, desirable, and in harmony with the American capitalist tradition. Business leaders succeeded in advancing their claim that industrial progress required the centralization of production in large corporations, with overall coordination pro-

[11]Weinstein, p. 162.
[12]Martin J. Sklar, "Woodrow Wilson and the Political Economy of Modern United States Liberalism," in James Weinstein and David W. Eakins, eds., *For a New America* (New York, 1967), pp. 46–100.
[13]Gardner Means, "Business Concentration in the American Economy," in Richard E. Edwards, Michael Reich, and Thomas E. Weisskopf, eds., *The Capitalist System: A Radical Analysis of American Society* (Englewood Cliffs, N.J., 1972), p. 148.

vided by the government. In fact, however, there was nothing inevitable about organizing production in large, privately-controlled corporations. Although it is widely believed that government limits and regulates big business, the irony is that it was the federal government's protection that sustained and strengthened corporate capitalism during the critical period.

THE GROWTH OF BIG BUSINESS AND BIG GOVERNMENT

The First World War

Government policies in support of corporate capitalism, a critical factor in explaining its initial success, have continued since then to aim at assuring conditions where corporations can prosper free from political challenge. The trend toward corporate dominance and government help accelerated during the First World War. During this time, the government expanded the regulatory machinery developed in preceding decades. Businessmen helped run the War Industries Board (WIB), which coordinated production and prices in an effort to expand output. The WIB functioned as a giant agency of central direction, formally part of the government, but in fact largely manned and controlled by business. To facilitate cooperation with industry, it encouraged the creation of trade associations within each sector of production. The WIB and trade associations took control of the entire economy—with the legitimacy and legal sanction conferred by government support. Thus, the government, in effect, turned over responsibility for mobilizing the economy to private business.[14]

Big business benefited handsomely from the arrangement. It added to its legitimacy by assuming a leading role in arming the country—and earned lavish profits from producing for war. The First World War opened the way to the development of today's military-industrial complex and to new cooperative arrangements between big business, big government, and big labor. From then on, the days of competition and relative equality were over. "Government and business were to be partners in the common

[14]Grant McConnell, *Private Power and American Democracy* (New York, 1966), p. 61.

enterprise of an ever-expanding economy."[15] The transformation took just twenty years.

Since the First World War, additional experimentation has led to new machinery for regulating and harmonizing the economy. Most of it has been a direct outgrowth of the earlier period. For example, when he was secretary of commerce after the First World War, Herbert Hoover encouraged trade associations to draw up codes of business practices and ethics that were then made official standards for industry by the government. The intent of these codes was to give government sanction to the attempt by business to limit competition and stabilize production.

The New Deal

During the Great Depression, which began in 1929, corporate capitalism was again in jeopardy. Following the stock market crash, production dropped sharply, unemployment soared, and there was widespread popular anger at the failure of business to bring about economic recovery. Elected in 1932, President Franklin D. Roosevelt might have been expected to attack corporate producers. Instead, he worked actively with businessmen to launch the National Recovery Administration (NRA) in 1933, which further extended the system of busines codes worked out by business in cooperation with government. It also set minimum prices and limited competition.[16] When the NRA was declared unconstitutional by the Supreme Court (dominated by those who harked back to the days when competition and small business prevailed), Roosevelt's next approach was to stress providing income directly to those in need through the Social Security programs. This move was interpreted by many (but not all) businessmen as antibusiness. Yet, although Roosevelt railed against the evils of big business, his New Deal legislation never attacked business interests and—in fields like banking, utilities, and finance—provided substantial help to corporations. Beneath an antibusiness rhetoric, the aim of the new measures was to restore prosperity, which meant high productivity and profits for corporate capitalism. This explains the support given liberal New Deal measures, such as the Wagner Act (protecting labor unions)

[15]Weinstein, *The Corporate Ideal*, p. 222.
[16]Ellis W. Hawley, *The New Deal and the Problem of Monopoly* (Princeton, 1966), Part I.

and the Social Security Act, by prominent businessmen like Averell Harriman, Barnard Baruch, Joseph Kennedy, and Adolf A. Berle, Jr., who understood better than those who opposed Roosevelt that the new legislation aimed to rescue corporate capitalism.

The New Deal accepted the basic legitimacy of corporate dominance. Aside from the government's one notable attempt to organize production directly (the Tennessee Valley Authority, which developed a system of flood control, and electric power and fertilizer production), the New Deal did not challenge corporate production. The top 100 corporations increased their control of all corporate assets during the New Deal, and the highest income group increased its share of the country's personal wealth.[17] The New Deal was an innovative attempt to save corporate capitalism when it was in deep trouble. As political scientist David Greenstone observes, "In general, the New Deal may have functioned to forestall radical change by eliminating the most unpopular features of American capitalism."[18]

Nonetheless, peacetime government expenditures failed to end the depression. "The Great Depression of the thirties never came to an end," John Galbraith has pointed out. "It merely disappeared in the great mobilization of the forties."[19]

The Second World War

The Second World War contributed even more than the First World War to a centralized economy. During the war, the government assumed the power to veto wage and price rises, ration civilian consumption, and decide what would be produced in the nation's factories; helped big business expand production; and purchased much of industry's output for the armed forces. Under the sponsorship of the Office of Production Management, over seven thousand advisory committees, composed mostly of businessmen, suggested economic priorities that the government promptly adopted. Industrial leaders were named to key positions in the executive branch while their salaries continued to be paid

[17]Kenneth Prewitt and Alan Stone, *The Ruling Elites: Elite Theory, Power, and American Democracy* (New York, 1973), p. 45.

[18]J. David Greenstone, *Labor in American Politics* (New York, 1969), p. 46.

[19]John Kenneth Galbraith, *American Capitalism: The Concept of Countervailing Power* (Boston, 1952), p. 69.

by their companies. (They were known as "dollar-a-year" men because they received no government salary.) Their efforts to further the interests of corporate capitalism thus became endowed with patriotic fervor.[20] Many measures that were illegal in peacetime were encouraged by the government in wartime, for example, price-fixing agreements and the sharing of markets by competitors (the attorney general issued a decree granting exemptions from the Sherman Antitrust Act).

Large firms benefited most from the wartime arrangements. They received the lion's share of the government's $200 billion in war contracts. After the war, big business bought (at bargain prices) most of the $16 billion of modern production facilities built by the government to speed wartime expansion. Companies like U.S. Steel, General Electric, and International Harvester got their biggest, most technologically advanced plants in this way. (For example, U.S. Steel purchased, for $40 million, the largest steel plant in the world, in Geneva, Utah, built by the government at a cost of $200 million, and was thereby able to break into the Western steel market and overcome small, independent steel producers.)[21]

The mobilized war economy provided lessons for both business and government; it established new patterns of cooperation in central coordination of the economy and set a precedent that would be used again, both in wartime (during the Korean and Vietnam wars) and in peacetime.

1945 to 1971

The history of the twenty-five years following the Second World War is one of continuing government expansion, largely in the service of big business, as well as increasing domination by the leading corporations. During this period, the federal government attempted to foster the prosperity of corporate capitalism not only by preventing economic decline and stagnation but also by preventing inflation and assuring economic expansion. As in the earlier period, federal innovations were often represented as limiting big business, but, in reality, they actually favored it. Influential new organizations of businessmen—like the Committee for Economic Development (CED), composed of the liberal

[20]McConnell, pp. 261–63.
[21]John Blair, *Economic Concentration* (New York, 1972), pp. 375, 381.

and forward-looking segment of the corporate sector—helped develop new regulatory mechanisms, and leading businessmen continued to be appointed to top government positions. The trend toward big government was not checked during this period—not by Republican President Eisenhower, under whose presidency federal expenditures increased by $10 billion, nor by Democratic President Kennedy, whose "new economics" assigned highest priority to using government power to help big business grow.

As a result of active government intervention, lavish military contracts to large firms, and economic expansion overseas, the corporate sector enjoyed unprecedented prosperity. Economic growth benefited government and corporate capital and trickled down to corporate labor and small capital. However, many small-capital and surplus workers benefited little, if at all, from economic expansion. Many Americans continued to live in near-poverty conditions despite the growth of new productive capacity. The paradox of the new era was captured by the publication—several years apart—of two books: *The Affluent Society,* in which it was argued that permanent and near-universal affluence had arrived; and *The Other America,* which portrayed the harsh reality of a large minority of poor in the United States.[22]

Nixon's New Economic Policy

Yet, even for the corporate sector, prosperity collided with inescapable difficulties. By the time President Nixon took office in 1969, the economic boom began to decline and crises developed. One reason was the Vietnam war, whose actual costs were concealed by Presidents Johnson and Nixon because of political opposition to the war. Of more long-term significance was the deterioration of American civilian productive capacity—caused by allocating resources to wasteful, nonproductive ends—the cost of supporting an immensely expensive military machine since the early 1950s, and a squeeze on natural resources, such as petroleum. In the 1970s, the United States faced the unprecedented situation of having inflation at the same time as widespread unemployment and underutilization of productive capacity. In an attempt to resolve the crisis and restore corporate prosperity, the federal government developed new devices that

---

[22]John Kenneth Galbraith, *The Affluent Society* (Boston, 1958); Michael Harrington, *The Other America* (New York, 1962).

further reinforced the trend toward government direction of the economy.

Wage and price control   Beginning in 1962, President Kennedy attempted to control inflation by exerting pressure on corporate management and labor to limit price and wage increases. Through "jawboning" (the use of persuasion, negotiations, and threats), Kennedy tried to prevent wage and price rises from exceeding guidelines established by economic advisers. The most famous case was in 1962, when Kennedy forced the United States Steel Corporation and other steel producers to postpone steel price rises.

Presidents Kennedy and Johnson were moderately successful in using jawboning to slow inflation. When President Nixon took office, however, a number of factors converged to produce galloping inflation. (The annual rise in the cost of living during the mid-1970s doubled from the decade before.) At first, he insisted that government should keep hands off "private" decisions such as the setting of wages and prices. But when prices shot up and consumer demand and employment fell, Nixon completely reversed his policy.

In August 1971, he acknowledged the failure of government nonintervention and adopted the "New Economic Policy." Going far beyond the jawboning approach, the new program gave government power to prohibit wage and price increases it judged excessive. The federal government thus became closely involved in one of management's chief tasks in a capitalist economy: setting wages and prices. Critics noted that, unlike wages and prices, corporate profits were exempt from government control. As a result, corporate profits in the early 1970s rose three times faster than wages. Nonetheless, government controls failed to control inflation: consumer prices shot up by 9 percent in 1973, while wages rose less than 6 percent—signifying a loss of purchasing power for most Americans.[23] Although controls were gradually abandoned by 1974, they can be reinstated when government chooses.

The widening scope of government economic activity Another major device gradually becoming standard in the federal regulatory arsenal is government allocation of productive resources. Two illustrations suggest government's vast power in this domain. Before the Second World War, corporate profits

[23]*New York Times,* January 6, 1974.

exceeded government purchases from industry. Thus, private corporations decided how new capital would be allocated. During the current period, mostly because of military spending, government expenditures for goods and services from the private sector are nearly double all after-tax corporate profits. The government has come to control an increasingly large proportion of the new capital used for expanding productive capacity.

A second illustration is the allocation of natural resources. In 1974, triggered by an apparent shortage of petroleum, the government issued orders to petroleum companies telling them how to allocate petroleum supplies for various uses (industrial fuel and power, home heating, gasoline for automobiles, and so on). The government also established quotas and priorities among various regions of the country. When truckers started blocking highways and refusing to make deliveries in protest against their low allocation of fuel and high fuel prices, the government conducted negotiations to end the disruption. Yet legal authority for such government activity does not exist. As a *New York Times* reporter noted, "The Government is not the truckers' employer and is supposed to enforce the laws rather than make 'offers' to satisfy the truckers."[24] However, this action was similar to previous occasions when, through the actions of the National Labor Relations Board and the Federal Mediation and Conciliation Service, the federal government attempted to stabilize and institutionalize capital-labor relations and minimize strikes.

These illustrations suggest how the federal government has become a central agency in organizing and directing the production, distribution, and (through tax policies to be discussed below) consumption of goods and services in the United States. Yet, rather than signifying an end to corporate power, the new arrangements are geared to expand the output and profits of large corporations.

The Corporate Complex

The steadily widening involvement of the state in the economy has occurred in periods of war and peace, of economic prosperity and decline, and under presidents of both parties and differing ideological outlooks. As a result, there is virtually no area of

[24]Philip Shabecoff, "The Truck Settlement: Complex, Difficult Negotiations," *New York Times*, February 13, 1974.

production and distribution of goods and services in which government is not integrated with private business. In some industries, such as banking, utilities, transportation, and military weaponry, government officials make key management decisions, including the setting of prices, targeting of profits, and whether a company can enter the market or close operations. Other industries, not directly controlled by government, depend on state services and are critically affected by government decisions regarding tariffs, interest rates, taxes, product safety, patents, environmental protection, and a host of other issues.

The effect has been to create a closely-knit tissue of government and corporate cooperation, in which each partner participates in the decisions made by the other, performs services of mutual benefit, and derives extraordinary power and financial rewards from the alliance. We designate this amalgam of government and large corporations the corporate complex. It connotes a strange hybrid of "private" socialism or "state" capitalism, in which the distinctions between public and private or politics and economics lose meaning. Government provides capital for investment, purchases corporate output, and stimulates corporate growth and profits; but benefits—in the form of profits, power, and status—continue to flow to those who own and control corporate capitalism.

Disagreements between government and corporate officials may occur, just as conflicts among corporations go on all the time. Government actions may favor some corporations and industries and harm others. Government policies may even appear to run counter to the interests of all corporate capital. There are several reasons for this. First, any particular government action cannot possibly be of equal benefit to all corporations. Further, government's perspective is different from that of any individual corporation. In attempting to safeguard long-term interests of corporate capital, the government may antagonize corporations. For example, product safety, pollution control, and environmental protection laws impose higher costs on corporate producers. But the ultimate effect reduces political opposition and thus strengthens corporate capitalism. Moreover, government must respond to pressures arising from other sectors of the society and may be forced at times to oppose corporate interests. Neither corporate capitalism nor government is all-powerful. Other forces, for example, small-scale capital, also have political power and may press demands that challenge corporate interests.

These factors help explain why big business frequently denounces federal government "interference." However, political scientist Grant McConnell points out that this opposition may be a verbal maneuver rather than a genuine grievance. McConnell suggests that business opposition to government intervention is intended to mislead public opinion, keep any potentially zealous government officials on the defensive, and forestall potential government action that might seriously jeopardize corporate interests.[25]

As a writer in a business publication admitted, "Clearly, businessmen have lost their old aversion to close ties with government."[26] Evidence that big business is basically content with existing arrangements and against a return to free enterprise is provided by the 1964 presidential election. Barry Goldwater, the Republican candidate, came closer than any major candidate had since the Second World War to advocating the abolition of the massive government regulatory machinery—and he was promptly deserted by big business (both in terms of campaign contributions and votes).

FEDERALISM AND SMALL-SCALE CAPITAL

Government in the United States means not *one* government but more than 80,000—ranging from tiny municipal and county governments and school and water districts up to the federal government with over two million civilian employees. Although such governments are linked, they are also distinct, responsible to different constituencies, and often display diverse and even conflicting purposes. The large number of governments in the United States contributes to the diversity and fluidity of American politics.

The United States Constitution assigns certain legal powers to the national government; others it assigns to the states; and some are assigned to both. This system is called federalism. The federal character of American government is among its most prominent features. In addition to the national government, there

[25]McConnell, pp. 293–94.
[26]Juan Cameron, "What Businessmen Like, and Don't Like, About Nixon," *Fortune* (July 1972), p. 108.

are fifty state governments, powerful entities in their own right. To this picture should be added the eighty thousand municipal governments, school districts, and other governmental entities that, although not formally included in the constitutional definition of federalism, are usually included in discussions of federalism and, in fact, outrank the national government in number of employees, revenue, and range of activities. Local governments (including all units but the federal) have three times as many employees as the federal government. Schoolteachers make up the single largest nonmilitary group of public employees, followed by other professionals, such as police, welfare workers, and administrators. Despite close involvement of the federal government in providing funds, specifying procedures, and setting standards, local governments carry out a large part of government activity in important fields like education, law enforcement, highway construction and maintenance, welfare, and licensing and regulating professions.

Although generalization is hazardous, local governments are responsive to a different set of interests than the national government. The latter is closely allied with corporate capital and, to a lesser extent, consumer and organized-labor interests. Local governments are more responsive to small-scale capital. In the nineteenth century, local governments were often captured by populist majorities of small farmers and workers who were opposed to business, particularly emerging large-scale capital. However, the erosion of radical working-class and populist agricultural organizations has left local governments largely in the hands of local politicians, local businessmen (construction companies, real-estate and insurance interests, retail trade), and middle-class professional groups (lawyers, doctors, and teachers). State and municipal governments permit the persistence of interests that were dominant prior to the rise of corporate capital. Federalism provides an institutional base for the protection of these interests, whose position in the economy has become subordinate. Despite the rhetoric of "grass roots democracy," local governments in the United States are not any more responsive than the national government to popular interests. Among the reasons that local governments are often even less representative than the national government are the lower degree of popular participation in local government (voting turnout is far lower for local than for national elections), the lower visibility of local governments, and the ease with which wealthy interests can make their influence felt at local levels.[27]

The power of local governments helps explain much that otherwise is puzzling in federal governmental activity. Small businessmen are able to obtain government help because they have access to the national government through influence over state and municipal governments, local political parties, and Congress.

The complex institutional patchwork of American government has another important consequence: it dilutes power and authority. For example, if a new force were to win the presidency, it would not necessarily be able to persuade Congress, local governments, and the courts to support its program. Because many agencies in different levels of government must approve a new government program, it is often easier to prevent action from being taken than to effect changes in existing practice. Groups who sponsor a new program must win acceptance for it every step of the way; groups who oppose a program need only defeat it at one stage. Sociologist David Riesman has suggested that American politics is dominated by "veto groups," who are quick to act in defense of their interests by blocking change.[28] Thus, one study found that 85 percent of all corporate communications to public officials was in opposition to proposed legislation.[29] The result is to preserve structural stability and make unlikely the redistribution of power and wealth through purely political means.

CLIENTELISM

From 1800 to the present, the federal government has grown from under three thousand civilian employees to well over two million. Nearly all the growth has occurred within the executive branch, which today is one of the largest organizations in the world. It includes executive departments, each with jurisdiction over a particular sector of the economy, presided over by a secretary

[27]McConnell, Chapter 6.
[28]David Riesman, Nathan Glazer, and Ruel Denney, *The Lonely Crowd* (Garden City, N.Y., 1953), pp. 246–59.
[29]Edwin M. Epstein, *The Corporation in American Politics* (Englewood Cliffs, N.J., 1969), p. 99.

who sits in the president's cabinet. Examples are the departments of Agriculture, Defense, Transportation, Interior, and Commerce. Each department in turn is composed of bureaus, which carry out the work of the department. In addition, some government agencies are located outside the regular executive structure. These include the so-called independent regulatory commissions, whose origins were discussed earlier: the Securities and Exchange Commission (SEC) for the financial and investment sector (created in 1934); the Federal Communications Commission (FCC) for radio, television, and telephone (1922); the Civil Aeronautics Board (CAB) for airlines (1938); the Interstate Commerce Commission (ICC) for rail and highway transportation (1887); the Federal Trade Commission (FTC) for commercial and manufacturing activity (1914); the Federal Power Commission (FPC) for energy—petroleum, electricity, and gas (1920); and the National Labor Relations Board (NLRB), for labor disputes (1934). The banking sector is also coordinated through the Federal Reserve Board (1913).[30]

Virtually every industrial and commercial activity has links to a government agency. Rather than government limiting the power of private interests, the relationship between a government agency and its private "clients" is one of mutual dependence and support. The close alliance between a government agency and its constituency (which is often organized through a professional association dominated by the most powerful firms of the sector) is a foremost characteristic of American political life. Joining this alliance are the House and Senate committees in Congress with jurisdiction over the government agency. The committee is usually dominated by congressmen who have informal ties to the industry and are sympathetic to its interests (for example, most members of the agriculture committees are from farm states). Together, agency, congressional committees, and the industry form a tight, mutually supportive coalition. Usually representatives from local governments also belong. One illustration, among countless, is the alliance that serves petroleum interests, which consists of the oil lobby (the large oil companies, organized into the American Petroleum Institute), the Department of the Interior, the House and Senate committees on the interior, and state government agencies (like the Texas Railroad Commission, which defends Texas oil interests). The oil industry represents

[30]Bernstein, pp. 8–9.

Figure 5-2
Governmental organization of
the United States

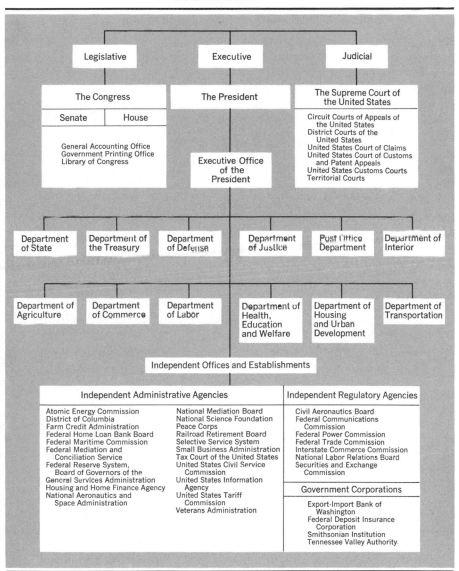

one of the mightiest forces in American politics. Contributions by oil company executives to President Nixon's 1972 election campaign totalled $6 million—one-tenth of his entire war chest. Petroleum companies have succeeded in obtaining favorable tax treatment. Joined with automobile companies, truckers, insurance companies, and others, they have been able to shape a transportation system based on the oil-hungry automobile and have obtained colossal sums from federal and local governments for highway construction and maintenance.

Some of the most important decisions affecting people's lives are made in the anonymous corridors of bureaucratic power. One scholar has noted that government policy is often best understood as "bureaucratic political outcomes."[31] The bureaucratic agency seeks autonomy, growth, and power. Its interest lies in strengthening the coalition of private forces linked to the agency. A government agency has much to gain from supporting its clients; conversely, the agency risks a stiff fight by opposing them.

Government agencies compete with each other in defense of the particular and often conflicting interests of their clients. As a result, government does not always speak with one voice. Thus, the Department of Health, Education, and Welfare warns the public about the dangers of smoking, while the Department of Agriculture provides subsidies to tobacco farmers and cigarette manufacturers. The Interstate Commerce Commission defends the interests of truckers while the Civil Aeronautics Board advances the interests of air transport and the National Maritime Commission subsidizes the merchant marine.

An agency's support for its constituency does not guarantee that the private interest will always get what it wants from government or that it will prosper. Overall government policy, such as budget requirements, may dictate a cutback in support for a particular industry. A corporation or an industry may require help from other government agencies than the one with primary jurisdiction; and these other agencies may be less sympathetic. Or, as we saw above, one agency-industry alliance may compete with others. Some industries may decline no matter how much help they get from government. Or public outrage may be strong enough to force an agency to act against an industry's interests. For example, despite strenuous opposition from both the tobacco

[31]I. M. Destler, *Presidents, Bureaucrats, and Foreign Policy* (Princeton, 1972), p. 64.

industry and television networks, the FCC banned cigarette advertising from television in 1969 on the grounds that smoking had been proven to be a health hazard.

Yet, particular setbacks aside, corporate capitalism receives a powerful boost from its friend in Washington. Most large corporations and industries are thoroughly dependent on the government's assistance and probably could not survive without its varied services. This does not mean, however, that government agencies control industry. In fact, most government agencies are likely to become captives of the interests that form their constituencies and act in concert with the corporate goals. The primary goal of the Federal Communications Commission regarding telephone communications is not to assure the best possible telephone service at least possible cost to the public, but to guarantee the American Telephone and Telegraph Company (and the few other telephone companies in the United States) a high (8 percent) profit and adequate funds for investment. Pentagon officials negotiate contracts that attempt to assure the prosperity of military contractors.

Within a given industry, the government agency usually favors large and established producers over small producers. For example, the Department of Agriculture gives little help to low-income and tenant farmers, who make up the majority of farmers; its price supports, technical assistance, and research programs are geared to the needs of large wealthy commercial farmers. (One-fifth of the nation's farmers get two-thirds of the government's agricultural subsidies.[32] One of the "farmers" getting the largest subsidy is Tenneco Corporation, a conglomerate that also ranks among the top ten military contractors.) The Food and Drug Administration requires drug companies to follow expensive testing procedures that favor large drug companies and brand name drugs. The Civil Aeronautics Board defends existing airlines and restricts entry of new airline companies. (The CAB has not licensed a new trunk airline since its creation in 1938.[33]) In the same way, the Federal Communications Commission favors existing radio and television networks over new applicants for broadcasting rights.

Why have consumers so little influence over the actions of the agencies presumably set up to protect their interests? To

---

[32]Martin Tolchin and Susan Tolchin, *To the Victor* (New York, 1971), p. 209.
[33]Mark J. Green, "Uncle Sam the Monopoly Man," in Mark J. Green, ed., *The Monopoly Makers* (New York, 1973), p. 22.

begin with, large numbers of small consumers have diffuse interests, and are less organized and cohesive than powerful producers. Corporate producers have the organization, money, staff resources, interests, contacts, and motivation to act effectively. They are well placed, in their day-to-day dealings with a government agency, to put across their point of view. When a government agency defends the interests of its private constituency, it is assured of powerful support, whereas defending broader interests (for example, consumer or worker interests) is sure to provoke a tough fight with its corporate constituency.

In the event of a conflict between the agency and its private clientele, staff resources are highly unequal. For example, the Antitrust Division of the Justice Department, whose responsibility is to review possible violations of antitrust laws occurring throughout the economy, has a yearly budget that is one-twentieth of Procter & Gamble's advertising budget. With fewer than four hundred professional personnel, it has jurisdiction over 1.5 million corporations, including more than 200 corporations whose assets each exceed $1 billion.[34] Whether it is government inspection of sanitary conditions in meatpacking plants, safety conditions in mines, or compliance by banks with banking laws, the government depends on the voluntary cooperation of private interests—and fears to provoke a confrontation with them.

Businessmen in Government

The way government agencies are staffed favors corporate interests. Top positions in government—members of the president's cabinet and the regulatory commissions and high positions within the bureaucracy—usually go to wealthy businessmen. One study of over one thousand appointees to top executive positions between 1933 and 1965 found that more than one-third had attended private preparatory schools, one-half were businessmen or lawyers, and the proportion of businessmen and lawyers among cabinet appointees was nearly two-thirds.[35]

There is a constant two-way flow of men between industry and government. The men appointed to head a government agency are usually corporate executives from the affected indus-

[34]Mark J. Green, with Beverly C. Moore, Jr., and Bruce Wasserstein, *The Closed Enterprise System* (New York, 1972), pp. 122–23.

[35]David T. Stanley, Dean E. Mann, and Jameson W. Doig, *Men Who Govern* (Washington, D.C., 1966), pp. 32, 132, 134.

try. In 1973, for example, the chairman of the Federal Power Commission, which sets gas and electric prices, was a former executive of a gas utility. The FPC's general counsel was from a Texas law firm with close links to a large oil company. Many members of the Federal Reserve Board are bankers, members of the Securities and Exchange Commission are financiers, and members of the Civil Aeronautics Board are airline officials. Most other members are lawyers, who are usually sympathetic to the interests of corporate leaders of the industry.

Conversely, when administrators leave government, they often take lucrative positions with firms in the industry with which they dealt while serving in government. Their knowledge of government procedures and contacts with the government agency enhance their value to industry. One month after James Boyd, secretary of transportation, approved a $25 million government grant to the Illinois Central Railroad, he resigned from government to become president of the company.[36] Clarence D. Palmby was a lobbyist for wealthy wheat farmers when he was appointed assistant secretary of agriculture. After Palmby played an important role in government negotiations with the Soviet Union for the sale of American wheat, he resigned from the government to become vice president of Continental Grain Company, one of the major companies benefiting from the wheat deal. Carl E. Bagge, president of the National Coal Association, was a Federal Power commissioner for six years. More than half the former FCC commissioners have gone to work for the communications industry after leaving government. All but two ICC commissioners in the 1960s took jobs in the transportation industry after leaving government.[37] General James Ferguson, former commander of the Air Force Systems Command, became vice president of United Aircraft Corporation, which holds large Air Force contracts. (More than two thousand retired high military officers currently work for the aerospace industry.) Part of the reason government agencies mirror industry's point of view is that the same men control both. The situation that exists flows quite naturally from America's political and economic structure. It stands to reason that the men appointed to government positions that deal with a particular industry or sector of economic activity should have expertise and experience in that field. Given the fact that production in the United States is

[36]Tolchin and Tolchin, p. 25.
[37]Green, *The Monopoly Makers*, p. 16.

organized in accordance with capitalist principles, this means that in most cases government officials will be recruited from private industry. Further, when leaving government positions, not only are they more valuable to private industry because of their knowledge and contacts—but where else could many government officials go? Once the principle of corporate capitalism is accepted, in which production is privately organized and controlled, clientelism follows not as an illogical exception but practically as a matter of course.

Getting Through to Government

There is an easy line of communications between industry and government. Most large corporations maintain a Washington office, whose job is to cover Congress and any government agency affecting corporate interests. (U.S. Steel's Washington office, for example, has seventeen staff members.) Company lobbyists maintain frequent contact with congressmen and bureaucrats, entertain them, and provide them with help when needed. Congressmen can have speeches written for them by company lobbyists and hop a company plane home if necessary. Corporate campaign contributions provide an even more effective way to open doors. Such courtesies create a quiet obligation toward the company. A company can get to top government officials fast if its interests are threatened. (When ITT feared the outcome of a government antitrust suit against the company, executives conferred with presidential aides and the attorney general and persuaded President Nixon to intervene on their behalf.) The chairman of Phillips Petroleum, who served on advisory committees to seven secretaries of the interior, explained what access can mean in a television interview: "Having gotten acquainted with so many people and knowing them on a personal basis, it made it real easy for me to go into government and discuss problems with them."[38] Getting into the right office to discuss problems and getting a friendly official to pick up the telephone to place a call is often half the battle.

Business access to government is facilitated by over five thousand advisory committees, mostly composed of businessmen, which exist at all levels of the bureaucracy. McConnell notes that these committees have "become an ingrained way of

---

[38]Television program on CBS reported in the *New York Times,* December 6, 1973.

government in the United States." Advisory committees exist for every conceivable industry, with their membership drawn mostly from the largest firms in the industry. Examples include the Aluminum Industry Advisory Committee, the Zinc Industry Advisory Committee, the Power Cranes and Shovels Industry Advisory Committee, and (to provide proper advice to the Department of Defense) the Industry Advisory Committee on Peanut Butter.[39] Advisory committees interlock business and government and provide business leaders with direct formal access to the executive bureaucracy to defend the industry's interests and suggest ways government can help the industry.

How Do Decisions Get Made? A Case Study

Evidence coming to light in the Watergate affair illustrates how government decisions are often the product of political as well as economic factors. Soon after Mr. Nixon entered the White House, Associated Milk Producers, the nation's largest milk cooperative, provided a $100,000 campaign contribution to the president's attorney—and pledged $2 million for the 1972 election campaign. ($400,000 was eventually contributed.) Because dairymen were dissatisfied with government decisions regulating milk prices, they requested, and were granted, a meeting with the president. In his meeting with the dairymen, a White House tape recording of their conversation revealed that Nixon praised the dairymen for their financial support: "Others . . . yammer and talk a lot but they don't do anything about it. But you do and I appreciate it. I don't need to spell it out." Soon after the meeting, Nixon overruled the Agriculture Department and substantially raised the government support price of milk. When the case came to light, the administration defended its actions on the grounds that it was a routine part of the political process for government decisions to be influenced by calculations regarding anticipated support or opposition.[40]

This defense was probably accurate. Associated Milk Producers executives later admitted that illegal contributions had also been made by the milk lobby to strategically placed Democrats. Commenting on the case, the *New York Times* declared in an editorial of March 28, 1974:

[39]McConnell, pp. 268, 274.
[40]*New York Times*, January 13, 1974.

What is most disturbing about this unsavory story of deceit, influence-mongering and illegality is that knowledgeable insiders in numerous other industries could tell similar stories, altering only the names and a few details.

Yet even more significant than the occasional public scandal or the incidents of wrongdoing that do not come to light is the routine—and mostly legal pattern—of business influence over government. Clientelism constitutes a comprehensive system of mutual support between government and corporate capitalism.

Clientelism at State and Municipal Levels

Business influence over government is also great at local levels. Ralph Nader's associates described Delaware as a "company state" because of the far-reaching influence exerted by E. I. Du Pont de Nemours, which is the world's largest chemical company and is headquartered in Delaware. Du Pont controls most of the state's economic and political life. Its annual sales are ten times larger than the state's tax revenues. The company employs over one-tenth of the state's work force and controls two of Delaware's four largest banks, the two largest newspapers, and the state's most important law firms, utilities, and charitable and cultural agencies. Delaware's single congressman is Pierre S. du Pont IV; in 1974, the governor and one United States senator were former Du Pont executives, and one-fourth of the state legislature is associated with the company.[41] Other states where one or two industries predominate include Montana (Anaconda Copper and Montana Power), Nevada (Las Vegas gambling interests), and Maine (seven paper companies own one-third of all land in the state). Numerous company towns exist throughout the country (for example Kodak in Rochester, New York, Boeing Aircraft in Seattle, and the insurance industry in Hartford, Connecticut) whose fortunes depend on decisions made by the local management or (more likely, in an era of corporate integration and concentration) by distant management in New York, Chicago, or San Francisco. Local power is translated into substantial benefits: low tax assessments for corporate property,

[41]James Phelan and Robert Pozen, *The Company State* (New York, 1973), *passim.;* and Ralph Nader and Mark J. Green, "Owing Your Soul to the Company Store," *New York Review of Books,* November 29, 1973.

favorable zoning laws, and public works projects facilitating company operations. Corporate capitalism thus is solidly entrenched in communities and states throughout the country.

However, as we have seen, small-scale capital and professional groups are also influential at the local level; these groups benefit from a clientele relationship with government. For example, when a state licenses a profession (and most states license dozens), it virtually turns over control of the profession to the private association of existing practitioners (such as the state medical association). One study found that, in over 700 of the 927 state licensing boards studied throughout the country, members of the profession held a majority on the state board. This system of private government (as McConnell has pointed out) limits entry into the profession—thereby keeping fees high—and makes outside scrutiny of professional standards difficult.[42]

Many government programs are not operated by the federal government, but by local government agencies with funds partly provided by the federal government. In recent years, as local governments have been unable to increase revenues through local taxes, the federal government has contributed a larger and larger share of local expenditures. A new approach to this grant-in-aid program has been named revenue sharing, and it will doubtless expand in the future. In part, the new funds represent a concession by the nationalizing forces of corporate capitalism and federal agencies to the influence of local political officials and small-scale capital. Economist James O'Connor has described the process as welfare for surplus capitalists, by which he means that many local contractors, law firms, insurance agencies, and banks survive largely through the funds they get from government contracts.[43] These clusters of small-scale capital interests are well situated to get government aid as a result of their solid institutional base in local governments and in Congress. Most state legislatures and state agencies are under the control of local business interests. Small-scale capital persists as a powerful force, in both the political and economic realm, largely because of its influence over thousands of political officials and agencies throughout the governmental apparatus.

[42]McConnell, p. 188.
[43]James O'Connor, *The Fiscal Crisis of the State* (New York, 1973), pp. 168–69.

Government Subsidies

Federal government help often goes beyond defending an industry's interest and may include providing direct subsidies to the industry. One form of subsidy is favorable tax treatment, such as that given the petroleum industry. For many years, petroleum companies have paid only 8 percent of their profits in American taxes, compared to the 40 percent paid by other corporations. An important factor has been the so-called oil depletion allowance, worth over $1 billion yearly. The depletion allowance is a tax break justified on the grounds that it encourages exploration for new petroleum sources. Yet one might ask why incentives to explore should be needed when the financial rewards of striking oil are so great. Moreover, the depletion allowance is a bad bargain, since the amount petroleum companies save in taxes far exceeds what they invest each year on new equipment and exploration. In reality, the explanation for federal generosity lies in the political power of the oil companies.

Existing oil companies have little incentive to expand production since together they exercise a monopoly over petroleum supplies. Their profits are already among the highest in the world: a dozen oil companies account for one-fifth of all profits of the 2,000 largest American companies. During the alleged energy crisis of 1974, petroleum companies suffered least of all, since the value of their oil resources zoomed. Despite decreased supplies, petroleum company profits were estimated as more than doubling from 1973 to 1974.[44]

Subsidies by the federal government exceed $60 billion per year.[45] Subsidized industries include shipping, air carriers, weapons manufacturers, and commercial agriculture. The federal government also provides billions of dollars annually to private firms for research and development. The firms use public funds to carry out their research, but any profits resulting from discoveries belong to private industry.

Subsidies go to a bewildering array of industries, seemingly without rhyme or reason. One explanation for specific subsidies lies in the give-and-take of interest group lobbying. Some industries have historically been successful in obtaining state or federal help. Since the late 1950s, the automobile lobby has been able to extract about $5 billion annually in federal funds to

[44]*New York Times,* January 8, 1974.
[45]*New York Times,* December 6, 1972.

subsidize the interstate highway system, the largest public works project in history. Once a subsidy is given, it tends to get renewed year after year. A second explanation for who gets subsidized distinguishes the privileged from the disadvantaged. According to democratic principles, power and resources should flow from the favored minority to the deprived majority. In fact, the opposite is more common. Subsidy programs for the wealthy and those with comfortable incomes are several times larger than welfare payments, low-income-housing subsidies, food stamps, and other government programs for small-scale-capital workers and surplus labor.

In extreme cases, the government may intervene directly in the production process. For example, if an industry cannot function profitably, the government may step in and help to pick up the bankrupt firms' debts. The firms continue to remain in private hands, with government benefits flowing to management and stockholders. (This happened in the case of unprofitable railroads in the Northeast.)

An even more extreme situation is military production; it is nearly completely organized by the government, with over two-thirds of the Pentagon's $40 billion procurement budget going to the 100 top military firms.[46] The largest military contractors, like Lockheed, McDonnell-Douglas, and Grumman, sell nearly all they produce to the government. In these cases, the result is to make government and private industry virtually indistinguishable.

The Tax System: Who Benefits?

About one-third the entire annual Gross National Product (GNP), the total value of the nation's annual output of goods and services, is collected by government in taxes.[47] The federal government receives about half of all taxes, local governments the rest.

The tax system is often presented as serving another purpose beyond providing government funds: it is said to help redistribute income from the wealthy to the poor. This principle is enshrined in the progressive income tax, which requires the wealthy to pay

[46]Larry Paul Ellsworth, "Defense Procurement: 'Everyone Feeds at the Trough,' " in Green, *The Monopoly Makers*, p. 229.
[47]Charles L. Schultze *et al., Setting National Priorities: The 1973 Budget* (Washington, D.C., 1972), p. 5.

a higher proportion of taxes than the poor. Prominent display is given each year to the federal income-tax rates on the tax forms sent to millions of families. The table shows that the tax rate for the lowest income groups is 15 percent, and it gradually increases to reach a hefty 70 percent for all taxable income earned over $100,000.

Figure 5-3
Tax table showing progressive feature of income tax

SCHEDULE X—Single Taxpayers Not Qualifying for Rates in Schedule Y or Z

If the amount on Form 1040A, line 16, is:	Enter on Form 1040A, line 17.

Not over $500....14% of the amount on line 16.

Over—	But not over—		of excess over—
$500	$1,000	$70+15%	$500
$1,000	$1,500	$145+16%	$1,000
$1,500	$2,000	$225+17%	$1,500
$2,000	$4,000	$310+19%	$2,000
$4,000	$6,000	$690+21%	$4,000
$6,000	$8,000	$1,110+24%	$6,000
$8,000	$10,000	$1,590+25%	$8,000
$10,000	$12,000	$2,090+27%	$10,000
$12,000	$14,000	$2,630+29%	$12,000
$14,000	$16,000	$3,210+31%	$14,000
$16,000	$18,000	$3,830+34%	$16,000
$18,000	$20,000	$4,510+36%	$18,000
$20,000	$22,000	$5,230+38%	$20,000
$22,000	$26,000	$5,990+40%	$22,000
$26,000	$32,000	$7,590+45%	$26,000
$32,000	$38,000	$10,290+50%	$32,000
$38,000	$44,000	$13,290+55%	$38,000
$44,000	$50,000	$16,590+60%	$44,000
$50,000	$60,000	$20,190+62%	$50,000
$60,000	$70,000	$26,390+64%	$60,000
$70,000	$80,000	$32,790+66%	$70,000
$80,000	$90,000	$39,390+68%	$80,000
$90,000	$100,000	$46,190+69%	$90,000
$100,000	....	$53,090+70%	$100,000

Table 5–1
Combined effect of federal individual income and payroll taxes
on the distribution of income, 1972

Income quintile	Percentage distribution	
	Total income before taxes	Total income after income and payroll taxes
Total population		
Lowest 20	1.7	1.8
20 to 40	6.6	7.0
40 to 60	14.5	14.8
60 to 80	24.1	24.4
80 to 100	53.1	51.9
Total	100.0	100.0

Source: Adapted from Edward R. Fried, Alice M. Rivlin, Charles L. Schultze, and Nancy H. Teeters, *Setting National Priorities: The 1974 Budget* (Washington, D.C., 1973), p. 50. © 1973 by the Brookings Institution, Washington, D.C.

A simple way to measure how well the progressive income tax redistributes income is to compare the distribution of income among different income groups before and after they pay taxes.

The surprising result is that tax laws have little effect on the relative distribution of income among most income groups. Most Americans—those earning between $2,000 and $30,000 annually—pay about the same proportion of their income in taxes (about one quarter). Those earning more than $30,000 pay a slightly higher tax—but nowhere near the rate given in the tax table. The cruelest irony is that the lowest income group, those with incomes under $2,000, also pay a higher proportion of taxes than many Americans. For most Americans, there are no progressive features built into the tax structure.

What accounts for the discrepancy? First there are a bewildering variety of other taxes beside the federal income tax. Most are regressive: instead of levying a higher rate on the wealthy, they levy a lower rate. One important example is payroll (social security) taxes, which are deducted directly from an employee's salary by his employer. Since social-security taxes are collected only on the first $13,200 of one's income, those earning above this amount pay proportionately less tax. (Nor is this a minor example: 31 percent of all federal tax revenue is now raised through payroll taxes.[48]) Local sales taxes, levied on clothing and other necessities, also fall more heavily on the poor.

[48]Schultze, p. 7.

Special features of the tax laws further permit the wealthy to shelter earnings from the progressive income tax. Such provisions, which result in a lower tax bill, are equivalent to granting a subsidy to affluent taxpayers. One example is a lower tax rate on income that comes from the sale of stocks (capital gains). If this income were taxed at the same rate as wages, it would produce $5 billion more in federal tax revenue. Who gets this $5 billion bonus? Three-quarters of it goes to .5 percent of the population—one in two hundred families.[49] Another example: dividends from state and municipal bonds—two-thirds of which are owned by .1 percent of the population—are not taxed at all.[50] Through such devices, the wealthy can exempt much of their income from high tax rates. Rather than redistributing income to the poor, two economists conclude that tax laws "provide a vehicle of redistribution to the wealthy."[51]

Here, as elsewhere, one should be wary of simplistic notions that only the very wealthiest benefit. Federal tax laws permitting taxpayers to deduct interest payments on mortgages from taxable income benefit middle-income homeowners, thus attracting their support for the existing tax system. But, of course, such a provision does not benefit those who cannot afford to buy their own home.

What can be concluded is that the tax system parallels other government activities in maintaining existing structural arrangements rather than in equalizing power.

Structural Consequences

Clientelism has long been recognized as a characteristic and important feature of American politics. Government help serves some structural interests and neglects or damages others. Amidst the myriad of government agencies, most represent large producers; few represent the far more numerous consumers, corporate workers, small-scale capital workers, or surplus labor. There are exceptions, but none so significant that they threaten corporate capitalism. The major exceptions are welfare and other agencies whose clients are workers, surplus labor, and the poor. Here, despite strains because of lower-level professional case workers'

---

[49]Martin Pfaff and Anita Pfaff, "How Equitable are Implicit Public Grants? The Case of the Individual Income Tax," in Kenneth E. Boulding and Martin Pfaff, eds., *Redistribution to the Rich and the Poor* (Belmont, California, 1972), p. 191.
[50]Philip M. Stern, *The Rape of the Taxpayer* (New York, 1973), p. 62.
[51]Pfaff and Pfaff, p. 201.

possible support for their clients, the agency's main aim is to prevent "welfare chiselers." The Department of Labor is closely tied to organized labor, although it is among the weakest government departments (and is allied with the most conservative elements in the labor movement). Small business has a voice through the Small Business Administration; the Department of Health, Education, and Welfare, the Environmental Protection Agency, and the Product Safety Commission provide some aid to consumers. Overall, however, government represents established powerful interests, particularly corporate capital.

Clientelism obscures this bias because the sprawling federal bureaucracy is so large and the constituencies organized and served are so many. But government service to corporate capital has become more clear with the emergence of a new layer of government activity above the particular government agencies that serve private groups. The development of federal planning mechanisms to coordinate the entire economy highlights the links between the federal bureaucracy and corporate capitalism.

PLANNING THE ECONOMY

A distinction can be made between government activity that is primarily designed to help particular industries and the new overall planning machinery that gives broad direction to the whole economy.

Most agencies of the federal and state governments serve the needs of particular sectors, both large and small-scale capital. The planning function is scattered throughout the bureaucracy, but it is centered in the presidency. In particular, agencies such as the Office of Management and Budget, the Council of Economic Advisers, and the Domestic Council—all located within the Executive Office of the President—attempt to provide overall coordination to the immense system.

Why plan? Planning becomes more and more necessary in an interdependent society. "The American economy is a gigantic, intricate machine. A serious malfunction of any one of its component parts affects, sometimes with a long delay, the working of all the other parts."[52] We have already alluded to the

[52]Wassily Leontief, "For a National Economic Planning Board," *New York Times*, March 14, 1974.

vast dislocations that can result from the disruption of corporate production. Another reason for planning is shrinking resources: a Federal Energy Office was created in 1973 to deal with energy shortages, and its powers include allocating petroleum among various uses (heating oil versus gasoline for automobiles) as well as among regions of the country.

These factors make understandable why Herbert Stein, a leading Republican economist and chairman of the Council of Economic Advisers, advocated the creation of "a huge planning agency" whose purpose would be to "coordinate and direct government economic policy."[53] Although unified government planning does not yet exist in the United States, the trend toward central planning has been rapid. For example, the severe inflation of the 1970s led to the creation by President Ford in 1974 of the Economic Policy Board, the White House Labor-Management Committee, and the Council on Wage and Price Controls.

What are the goals of federal planning? The major aim is to assure stability, growth, and profits to the corporate sector as well as the political acquiescence of small capital, labor, and other groups. A variety of government policies are directed to this end. Among the many aspects of the economy that the federal government attempts to regulate are wages, prices, overall (aggregate) demand, employment, interest rates, money supply, and production. Government's own tax, fiscal, and employment policies have enormous impact due to the federal government's large size and vast resources.

Federal expenditures have climbed to $300 billion per year, one-fifth of America's total production. And national and local government expenditures are rising steadily: by more than one-third between 1969 and 1973. Government expenditures contribute to growth by injecting purchasing power into the economy and providing demand for corporate output.

In addition, the government tries to achieve its planning goals through adroit use of federal powers, for example, manipulation of interest rates charged by the Federal Reserve Board to private banks. This approach has been called "fine tuning" the economy. Government planning agencies use sophisticated economic techniques in an attempt to achieve growth without rapid inflation.

If growth is a necessity for corporate capitalism, it is justified on the grounds that it benefits everyone. President Nixon

[53]*New York Times,* December 30, 1973.

explained why in a radio address on October 7, 1971:

> All Americans will benefit from more profits. More profits fuel the expansion that generates more jobs. More profits means more investment, which will make our goods more competitive in America and in the world. And more profits means there will be more tax revenues to pay for the programs that help people in need. That's why higher profits in the American economy would be good for every, person in America.

In the ideology of corporate capitalism, higher profits and economic growth replace reform as a way to help the under-privileged. It is assumed that the growth of the corporate complex will benefit everyone—but, as was already indicated, much of the fruits from economic growth go to those who own and control the means of production. Increased production and the distribution of profits from that increased production are two different matters. Particularly in an era of advanced technology, economic growth can occur without alleviating widespread poverty and unemployment, for overall growth is sparked by the corporate sector—a declining area in terms of employment (Unemploy ment in the 1970s remains high at the same time that industry booms and profits grow.)

Aside from how the fruits of state-sponsored economic growth are distributed, other objections exist to accepting eco-nomic growth as the highest good. Growth is a quantitative, not a qualitative goal: expenditures for weaponry, advertising, and luxury cars help push up the growth rate as much as expenditures for cancer research or clothing. The government is more commit-ted to forcing perpetual growth than to questioning the *wisdom* of how resources in America are being allocated. In effect, this means accepting as desirable the way resources are presently being used. And this, in turn, means accepting the right of the corporate complex to decide the question.

Furthermore, the goal of growth may be questionable and even immoral in a world of shrinking resources. Increased production means increased consumption of raw materials. The United States is by far the world's largest consumer of raw materials: with 6 percent of the world's population, the United States consumes over one-third of the world's raw materials used annually.

Energy is one important example. The average American annually uses more than twice as much energy as the average Englishman, nearly three times as much as the average Russian, and six times as much as the average Indian. Oil consumption in the United States has doubled in a generation. Yet much of the energy consumption is unnecessary: homes overheated in winter and overair-conditioned in summer, overreliance on inefficient automobile transportation, and excessive lighting in office buildings. Putting high priority on growth and private consumption encourages waste. The corporate complex, with the government's blessing, artificially stimulates the consumer demand for goods (through advertising) and then argues that it should be allowed to meet this demand through wasteful production. The petroleum industry, for example, advocated opening up new oil fields in Alaska and off the Atlantic coast to resolve the energy crisis; electric companies make the same argument in pressing for the right to build new power plants. But rather than adopting growth and high consumption as a goal, the wise policy in a world of scarce resources would be precisely opposite: to learn how to conserve resources and live on less. Such a policy, however, would strike at the core of corporate capitalism, whose profits depend on expanding production, and would also threaten the position of corporate labor, affluent professionals, and small business.

By making growth the main yardstick of economic success, the government contributes to the waste of valuable resources, ignores basic questions about the quality of life and control over what the United States will produce, and bolsters the power of corporate capitalism. Yet, in a system of corporate capitalism, the state has no viable alternative but to foster the expansion of production.

Economic growth in the United States has depended, especially in the period following the Second World War, on an international situation favorable to American corporate interests. Prosperity occurring within the United States can partly be traced to the advantages American corporations extracted from other countries. In order to maintain this state of affairs, the United States mounted the largest military establishment in history and intervened in countries throughout the world. Yet the system of production fostered by the corporate complex within the United States has become more difficult to maintain in recent years, as America's dominant position in the international system is threatened. Since the current crisis of American capitalism is partly the result of the changing balance between the United States and other countries, we turn now to the corporate complex abroad.

6

the corporate complex abroad: military and foreign policy

AMERICA AND THE WORLD

Some statistics provide the context for understanding American foreign policy: with 6 percent of the world's population, the United States accounts for the annual consumption of over half the world's manufactured products, one-quarter of the world's steel and fertilizer, and one-third of the world's tin, tractors, rubber, and television sets. Nearly one-half of all telephones are in the United States. The United States consumes one-third the world's total energy; the average American uses six times the world average. Well over half of all airline passengers each year are American. Nearly half of all Americans between the ages of 20 and 24 are enrolled in an institution of higher education; the comparable proportion for Europe is less than one-quarter, for Latin America, Asia, and Africa, it does not exceed one-twentieth. Per capita income in the United States is $4,100 yearly; it is $2,100 in Western Europe, $460 in Latin America, and $170 in Africa.[1] Overall, most Americans are wealthier, better-fed, and

---

[1]United Nations, *U.N. Statistical Yearbook, 1972,* pp. 6, 37, 621; *New York Times,* October 2, 1972.

receive more education, material benefits, and services than most people in the world. Although these figures do not take note of the extensive inequalities *within* the United States, which are the subject of other chapters, they suggest that even greater inequalities exist between the United States (along with the capitalist countries of Western Europe and Japan, to a lesser extent) and the rest of the world. When American political leaders talk of the need to maintain world order and stability, they are referring to a world based on this inequality. Stability means the persistence of United States privilege.

However, a situation of inequality is not natural or inevitable. In Chapter 1, it was suggested that in order to maintain stability, the structurally dominant in America exert power to overcome the resistance of subordinates. The United States functions in much the same way in its relations to other countries, by the manner in which it uses its great political, military, and economic influence throughout the world.

Just after the Second World War, the United States rapidly attained a position of unprecedented world power. American dominance has rested on two pillars, described by political scientist Samuel Huntington as "U.S. military superiority over the Communist world and U.S. political-economic hegemony in the noncommunist world."[2] To put it another way, American dominance has consisted of United States corporate penetration of other countries coupled with the use of the government's political and military power abroad. The linkage of corporate capitalism and government within the United States has been described as the corporate complex. This chapter describes how the corporate complex functions abroad and shapes American foreign policy.

A common view holds that after the Second World War the United States did not deliberately seek to extend its power, but, "having many obligations and vast responsibilities in the world," was forced to "adopt a policy not dictated by any American material needs and certainly not in response to any American ambition or desire."[3] President Lyndon B. Johnson proudly stated, "History and our own achievements have thrust upon us

[2]Samuel P. Huntington, "After Containment: The Functions of the Military Establishment," *The Annals* 406 (March 1973): 4.
[3]Charles E. Bohlen, *The Transformation of American Foreign Policy* (New York, 1969), p. 124.

the principal responsibility for the protection of freedom on Earth."[4] Writing in the fiscal 1975 annual Defense Department report, the secretary of defense observed:

> The United States today, as opposed to the period before 1945, bears the principal burden of maintaining the worldwide military equilibrium which is the foundation for the security and the survival of the free world. This is not a role we have welcomed; it is a role that historical necessity has thrust upon us. . . . There is nobody else to pick up the torch.

Nonetheless, the facts remain that the United States has emerged as the foremost power in the world, that it has devoted many resources to maintaining dominance, and that it has derived rich benefits from its position. American military, diplomatic, and economic influence is visible in virtually every country. The United States leads all other countries in investments abroad and in military power. This power is consistently used to contain challenges throughout the world to the American corporate complex.

However, no country can maintain dominance indefinitely. In both the political and economic spheres, American power has been shrinking. The most dramatic illustration is America's defeat in Vietnam. More broadly, "While American military power has declined relative to that of the Soviet Union, American economic strength has declined relative to that of Europe and Japan. . . . The United States remains the strongest power in the world. But the preeminent feature of international politics at the present time is the relative decline in American power."[5]

On the most general level, United States actions represent no more (nor less) than the age-old attempt by a major power to extract the political, military, and economic advantages that dominance brings. Whether the country be Athens in the fifth century B.C., Rome during the Roman Empire, or Great Britain in the nineteenth century, the international system has often been dominated by a single country. The United States is not the first nation to attempt to maximize its power position in the international area, and it will not be the last. Thus, on the one hand, despite the protestations of American leaders that the United

[4]Quoted in Richard J. Barnet, *Roots of War* (New York, 1972), p. 19.
[5]Huntington, p. 5.

States is historically unique in neither seeking world power nor profiting from hegemony, the worldwide influence the United States has exercised in the past thirty years qualifies it as an imperialist power.

However, on the other hand, such an abstraction misses the specificity of history, the unique characteristics that differentiate United States dominance from that exercised by other imperial powers. American hegemony is not traditional imperialism: it is both more global in scope and more far-reaching within individual countries than past imperial situations, and yet it is exercised through informal influence rather than formal colonial arrangements. What must be examined, then, are the specific new features of American dominance, which are linked to corporate capitalism, rapid communications, and military technology.

American Foreign Policy Before the Second World War

During the eighteenth and nineteenth centuries, the United States was far removed from world power struggles. In his farewell address, George Washington advised the country to profit from the good fortune that geographic accident provided and not to get involved in "entangling alliances." For more than a century afterward, the United States attempted to derive maximum benefit from her geographic isolation and refused to ally for long with any European power.

During the eighteenth and nineteenth centuries, United States expansion was toward the vast western frontier. Although this differed from the overseas expansion and the search for colonies of European powers during the same period, it represented imperialism none the less—and on a continental scale. Nor is the American past the inspiring picture sometimes painted of a free people braving hardships to create a democratic society. American history cannot be separated from the conquest and extermination of Indians, the enslavement of blacks as a source of cheap labor, and war with Mexico in 1846 (which resulted in the annexation of a substantial portion of that country, including the area that is now California, New Mexico, Utah, Arizona, and Nevada). In the 1840s, the United States and England came close to war over the western boundaries between the United States and Canada. Other examples of territorial expansion include the taking of Florida from Spain and the annexation of Texas in 1845.

Furthermore, isolation from Europe did not mean abstaining from other international intervention. Uninterested in Europe's struggles, the United States attempted to stake out its own sphere of influence close to home. In 1823, President Monroe issued a proclamation warning European powers not to intervene in Latin America. "But it is not the negatives [in the Monroe Doctrine] that really count. It is the hidden positive to the effect that the United States shall be the only colonizing power and the sole directing power in both North and South America."[6]

In the half century between the Spanish-American War in 1898 and the Second World War, the United States vacillated between a new expansionism overseas and an inward-looking isolationism. War with Spain resulted in United States control over the Philippines, Puerto Rico, and Guam. Gunboat diplomacy in Latin America insured that this area would remain a preserve for United States business interests. The navy and marines overthrew "uncooperative" governments and installed and kept in office puppet regimes. For example, American marines occupied and governed Nicaragua between 1926 and 1932. President Theodore Roosevelt maneuvered to build the Panama Canal by carving up Colombia and creating the client state of Panama, which quickly ceded to the United States sovereignty over the land for the canal.

United States influence was mostly confined to the Western Hemisphere until the two world wars made the United States a global power, although American political leaders had a lively interest in Asia (for example, President McKinley dispatched five thousand troops to China to help crush the Boxer Rebellion in 1900). The wars resulted in a weakening of the leading European states; the United States did not enter either war until years after it began, and it was an ocean away from the actual fighting. The Second World War was decisive, for it signified the irrevocable decline of Great Britain, the dominant capitalist power and the hub of world production, commerce, and banking.

The Soviet Union (USSR), Japan, Germany, and France—the other major industrialized countries—all suffered direct damage from the war. The United States was the only country to emerge unscathed. Indeed, in 1945 the United States was far stronger than before the war, partly because the government-

[6]Richard W. Van Alstyne, *The Rising American Empire* (Chicago, 1965), p. 99.

sponsored wartime expansion of productive capacity was quickly converted to peacetime production and overseas expansion when the war ended.

After the Second World War, there was no question of returning to the isolation of the Western Hemisphere. Europe's decline, the existence of a political and ideological rival in the Communist regime of the Soviet Union, and the fear by American officials that a domestic depression would recur unless the United States expanded outward, resulted in the transformation of the United States from a powerful, but insular, country to the dominant force shaping the world political and economic system.

Cold War Rivalry

In 1945, United States officials hoped to create a peaceful, stable world free for international trade and open to American influence. The new world would be one of formal equality among nations. Like Woodrow Wilson after the First World War, American leaders after the Second World War pressed the colonial powers (Great Britain, France, and the Netherlands) to dismantle their empires. Only one country threatened the vision of an integrated capitalist world order: the USSR.

As a Communist country, the USSR opposed a capitalist trading bloc. The Soviet Union was also perceived as a potential aggressor, bent on territorial conquest in Europe. American foreign policy since the Second World War, which has depended heavily on military power, has usually been interpreted as an attempt to counter the threat of Communist aggression around the world.

After the Second World War, the Soviet Union was prostrate. "The moment of victory was to find the Soviet Union enfeebled and devastated on a scale unprecedented in the past by countries *defeated* in a major war."[7] Soviet losses far exceeded those of the other allied powers.

> For three years, from June of 1941 to June of 1944, the Soviet Union carried the main burden of the fight against Hitler. . . . Partly because of Russian military successes, the United States

[7]Adam Ulam, *The Rivals: America and Russia Since World War II* (New York, 1971), p. 11.

Army got through the war with less than half the number of divisions prewar plans had indicated would be necessary for victory. Casualty figures reflect with particular vividness the disproportionate amount of fighting which went on in the east. A conservative estimate places Soviet war deaths—civilian and military—at approximately 16 million. Total Anglo-American losses in all theaters came to less than a million.[8]

In 1945, Soviet industrial output was only 58 percent of the 1940 level, and the country faced famine because of drought and destruction of its agriculture.[9] This contrasted sharply with the United States, whose industrial base had expanded during the war and whose military strength was enhanced by exclusive possession of atomic weapons. Most historians "now generally agree on the limited nature of Stalin's [postwar] objectives."[10] Invaded twice from the West within a generation, Russia aimed to create a buffer zone under her control in Eastern Europe. Regardless of the ethics, legality, or wisdom of this goal, it was far from an attempt to foment global revolution. Indeed, Premier Joseph Stalin restrained Communists in Western Europe, Yugoslavia, and China from seeking power.

In part, American political leaders probably sincerely misjudged Soviet intentions after the Second World War when they continually alarmed Americans with the prospect of a Soviet invasion of Western Europe.[11] In part, however, the Soviet threat was used to frighten Americans into supporting activist policies. "Scare hell out of the country," Senator Vandenberg advised President Truman. Truman heeded the advice and went to Congress in 1947 to advocate passage of his Truman Doctrine, which symbolized American expansionism. Just three years after the United States and the Soviet Union were wartime allies, the

---

[8]John Lewis Gaddis, *The United States and the Origins of the Cold War, 1941-1947* (New York, 1972), pp. 79–80.

[9]Joyce Kolko and Gabriel Kolko, *The Limits of Power: The World and United States Foreign Policy, 1945–1954* (New York, 1972), p. 53.

[10]Gaddis, p. 355, fn 2.

[11]Many of those influential in shaping the containment policy have subsequently admitted their error in judgment. See, for example, Dean Acheson, *Present at the Creation* (New York, 1969), p. 753; George Kennan, " 'X' plus 25: Interview with George F. Kennan," *Foreign Policy* no. 7 (Summer 1972): 14; and others cited in Ronald Steele, "The Power and the Glory," *New York Review of Books*, May 31, 1973, p. 30, fn 3.

cleavage between the two hardened into what English leader Winston Churchill called the "iron curtain."

More important than the question of which country "started" the cold war is the ensuing and continuing destructive spiral of arms production, which has maintained world tensions at a dangerous pitch. The period soon after the war ended saw the emergence of a relentless and unlimited arms race, for which the United States shares responsibility.

Global Expansion

Focusing on the US–USSR cold-war rivalry—important as the issue is—may obscure another development possibly of greater importance that occurred following the war. Joyce and Gabriel Kolko have suggested that the most important aspect of American foreign policy during the last thirty years has not been US–USSR hostility but the postwar quest of the United States for worldwide domination.[12] As restated by foreign-policy analyst Graham Allison, "Historians in the year 2000, looking back with detachment on the cold war, are apt to conclude that the main feature of international life in the period 1945–1970 was neither the expansion of the Soviet Union nor Communist China. Instead, it was the global expansion of American influence: military, economic, political and cultural."[13]

Underlying the new expansionism—a process that was already underway when the United States began to pick up the slack left by England, France, and Germany after the First World War—was a fear shared by political officials and corporate leaders that the depression, which had sapped the United States economy in the 1930s and had ended only when war needs created new demand, would recur. "Fully aware that the New Deal had not solved the problem of unemployment in peacetime, Roosevelt and his associates hoped that foreign markets would help absorb the vast quantity of goods which would have to be produced if employment levels were to be maintained after the fighting had stopped."[14]

[12]Kolko and Kolko, *passim.*
[13]Graham Allison, "Cool it: The Foreign Policy of Young America," *Foreign Policy* No. 1 (Winter 1970–71): 144–45.
[14]Gaddis, p. 21.

Figure 6–1
Foreign investments of capital-exporting countries

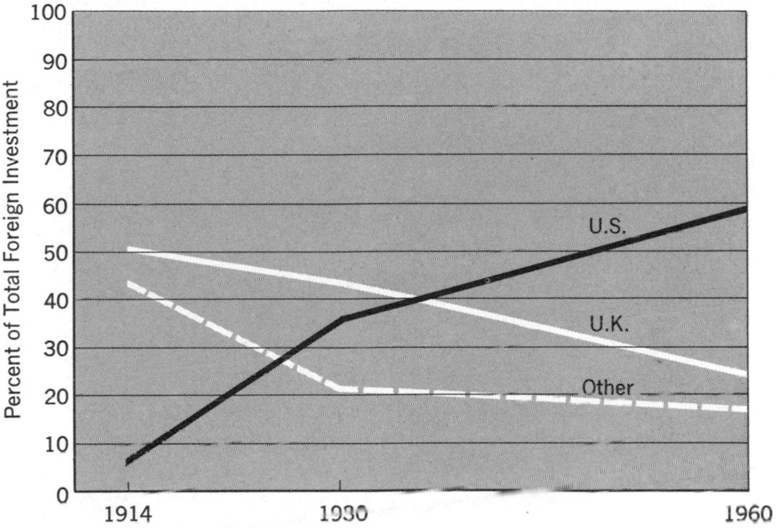

Source: Adapted from William Woodroot, *Impact of Western Man* (New York, 1966), p. 150.

The search for foreign markets and spheres of influence took several forms.

Replacing Western Europe as a world power Before the Second World War the capitalist countries of England, France, Germany, Belgium, Italy, and the Netherlands were the leading world producers, traders, and colonial powers. All were severely weakened by the war. Within a few years, the United States moved into the vacuum thus created—and used economic aid and political pressure to hasten the process.

The United States set out to replace England, which had been the keystone of the former international capitalist system and the largest trader, banker, and colonial power. This was the price England was forced to pay for American assistance in the desperate years after the war. Historian John Gaddis notes that "blunt pressure from the [American] negotiators eventually forced London to accept most of Washington's plans. Dependent on American aid for both its war effort and postwar reconstruction, Great Britain was in no position to resist."[15] Within a few years, the United States succeeded in supplanting England as international trader and banker. By the Bretton Woods agreement of 1944, the dollar replaced the British pound as the international currency, providing the United States with substantial benefits. (For example, other countries must maintain reserves in dollars, which results in the equivalent of a several-billion-dollar low-interest loan to the United States each year.) As for foreign investment, the table shows how rapidly the United States replaced European countries as the leading world investor.

The Third World   With Latin America already to a large extent under informal American control, the United States expanded into other resource-rich areas. Particularly important was the Middle East, which contained vast petroleum deposits that American petroleum companies soon dominated, as well as countries in Africa and Asia with mineral deposits. In 1940, Great Britain controlled 72 percent of Middle East oil reserves; the United States, 10 percent; and other countries, the rest. By 1967, Great Britain controlled 29 percent; the United States, 59 percent; and other countries, the remainder.[16] Since European countries needed all their available resources to rebuild after the Second World War, American business was uniquely situated to expand into other areas. American aims in the Third World were to open up these areas to investment by American corporations and to prevent local government control by regimes that might challenge foreign (particularly American) interests. (The Third World is usually defined as the rural, poor countries in Asia, Africa, and Latin America, who are aligned neither with the Communist nor Western capitalist bloc. Yet nearly all countries in the Third World are tied—by trade, investment, political, and military links—to the capitalist bloc under United States direction.)

Containment   The new expansionism required checking potential challengers. Both because the Communist Trading bloc represented an alternative to the Western capitalist trading bloc, and, from a fear of Soviet expansion, American policy aimed to confine Soviet influence to Eastern Europe, reserving the rest of

[15]*Ibid.*, p. 22.
[16]Harry Magdoff, *The Age of Imperialism: The Economics of U.S. Foreign Policy* (New York, 1969), p. 43.

the world for capitalist economic development and political control. The world was thus divided into two areas: the Communist countries of the Soviet Union, Eastern Europe, and (after 1948) China; and the capitalist areas (both industrialized and agricultural).

Priority was first given to rebuilding war-torn Europe, militarily, economically, and politically, in order to assure reliable and prosperous allies among the industrialized nations. In 1948, Secretary of State George Marshall proposed a program of American financial and technical aid to Europe. Marshall defended his plan to Congress on the humanitarian ground that famine was sweeping Europe. Moreover, he warned, unless the United States helped other countries to recover, "the cumulative loss of foreign markets and sources of supply would unquestionably have a depressing influence on our domestic economy. . . ." [17] The secretary of the interior also defended the plan as essential to America's continued productivity and prosperity.

The Marshall Plan was further justified as a way to prevent socialist regimes from taking power in Western Europe and to stop the spread of communism. Marshall Plan funds were provided to Germany, America's enemy in the war, but conditions imposed on funds offered to the Soviet Union, the wartime ally of the United States, virtually insured the USSR's refusal. At the same time that the Marshall Plan was launched, a series of military initiatives were also taken by the United States, notably, the Truman Doctrine, which provided military aid to Greece and Turkey, and justified aid and intervention abroad on the grounds that they were necessary to bolster regimes against domestic challenge; and the North Atlantic Treaty Organization (NATO), which linked the United States and Western Europe in an anti-Soviet military alliance.

The twin motivation behind the first thrust of American international expansion after the Second World War still underlies American policies: to strengthen the prosperity of the corporate complex at home through economic penetration abroad, and to assure American influence over other countries through political and military means. The two aims are closely linked. However, to simplify presentation, they will be described separately.

[17]William Appleman Williams, *The Tragedy of American Diplomacy* (Cleveland, 1959), p. 177.

ECONOMIC PENETRATION AND
MULTINATIONAL CORPORATIONS

American corporate capitalism has expanded outside the United States in response to three internal dilemmas. Each one has shaped a different form of American economic expansion.

Dependence on raw materials   The United States is among the countries best endowed with natural resources. It has some of the world's largest deposits of coal, copper, natural gas, iron, petroleum, and aluminum. The United States is also among the world's leading food producers; for example, it is the largest producer of corn, soybeans, cotton, and oranges, and the largest exporter of wheat and rice.[18] However, no country is fortunate enough to contain within its borders all the raw materials it needs for modern industrial production—and the United States is no exception. Moreover, through heavy, often inefficient and wasteful use, the United States has begun to deplete many of the natural resources it once contained in abundance. Both factors produce a growing dependence on other countries for essential raw materials.

The speed with which the United States has come to rely on other countries for raw materials can be seen from the following figures: of the thirteen minerals considered essential for a modern industrial economy, the United States had to import only four in 1950; yet by 2000, estimates are that the number will have climbed to twelve. The United States already imports all its natural rubber, over 90 percent of its manganese, cobalt, and chromium, and over half its aluminum, platinum, tin, nickel, antimony, bismuth, mercury, and zinc.[19] Most of these raw materials come from less developed countries in Latin America, Asia, the Middle East, and Africa.

The American corporate complex, both corporations and government, seeks to assure a cheap and adequate supply of minerals and other natural resources flowing to the United States. The most effective way in the past has been for American corporations to invest in the Third World and to gain direct control over foreign raw materials. Thus, Kennecott and Anaconda control much of the world's copper deposits, located in

---

[18]*New York Times*, January 6, 1974; Emma Rothschild, "The Politics of Food," *New York Review of Books*, May 16, 1974, p. 17.
[19]*New York Times*, November 5, 1972; December 22, 1973.

Zambia, Chile, and elsewhere. And a handful of American petroleum corporations (and a few foreign companies) control most of the world's petroleum supplies, located in the United States, the Middle East, and Venezuela.

However, countries containing raw materials have begun in recent years to resist American control of their vital resources, and the era of American domination of world commodities and low prices may be drawing to a close. The most dramatic change has been the steep rise in the price of petroleum charged by Middle East oil-producing countries. The United States paid $25 billion for petroleum imports in 1974 and will be paying double that amount by 1980.

*Foreign trade: export of manufactured products and food-*The United States imports many of the commodities needed in modern industry. (Commodities refer to food, fiber—wool and cotton—and minerals, including steel, aluminum, rubber, and so on.) At the same time, much of what American industry produces cannot profitably be sold at home. Not that millions of Americans do not lack basic necessities, including adequate food, medical care, and housing. The need is there—but many do not have the income to buy. Thus, following the logic of profit, not need, American industry has begun to look elsewhere to find lucrative outlets for surplus American productive capacity. The government, as a buyer of goods such as military weaponry, represents one additional market for American corporate capitalism. Foreign countries represent another.

In 1973, American business exported $70 billion worth of goods produced in the United States. The economic expansion to foreign countries has not been carried out by all segments of American business. It takes capital, expertise, and organization to establish trade abroad. It follows, then, that most foreign activity is organized within the sector of corporate capital. Encouraged by government help, including tax incentives, technical assistance, insurance against political difficulties, and, most important, a foreign policy that aims at creating conditions throughout the world favorable to American corporations, the expansion of America's foreign trade has been rapid. For large corporations, overseas sales often mean the difference between profit and loss.

Capital export: foreign investment In recent years, American corporations have found it more profitable to invest capital in building new factories abroad rather than to expand manufacturing at home and export the products abroad. Foreign investments give American corporations easier access to foreign markets and a direct hold over the economies of other countries. When manufactured products or food are exported, the transaction ends once they are purchased by foreign customers. However, when capital and technology are exported, and an American corporation creates a foreign manufacturing subsidiary, the transaction only *begins* with the initial investment: the foreign subsidiary remains year after year, continuing to produce and sell goods that make a profit for the American home company. American corporations began investing heavily in foreign manufacturing subsidiaries during the 1950s and a substantial investment has piled up abroad. Between 1950 and 1971, direct overseas investment by American corporations increased from $12 billion to $86 billion, and foreign investment continues to rise at the rate of about $8 billion yearly. American subsidiaries produce far more abroad than the $70 billion in goods annually exported from the United States. In 1970, $200 billion in goods were produced by American-owned corporations in foreign countries, making this economic unit one of the six largest productive units in the world. [20]

American corporations invest abroad for the same reason they invest at home: to make a profit. Profits on foreign investments represent a growing proportion of total American corporate profits. The share of after-tax corporate profits accounted for by foreign investment went from 7 percent of all corporate profits in 1950 to 18 percent in 1970.[21] Foreign profits amounted to $13 billion in 1971. Many of these profits—$5 out of the $13 billion in 1971—flow back to the United States. The rest remain abroad and represent new foreign investment added to existing investments. Foreign investments enable American corporations to influence the economies and obtain the resources of foreign countries.

Overseas investment has rapidly transformed both the American and the world economy. American corporate capitalism reaches throughout the world and has become part of the

---

[20]Neil H. Jacoby, *Corporate Power and Social Responsibility: A Blueprint for the Future* (New York, 1973), p. 99.

[21]Thomas E. Weisskopf, "United States Foreign Private Investment," in Richard E. Edwards, Michael Reich, Thomas E. Weisskopf, eds., *The Capitalist System: A Radical Analysis of American Society* (Englewood Cliffs, N.J., 1972), p. 428.

fabric of foreign countries. American corporations attempt to create conditions elsewhere similar to conditions within the United States favoring corporate success. The foreign policies of the American government are geared to assisting corporations abroad in much the same way that domestic policies help corporations at home. The expansion of American government power abroad has gone hand in hand with corporate expansion abroad.

The term *multinational corporations* has been coined to describe corporations heavily involved in foreign operations. Multinationals are the new Goliaths of the present era. In 1970, 51 corporations ranked among the world's 100 largest economic units (measured by countries' GNP and corporate sales). [22]Multinational corporations straddle countries. They make decisions about research, investment, manufacturing, and sales without much regard for national boundaries: decisions are governed by profitability. For example, the choice of a location for a new factory is often based on where wages are lowest. A multinational corporation may carry out product research in one country, obtain raw materials from another, manufacture the product in a third country, and market it in a fourth. Multinational corporations carry further the principle of integration and planning described in Chapter 3. Their unique situation provides them with benefits at every stage of the manufacturing process.

Economist Daniel R. Fusfeld explains that the multinational corporation

> was made possible by advances in the technology of transportation and communication after World War II (jet aircraft and automatic data communication, for example). U.S. corporations were able to take advantage of the new technology much more readily than foreign corporations, in part because much of that technology was developed here, but chiefly because of the predominance of the United States in world trade and international finance.[23]

Most huge American corporations are multinational and most American investments abroad are carried on by the largest

[22]U.S. Congress, Senate, Select Committee on Small Business, Subcommittee on Monopoly, *The Role of Giant Corporations in the American and World Economies*, 92nd Cong. 1st sess., November 9 and 12, 1971, p. 1043.

[23]Daniel R. Fusfeld, *The Rise of the Corporate State in America* (Andover, Mass. 1973), p. 3.

corporations and financial institutions. 71 of the top 100 American manufacturing corporations have over one-third of their payroll employed overseas. Some of the largest American corporations, including Exxon, Mobil Oil, Woolworth, National Cash Register, Burroughs, Colgate-Palmolive, and Singer have larger sales abroad than at home. By the late 1960s, nearly all the top 25 corporations, 80 of the top 200, and one-fifth of the 500 largest corporations had over one-quarter of their assets abroad. Foreign investments are heavily concentrated among these large corporations: the top 200 American corporations account for over three-quarters of all foreign investment. Three American banks (Bank of America, First National City Bank, and Chase Manhattan) accounted for 259 of the 298 branches of American banks abroad in 1967.[24]

Further, a majority of multinational corporations are based in the United States, and their stockholders and managers are mostly American. Some multinational corporations, including Nestlé, Phillips, Sony, and Royal Dutch Shell, are based in Europe and Japan. However, American corporations took an early lead: among the 300 largest multinationals, 187 are American.[25]

Overall, the United States is being transformed into a headquarters economy: for many corporations, "the headquarters and staff operations remain in the United States, as directing and service facilities, while manufacturing operations are extended abroad."[26] However, the process of foreign expansion has begun to produce opposition both within the United States and abroad. When corporations create new jobs abroad, there are fewer jobs in the corporate-labor sector in the United States; and American workers are forced to take low paying jobs in the spheres of small-scale capital or marginal labor, or remain unemployed. As a result, American trade unions have begun to oppose foreign corporate expansion. At the same time, the influence of American multinational corporations over the productive apparatus of other countries has created resistance from groups within these countries.

[24]Statistics based on Barnet, p. 230; Richard J. Barber, *The American Corporation: Its Power, Its Money, Its Politics* (New York, 1970), p. 251; Weisskopf, p. 432; and *Business Week*, December 19, 1970, p. 58.
[25]Daniel Bell, *Toward a Post-Industrial Society* (New York, 1973), p. 484.
[26]*Ibid.*, p. 485.

Trends in Corporate Trade and Investment Abroad

In the Third World   In the early years of United States foreign expansion, most investments were directed toward gaining control of the mineral resources of Third World countries. In recent years, however, corporations have also been investing in the manufacturing sector in these countries. Setting up a factory in Brazil or Hong Kong (rather than Ohio, for example) provides attractive advantages, including lower wages paid to workers, low taxes, and few outlays for pollution control and safety devices.

At the extreme, one can speak of company countries, where foreign-owned (often United States) corporations monopolize the country's raw materials and manufacturing sector. An example is provided by Chile, where a few American mining companies (Anaconda and Kennecott) control half the country's extractive industries—on which Chile relies for nine-tenths of her exports. ITT owns the Chilean telephone and electric companies, two Sheraton hotels, and a radio station. Most Chilean shipping is controlled by W. R. Grace, an American shipper. Multinational corporations are among the best organized, wealthiest, and most powerful forces within many Third World countries. In addition, through the development of a local capitalist group whose interests are tied to the foreign corporate sector, political conditions favorable to multinational corporations are fostered.

In the attempt to create demand for American products, American companies alter cultural patterns as well. A comment made by economist Neil Jacoby illustrates their impact:

> The cultural consequences of American corporations' penetration of the poor countries can be plainly seen in the ready acceptance by native peoples of soft drinks, packaged foods, electrical appliances, automobiles, brand names and advertising, and much of the paraphernalia of American life. . . . Such changes ultimately should reduce barriers to communication between peoples and lay a common basis for a stable world order.[27]

In Industrialized Nations   In the past several decades, most new American investments have gone to Europe and Canada rather than the Third World. Since Third World resources are

[27]Jacoby, p. 106. But notice who controls and benefits from the stable world order described by Professor Jacoby.

Table 6–1

Value of U.S. direct foreign private investment by area, 1929–1969 (all figures in millions of dollars)

	1929	1950	1959	1969
All Countries	7,528	11,788	29,735	70,763
Latin America	3,519	4,576	8,990	13,811
Africa[1]	25	147	520	2,215
Asia [2]	334	982	2,026	3,974
Canada	2,010	3,579	10,171	21,075
Europe	1,353	1,733	5,300	21,554
Other areas[3]	287	771	2,728	8,133

[1]Excluding South Africa.
[2]Excluding Japan.
[3]Including international.
Source: Thomas E. Weisskopf, "United States Foreign Private Investment," in Richard C. Edwards, Michael Reich, and Thomas E. Weisskopf, eds., *The Capitalist System: A Radical Analysis of American Society,* © 1972, p. 430. By permission of Prentice-Hall, Inc., Englewood Cliffs, N.J.

already controlled, industrialized countries now offer more new investment opportunities, higher consumer demand, and more stable political situations. American multinational corporations have gained an important role in these countries. Some of the most advanced industrial sectors in Western Europe are under American control, including 80 percent of the market for computers, 95 percent of integrated circuits, 50 percent of semiconductors, and an important share in automobiles, electronics, and home appliances. American corporations control 10 percent of England's total production. The most extreme case is Canada, where United States corporations control half of the country's manufacturing.[28]

Although far more is invested in industrial capitalist countries than in the Third World, American firms derive nearly equal income from their investments in the two areas. This suggests their greater power in less developed societies.

In the Soviet Union, China, and Eastern Europe   The rapid

[28]*Ibid.,* p. 99; Raymond Vernon, *Sovereignty at Bay: The Multinational Spread of U.S. Enterprises* (New York, 1971), p. 20.

Table 6-2
Earnings on U.S. direct foreign private investment by area, 1959 and 1969

	Reported Earnings (millions of dollars during year)	Value of Investment (millions of dollars at year-end)	Rate of Earnings (%)
1959			
Underdeveloped countries	1,615	11,536	14.0
Developed countries	1,640	18,199	9.0
Total investment	**3,255**	**29,735**	**11.0**
1969			
Underdeveloped countries	3,747	20,000	18.7
Developed countries	4,208	50,763	8.3
Total investment	**7,955**	**70,763**	**11.3**

Source: Thomas E. Weisskopf, "United States Foreign Private Investment," in Richard C. Edwards, Michael Reich, and Thomas E. Weisskopf, eds., *The Capitalist System: A Radical Analysis of American Society,* © 1972, p. 430. By permission of Prentice-Hall, Inc. Englewood Cliffs, N.J.

economic growth of Western Europe and Japan has challenged the dominant position of American multinationals. In an attempt to find new outlets, American business has turned to Communist countries, with whom there were few economic ties before the 1970s. The decision to increase trade between the United States and Communist countries was part of a more general policy of détente, which signifies a decline of the virulent rhetoric of the cold war. East-West trade has boomed following a trade agreement between the United States and the USSR signed in 1972. American exports to the Soviet Union and Eastern Europe climbed from $400 million to nearly $2 billion yearly between 1971 and 1973. One of the newest branch offices of the Chase Manhattan Bank (whose board chairman, David Rockefeller, comes from a family that epitomizes Western capitalism) is located at 1 Karl Marx Square, a block from the Kremlin. As reporter Harvey D. Shapiro put it, "Alexei Kosygin has a friend at Chase Manhattan."[29] International Harvester, G. E., and other

[29]Harvey D. Shapiro, "Alexei Kosygin has a friend at Chase Manhattan," *New York Times Magazine,* February 24, 1974.

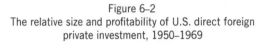

Figure 6–2
The relative size and profitability of U.S. direct foreign
private investment, 1950–1969

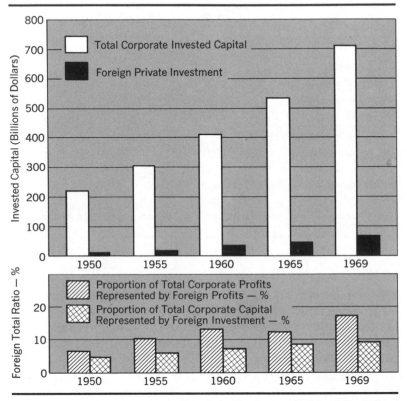

Source: Adapted from Thomas E. Weisskopf, "United States Foreign Private Investment," in Richard C. Edwards, Michael Reich, and Thomas E. Weisskopf, eds., *The Capitalist System: A Radical Analysis of American Society,* © 1972, p. 429. By permission of Prentice-Hall, Inc., Englewood Cliffs, N.J.

large American corporations have opened offices in Moscow to facilitate the export of goods and technology to the Soviet Union. Trade with the People's Republic of China is less extensive but also on the upswing.

The significance of American corporate expansion abroad cannot be overestimated. The prosperity of American corporate capitalism has become closely linked to overseas operations, whose expansion has been far more rapid than growth within the United States. Between 1957 and 1971, the overseas assets of

American manufacturers increased more than 500 percent, compared to a 90 percent rise in domestic assets. Foreign investments are particularly attractive because their rate of profit is about double that on domestic investments.[30] Multinationals produce goods for distribution within other countries, and they help transfer technological know-how abroad. But they levy a heavy price in return in the form of profits for American owners of capital, the political and economic influence they exert within foreign countries, and the cultural values they purvey.

Government Protection

Multinational corporations and the United States government share interests abroad just as they do at home. What the government presents as American national interests are above all the interests of the American corporate complex. American foreign policy attempts to create conditions where multinational corporations can operate freely and profitably. By furthering the interests of corporate capitalism, the government is also protecting the key group on which its resources and power depend.

This does not mean that every action of the American government can be explained as helping multinational corporations. Some government actions may conflict with the particular interests of corporations at a given time. However, this need not mean that the government is undermining the interests of corporate capital. As within the United States, the government's own interest lies in representing the broad, long-term interests of corporate capitalism. To illustrate: during the late 1960s, the government restricted corporate investment abroad in order to protect the American dollar. Although corporations protested the move, it was a policy clearly designed to strengthen the United States international economic position—and therefore the long-range interests of large corporations. Similarly, although American military policies may not represent an attempt to secure particular benefits for American corporations, their broad aim is to assure compliant regimes in foreign countries who will not challenge American interests. Yet the fact that corporate capitalism and government try to shape a world to their interests does not mean they will necessarily succeed.

[30]Barber, p. 256; Weisskopf, p. 428.

THE SEARCH FOR MILITARY
AND POLITICAL SUPREMACY

The United States has a vast military establishment, the largest and most powerful in the world. It maintains nearly four hundred major military bases around the globe as well as several thousand smaller ones. Over one-half million troops are stationed abroad; the navy has patrols in every ocean; reconnaissance satellites circle the world. American military missions are stationed in fifty foreign countries.[31] Military treaties link the United States to the regimes of over forty countries in Europe, Asia, and Latin America. Each year, an immense sum is spent to support the armed forces and purchase new weapons.

The Arms Race with the Soviet Union

Much of the American military budget has gone to develop sophisticated thermonuclear weapons directed mainly against the Soviet Union. Beginning with the cold war arms race in the 1950s, there has been a never-ending search by each country for military advantage. The result has been to create a world permanently poised for war and total devastation. Each country possesses a staggering "overkill" capacity: the United States possesses the equivalent of 30,000 Hiroshima nuclear blasts in its stockpile of atomic weapons. For example, the multiple warhead MIRV missiles from one Poseidon submarine could destroy about one-quarter of Soviet industry; in 1975, the United States possessed about 40 Poseidon submarines equipped with MIRVs, along with sufficient long-range bombers and missiles to destroy the Soviet Union many times over. And the United States and the Soviet Union continue to develop new weaponry, each attempting to secure an advantage over the other. One goal is a *second*-strike capability: the development by a country of a strategic force sufficiently invulnerable and powerful that it could survive a nuclear attack and be launched in deadly retaliation against the attacking country. Another goal is *first*-strike capability, enabling a country to launch a preemptive attack that could destroy the other country's second-strike force, and thus not incur a nuclear counterattack in return. Yet the cruel irony is that

[31] Adam Yarmolinsky, *The Military Establishment* (New York, 1971), p. 115.

the *more* weapons produced, the *less* security exists because of the greater danger that (through accident or intention) the deadly weapons will be used by one side, inviting retaliation by the other and resulting in the destruction of both.

The arms race produces stalemate (what has been called the "balance of terror"), but it is not a static one. As each country develops newer, costlier, and more dangerous weapons, it drains productive resources for military purposes, without increasing security or effective power. In a belated response to this dangerous and irrational situation, and as a result of popular and congressional pressure, attempts were initiated in the 1970s to limit new weaponry. Strategic arms limitation talks in 1972 (SALT I), extended by accords concluded in 1974, resulted in an agreement between the United States and the USSR to regulate arms buildups. The agreements provided for ceilings on the total number of intercontinental missiles and MIRVs allowed each side. However, the ceilings were high enough to allow substantial expansion of existing strategic weapons systems for both countries. New weapons systems, including the B-1 bomber and the Trident submarine, are still in the process of development and production, and the number of United States strategic warheads increased by a thousand in 1973 and 1974. The focus of the arms race appears to have shifted from quantitative to qualitative factors—measured by the accuracy and sophistication of weapons. But it is doubtful whether a turning point in the arms race has been reached.

Developing Compliant Regimes

Although the methods used are less dramatic than nuclear confrontation, American power is directed against many countries other than those in the Communist bloc: the American government seeks to influence regimes throughout the world.

American foreign policy has undergone many shifts since the Second World War. But its basic aim has remained the same: to use American political, military, and economic power to assure "friendly" foreign regimes. Whether a government is friendly or not depends on whether it permits American corporations to operate freely within its borders to obtain raw materials, trade, and investment opportunities; and whether it supports the United States position in the international arena. Note that Third World regimes friendly to the United States are likely to be reactionary and repressive: no democratic government could permit its country's resources to be developed on terms favorable to American corporate and governmental interests. It is no accident that America's closest allies in the Third World are among the most authoritarian regimes: South Korea, South Africa, South Vietnam, Indonesia, Brazil, and Taiwan. Conversely, countries struggling to overcome internal inequality and Western control (including Cuba, Tanzania, North Vietnam, and Chile, when it was under the Socialist regime of Salvador Allende Gossens) have become opponents of the United States.

In the strange logic of American foreign-policy makers, the United States represents democracy and protects freedom in the world. Therefore, any actions are justified. The double standard has been described by historian Henry Steele Commager:

> When the Soviet Union intervenes in Czechoslovakia, that is naked aggression, but when we land 22,000 marines in Santo Domingo, that is peace keeping. When communist countries carry on clandestine activities abroad, that is part of an 'international conspiracy,' but when the CIA operates clandestinely in sixty foreign countries, that is a legitimate function of our foreign policy. When Russia establishes a missile base in Cuba (on the invitation of Cuba), that is an act of war which must be met with all the force at our command, but when we build the largest airbase in the world in Thailand, that is part of our ceaseless search for peace.[32]

Political Influence

The government attempts to influence other countries through a variety of institutional mechanisms. Financial agencies, including the Agency for International Development (AID), the Export-Import Bank, and the Overseas Private Investment Corporation, provide aid and loans to foreign governments and technical help and insurance to American businesses in an attempt to facilitate American business operations abroad. The United States uses its preponderant influence within international financial institutions, including the International Monetary Fund, the Organization for Economic Cooperation and Development, and the International

---

[32]Henry Steele Commager, "The Defeat of America," *New York Review of Books*, October 5, 1972, p. 12.

Bank for Reconstruction and Development (also called the World Bank, whose current president is Robert S. McNamara, former United States secretary of defense), to regulate an international capitalist order within which American business can prosper. The United States exerts influence through its participation in military alliances (NATO and the Southeast Asia Treaty Organization—SEATO) and international organizations including the Organization of American States, the United Nations General Assembly, the Security Council, UNESCO, and the International Labor Organization.

Other mechanisms used to shape world opinion are the day-to-day operations of American embassies in other countries and public and private statements by American officials. The process might be considered a normal part of the give-and-take of international politics—except that American power over most other countries is far greater than their power over the United States. As in the United States, there is a structure in the international arena that both shapes and reflects the contours of international power. Through the normal mediations of international politics and diplomacy, the United States attempts to maintain structural dominance in the world. More intensive means of influence include foreign aid and military intervention.

Foreign Aid

The foreign aid program of the United States operates in over sixty countries of Africa, Asia, and Latin America. Between 1946 and 1971, the United States gave $149 billion in grants and loans to foreign regimes. This figure includes Marshall Plan grants to Europe. The purpose is presumably to help poorer nations develop. But the interests of the American corporate complex were often a more important reason. Foreign aid is mainly a lever used to extract concessions from other countries to assure cooperation with the American corporate complex.

Military assistance   This form of foreign aid is given not to help countries industrialize and achieve self-sufficiency, but to build foreign armies who protect multinational corporations and regimes favorable to the United States in these countries. Over half the $5 billion appropriated in foreign aid in 1973 went for military assistance.[33] Military aid goes to equip and train foreign

[33] *New York Times*, December 23, 1973.

military personnel each year, as well as foreign police forces. More than 250,000 foreign military officers were trained by the United States between 1950 and 1968.[34] Thus, when regimes that are friendly to the United States are threatened by internal challenge, foreign armies and police are ready to defend those in power and to safeguard American interests.

Economic assistance   It is widely assumed that foreign aid for economic development is evidence of American altruism. However, aid is given in the form of loans, which must be repaid with interest. These countries must thus use their resources to repay the interest on American loans. And the more loans given, the more interest charges pile up. In 1956, the underdeveloped countries used about 4 percent of their exports to repay past loans; this figure had risen to 10 percent by 1967 and stands at 20 percent in 1975. In 1970, repayment of past debts to the United States exceeded new aid by over $1 billion. One of the most important effects of foreign aid is to create dependence on the United States. [35]

Much foreign aid is given to develop services for multinational (usually American) corporations, for example, transportation facilities to mining operations. The major need in many Third World countries is to increase food supplies: more than half the 2.5 billion people living in the Third World suffer from malnutrition. But, as an exporter of food to these areas, the United States government prefers not to devote many resources to improving agriculture. Furthermore, in order to receive foreign aid from the United States, countries must agree to two conditions. First, they must agree to "buy American," that is, use American aid to buy American products wherever possible. A substantial portion of foreign aid is used to buy goods made in the United States. Foreign aid thus increases the demand for American products and represents a hidden subsidy to American producers. The second condition countries must accept in order to qualify for foreign aid is not to take over American companies operating in the country without generous compensation.

Countries accepting American assistance are shaped to

[34]Yarmolinsky, p. 146; Michael T. Klare, *War without End: American Planning for the Next Vietnams* (New York, 1972), p. 241.

[35]Gabriel Kolko, *The Roots of American Foreign Policy* (Boston, 1969) p. 72; Magdoff, p. 150; and Michael Hudson, *Super-Imperialism: The Economic Strategy of American Empire* (New York, 1972), pp. 118, 166.

American interests. Their governments are encouraged to be receptive to American multinational corporations. Their economies are interwined with the corporate complex. A principal mission of their armed forces is to support United States goals. And American aid does not help much to solve the basic problems: grinding poverty and political dependency.

Intervention: Chile and Vietnam

The routine operation of United States influence usually insures regimes favorable to United States interests. The result can be considered a form of imperialism, in which countries remain legally sovereign in principle but dependent on the United States in fact. When cooperative foreign regimes are threatened or an unfriendly regime takes power, the United States may intervene more actively. United States forces invaded Lebanon in 1958, the Dominican Republic in 1965, and Laos, Cambodia, and Vietnam from the 1950s to the present. American-financed armies have intervened against civilian regimes in Iran in 1953, Cuba in 1961, and Indonesia in 1966. In addition, the Central Intelligence Agency (CIA) operates in more than sixty countries, using bribery, subversion, espionage, and "dirty tricks" to influence politics in these countries. The CIA has supported pro-American political parties, labor unions, and media in foreign countries. It has carried on its own secret war in Laos, overthrown the government of Guatemala (1954), helped plan the 1961 Bay of Pigs invasion of Cuba, and organized the capture and murder of Ernesto "Ché" Guevara in Bolivia (1967).[36]

Two recent examples illustrate the "soft" and the "hard" types of United States intervention.

Chile Although the United States did not send troops to invade Chile in the early 1970s, the interwining of American government and corporate activity in Chile illustrates the soft face of foreign intervention by the corporate complex.[37]

---

[36]Richard J. Barnet, *Intervention and Revolution: The United States in the Third World* (New York, 1968); and two books by Daniel Wise and Thomas B. Ross: *The Invisible Government* (New York, 1964), and *The Espionage Establishment* (New York, 1967).

[37]This account is based on Jeffrey L. Kessler, "The Relationship of U.S. Multinational Corporations with Chile during the Allende Years," unpublished paper; *New York Times*, April 1, 1973; April 3, 1973; September 24, 1974.

In July 1970, Harold S. Geneen, board chairman of ITT, secretly offered the CIA $1 million to bribe Chilean politicians and sabotage Allende's election in Chile's presidential elections the following November. ITT made the offer because it feared its Chilean investments would be endangered by a victory for Allende, whose program included the expropriation of foreign companies. In seeking CIA help to prevent free elections in a foreign country, ITT had excellent access to the CIA: ITT's offer was personally delivered to Richard Helms, CIA director, by John A. McCone, a member of ITT's board of directors and Helms's predecessor as director of the CIA. The CIA turned down the offer, although it did spend $400,000 in the election campaign to buy newspaper advertising in an unsuccessful attempt to defeat Allende. However, after the election, the CIA approached ITT with a plan of its own: ITT and other American corporations with investments in Chile should delay deliveries of spare parts to Chile, withdraw credit, and bring home American technical personnel. An ITT vice president later expanded the plan in an attempt to insure, in his words, "that Allende does not get through the next six months."

Under ITT's leadership, American banks in Chile and American multinationals slowed down their operations in Chile, stopped all further investments there, withdrew technical aid and personnel, and reduced United States trade with Chile. Among United States government actions were the cutting off of all loans to Chile by the government and international financial agencies, in which the United States plays the leading role, and supporting American multinationals in United States courts when they sued the Chilean government.

The result was a veritable economic blockade of Chile. The actions of the United States government and multinational corporations helped produce severe economic dislocations, difficulties in production, inflation, a shortage of international credit, and a lack of spare parts and technical personnel for Chilean industry. The only United States government aid that did not cease (in fact it doubled) was to the Chilean military. Allende was overthrown by a military coup in September 1973. The military junta, which continued for over a year to carry out systematic torture and killing, immediately invited back American multinational corporations. It was rewarded with loans by American banks and government agencies and with new investment in Chile by American companies.

Although American government officials repeatedly denied any direct United States government intervention in Chilean domestic affairs and any responsibility for Allende's downfall, a more accurate picture was provided by the disclosure in 1974 of secret congressional testimony by CIA Director William Colby. Beginning prior to Allende's election and accelerating in 1972 and 1973, the CIA (at the direction of Secretary of State Henry Kissinger) spent $8 million for espionage, subversion, and other efforts aimed at overthrowing the Allende regime. Most of the money was spent to bribe Chilean politicians and newspapers and to encourage strikes by truckers and shopkeepers. The result of the CIA's activities was to disrupt the Chilean economy and thus increase the likelihood that Allende would be driven from office. The combination of United States multinational corporation efforts, withdrawal of United States government economic assistance, CIA subversion, and increased government aid to the Chilean military was instrumental in leading to the bloody suppression of Chile's experiment in democratic socialism.

When President Gerald Ford was asked at a 1974 press conference about the CIA's illegal activities, he replied that the CIA had acted "in the best interest of the people in Chile, and certainly in our best interest." He failed to explain, however, how the American government was better qualified to discern Chilean interests than Chile's own democratically elected government, or how United States interests were furthered when the American government conspired illegally to overthrow a democratic regime.

A clue to the motivations of American policy makers was provided by investigative reporter Seymour Hersh. In an analysis appearing in the *New York Times* of September 24, 1974, Hersh described American officials as "concerned that if the United States continued to appear 'soft' toward underdeveloped countries that expropriated American assets, a rush of similar actions would be precipitated [in other countries]."

Vietnam The Vietnam war, the longest war in American history, began as a conflict no different than many others in which small numbers of American military advisers attempted to prop up weak, undemocratic, and corrupt regimes. American involvement in the war began long before the first American combat soldier ever set foot in Indochina—the area that is presently Vietnam, Laos, and Cambodia. In 1950, the United States began to supply military aid to France, who was fighting in Indochina to reestablish the colonial control that she lost during the Second World War. By the time the French admitted defeat in 1954 and withdrew, unable to overcome the Viet Minh insurgent forces led by Ho Chi Minh, the United States was paying most of the costs of the French colonial war.

For the next several years, a civil war was fought in Vietnam between insurgent forces in the South and an American-supported-and-financed puppet regime. As this government crumbled, American intervention was stepped up. What makes Vietnam unusual, however, is not that the United States intervened—this happened in a variety of ways in a number of other countries. The difference is that, after the Vietnam conflict erupted into a war, the United States was unable to crush insurgent forces, either through backing a pro-American repressive government or through direct military involvement.

As resistance continued American involvement increased. There were 1,000 American military personnel in South Vietnam when President Kennedy took office; the number increased to 16,000 by the time he was assassinated. The greatest escalation occurred under President Johnson. During the height of the American invasion in 1968, more than 500,000 American troops fought in South Vietnam. Perhaps even more devastating than the killing and damage resulting from ground combat was the destruction caused by the American aerial bombardment, the most massive in history.

From air bases in Vietnam, Thailand, and Guam, the latter thousands of miles from Vietnam, the United States dropped over seven million tons of bombs in Indochina—the equivalent tonnage of 350 Hiroshima blasts and more than three times the tonnage of all bombing in the Second World War.[38] In order to destroy the rural strongholds of the Vietcong insurgent forces, the Vietnamese countryside was ravaged: between 1961 and 1970, the United States applied twenty-seven pounds of herbicides, defoliants, and poisons per acre in South Vietnam. Defoliation destroyed 15 percent of South Vietnam's forests and 7 percent of

[38]*New York Times*, December 26, 1972.

its arable land; as well as over one-third the forests and arable land of North Vietnam.[39] Formerly an exporter of rice, Vietnam is now forced to import rice and faces the prospect of famine. An even greater cost was paid in human life. One million people were killed in Vietnam, several million were injured, and ten million were made homeless. While several massacres of villages by American troops were publicly reported, including My Lai and Song My, American forces engaged daily in aerial bombardment, search-and-destroy missions, and "interrogations" that maimed and killed far more people with no more legality or military justification.

Despite overwhelming military superiority, the prolongation and brutality of the war, the United States was unable to crush the Vietcong or the Democratic Republic of Vietnam. Continued defeat in Vietnam and opposition within the United States to American involvement forced Lyndon Johnson to renounce his candidacy for reelection in 1968 and call for peace negotiations, and led Richard Nixon, his successor, to announce the phased withdrawal of American combat troops. In 1973, the United States signed an armistice agreement.

The war is far from over. "Peace with honor," the phrase used by President Nixon to describe the settlement, has brought neither honor to the United States nor peace to Vietnam. The civil war in Vietnam continues, with the American-backed South Vietnam regime still unable to overcome the opposition. Nor has America's involvement ended: extensive American economic and military aid continues to flow to Vietnam. In 1973, several billion dollars in aid was given to the puppet regime in South Vietnam, 90 percent of whose civilian expenditures and most of whose military outlays are paid for by the United States.[40] Moreover, in violation of the peace agreement, 2,800 private American technicians paid by the Pentagon remained in South Vietnam one year after the Paris Accords as essential parts of the South Vietnamese supply, transport, and intelligence systems.[41]

While American influence over regimes around the globe continues, and United States intervention on a smaller scale and

[39]Barry Weisberg, *Beyond Repair: The Ecology of Capitalism* (Boston, 1971), pp. 88–90.
[40]Fred Branfman, "Vietnam: The Aftermath," *The Progressive* 37 (November 1973); 30; *New York Times*, March 20, 1974.
[41]*New York Times*, February 25, 1974.

in a quieter manner remains a characteristic feature of contemporary world politics, America's defeat in Vietnam may possibly indicate a trend. Vietnam may demonstrate that a foreign army cannot impose its will against well-organized native forces supported by the local population. In a statement of foreign policy aims in 1969, President Nixon announced that henceforth the United States would continue to supply military aid and equipment, including aerial support, to military operations by allied governments. However, the Nixon Doctrine stated that the United States would not commit American combat troops in Third World counterinsurgent operations. Vietnam thus may represent what Joyce and Gabriel Kolko describe as the limits of American power. Although the United States will continue to attempt to control world affairs, the gap of inequality between the United States and other countries may be narrowing.[42]

THE MILITARY-INDUSTRIAL COMPLEX

The growth of a powerful domestic military sector is quite recent. Throughout most of American history, the military has been viewed with suspicion. Except during wartime, the armed forces were small and few resources were devoted to their maintenance. Planning and preparation for war were relatively easy because military technology was simple, and a wartime economy was quickly demobilized when peace arrived. As recently as the period just before the Second World War, the economy was on a peacetime basis, with little military production. In 1918, it took only several months to mobilize and retool civilian industry for the production of war matériel. And several months after the war ended, the economy returned to peacetime patterns.

The Second World War represented a transition in the history of warfare. Military technology advanced enormously, with such innovations as radar, missiles, mechanized warfare, and, perhaps the greatest advance in the science of destruction, atomic weapons. General Dwight D. Eisenhower, the top-ranking Army officer after the Second World War, understood the

---

[42] Kolko and Kolko, *The Limits of Power, passim.*

fundamental implications of the change in military technology that had occurred as a result of the war. In a memorandum entitled "Scientific and Technological Resources as Military Assets," he wrote:

> The recent conflict has demonstrated more convincingly than ever before the strength our nation can best derive from the integration of all of our national resources in time of war. It is of the utmost importance that the lessons of this experience be not forgotten in the peacetime planning and training of the Army. The future security of the nation demands that all those civilian resources which by conversion or redirection constitute our main support in time of emergency be associated closely with the activities of the Army in time of peace.
>
> The lessons of the last war are clear. The military effort required for victory threw upon the Army an unprecedented range of responsibilities many of which were effectively discharged only through the invaluable assistance supplied by our cumulative resources in the natural and social sciences and the talents and experiences furnished by management and labor. . . . This pattern of integration must be translated into a peacetime counterpart which will . . . draw into our planning for national security all the civilian resources which can contribute to the defense of the country.[43]

The peacetime cooperation among the armed forces, business, and science advocated by General Eisenhower began soon after the Second World War. In the decades since then, the new partnership has become a permanent part of the American political and economic system.

Fifteen years after he had written his memorandum, General Eisenhower returned to the subject. Yet this time, in his farewell address after eight years as president, he expressed alarm about the new trend:

> Our military organization today bears little relation to that known by any of my predecessors in peacetime, or indeed by the fighting men of World War II and Korea.
>
> Until the latest of world conflicts, the United States had no armaments industry. American makers of plowshares could, with time and as required, make swords as well. But now we can no longer risk emergency improvisation of national defense; we have

[43]Seymour Melman, *Pentagon Capitalism* (New York, 1970), pp. 231–32.

been compelled to create a permanent armaments industry of vast proportions. . . .

The conjunction of an immense Military Establishment and large arms industry is new in the American experience. . . . In the councils of government we must guard against the acquisition of unwarranted influence whether sought or unsought, by the military-industrial complex. The potential for the disastrous rise of misplaced power exists and will persist.

The term *military-industrial complex* refers to the alliance of government, business, and science devoted to war preparation. It is a mighty alliance: the annual budget of the Department of Defense (DOD) exceeds $100 billion, which constitutes 60 percent of the budget for all federal executive agencies, substantially more than the net income of all American corporations, and more than the total annual production of all but eight nations. Military spending constitutes the single largest item in the federal budget. Military agencies, including the National Security Agency, the Department of Defense, CIA, and military components of the Atomic Energy Commission (AEC) and National Aeronautics and Space Administration (NASA), rank among the most powerful groups in the federal bureaucracy.

Business: Military Production and Profits

Sociologist Daniel Bell lists the development of a mobilized war economy as one of the three major changes in American society in the past thirty years.[44] (The other two are a managed, planned economy described in Chapter 5, and the welfare state, described in Chapter 13.) Producing for war is the biggest industry in the United States: over 5 percent of the labor force is engaged in military activity. More than two million Americans serve in the armed forces, another million civilians work for the Pentagon (the Department of Defense), and another two million civilian workers are engaged in military production.

The military sector has close links with corporate capitalism and reaches throughout American society. The Department of Defense is the single largest customer in the world: it purchases 15 percent of American manufactured goods.[45] The Pentagon is

[44]Bell, pp. 360–61.
[45]Tom Christoffel, David Finklehor, Dan Gilbarg, "Corporations and Government," in *Up Against the American Myth* (New York, 1970), p. 101.

Figure 6-3
U.S. military expenditures, 1800–1970

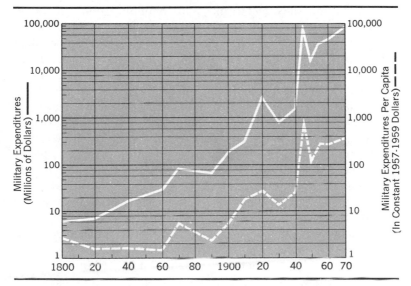

Source: Adapted from James L. Clayton, "The Fiscal Cost of the Cold War to the United States: The First 25 Years, 1947–1971," *Western Political Quarterly* 25 (September 1972): 380.

the nation's largest landlord, owning $40 billion in property. Through the post-exchange (PX) system, it is the third largest retail distributor, after A&P and Sears, Roebuck.

A war economy differs from civilian manufacturing in important respects. What is produced for military purposes cannot be eaten, worn, lived in, or used in the manufacture of other products. Since the end of the Second World War, nearly $2 trillion have been spent for missiles, nuclear warheads, radar, submarines, tanks, and military personnel.[46] The magnitude of such an amount is hard to grasp. Written out, it looks like this: $2,000,000,000,000 and represents the value of all homes and business structures in the United States.

Although the $40 billion of military weapons and equipment purchased annually by the Pentagon is distributed throughout the economy, military spending is particularly concentrated in the

[46]James L. Clayton, "The Fiscal Cost of the Cold War to the United States: The First 25 Years, 1947–1971," *Western Political Quarterly* 25 (September 1972); 375–94.

most technologically advanced sectors. Three-quarters of defense spending in the civilian sector is located in three industries: aircraft and missiles, electronics and communications, and shipbuilding and repairing. Some high-technology industries are nearly captives of the Pentagon, since large proportions of their sales are to the Defense Department. The military purchases 60 percent of the output of the shipbuilding industry, 87 percent of aircraft, 41 percent of communications equipment, 39 percent of electronics, and 30 percent of scientific and control instruments.[47]

Many large corporations benefit heavily from military contracts. Among the 100 largest corporations in the country, 65 are significantly involved in military production. Among the 25 largest corporations, all but 5 were on the list of the top 100 firms receiving DOD contracts. Thus, there is extensive overlap between the largest military firms and the largest firms in the country.

The military industry is concentrated. Most military purchasing occurs through the Defense Department awarding prime contracts for large weapons systems—nuclear-powered submarines, missile launchers, radar equipment, and space stations—to a single firm. The firm receiving the prime contract is responsible for the overall work. Prime contracts involve hundreds of millions of dollars. For example, two new aircraft carriers (the *Nimitz* and the *Eisenhower*) cost $1 billion apiece. And most prime contracts go to a handful of firms.

A company with nearly $2 billion in annual sales is immense: Lockheed Aircraft Corporation received $1.71 billion in Pentagon procurement awards in 1972. Lockheed is not alone in obtaining lavish military contracts: six other companies each won over $1 billion in Pentagon awards. These seven firms, with nearly $10 billion in military contracts, received one-quarter of the total military procurement in 1972. The top 100 companies received nearly three-quarters of the $40 billion in prime contracts in 1972 and virtually all the military grants to industry for research and development. However, from another perspective, only a few among the top corporations produce exclusively for the military. Among the 100 largest corporations in 1968, 5 sold over half their total putput to the Defense Department, 47 sold between 5 and 50

[47]Paul M. Sweezy and Harry Magdoff, *The Dynamics of U.S. Capitalism: Corporate Structure, Inflation, Credit, Gold and the Dollar* (New York, 1972), p. 11; Seymour Melman, *Our Depleted Society* (New York, 1965), p. 225.

percent, and the remaining 48 sold less than 5 percent of their output to the military.[48]

Although the largest firms derive greatest profit from military production, small companies throughout the United States also benefit, since giant firms subcontract out much of the actual work on prime contracts. Twenty thousand firms throughout the country are engaged in production for the military, integrating communities and small business into the war economy.

Regional Concentration In every state, there are firms engaged in military production, providing ammunition, bomb sites, electronic equipment, and aircraft parts. Several regions have particularly high concentrations of military production. With 26 percent of the country's population, the South received 38 percent of the Pentagon's 1971 procurement—and 40 percent of the nation's military personnel stationed in the United States are in bases in the South.[49] (One reason for the South's ability to attract military spending is the domination of the congressional military appropriations committees by Southern congressmen.) In Virginia, Utah, Washington, California, Alaska, Hawaii, Arizona, Colorado, Maryland, Massachusetts, and Connecticut, military spending exceeds 10 percent of the state's economic activity.[50]

The military lobby Military spending is high in part because it is popular. Military dollars provide business to corporations and communities all over the country. Military spending represents subsidies to diverse elements in large and small-scale capital as well as to corporate labor. Thus, there is a built-in lobby for militarism that comes from labor unions, local businessmen, congressional and other local political officials, as well as from the Pentagon and the large military firms who benefit most.

Military gravy Military production is a lucrative business. One study found that the profits of military contractors are 18 percent compared to 11 percent for large firms producing civilian goods.[51] This is primarily the result of government generosity. (It is also an extreme instance of how corporate costs are socialized while profits remain private.) Payments for cost overruns, which

[48]Stanley Lieberson, "An Empirical Study of Military-Industrial Linkages," *American Journal of Sociology*, 76 (January 1971): 568.
[49]Institute for Southern Studies, *Southern Militarism* (Atlanta, 1973).
[50]Yarmolinsky, p. 254.
[51]Murray Weidenbaum, *The Modern Public Sector* (New York, 1969), p. 56.

in recent years have amounted to $31 billion on the forty-five major new weapons systems, are the most dramatic instance of government generosity to military contractors. For example, the C-5A transport plane produced by Lockheed cost the government $2 billion more than the original estimate. The C-5A case was brought to light by A. Ernest Fitzgerald, when he was deputy secretary for management systems in the Air Force. He described the cost-plus procedures, which reward inefficiency and provide bonuses for firms that find ways to pad costs, and revealed the collusion between the Pentagon and Lockheed to conceal the mounting overruns. As a result of his disclosures, Fitzgerald was fired from his position at the Pentagon.[52]

The government is also magnanimous in its loans of factories, equipment, and capital to military contractors. In 1971, Lockheed and the General Dynamics Corporation were each using over $200 million worth of government plants and equipment—one-quarter of each firm's total manufacturing assets.

Focusing on costs, however, misses the major point. Neither the Pentagon nor military producers have an incentive to keep costs low. Quite the contrary. The Pentagon is mainly interested in insuring a steady flow of funds to military producers. These payments can be considered a subsidy to support a constituency for militarism. Both the Pentagon and military contractors share an interest in maximizing the threat of war—which in turn generates support for more military spending.[53]

Science: The Knowledge Industry

Without the participation of scientists, engineers, professors, specialized planners, and social scientists, the military-industrial complex would not exist.

As superiority in the science of weaponry has become the criterion of military power, the arms race has become largely a scramble to develop ever more technologically advanced weapons. Scientists, engineers, and other technical personnel are crucial to the design and production of missiles, sensor devices,

---

[52]Fitzgerald describes the story in his *The High Priests of Waste* (New York, 1972).

[53]Melman, *Pentagon Capitalism, passim,* and *The Permanent War Economy* (New York, 1974).

unmanned bombers, electronic homing devices, reconnaissance satellites, and antipersonnel weapons.

Social scientists also have an important role in the military-industrial complex. They are called upon to find ways to secure reliable allies among foreign countries by gathering information, analyzing problems, and suggesting alternatives. Anthropologists have developed ways to penetrate Third World cultures and mobilize groups against insurgent movements. Political scientists have elaborated strategic doctrines, such as first-strike capabilities and flexible response. Experts in propaganda, linguistics, psychological warfare, cartology, cryptology, and geographic regions have contributed their skills. The flavor of their efforts is captured by a research proposal submitted to the Department of Defense in 1967 by the American Institute for Research:

> The struggle between an established government and subversive or insurgent forces involves three different types of operations. The first is to make inputs into the social system that will gain the active support of an ever-increasing proportion of the local population. Threats, promises, ideological appeals, and tangible benefits are the kinds of inputs that are most frequently used. The second is to reduce or interdict the flow of the competing inputs being made by the opposing side by installing anti-infiltration devices, cutting communications lines, assassinating key spokesmen, strengthening retaliatory mechanisms, and similar preventative measures. The third is to counteract the political successes already achieved by groups committed to the "wrong" side. This typically involves direct military confrontation.[54]

Yearly expenditures in the United States for research and development (R and D) amount to $30 billion, about two-thirds of which are provided by the federal government. The intellectuals and scientists who are the major beneficiaries of these funds move back and forth between universities and private industries, think tanks and government. Some statistics suggest the interlocking relationship between science, industry, government, and war. Over half the 250,000 scientists in the United States and a higher proportion of engineers work on projects supported with federal funds. Two-thirds of all university research funds are provided by the Defense Department, AEC, and NASA. Although the proportion has declined slightly from the post-Sputnik

[54]Klare, p. 116.

peak, four-fifths of federal funds for research and development are spent for military-related research.[55]

The United States spends more on research and development than any other country in the world. However, Western Europe and Japan spend about twice as much per capita as the United States on civilian research and development and half as much per capita on the military. Among the reasons why Japan and West Europe are able to devote more effort to civilian production is because the United States acts as their army. America's scientific resources are thus geared primarily to nonessential military production. American industry has been steadily deteriorating and growing less competitive than foreign industry partly because American scientists devote their talents to improving weapons rather than improving the production of peacetime goods.

Government: The Foreign-Policy Establishment

Just as there is an interchange of leaders between corporations and government agencies concerned with domestic policy, so too the men who shape American foreign policy have close links with big business, finance, and law. Many of them also come from upper-class social backgrounds. They circulate among the different sectors of industry, government, education, and foundations, and share a common outlook and interests.

They also tend to monopolize positions in the foreign-policy establishment: the same men who are appointed to presidential commissions to review foreign aid, military policy, and intelligence work, are chosen for high positions in the Department of Defense, State Department, and CIA. The prominent business connections of America's foreign-policy makers can be seen from the fact that, of the men who were secretaries and undersecretaries of state and defense, secretaries of the three armed services, chairmen of the AEC, and directors of the CIA between 1940 and 1967, seventy out of ninety-one came from big business and finance.[56] Party ties are less important than "safe" opinions: many have served in both Democratic and Republican administrations. Some specific examples of these interconnections are:

[55]Melman, *Pentagon Capitalism*, p. 97; Barber, p. 137; and Bell, p. 253.
[56]Richard J. Barnet, "The National Security Managers and the National Interest," *Politics and Society* 1 (February 1971): 257–68.

Robert S. McNamara: Secretary of Defense, 1961–1967; president and member of the board of directors of the Ford Motor Company; member of the board of directors of Scott Paper Company; president of the World Bank, 1967 to date.

John Foster Dulles: Secretary of State, 1953–1959; partner of Sullivan and Cromwell (one of twenty largest law firms on Wall Street); member of the board of directors of the Bank of New York, of the Fifth Avenue Bank, the American Bank Note Company, of the International Nickel Company of Canada, Babcock and Wilson Corporation, Gold Dust Corporation, the Overseas Security Corporation, Shenandoah Corporation, United Cigar Stores, American Cotton Oil Company, United Railroad of St. Louis, and European Textile Corporation. He was a trustee of the New York Public Library, the Union Theological Seminary, the Rockefeller Foundation, and the Carnegie Endowment for International Peace; a delegate to the World Council of Churches.

Clark Clifford: Secretary of Defense, 1967–1969; senior partner of Clifford and Miller (Washington law firm); member of the board of directors of the National Bank of Washington and the Sheridan Hotel Corporation; Special Counsel to the President, 1949–1950; member of the board of trustees of Washington University in St. Louis.

W. Averell Harriman: U.S. Ambassador-at Large and Under Secretary of State for Political Affairs, 1961–1969; chief United States negotiator at Paris Peace Conference on Vietnam; former Governor of the State of New York, 1955–1958; former chairman of the board of directors of the Union Pacific Railroad and the Merchant Ship Building Corporation; partner in Brown Brothers, Harriman, and Company (Wall Street investment firm).

John J. McCloy: Special Adviser to the President on Disarmament, 1961–1963: chairman of the Coordinating Committee on the Cuban Crisis, 1962; member of the President's commission on the assassination of President Kennedy; U.S. High Commissioner for Germany, 1949–1952; President of the World Bank, 1947–1949; partner in Milbank, Tweed, Hadley, and McCloy (Wall Street law firm); member of the board of directors of Allied Chemical Corporation, American Telephone and Telegraph Company, Chase Manhattan Bank, Metropolitan Life Insurance Company, Westinghouse Electric Corporation, E. R. Squibb and Sons; member of the board of trustees of the Ford Foundation, the Council of Foreign Relations, and Amherst College.

Arthur H. Dean: chairman of the U.S. Delegation on Nuclear Test Ban Treaty; chief U.S. negotiator of the Korean Armistice Agreement; partner, Sullivan and Cromwell (Wall Street law firm); member of the board of directors of American Metal Climax, American Bank Note Company, National Union Electric Corporation, El Paso Natural Gas Company, Crown Zellerback Corporation, Campbell Soup Company, Northwest Production Corporation, Lazard Fund, Inc., and the Bank of New York; a member of the board of trustees of New York Hospital, Cornell Medical Center, Cornell Medical College, Cornell University, the Carnegie Foundation, and the Council of Foreign Relations. [57]

Some of Kennedy's top advisers described themselves as "the brightest and the best" of their generation. As described by an outside observer, "They were Rhodes Scholars, university professors, business leaders, war heroes—all men who had succeeded brilliantly in their careers . . . models of respectability and achievement. They were superior by almost any accepted definition of the society. They performed well on tests. They knew how to make money."[58]

Yet at the same time one might wonder whether they had lost a basic sense of humanity. The problem with the military-industrial complex is not, as sometimes alleged, that the military got the upper hand, but that *militarist thinking* characterized the top civilian echelons. It was this kind of thinking that led the men at the top to calculate the most efficient means to attack countries thousands of miles away and to take pride in tough-mindedly thinking the unthinkable. An illustration of their approach is provided in a memorandum written by Assistant Secretary of Defense John McNaughton during the Vietnam war. McNaughton speculated that a possible tactic was "shallow-flooding the rice paddies [which] leads after time to widespread starvation (more than a million?) unless food is provided—which we could offer to do at the conference table."[59]

Is Military Spending Essential to American Capitalism?

Despite the fact that many large corporations produce for the military, economist Seymour Melman asserts that military production is detrimental to corporate capitalism in the United

[57]Thomas R. Dye and L. Harmon Zeigler, *The Irony of Democracy; An Uncommon Introduction to American Politics* (North Scituate, Mass., 1971), pp. 97–98.
[58]Barnet, *Roots of War*, p. 16.
[59]*The Pentagon Papers—The Senator Gravel Edition* (Boston, 1971), vol. 4, p. 43.

States. It has absorbed resources—capital, technology, raw materials, and scientific personnel—that might have been used to increase the country's civilian production. America's competitive economic position has thus been weakened by a decline in United States productivity and efficiency.[60] Other capitalist countries, which are not saddled with high military budgets, are in a good position to challenge American economic dominance. With a combined population for exceeding that of the United States, the major countries of Western Europe and Japan have a total military budget one-quarter as large.

If military production is not directly helpful and is even possibly harmful to corporate capitalism, why is military spending so high and why does it continue to climb?

Two reasons can be advanced. First, as we have seen, the sectors that benefit from military spending are among the most influential forces in the United States: military firms, key congressmen, the Department of Defense, organized labor, and localities throughout the country with military installations and factories.

However, there is an even more important reason for high military spending. Although it may adversely affect productivity in the United States, it protects American business interests abroad. The vast military establishment enables the government to hold a commanding position in the world and the corporate complex to operate freely in foreign countries. Military spending can thus be considered an "overhead cost" of maintaining American privilege at the expense of other countries.

In an attempt to resolve the contradiction between the need to use military power to maintain an international capitalist sphere and the costly drain this imposes on America's resources —and also because of the United States defeat in Vietnam, the rapidly increasing costs of weaponry, and the growing opposition to military spending by Congress and other groups—the United States has sought ways to slow down the expansion of military spending. It has tried to persuade other capitalist countries (notably West Germany and Japan) to share the expenses of maintaining American troops stationed abroad, slightly scaled down its foreign-policy aims, and reached limited agreements with the Soviet Union and China.

---

[60]Melman, *Pentagon Capitalism*, as well as his *Our Depleted Society* and *The Permanent War Economy*.

The arms race probably now represents in good part a subsidy to powerful interests within the United States. Many who formerly favored high military spending have revised their views. According to George Kennan, who helped develop the policy of "containing" the USSR through military threats, the arms race between the United States and the Soviet Union "is simply riding along on its own momentum, like an object in space. It has no foundations in real interests."[61]

Current trends, however, should provide no cause for complacency. Military spending remains high and continues to increase each year, the arms race has not ended, and the danger posed by thermonuclear holocaust has not diminished. The military budget might be compared to a runaway truck that, after accelerating at an increasing rate, continues to accelerate—but less rapidly.

CHALLENGES TO AMERICAN DOMINANCE

For thirty years, American dominance rested on the head start that the United States enjoyed after the Second World War both as a result of the war itself and other advantages the United States possessed: a vast market, a skilled labor force, and abundant natural resources. The United States remains today the most powerful nation in the world. However, the 1970s have witnessed a relative decline of American military and economic supremacy. The gap between the United States and some other countries has begun to narrow, and American dominance has become increasingly more difficult to maintain.

Militarily, the USSR has drawn closer to the United States in recent years. "There was only one global power in 1947; today there are two."[62] In 1964, the United States had five times more intercontinental missiles than the USSR. Today it has fewer than the Soviet Union. The SALT agreement symbolizes United States acceptance of the narrowing military gap with the USSR rather than superiority. (However, the United States continues to

[61]Kennan, p. 11.
[62]Raymond Aron, *The Imperial Republic: The United States and the World, 1945–1973* (Englewood Cliffs, N.J., 1974), p. 149.

Table 6–3
Gross domestic product (GDP) as percentage of U.S. GDP

	1950	1960	1969	1972
France	9.7	12.0	15.1	16.5
West Germany	8.1	14.1	16.5	22.2
Italy	4.9	6.8	8.8	10.1
Japan	3.8	8.5	18.0	23.9
United Kingdom	12.6	14.0	11.7	13.6
All Five	39.1	55.4	70.1	86.3

Source: Albert Szymanski, "The Decline and Fall of the U.S. Eagle," *Social Policy* (March–April 1974): 6. Based on U.N. and I.M.F. data. *Social Policy* published by Social Policy Corporation, New York, New York 10010. © 1974 by Social Policy Corp.

have a decisive lead in the quality of weaponry and in the total number of strategic warheads and nuclear-powered submarines.) To maintain superiority in all categories of strategic weapons, the United States would have to reduce spending in other areas (for example, welfare programs) or raise taxes. Yet the political opposition that would be generated by such measures limits the possibility of increasing military spending indefinitely.

The United States has experienced intense economic competition from other major capitalist countries. In 1959, the combined production of the five other major capitalist countries was equivalent to only 39 percent of United States production; by 1972 the figure had risen to 86 percent.

The United States rate of growth, both per capita and total growth, lags behind most other Western capitalist countries.

Worker productivity in other capitalist countries as well as in the USSR has risen faster than in the United States. Japan has grown at an especially rapid pace and may achieve economic parity with the United States within several decades.

These overall figures are reflected in the changing pattern of multinational corporate competition and in particular industrial sectors. Whereas in 1969, only 2 of the world's 20 largest corporations were non-American, by 1973 there were 5 non-American firms among the top 20. Between 1950 and 1970, American share of world steel production fell from 55 percent to 20 percent, its share of world automobile production from 82 percent to 29 percent. In 1948, the United States exported twice

Table 6–4
The economics of developed capitalist economies

Country	GNP per capita US $ 1969	Growth of GNP per capita per annum 1960–70	GNP growth per annum 1960–70
USA	4664	3.2	4.4
Japan	1626	9.6	10.6
W. Germany	2512	3.5	4.5
France	2783	4.6	5.6
UK	1976	2.2	2.8
Italy	1548	4.6	5.4
Canada	3260	3.6	5.4
Australia	2660	3.1	5.1
Spain	872	6.1	7.2
Netherlands	2196	3.9	5.2
Sweden	3490	3.8	4.5

Source: Bill Warren, "Imperialism and Capitalist Industrialization," *New Left Review* no. 81 (September-October 1973): 9. Based on U.N. data.

as much as the original six countries of the European Economic Community; in 1972, these countries exported two and one-half times more than the United States.[63]

Another illustration of Europe's and Japan's growing economic power is that their multinational corporations are beginning to penetrate the American market. Sony (a Japanese producer of television receivers) and Michelin (a French tire company) are among the foreign corporations who have recently built large factories in the United States. In 1973, foreign investment in the United States was over $3 billion.

There is also growing resistance to multinational economic control in the Third World. Countries producing petroleum, bauxite, and other commodities have begun organizing to resist American and European control of their resources. The three major techniques they use all strike at multinational corporations:

[63]Albert Szymanski, "The Decline and Fall of the U.S. Eagle," *Social Policy* (March–April 1974): 7–8.

raising the price of raw materials charged to foreign firms, processing the raw materials locally rather than exporting them for processing elsewhere, and gaining national control over their resources rather than allowing multinational companies to exercise control.[64]

Note that the new developments do not necessarily spell an end to capitalism, nor to inequalities within or among countries. In fact, what often occurs is local capitalist development in the Third World and the creation of locally powerful capitalist classes. Within countries, these local capitalist classes may exercise harsh control and maintain class and ethnic inequalities. Among nations, the gap between wealthy capitalist countries and many poor countries is increasing. But some Third World countries are displaying patterns of rapid economic growth. During the decade from 1960 to 1970, for example, the following countries achieved higher per capita growth rates than the United States: Taiwan, South Korea, Thailand, the Ivory Coast, Tanzania, and the petroleum-exporting countries of the Middle East. The other side of the coin of investment by multinational firms has been industrialization in these countries. However, other countries, including India, Indonesia, Nigeria, and Morocco, barely grew at all during this period if population increases are taken into account. There is thus increasing inequality *among* Third World countries.

The future is uncertain. For example, Third World nations may use the profits from the sale of commodities to hasten the development of their own manufacturing and high-technology sectors, thus shutting out multinational corporations. Or multinational corporations may succeed in allying with Third World commodity producers *against* the rest of the world to the benefit of capitalist groups both in the Third World and the West. A third possibility is that insurgent forces may wrest control over their country away from local capitalist groups and multinational corporations. What is apparent at the present time is that American efforts have failed to fashion a stable, integrated capitalist world order with the United States in the commanding position. Whatever else the future holds, it will doubtless witness further challenges to American power.

---

[64]Bill Warren, "Imperialism and Capitalist Industrialization," *New Left Review* no. 81 (September–October 1973): 3–44, has analyzed the new trends.

7

the president as manager of the corporate complex

When delegates to the Constitutional Convention were meeting in Philadelphia in 1787 to consider ways to revise the Articles of Confederation, Alexander Hamilton, a thirty-year-old delegate from New York, shocked the gathering by praising the British monarchy—against whom the colonies had revolted a mere decade before—as "the best in the world." Recognizing that hereditary monarchy would never be accepted in America, Hamilton suggested that the new federal government should be directed by an elected monarch, holding office for life. Hamilton later returned to this idea in *The Federalist* No. 70, one of a series of papers written by Hamilton, James Madison, and John Jay to persuade voters to ratify the proposed Constitution.

Hamilton's proposal was not even considered by the Convention and it occupies barely a footnote in histories of the founding period. Instead, the Constitutional Convention proposed a government of separated institutions, embodying the delegates' belief in the necessity for a system of checks and balances to prevent any one branch from overpowering the others and gaining the chance to exercise tyranny.

Yet, aside from the fact that the president is elected every four years, rather than holding office for life as Hamilton favored, the term *elected monarch* is as accurate as any to describe the contemporary presidency. Senator Jacob Javits recently observed that the United States had lodged "more power in a single individual than any other system of government that functions today," a strange irony in a country that once prided itself on limited government and that regarded "the accumulation of all powers, legislative, executive, and judiciary in the same hands," according to James Madison's formulation in *The Federalist* No. 47, as "the very definition of tyranny."[1] Contrary to the intention of the framers—who attempted to distribute the legislative (policy making), executive, and judicial functions of government among separate branches of government, with the three responsive to different constituencies but sharing the functions of government—the contemporary presidency has substantially absorbed many of the powers of government.[2]

The modern presidency is at the center of the executive branch of the government, numbering more than two million civil servants. The presidency has taken over much of the function of policy initiation—although Congress may amend or reject presidential proposals, the president largely determines the legislative agenda. In recent years, the courts have curbed presidential power only in extreme instances, such as Watergate. Nor have the sovereign people posed major obstacles to presidential power. In all but two of the twelve cases in the twentieth century where incumbent presidents have sought reelection, they have been successful. But in recent years, public opinion has played a major role in the downfall of two presidents: Lyndon Johnson's decision not to seek reelection in 1968 was the result of public opposition to his conduct of the Vietnam war; and Richard Nixon's resignation was brought about by public indignation about Watergate.

Although Nixon's defiance of democratic procedures, constitutional and legal restraints, and the legislative and judicial branches of government in the Watergate affair eventually pro-

[1]*New York Times*, April 28, 1974.
[2]This is one of the themes in James MacGregor Burns, *Presidential Government* (Boston, 1965), pp. 124–54.

voked resistance, the basic nature of the presidency remains unchanged. Future presidents will take care to observe standards of legality and probity, but the overweening power of modern presidents preceded Watergate, derives from sources quite unrelated to the Watergate excesses, and persists in the aftermath of Watergate.

The presidency did not assume its present character overnight nor was the development inevitable. In constitutional doctrine and in political practice through much of American history, the three branches of government have been relatively coequal. Prior to the twentieth century, most presidents exercised few powers, and the entire national government had a limited influence. Bold innovators like Andrew Jackson, Abraham Lincoln, Theodore Roosevelt, and Woodrow Wilson were the exception, not the rule.

As late as the end of the nineteenth century, the presidency was viewed by many scholars as a weak branch of the government. In 1885, a young Princeton professor published an influential study of American politics, entitled *Congressional Government,* in which he asserted that Congress was the foremost policy-making institution of American government. Indeed, the president was powerful only to the extent that he participated, by his limited veto power over bills passed by Congress, in the legislative domain. Twenty-three years later, the author changed his view and, in *Constitutional Government in the United States,* developed a far more expansive theory of the presidency. Soon after, Woodrow Wilson, the former Princeton professor, contributed even more directly to the creation of a powerful presidency by his actions as president.

Through much of the nineteenth and early twentieth century, there were cyclical swings between strong and weak presidents, between presidential and congressional supremacy, and between an interventionist and a restrained federal government. Underlying the particular changes, however, was the slow but steady growth in size and power of the federal government. A decisive shift occurred in the early twentieth century. The development of the modern presidency has accompanied the growth of big government, which, we saw in previous chapters, was a product of the rise of corporate capitalism within the United States and its penetration abroad. Particularly since Franklin D. Roosevelt, the balance of power among the three branches of government has tilted toward the president.

The rapid growth in size and power of the presidency can be illustrated by one statistic. When Herbert Hoover served as president from 1928 to 1932, he was aided by a personal secretary and two assistants. Less than half a century later, the Executive Office of the President (EOP) exceeds five thousand staff members, including six hundred members of the White House staff.[3]

Every president for nearly half a century has probably been more powerful than even the most powerful presidents of the nineteenth century. The bold innovations of one president have come to be accepted as a normal feature of presidential rule by the next. "In instance after instance," Richard Neustadt, a student of the presidency, has observed, "the exceptional behavior of our earlier 'strong' Presidents has now been set by statute as a regular requirement."[4]

Until the Watergate scandal, it was fashionable for presidents unabashedly to proclaim the need for wide-ranging power. The president, stated John F. Kennedy during the 1960 presidential campaign

> must be prepared to exercise the fullest powers of his office—all that are specified and some that are not. . . . For only the president represents the national interest. And upon him alone converge all the needs and aspirations of all parts of the country, all departments of the government, all nations of the world.[5]

During a television interview in 1964, Lyndon Johnson asserted:

> The office of the Presidency is the only office in this land of all the people. . . . At no time and in no way and for no reason can a President allow the integrity or the responsibility or the freedom of the office ever to be compromised or diluted or destroyed, because when you destroy it, you destroy yourselves.[6]

In a 1968 election campaign address, Richard Nixon stated:

> The days of a passive Presidency belong to a simpler past. Let me be very clear about this. The next President must take an activist view of his office. He must articulate the nation's values, define its

[3]Arthur M. Schlesinger, Jr., *The Imperial Presidency* (Boston, 1973), p. 221.
[4]Richard E. Neustadt, *Presidential Power: The Politics of Leadership* (New York, 1963), p. 5.
[5]Campaign speech by John Kennedy, quoted in Robert S. Hirschfield, ed., *The Power of the Presidency: Concepts and Controversy*, 2d ed. (Chicago 1973), pp. 130, 133.
[6]*Ibid.*, p. 150.

goals and marshal its will. Under a Nixon Administration, the Presidency will be deeply involved in the entire sweep of American public opinion.[7]

On another occasion, Nixon suggested, "Only the President can hold out a vision of the future and rally the people behind it."[8]

All modern presidents aim to be remembered as innovators. It has become standard to group an assortment of policy recommendations and present the package as an original program of the president. The precedent was set by Theodore Roosevelt's Square Deal, followed by Woodrow Wilson's New Freedom, Franklin Roosevelt's New Deal, Truman's Fair Deal, Kennedy's New Frontier, and Johnson's Great Society. Richard Nixon continued this tradition when he proclaimed, "This will be known as an Administration which advocated . . . more significant reforms than any Administration since Franklin Roosevelt in 1932."[9]

Yet, however powerful the president, there are limits as well. Presidents Johnson and Nixon could order aerial bombardments of Indochina, but this did not assure victory. Presidents can prepare economic plans, but this may not prevent inflation. They can submit legislation to Congress, but they cannot compel congressional consent. And, as Nixon discovered, although a president can pursue his goals by a variety of means, he violates the standards of procedural democracy at his peril.

A good way to understand the political significance of the presidency is to study the various areas in which the president exercises power. Different scholars have suggested alternative classifications. Clinton Rossiter, a long-time student of the presidency, identifies various "hats" or roles of the president, including (following Rossiter's terminology) chief of state, chief executive, commander in chief of the armed forces, chief diplomat, chief legislator, chief of party, voice of the people, protector of the peace, manager of prosperity, and world leader.[10] Political scientist Thomas Cronin describes four spheres, or subpresidencies: foreign policy, aggregate economic functions, domestic-policy functions, and symbolic and moral leadership.[11] Aaron

[7]*New York Times,* March 4, 1973.
[8]Hirschfield, p. 165.
[9]*New York Times,* November 10, 1972.
[10]Clinton Rossiter, *The American Presidency,* revised ed., (New York, 1960), chapter 1.
[11]Thomas E. Cronin, "Presidents as Chief Executives," in Rexford G. Tugwell and Thomas E. Cronin, eds., *The Presidency Reappraised* (New York, 1974), p. 235.

Wildavsky, dean of the school of public policy at the University of California, Berkeley, has pointed to two presidencies, one for foreign and the other for domestic affairs.[12]

Adapting these classifications, we suggest three broad purposes on behalf of which contemporary presidents exercise power: to assist corporate production at home, defend the corporate complex abroad, and maintain social control. The three represent major founts of modern presidential power, resulting from the growth of corporate production, corporate and government expansion abroad, and the nationalization of American political and cultural life through the mass media. Each sphere can be identified with particular constitutional grants of authority and particular agencies within the Executive Office of the President.

Richard Neustadt has questioned the validity of dividing the presidency into separate roles. In his view, the classification of presidential activity into various functions or powers conveys the misleading impression that the spheres exist in isolation from one another. Neustadt emphasizes that the various presidential functions are woven together into an indistinguishable whole. The common ingredient that gives presidential actions their coherence, according to Neustadt, is the exercise of presidential power. Presidential activity can be understood better as the attempt to exert influence rather than the mechanical performance of separate roles.[13]

In our view, Neustadt is correct in stressing the need to understand the overall coherence of presidential activity. Yet he does not specify what ends are served by the successful exercise of presidential power. Unless one can supply an answer, the exercise of presidential power appears meaningless, like a dog chasing its tail. Our interpretation is that presidential power can best be understood as exercised on behalf of the corporate complex. The president's interest is closely bound up with the interest of the corporate-state alliance described in previous chapters.

An illustration is provided by a comment made by President Lyndon Johnson during a television interview. Note how Johnson links government to corporate-capitalist production and foreign involvement in a paean to the United States, thus weaving

---

[12]Aaron Wildavsky, "The Two Presidencies," *Trans-action* (December 1966): 7–14.
[13]Neustadt, chapter 3.

together what we identify as the three major presidential functions:

> I am so proud of our system of government, of our free enterprise, where our incentive system and our men who head our big industries are willing to get up at daylight and get to bed at midnight to offer employment and create new jobs for people, where our men working there will try to get decent wages but will sit across the table and not act like cannibals, but will negotiate and reason things out together. . . . We have one thing they [the USSR] don't have and that is our system of private enterprise, free enterprise, where the employer, hoping to make a little profit, the laborer, hoping to justify his wages, can get together and make a better mousetrap. They have developed this into the most powerful and leading nation in the world, and I want to see it preserved. And I have an opportunity to do something about it as President. And I may not be a great President, but as long as I am here, I am going to try to be a good President and do my dead-level best to see this system preserved.[14]

This chapter examines how the president carries out the three broad functions of defending the corporate complex abroad, assisting corporate capitalism at home, and maintaining social control.

THE IMPERIAL PRESIDENT AND THE IMPERIAL REPUBLIC

The rise of the modern presidency has been inseparable from the rise of the United States as an imperial power. Presidential power has thrived on foreign involvement, crisis, and war. The titles of two books published a few months apart—*The Imperial Presidency* by historian Arthur Schlesinger, Jr., and *The Imperial Republic* by French scholar Raymond Aron—evoke the parallel expansion of the presidency within the government and the United States in the world.[15] Presidential power has taken a quantum leap each time the United States has expanded abroad or been involved in a military, diplomatic, or commercial crisis.

[14]Hirschfield, pp. 147–48.
[15]Schlesinger, *The Imperial Presidency*; Raymond Aron, *The Imperial Republic* (Englewood Cliffs, N.J., 1974), first published in France in 1973.

One of the chief pegs on which increased presidential prerogative has been hung is the president's role in foreign affairs, including the constitutional power to negotiate treaties, receive ambassadors from foreign countries (which implies the right to recognize or refuse to recognize the regime of a particular country), and, above all, command the armed forces. The framers intended the president's power as commander in chief to be confined to the limited authority of a military leader to issue orders once hostilities exist. The Constitution granted Congress, not the president, the power to declare war and appropriate funds for military expenditures.

Early presidents soon expanded their power as commander in chief—and thereby the power of the presidency as a whole—by deploying American troops in pursuance of their foreign policies. James K. Polk, for example, provoked war with Mexico in 1846 by sending American troops into disputed land between Texas and Mexico. When the troops were fired upon by Mexican forces, Polk quickly extracted from Congress a declaration of war. Polk's actions brought forth an angry reaction from a young Illinois congressman, "Allow the President to invade a neighboring nation, whenever *he* shall deem it necessary to repel an invasion . . . and you allow him to make war at pleasure. Study to see if you can fix *any limit* to his power in this respect."[16]

Abraham Lincoln's words proved prescient. The scenario was repeated over a century later when, in 1964, President Johnson ordered naval destroyers deployed close to the coast of North Vietnam, in the Gulf of Tonkin, and provoked an encounter with North Vietnamese forces. The incident was quickly used to obtain from Congress a resolution drafted by the executive (ostensibly in the heat of the crisis—it was later revealed that the resolution had been prepared long in advance) authorizing the president "to take all necessary measures" to pursue the war. The Gulf of Tonkin resolution paved the way to American aerial bombardment of North Vietnam the following year.

Lincoln himself, when president, used presidential war powers during the Civil War in a drastically expanded manner. During the first months after the war broke out, Lincoln refused to call Congress into special session. Among the unauthorized measures he took were the blockading of Southern ports, suspending constitutional rights in judicial proceedings, expanding

---

[16]Schlesinger, p. 42, italics in original.

the armed forces beyond their congressionally prescribed size, and spending money for purposes not approved by Congress. During the course of the war, Lincoln took additional measures without congressional approval: he proclaimed martial law behind the lines, arrested people without following judicial procedures, seized property, suppressed newspapers, and laid out a plan for reconstruction.[17] Edward Corwin, a scholar of constitutional law, notes that Lincoln's actions "assert for the President for the first time in our history, an initiative of indefinite scope . . . in meeting the domestic aspects of a war emergency."[18]

Woodrow Wilson was prophetic when, as a professor, he wrote of the president's new position arising from American power internationally:

> The President can never again be the mere domestic figure he has been throughout so large a part of our history. The nation has risen to the first rank in power and resources. . . . Our President must always, henceforth, be one of the great powers of the world, whether he act greatly and wisely or not. . . . We can never hide our President again as a mere domestic officer. . . . He must stand always at the front of our affairs, and the office will be as big and as influential as the man who occupies it.[19]

Chapter 6 described how presidents in the twentieth century have promoted expansion of American power abroad. Following a policy of "gunboat diplomacy" in the early part of the century, presidents ordered American forces to Latin America to "collect debts for American banks and enforce the will of American sugar, fruit, and other interests."[20] President Wilson during the First World War and President Roosevelt during the Second World War exercised wide-ranging powers as military leaders. Through the destroyer deal with Great Britain, in which (by executive agreement) Roosevelt exchanged United States destroyers for the use of British naval bases, the president circumvented Congress to accelerate military preparations. During the war he relocated the entire Japanese-American population

---

[17]*Ibid.*, p. 58.
[18]Edward S. Corwin, *The President: Office and Powers, 1787–1957* (New York, 1957), p. 232.
[19]Woodrow Wilson, *Constitutional Government in the United States* (New York, 1908), pp. 78–79.
[20]I. F. Stone, "Can Congress Stop the President?" *New York Review of Books,* April 19, 1973, p. 23.

(70,000 people) living on the West Coast to makeshift intern camps in California and elsewhere; he created wartime agencies on his authority to regulate prices, rents, and raw materials; and he seized sixty strike-bound plants to force workers to return to their jobs. After the Second World War, President Truman enunciated the Truman Doctrine on his own authority; its pledge to intervene militarily anywhere in the world represented a basic shift in American foreign policy.

Presidents nowadays justify their increased power by reference to the litany of the cold war, the threat of nuclear destruction, the requirements of national security, and the need for speed and secrecy. In Neustadt's words, "Technology has modified the Constitution. The President . . . becomes the only . . . man in the system capable of exercising judgment under the extraordinary limits now imposed by secrecy, complexity, and time."[21]

Presidents frequently defend their actions on the basis of their unique access to secret information. "If you knew what I know," asserted Lyndon Johnson, "then you would be acting in the same way." [22] Yet "backstage" glimpses of workings of the presidency, such as those provided by the Pentagon Papers and the transcription of the White House tapes in the Watergate affair, reveal the limited role of superior information. Moreover, Johnson's argument has a suspiciously self-serving ring. First, presidents do their utmost to withhold information (the top-heavy security-classification system is an example)—and thus try to prevent citizens from knowing what presidents know. Further, the quality of this inside information can be questioned: "I used to imagine when the government took actions I found inexplicable that it had information I didn't have," relates Charles Frankel, who served as an assistant secretary of state under President Johnson. "But after I had served in the government for some months, I found that the information was often false!"[23] George Reedy, press secretary to President Johnson, notes, "The most easily observable fact about 'secret diplomacy' is that it has not worked very well."[24]

---

[21]Richard Neustadt, "Testimony of Richard Neustadt Before the Senate Subcommittee on National Security Staffing and Operations," In Aaron Wildavsky, ed., *The Presidency* (Boston, 1969), p. 516.

[22]Robert T. Nakamura, "Congress Confronts the Presidency," in Robert Paul Wolff, ed., *1984 Revisited: Prospects for American Politics* (New York, 1973), p. 82.

[23]Charles Frankel, *High on Foggy Bottom* (New York, 1969), p. 78.

[24]George Reedy, "On the Isolation of Presidents," in Tugwell and Cronin, p. 130.

The major consequence of the presumed need for secrecy and the secret information presidents possess is to shield presidential activity from public scrutiny. An extreme illustration is the secret air wars President Nixon conducted in Cambodia during 1969–70 and 1973. (When announcing an American ground invasion of Cambodia in April 1970, Nixon stated that until then the United States had "scrupulously respect[ed] the neutrality of the Cambodian people," and had done nothing "to violate the territory of a neutral nation.") So expansive had the president's war power become that the House Judiciary Committee investigating possible grounds for presidential impeachment in 1974 decided that Nixon's actions and duplicity regarding Cambodia did not constitute grounds for impeachment.

The need for speed as a justification for presidential power is also open to doubt. Presidential decisions rarely need to be made in a hurry. The usual process is policy making by accretion, in the words of former Senator William Fulbright. Foreign engagements such as Vietnam occur through a slow process of escalation, not as the result of a crisis demanding a rapid decision. The image of the finger on the nuclear button has been unjustifiably extended to the entire range of presidential activity. The president's expanded powers in the exceptional conditions of wartime have become standard in an era where the economy is permanently mobilized, American corporations routinely operate throughout the world, and the armed forces are stationed in every continent and are on the brink of war twenty-four hours a day. Presidential power is given an awesome boost by the fact that the United States is a militarized economy.

As commander in chief and chief of the executive branch, the president is in overall control of the military-industrial complex; he can be considered board chairman of the military establishment. His reach is extended through staff members in the Executive Office of the President, notably the National Security Council, whose members include the secretaries of state and defense, the director of the CIA, and the president's personal national security adviser. The president must contend with conflicting interests among the army, navy, and air force as well as the entrenched power of the service chiefs, key congressmen, and corporate military producers, and he must bargain and compromise to develop policies. Nonetheless, the president is at the apex of the most powerful military machine in history.

Although national security is the standard usually invoked to justify this vast enterprise, the increasing dependence of American corporations on foreign operations means that presidential policies are formulated with an eye to the overseas interests of the corporate complex. Foreign-investment policies, tariffs, and decisions about currency and other economic matters aim to strengthen American multinational corporations in their worldwide activities. The previous chapter reviewed how anticommunism and foreign economic penetration were intertwined as twin justifications for international expansion. The president manages the vast foreign policy and military establishment that has been developed to achieve these goals.

Acting as protector of America's national security strengthens the president at home. "Don't bother the president," presidential adviser Sherman Adams was fond of telling visitors who wanted to see Eisenhower. "He's busy trying to keep us out of war." But national security and international tensions may be invoked for reasons having more to do with presidential interests than with the survival of the United States. The Watergate affair provides a good illustration. In a speech in May 1973 minimizing the gravity of the events, President Nixon mentioned national security thirty-one times.[25]

Even when a president does not consciously exaggerate the danger of war and the need for a free hand abroad, his power is greater in foreign affairs, where there are fewer internal obstacles, than in domestic affairs. Aaron Wildavsky suggests that the president's "scoreboard" of success with Congress in foreign affairs is nearly twice as high as in domestic affairs.[26] Congress is more fearful of questioning the president on foreign policy, where the danger seems greater and congressional expertise less sure. As the automobile industry thrives on traffic accidents and the FBI on crime, so the president is a principal beneficiary within the government of the growth of the military-industrial complex, the cold-war crisis, and America's expanded role abroad.

Limited recognition of the need to restrict presidential freedom in foreign affairs was demonstrated in November 1973, when Congress passed the War Powers Act over President Nixon's veto. The law requires congressional approval of the use

[25]Charles M. Hardin, *Presidential Power and Accountability: Toward a New Constitution* (Chicago, 1974), p. 24.
[26]Wildavsky, "The Two Presidencies."

of American forces in hostilities beyond a certain period. However, the reaction against presidential abuse of authority in foreign affairs is limited for three reasons. First, a president can easily evade a congressional injunction by invoking a crisis or an emergency. Congress would not dare question a president's judgment during the heat of a crisis. Second, the most significant feature of presidential power in foreign affairs is not the sudden and dramatic resort to military force. Instead, presidential activity is part of an institutionalized process directed to the defense of the corporate complex abroad. There are few dramatic acts in this vast domain comparable to the escalation of the Vietnam war, against which Congress or American citizens can react. Third, current debates about whether Congress or the president should exercise greater power in foreign affairs overlook the substantial measure of agreement between the two branches of government on the aims of America's actions abroad. Despite some confrontations between Congress and the president on foreign and military policy, the usual situation is the predominance of a "hard line" in both branches and agreement on the desirability of corporate expansion abroad.

MANAGING THE MANAGED ECONOMY

The modern presidency has been pictured as a series of concentric circles, with the president himself at the center. Surrounding the president are his most trusted personal advisers in the presidential agency—the White House staff. Close to these personal advisers are agencies in the Executive Office of the President. The contemporary presidency is not one person but the several thousand who make up the EOP. Another ring is constituted by the cabinet: the secretaries of the eleven executive departments. They are followed by the "permanent government": the over two million civil servants who work in the bureaus and other agencies within the executive departments.

While this scheme provides a useful guide, it is oversimplified—the modern presidency cannot be reduced to neat organizational charts. Formal positions may be a misleading guide to informal influence. A president may rely heavily on a particular department head, as President Kennedy did on the attorney general (who also happened to be his brother) or as President

Figure 7–1
The Executive Office of the President

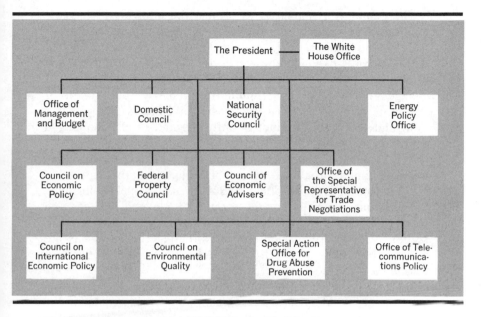

Source: *United States Government Manual, 1973 1974* (Washington, D.C., 1973), p. 78.

Nixon did on his first attorney general (who was his former law partner). Informal advisers without a position in government may be more powerful than officially designated counselors. A presidential task force may be more influential in initiating a new policy than the government agency with official responsibility in that area.

Chapter 5 described the process of clientelism—in which, under the guise of regulating business, government agencies defend and promote specific economic sectors. The sprawling, diverse bureaucracies in the executive give to the government its proverbial character of being slow to act, internally divided, and formless. Yet one agency within the executive does represent the interest of the whole system of established arrangements and attempts to safeguard these arrangements: the presidency. Given the central structural dichotomy in corporate capitalism between capital and labor, between those who organize, own, and control production, and those who work for a wage or salary, the president cannot neutrally represent both. Since the president's foremost interest lies in stabilizing the capital-labor opposition, he must side with and defend the interests of corporate capital.

The economy is managed to protect the interests of the few hundred largest corporate producers. The institutionalized presidency is the manager of the managed economy. As in the case of the president's expanded power in foreign affairs, the expanded presidential reach in domestic affairs is partly the result of changes outside the government (particularly the growth of corporate capitalism), partly the result of congressional delegation, and partly the product of informal and rarely challenged accretion of power.

Whereas the agencies comprising the executive branch carry out government programs, overall planning is mostly centered in the institutionalized presidency. Sociologist Daniel Bell notes, "In the long run, it is not the growth of personal powers and prestige of the President that is important, but the institutionalization of such crucial control and directing functions—as are now carried out by the Budget Bureau and the Council of Economic Advisers—in the executive"[27]

The Constitution provides ample latitude for the expansive exercise of presidential power. Executive power is vested in the president as well as the power to nominate high officials in the executive and judiciary. The president is instructed to deliver an annual state-of-the-union address and is given a qualified veto over congressional legislation. (For a bill to pass over a presidential veto, a two-thirds vote is required by both the House and the Senate.) An elastic provision empowers the president to take care that laws are faithfully executed and represents an open-ended invitation to presidential discretion.

Congress has played an important role in expanding presidential policy planning and management of the economy. Numerous laws make the president responsible for wide-ranging planning functions. The Budget and Accounting Act of 1921 instructs the president to prepare the annual budget and created the Bureau of the Budget (since renamed the Office of Management and Budget—OMB) to assist him in its preparation. Preparing the budget is important because the budget signifies government in action: what government will do. With over six hundred staff members, the OMB is among the most powerful agencies in the executive. Working closely with the president, it reviews budgetary requests and proposed legislation from the departments.

[27]Daniel Bell, *Toward a Post-Industrial Society* (New York, 1973), p. 312.

OMB control is limited by the fact that departments can "end run" their proposals to Congress, thus by-passing presidential control. Moreover, there is usually little change from the previous year in the amount of money requested by most government agencies.[28] But the fact that the OMB prepares the federal budget and preclears proposed legislation considerably increases presidential control over the administration, Congress, and (given the mammoth size of the federal budget: 20 percent of GNP) the whole economy as well. In the "new economics," which calls for federal expenditures to be used to regulate overall economic conditions, control of the budget and legislative clearance are among the important tools of presidential power.

The OMB exercises surveillance and control over the entire executive establishment. The power of the anonymous members of the presidential office can be seen from one account, which describes the OMB associate director as having "negotiated agreements with Congress, initiated programs, blocked proposals from agencies, decided disputes between departments, brought about the impoundment or release of funds and precipitated presidential vetoes."[29]

Another landmark piece of legislation contributing to the transformation of the presidency into an agency responsible for overall direction of the economy is the Employment Act of 1946, which instructs the president to take steps to maintain high employment and production, combat inflation, and satisfy economic needs. The act created the Council of Economic Advisers (CEA), a group of three professional economists with staff assistance, within the Executive Office of the President. Other congressional legislation that delegates responsibility for economic planning includes the Trade Expansion Act of 1962, which empowers the president to negotiate tariffs with other nations, and the Economic Stabilization Act of 1970, which grants the president broad authority to "issue rules and regulations as he may deem appropriate to stabilize prices, rents, wages, and salaries."

Presidential planning has become an essential feature of corporate capitalism. It functions routinely and during crises.

---

[28]Aaron Wildavsky, *The Politics of the Budgetary Process* (Boston, 1964), pp. 13–16.

[29]John Herbers, "The Other Presidency," *New York Times Magazine*, March 3, 1974, p. 34.

During the fuel shortage of 1973, the president created an Energy Administration within the EOP, whose powers included allocating petroleum among industrial and household consumers and different geographic regions.

Annual presidential messages concerning the state of the union, the budget, and the economy enable the president to provide a unified coherent program. These messages offer comprehensive guidelines for the attempt to manage the corporate complex.

The result of these developments is that the presidency has become the nerve center of corporate capitalism. Through law and custom, it is widely accepted that the president will be in overall charge of coordinating the corporate economy.

Outside the EOP, but partially subject to control by the president and agencies within the EOP, is the group of department heads collectively known as the cabinet. Most departments represented in the cabinet are concerned with aspects of the economy: agriculture, commerce, labor, housing and urban development, treasury, transportation, and so on. Partial exceptions are the departments of state and defense, whose bailiwick is American interests abroad.

Cabinet members are appointed by the president and can be removed by him. However, cabinet secretaries are rarely in close communication with the president, and they have separate interests that derive from their administrative positions as heads of a large departments. A cabinet secretary's day-to-day work consists of supervising the thousands of civil servants within his or her department. Presidential control and planning may be diluted by the fact that cabinet secretaries (and bureau chiefs and others within the bureaucracy) may oppose presidential directives. However powerful the president, the impression should not be given that presidents can have orders obeyed at a wave of the hand. If the president can issue directives to cabinet members, they may find ways to evade presidential instructions. Commands issuing from the top levels of the bureaucracy have a curious way of being distorted or ignored at the bottom. So powerful is the bureaucracy that it has been called the "fourth branch of government."

Neustadt asserts that presidential power usually amounts to little more than the power to persuade.[30] It is true that, in order to

[30]Neustadt, *Presidential Power, passim.*

accomplish his goals, the president is forced to bargain and compromise with influential public and private officials who are in a position to help or impede the president's efforts. Yet, although the president is far from all-powerful, he is well endowed—as a result of staff assistance, constitutional power, congressionally delegated authority, and public standing—to bargain with others on favorable terms. As a result, the initiative in policy planning in the United States is mostly centered in the White House. In a study of domestic-policy innovations developed during the Kennedy and Johnson years, former presidential aide James Sundquist notes that

> the major legislative impulse of the 1961–66 period came from a single source—the White House. Members of Congress could retard, accelerate, or deflect these impulses, and they could expand, limit, or modify the specific proposals initiated from the White House. But they could not set in motion the legislative stream itself. Constitutionally, they had every right to do so. Theoretically, perhaps, they had the opportunity. Practically, they did not.[31]

Chapter 5 described the connection between corporate capitalism and government and analyzed the interests that gain and lose from government activity. Overall, government planning is primarily geared to facilitate corporate production. The means include fiscal policy (the use of government expenditures to assure a stable economy), monetary policy, grants to particular corporations and industries, tax policies, patents, and a myriad of other measures.

The president's control over the economy is limited by a welter of conflicting forces in the federal bureaucracy, state and local governments, political parties, and private sectors. No private group ever proclaims itself satisfied by government action. Similarly, presidents and their supporters never admit that they have adequate power—they often complain that the real problem is not that the president has too much power but too little. For the president to accomplish broad national purposes, it is argued, immense resistance must be overcome—or simply tangle, complexity, and inertia.

Yet the job of sorting out presidential goals and evaluating presidential power, cannot be carried out in a vacuum. Although

[31]James Sundquist, *Politics and Policy: The Eisenhower, Kennedy, and Johnson Years* (Washington, D.C., 1969), p. 489.

the cumulative effect of the formal and informal economic-planning authority the presidential office has acquired over the years is immense, this authority is not carried out by presidential whim. For, as described in Chapter 3, America's productive apparatus is controlled to a considerable extent by a few hundred large corporations. If the president were not to gain that intangible factor called "business confidence"—the support of the corporate sector—no amount of government planning, tinkering, or regulating could succeed. Thus, presidential success is closely tied to the success of corporate capitalism. The alternative to not helping corporate capitalism flourish is economic dislocation—recession, unemployment, inflation—as well as political opposition. Just as in foreign affairs there is a close connection between the president and corporate capitalism abroad, so in domestic affairs there is a convergence between the president's personal interest as economic planner and the interests of the corporate sector—the president stands to gain when corporate capitalism gains.

SOCIAL CONTROL: MANAGING DISCONTENT AND PACKAGING THE PRESIDENT

Because of the fundamental conflict of interest between capital and labor, and the necessity for presidents to foster corporate success to insure their own success, a third arena of presidential activity consists of containing the discontents generated by capitalist production. Thomas Cronin suggests that "calibration and management of conflict is the core of presidential leadership."[32] The president's concern in this arena is to keep conflict from threatening structural stability and is centered on those who do not control corporate capital: small-capital businessmen, wage earners, racial minorities, the unemployed, and consumers.

When discontented groups express grievances, the president often takes to the media. In a public address, sympathetic

[32]Thomas E. Cronin, " 'Everybody Believes in Democracy Until He Gets to the White House . . .': An Examination of White House-Departmental Relations," *Law and Contemporary Problems*, 35 (Summer 1970): 575.

symbolic gestures are made on behalf of the aggrieved group. Persistent opposition may be met by more tangible measures: the president may develop new policies, programs, and institutions to deal with the crisis. Illustrations are provided by presidential reactions to the urban crisis, poverty, and civil rights.

When groups are strong, angry, and determined, they may succeed in wresting real benefits from government. Often, however, they can be subdued by symbolic means or repression. Consider, as an illustration of presidential approach to crisis, the issue of black insurgency in Northern cities during the 1960s. The "urban crisis" was viewed by several presidents less as the impoverished and disadvantaged conditions in which a large proportion of blacks lived than as the political challenge posed by black militancy. By a combination of government aid, institutional innovation, and police repression, Presidents Kennedy, Johnson, and Nixon managed to get confrontation out of the streets without substantially altering the conditions that caused the challenge. In 1972, President Nixon declared that the "urban crisis has passed" and that the "ship of state is no longer in danger." Given the fact that the social, economic, and political situation of black and Spanish-speaking urban groups had declined, not improved, since the late 1960s, the president's declaration represented an exercise in public relations. But the kernel of truth contained in his statement—that black insurgency has been overcome—is revealing of how presidents define crisis. No matter how deprived and powerless a group is, a crisis does not exist (according to this view) until the group takes militant action to remedy its situation. And the president regards crisis as resolved when order is restored.

The president is the foremost defender of established arrangements. He attempts to reassure Americans (and the world) that established arrangements are basically sound—and whatever problems do exist will be solved if his proposals are accepted. Whether he claims that America's invasion of Vietnam has ended in "peace with honor," or that government-imposed wage and price controls further a free economy, or that the national interest requires reducing federal subsidies to the poor, the president's aim is to legitimize and preserve established arrangements—in other words, to defend the interests of the corporate complex. When the president calls on all Americans to work together to support the country, he is in fact asking them to support the capitalist system despite the conflicts of interest that divide Americans. The president has unique opportunities to provide an authoritative interpretation of the political and economic situation through his reports and recommendations to Congress, his ceremonial role as chief of state, and his instant access to the media.

A president's staff contains specialists in legitimizing established arrangements and packaging the president. Speechwriters, press secretaries, and media consultants strive to present the president and his policies in a favorable light. The methods used to sell the president are not fundamentally different from those used to sell toothpaste. At the extreme, as in the Watergate affair, they may include outright deceit, the suppression of damaging information, and the stretching of truth to suit the president's interests. But the routine activity is more significant than the extreme case. Much presidentail action represents an exercise in public relations. Presidential use of the media, especially television, is particularly important. In the electronic age, presidents can reach out to millions of homes to present the presidential message. No other person in the world can command comparable access to the media. Prime-time speeches, presidential press conferences, and other public appearances all provide occasions for packaging the president.

An illustration of packaging techniques was the manner in which Richard Nixon nominated Gerald Ford to succeed Spiro Agnew as vice president in October 1973. During the speech announcing his choice of Ford, carried live by the three major television networks, Nixon never mentioned that Agnew was the first vice president in American history to resign from office because of criminal misconduct. (Agnew pleaded no contest to a criminal charge involving nonpayment of income taxes, amid extensive evidence of accepting bribes.) Instead, the president turned the occasion into a celebration—a "fiesta" in the words of CBS correspondent Dan Rather.

The president can draw upon the salience and pomp of the presidential office and thereby link up with the secular rituals of patriotic America. He issues a national proclamation on Thanksgiving, the Fourth of July, and New Year's Day. In a country without a state religion, patriotism has taken its place—with the president as high priest.[33] Another analogy, with which we

[33]Henry Fairlie develops the point in *The Kennedy Promise: The Politics of Expectation* (New York, 1973).

opened the chapter, is to be an elected monarch. One account of White House personnel enumerates

> seventy-five retainers, including forty-two mechanical and mainte-
> nance workers, thirty domestic employes, and three civil servants
> on loan from other Federal agencies. Among the seventy-five are:
> a head butler and four butlers; a chief floral designer; four
> doormen; a foreman of housemen and six housemen; six maids, a
> pantryman and a pantrywoman; a *maître d'hôtel;* a chef, an
> assistant chef, a second cook, a pastry chef, and two kitchen
> stewards; a head laundress, an assistant laundress, and a combined
> porter and laundryman. There are also a transportation specialist, a
> film projectionist, three operating engineers, and someone with the
> title of "principal foreman operating engineer."
>   Not included are extra waiters and other help recruited for
> special events, U.S. military personnel assigned to the White
> House, Secret Service agents, Navy cooks for the White House
> staff mess, fifteen gardeners, Executive Protection Service
> officers, General Service Administration employes who handle the
> West Wing business office area, and the President's executive
> staff.[34]

Scholarly writing on the president from Franklin D. Roosevelt until the early 1970s has been close to unanimous in its celebration of strong presidents. For a generation, political scientists have equated strong presidents with good and wise presidents. Theodore Sorenson, staff aide to Presidents Kennedy and Johnson, notes "A president cannot afford to be modest. No one else sits where he sits or knows all that he knows. No one else has the power to lead, to inspire, or to restrain the Congress and country. If he fails to lead, no one leads."[35] According to Richard Neustadt:

> The more determinedly a president seeks power, the more he will
> be likely to bring vigor to his clerkship. As he does so he
> contributes to the energy of government. . . . The contributions
> that a President can make to government are indispensable. . . . In
> a relative but real sense one can say of a President what Eisenhow-
> er's first Secretary of Defense once said of General Motors: what
> is good for the country is good for the President, and vice versa." [36]

[34]Dom Bonafede, "The Keeping of the President," *The Progressive,* February 1974, p. 45.
[35]Theodore E. Sorenson, *Decision-Making in the White House* (New York, 1963), p. 83.
[36]Neustadt, *Presidential Power,* p. 185.

Clinton Rossiter marvels that the presidency is "one of the few truly successful institutions created by men in their endless quest for the blessing of free government."[37] One scholar laments that the American president's power "is seldom fully available or appropriate for the worst problems he must cope with."[38] Another declares, "Measured against the opportunities, the responsibilities, and the resources of others in our political system and in other nations, the powers of the Presidency are enormous. It is only when we measure these same powers against the problems of our age that they seem puny and inadequate."[39]

Political science textbooks reflect the orientation of the majority of scholars to a strong presidency. Thomas Cronin has questioned the picture of the president presented in most textbook accounts. He finds that textbooks present

> inflated and unrealistic interpretations of presidential competence and beneficence. . . . What is needed, most texts imply, is a man of foresight to anticipate the future and the personal strength to unite us, to steel our moral will, to move the country forward and to make this country governable. The vision, and perhaps the illusion, is that if only we can identify and elect the *right* man—our loftiest aspirations can and will be accomplished.[40]

One reason many textbooks present the president in such a light, according to Cronin, is that political science courses train citizens as well as communicate truth. In unvarnished language, this amounts to deceiving students by exaggerating the merits of presidents and concealing the deficiencies of American politics.

Thanks to his vast powers and the attention lavished on him by the media, a president quickly becomes a mythical figure. Nearly any personal qualities can be made the stuff of myth. For example, it would be hard to exaggerate the contrast between John Kennedy and Gerald Ford. Yet each was mythologized after his election: Kennedy on the basis of his aristocratic manner, his dash and sparkle, and his glamorous wife; Ford (who went virtually unnoticed during twenty years in Congress) because of his homely virtues (one of which was the fact that he prepared his own breakfast). Much of the mythology surrounding presidents is

[37]Rossiter, p. 13.
[38]Louis W. Koenig, *The Chief Executive* (New York, 1968), p. 1.
[39]Nelson Polsby, *Congress and the President* (Englewood Cliffs, N.J., 1964), p. 30.
[40]Thomas E. Cronin, "The Textbook Presidency and Political Science," *Congressional Record,* October 5, 1970, S17102–03.

humbug, and there is no particular reason to exaggerate the importance of the qualities presidents actually do possess. Save for the exceptional Lincoln or Franklin Roosevelt, most presidents are quite ordinary men.

Yet the result of this mythology is that the president usually occupies a position at the top of the pantheon of American heroes. Nearly every year the president emerges as "most admired man of the year" in the annual Gallup poll survey. However, several events in the 1970s, notably the Vietnam war, inflation, and Watergate, heavily tarnished the myth of presidential perfection. Several studies have recently been published challenging the dominant view. Among those who now stress the need for limits to presidential power are historians Henry Steele Commager and Arthur Schlesinger, Jr., both of whom were among the champions of a "strong president."[41]

WATERGATE

Given the preeminent role of the president in the popular mythology that sustains established arrangements, political stability is threatened if the impression becomes widespread that a president has violated democratic procedures. Like Caesar's wife, the president must be above suspicion. Thus, selling the president *does* differ from selling toothpaste, for advertisers are expected to lie—but not presidents. It may have been Richard M. Nixon's failure to grasp this distinction that explains why even moderate and conservative groups supported his ouster in 1974. The far-flung events grouped together as Watergate represented the greatest political scandal in the history of the United States. The drama unfolded in three acts: the background, break-in at the Watergate headquarters of the Democratic National Committee, and initial cover-up; investigations of misconduct by the Senate Select Committee on Presidential Campaign Activities and by

[41]Schlesinger, *The Imperial Presidency;* Henry Steele Commager, "The Presidency After Watergate," *New York Review of Books,* October 18, 1973, pp. 49–53. Also see Fairlie, *The Kennedy Promise;* George E. Reedy, *The Twilight of the Presidency* (New York, 1970); and Tugwell and Cronin, *The Presidency Reappraised.*

special prosecutors; and the impeachment investigation by the House Judiciary Committee culminating in the forced resignation of Richard Nixon and his replacement by Gerald Ford.

Background, Break-in, and Cover-up

On the evening of June 17, 1972, a security guard noticed a door suspiciously taped open in the luxurious Washington office building where he worked. When police responded to his telephone call, they spotted lights in an eighth-floor office, where they surprised and arrested five burglars. America's greatest political scandal began with an incident outwardly no different from thousands that occur in any city every year. Except that the office was the headquarters of the Democratic National Committee, the burglars were directed by close associates of the president, and the president himself soon helped to direct a criminal conspiracy to obstruct justice and cover up responsibility for the burglary.

The series of events that came to be known as the Watergate affair (the name of the building where the break-in occurred) stretched over years. Indeed, its roots were so deep and its consequences so wide that it is hard to distinguish Watergate from the administration of Richard Nixon. During the course of the investigations, massive evidence accumulated of the abuse of federal agencies for partisan purposes, sale of political favors, use of government and campaign funds for private gain, bribery, campaign finance violations, burglary, forgery, perjury, wiretapping, and obstruction of justice; more than a dozen of the president's closest advisers (including the highest members of the White House staff, cabinet officers, and presidential campaign officials) as well as a score of lesser officials were convicted of criminal acts; and—as a result of his own personal misconduct in office—Richard Nixon became the first American president ever to be forced from office.

Soon after entering the White House in 1969, Nixon approved a plan submitted to him by a staff aide that, in the name of national security, provided for widespread domestic spying operations (including operations clearly identified as illegal). At the president's direction, and prompted by newspaper accounts of secret United States bombing missions in Cambodia that Nixon wished to conceal, the FBI had already begun wiretapping the telephones of eighteen reporters and White House officials. (Wiretaps remained on the telephones of two officials after they left government service and became active in Senator Edmund Muskie's campaign for the 1972 Democratic presidential nomination.) The FBI provided the president's political aides with wiretap reports, which they used for partisan purposes. But in 1971, after the FBI balked at participating in the overall domestic surveillance plan, Nixon created a secret White House agency, the Special Investigations Unit. Informally known as the plumbers because its purpose was ostensibly to plug security leaks, the agency was mostly financed by illegal election campaign contributions. Top White House aide John Ehrlichman was in overall charge of the plumbers. Among those hired for the unit were former CIA agent E. Howard Hunt, Jr., and former FBI agent G. Gordon Liddy, both of whom later directed the Watergate burglary.

With technical assistance and equipment that Ehrlichman ordered the CIA to provide, Hunt, Liddy, and others burglarized the office of Daniel J. Ellsberg's psychiatrist in 1971, after Ellsberg made the Pentagon Papers available to newspapers. In a secret memo, a White House aide stated that the aim of the burglary was to obtain information to discredit Ellsberg, the peace movement, the Democrats, and the press. Although the links between these groups and national security seem obscure, those in the White House (from the president down) appear to have sincerely believed that they were up against a subversive plot, which justified illegal retaliation. National security and partisan politics thus became intertwined for these men.

As the 1972 election approached, President Nixon's hope for reelection became his major concern. Again, he and his advisers appear to have believed that his reelection was necessary to save the country from Democratic-sponsored subversion. Officials in the president's campaign organization, the Committee for the Reelection of the President (CRP), developed a plan for illegal political espionage and sabotage against the Democrats, and it received the personal approval of CRP director John Mitchell, who as former attorney general had been the nation's chief law enforcement official. The goal was to throw the Democrats into disarray, discredit Muskie, and influence the nomination of a weaker candidate. Members of the White House plumbers were transferred to CRP to help. CRP funds (obtained through large, often illegal, gifts) were used to plant political spies in the organizations of the candidates for the Democratic nomination. CRP saboteurs stole records from the Democratic candidates' offices, spread scurrilous information about the candidates, disrupted their campaign activities, rigged public-opinion polls, and engaged in other "dirty tricks." John Ehrlichman repeatedly pressed the Internal Revenue Service (IRS) to investigate the tax returns of Democratic chairman Lawrence O'Brien in the hope of turning up incriminating evidence before the election.

The break-in at the Watergate was thus only one of many illegal and unethical activities sponsored by CRP and the White House. What distinguished the break-in from other illegal activities was that the Watergate burglars were caught and eventually traced to CRP and the White House, and the president subsequently attempted to cover up high-level involvement in the event. According to Jeb Magruder, CRP chief of staff, the decision to conceal the break-in was "immediate and automatic; no one ever considered that there would *not* be a cover-up."[42] Starting immediately after the arrest of the Watergate burglars, leading government officials destroyed incriminating evidence and committed perjury in interviews with FBI investigators in an attempt to conceal the origins of the break-in. An order went out from the White House to the FBI to limit its investigation on the grounds that unrelated CIA operations might be uncovered. Although at first the CIA went along with the story, this allegation was false and was repeated even after it was later denied by CIA officials. More than two years after the Watergate break-in, a trail of evidence strongly suggested that the man who ultimately directed the cover-up attempt was the president of the United States.

At first, however, the cover-up succeeded, in part because a several-hundred-thousand-dollar CRP "slush fund" was given to Watergate defendants to pay their legal costs and buy their silence. The presidential press secretary's initial characterization of the incident as a "third-rate burglary attempt" was nearly universally believed. Watergate was regarded as a "caper" by most Americans, and it failed to mar Richard Nixon's triumphal reelection in November 1972.

Nonetheless, from the very beginning, evidence began to accumulate that Watergate was far more than a harmless prank: it

[42]Jeb Stuart Magruder, "Means," *New York Times Magazine,* May 19, 1974, pp. 104, 108.

was revealed that the CRP security director was among the burglars; the electronic gear they installed suggested skilled help and ample funds; one of the burglars carried an address book containing Hunt's name and White House office address; and the bail money paid to free the defendants after their arrest was traced to CRP. Relentless investigations by two young reporters for the *Washington Post,* Carl Bernstein and Robert Woodward, and damaging information provided them by a highly-placed confidential informant (whom they nicknamed "Deep Throat") kept the memory of Watergate alive. As a result, the Senate unanimously voted in February 1973 to create the Select Committee on Presidential Campaign Activities (usually called the Senate Watergate Committee or the Ervin Committee, after its chairman, Senator Sam J. Ervin, Jr., of North Carolina) to investigate 1972 campaign irregularities.

In March 1973, two major breakthroughs occurred that led to a veritable explosion of Watergate into public consciousness. As the result of pressure by John J. Sirica, the federal judge presiding at the trial of the Watergate burglars, one of the defendants finally admitted CRP involvement in the planning and cover-up of the Watergate affair. Attention was directed even higher—to the White House itself—by the admission of L. Patrick Gray, III, Nixon's nominee as director of the FBI, that presidential counsel John W. Dean, III, had "probably lied" to FBI agents during the post-Watergate FBI investigation. (Gray himself admitted to destroying incriminating evidence in the Watergate affair at the direction of White House aides, a criminal offense, and he withdrew from consideration as FBI director.)

Investigating the Cover-up

Public outrage at these revelations forced the appointment of a special prosecutor for Watergate-related crimes in May 1973, and Archibald Cox, a Harvard law professor chosen for the position, immediately began an intensive investigation. But it was the Ervin Committee hearings in the summer of 1973 that riveted public attention on Watergate and transformed it into a major political crisis. Hoping for lenient treatment from federal prosecutors in return for providing evidence, a parade of White House and CRP officials testified in detail (before a nationwide television audience) about their part in Watergate.

The most serious allegation made at the Watergate hearings

came from John Dean. Whereas other witnesses pointed to wrongdoing among presidential staff members and other high officials, Dean charged wrongdoing by the president himself. He disclosed the existence of lists of political enemies drawn up by the White House against whom the president ordered retaliation by government agencies. (At one point, White House transcripts of presidential conversations show Nixon asking Dean: "Do you need any IRS stuff?") As for the Watergate break-in, Dean described conversations he held with the president that directly implicated Nixon in the cover-up and squarely contradicted Nixon's repeated assertions of ignorance concerning high-level involvement in the affair. If Dean's testimony was accurate, the president of the United States was part of a criminal conspiracy to obstruct justice.

It was Dean's word against Nixon's—until, on July 16, 1973, a junior White House aide dropped a bombshell at the Watergate hearings when he revealed that, in 1971, President Nixon had secretly initiated the practice of tape recording all conversations in the president's office. From that moment, the Ervin Committee and the special prosecutor sought to obtain the tapes in order to examine them for incriminating evidence. At one stroke, there appeared to be a way to determine the truthfulness of Dean's allegations.

But for one thing: the president refused to release the Watergate tapes, arguing that they contained sensitive material bearing on national security and that the separation of powers, executive privilege, and the need for confidentiality of presidential conversations justified withholding the tapes. Furthermore, he asserted, the tapes backed up his claim of innocence anyway, so no useful purpose could be served by releasing them. Cox sought to get the tapes by issuing a subpoena against the president (the first issued in over a century) and sued in court to have it enforced. Nixon ordered Cox to stop pressing court action. When Cox refused, Nixon fired him on Saturday, October 20, 1973, and abolished the office of special prosecutor. The "Saturday night massacre" set off a wave of protest that forced the president to comply with the federal court order Cox had obtained to turn the tapes over to the court. Nixon also bowed to public and congressional pressure and appointed a new special prosecutor, Texas lawyer Leon Jaworski. Jaworski soon pressed for additional tapes and, when the president again refused, Jaworski followed Cox's example and sued the president.

Impeachment and Resignation

The Saturday night massacre led congressional leaders to initiate the impeachment process, the first time that Congress had undertaken a presidential impeachment inquiry since 1868, when President Andrew Johnson was impeached. Impeachment and conviction, which results in the president's removal from office, is a cumbersome process: impeachment occurs if the House Judiciary Committee votes to recommend articles of impeachment to the full House of Representatives and the House approves by a majority vote. Conviction and removal from office require a trial by the Senate and a two-thirds vote of the Senate for conviction.

Different views exist on the exact meaning of the phrase *Bribery, or other high Crimes and Misdemeanors,* the grounds specified in the Constitution for impeachment and conviction. A broad view is that impeachable offenses include grave violations of the president's oath of office and his misuse of power even where he has not specifically broken criminal laws. A narrow view, defended by Nixon, is that impeachment is possible only if actual evidence exists of serious criminal misconduct by the president—the "smoking pistol." A middle view on impeachment, formulated in 1974 by a Republican member of the House Judiciary Committee, is that an impeachable offense is an extremely serious offense against the political process or the Constitution and one that is recognized to be such by a broad majority of citizens.

During the spring of 1974, the Judiciary Committee investigated allegations of possible presidential wrongdoing, including the Watergate cover-up, the abuse of federal agencies by the president, irregularities in Nixon's income-tax situation (he was assessed nearly one-half million dollars in back taxes in 1973, and the possibility existed of tax fraud), his unauthorized bombing of Cambodia, and possible favors granted ITT and the dairy lobby for their campaign contributions. The presidential tapes continued to be at the center of the controversy, for many of the charges might be proved or laid to rest with evidence in the tapes. The Judiciary Committee's attempts to obtain the tapes proved only slightly more successful than other investigative bodies, despite the fact that the Constitution gives the House of Representatives sole authority to impeach and that constitutional scholars consider that an impeachment inquiry takes precedence over other claims. In April 1974, in an attempt to engineer a compromise with the committee and quiet the charge that he was trying to suppress incriminating evidence, the president dramatically released censored transcripts of presidential conversations. The transcripts were incomplete and peppered with deletions (for example, at one point, the White House transcript has the president saying: "(expletive deleted)! (unintelligible)"). Both the committee and special prosecutor continued to press for the actual tapes.

Yet even the mutilated version released by the White House contained enough evidence of presidential misconduct to add fuel to the impeachment flames. The transcripts showed a president who was cavalier about the law, deceitful, and vulgar; who calmly discussed how to commit perjury; and who ordered the payment of "hush money" to cover up the investigation. Here, for example, in a discussion with Dean and chief of staff H. R. Haldeman on March 21, 1973, is how the president concocted national security as a pretext for the burglary of the office of Dr. Ellsberg's psychiatrist:

P. What is the answer on this? How you keep it out, I don't know. You can't keep it out if Hunt talks. You see the point is irrelevant. It has gotten to this point—
D. You might put it on a national security grounds basis.
H. It absolutely was.
D. and say that this was—
H. (unintelligible)—CIA—
P. National security. We had to get information for national security grounds.
D. Then the question is, why didn't the CIA do it or why didn't the FBI do it?
P. Because we had to do it on a confidential basis.
H. Because we were checking them.
P. Neither could be trusted. . . . With the bombing thing coming out and everything coming out, the whole thing was national security.
D. I think we could get by on that.

Regarding the payment of hush money to Howard Hunt, the following discussions occurred on March 21, 1973:

P. How much money do you need?
D. I would say these people are going to cost a million dollars over the next two years.

P. We could get that. On the money, if you need the money you could get that. You could get a million dollars. You could get it in cash. I know where it could be gotten. It is not easy, but it could be done. But the question is who the hell would handle it? Any ideas on that?

*   *   *

P. Just looking at the immediate problem, don't you think you have to handle Hunt's financial situation damn soon? . . . It seems to me we have to keep the cap on the bottle that much, or we don't have any options.

*   *   *

P. That's why for your immediate things you have no choice but to come up with the $120,000, or whatever it is. Right?
D. That's right.
P. Would you agree that that's the prime thing that you damn well better get that done?
D. Obviously he [Hunt] ought to be given some signal anyway.
P (Explotive deleted), get it. [When the actual tapes were eventually made available, Nixon's complete statement was: "You better damn well get that done but fast. . . . For Christ's sake, get it."]

In a conversation with John Mitchell (on a portion of the tapes that were not released at first and were later provided by accident), Nixon declared: "I want you all to stonewall it, let them plead the Fifth Amendment, cover up or anything else, if it'll save it—save the [cover-up] plan. That's the whole point."

The tapes reveal that Nixon worked ceaselessly to suppress the true story. He invented pretexts for concealing evidence, counseled how to evade investigators' questions, and fabricated a story that would cast him in the best light. (At one point he asked Ehrlichman and Haldeman: "How has the scenario worked out? . . . How do I get credit for getting Magruder to the [witness] stand?" In fact, Nixon had no part in Magruder's decision to testify.)

Following release of the tapes, even conservative sectors, including newspapers that had supported Mr. Nixon's reelection in 1972, called for his resignation or impeachment.

After examining the mountain of evidence gathered from the Ervin Committee hearings, the White House tapes, and other sources, the House Judiciary Committee voted three articles of impeachment charging the president with violating his oath to defend the Constitution and his constitutional duty to take care that the laws are faithfully executed. The first article charged the president with participating in a cover-up plan to obstruct the government's investigation of the Watergate break-in. Included in the charge were allegations of false or misleading statements, withholding evidence, counseling perjury, interfering with government investigative agencies, and approving the payments of money to buy the silence of witnesses. The second article accused the president of using the Internal Revenue Service to violate the constitutional rights of citizens, ordering the FBI to carry out electronic surveillance unrelated to national security or law enforcement, suppressing incriminating evidence, and interfering with the lawful operation of executive agencies. The third article of impeachment charged the president with failing to provide evidence subpoenaed by the House Judiciary Committee in the course of its impeachment inquiry. The articles were voted by bipartisan majorities of congressmen from all sections of the country, with the vote reaching twenty-eight to ten on the second article, alleging abuse of presidential power (all twenty-one Democrats combining with seven of the seventeen Republicans). The final report of the Judiciary Committee unanimously charged that Mr. Nixon was responsible for "deliberate, contrived, continued deception of the American people." Obstruction of justice, abuse of power, and withholding evidence: these were weighty charges to be brought against a president by moderate congressmen, including members of his own party.

Yet, for some people, lingering doubt remained of the president's personal responsibility for the illegal actions committed by his associates. However imprudent or mistaken the president had been, did this justify impeachment and removal from office? Diehard opponents of impeachment insisted on the necessity of incontrovertible evidence—the "smoking pistol." Then, days after the Judiciary Committee vote, it was found. The new evidence came from tapes subpoenaed by special prosecutor Jaworski. Following the precedent set by Cox, Jaworski had sued in federal court for additional tapes. In July 1974, the Supreme Court unanimously decided in Jaworski's favor against the president's claim of executive privilege. To withhold the tapes after a definitive ruling by the Supreme Court would have meant certain impeachment and conviction.

Nixon's determined, year-long resistance to making the tapes available became understandable when a transcript was released of a conversation between Nixon and Haldeman on June 23, 1972, only days after the Watergate break-in. Despite Nixon's attempt to explain away the evidence on this tape by invoking faulty recollection, even he was forced to admit that it contradicted his repeated public statements. Here is a portion of the conversation:

H. You know the Democratic break-in thing. We're back in the problem area because the FBI is not under control. . . . The way to handle this now is to have [deputy CIA director] Walters call [acting FBI director] Gray and just say, "Stay to hell out of this—this is, ah, business here we don't want you to go any further on it."

P. What about Pat Gray? You mean Pat Gray doesn't want to?

H. Pat does want to. He doesn't know how to, and he doesn't have any basis for doing it.

* * *

H. And you seem to think the thing to do is get them [the FBI] to stop?

P. Right, fine.

The tape gave the lie to Nixon's many assertions that he had not learned of the cover-up until nine months after it occurred and that his main aim had always been to make sure the truth came out. Nixon admitted that the tapes proved his deception when he repeatedly denied any involvement in the cover-up. But he argued that this did not justify his removal from office.

Few agreed with his position. The president's support, even among his attorneys and staunch defenders, melted away. The Republicans on the House Judiciary Committee who had voted against impeachment announced they would support Nixon's impeachment in the full House deliberations. Delegations of senior White House officials and influential Republican congressmen as well as Secretary of State Kissinger reported to Nixon that his impeachment and removal from office were now a certainty. Rather than suffer the disgrace of being the first American president convicted of impeachment charges, Nixon became the first American president to resign from office.

When, on August 8, 1974, Nixon announced his decision to the largest television audience in history (135 million), he explained his resignation merely by noting that his "political base" in Congress had eroded. What Nixon failed to point out—possibly even failed to realize, so isolated had he become—was that his political base vanished because of firm evidence of criminal wrongdoing. Nonetheless, for most Americans, the president stood exposed for what he had belligerently denied he was in an earlier television address—a crook. In a way very different from what he had promised in his 1968 campaign slogan, Richard Nixon had been able to "bring us together."

The transition occurred smoothly and rapidly. Vice President Gerald Ford, the man Nixon had picked to replace Spiro Agnew, took office on August 9, 1974. Although Ford was the first president not to be elected by the people, and his record as congressional leader was undistinguished, he seemed a decent, honest man; he was greeted by a groundswell of support.

For several weeks Watergate was absent from the front pages of the newspapers, and the transition was hailed by a *New York Times* editorial as "a triumph for America." But Watergate was too great a political scandal to disappear without a trace. It was revived by President Ford's unexpected announcement in September 1974 that he was granting Mr. Nixon a "full, free and absolute pardon" for any federal criminal offenses Mr. Nixon may have committed while president. Among the possible crimes covered by the pardon were Mr. Nixon's participation in the conspiracy to obstruct justice in the Watergate cover-up; his responsibility for irregularities in his income tax returns and real estate and business affairs; his use of government agencies for reprisals against political enemies; his role in the Ellsburg, ITT, and milk cases; and other activities by Mr. Nixon that special prosecutor Jaworski indicated were under investigation.

Mr. Nixon's timely resignation headed off impeachment and conviction by Congress. Once he was pardoned before even being indicted and tried in a court of law, no authoritative body would pass judgment on his misconduct. Thus, although Mr. Nixon's misdeeds were apparent, it would be more difficult to refute his contention that he was responsible only for what he termed (in a statement he issued after accepting the pardon) "mistakes and misjudgments." Some interpreted the pardon as a further attempt to cover up the Nixon administration's wrongdoing, a cover-up that continued long after he left office. An additional consequence of the pardon was to dispel any illusion that the simple personal qualities of Mr. Ford signified an end to the imperial presidential style.

The Significance of Watergate

The primary cause of Nixon's downfall was his criminal misconduct and abuse of power—the charges forming the basis for the impeachment articles voted by the House Judiciary Committee. Cynical critics to the contrary, President Nixon's actions were not typical of American politics. Although earlier presidents can be accused of many of the charges laid at Nixon's door—lying to Congress and the American people, rewarding political contributors with ambassadorships, and using government agencies to hound opponents—the cumulative total of the excesses committed by Nixon during his presidency was unprecedented, consisting not of just one or two misdeeds but a vast web of political and criminal misconduct. Nonetheless, chance also played a role in Nixon's departure, starting with the accidental discovery of an inept burglary and culminating in irrefutable proof of presidential deceit.

But there were other, less obvious reasons for Nixon's downfall. Once public confidence in Nixon dropped below a certain point, his ability to legitimize established arrangements disappeared. The danger arose that the mass electorate would become openly disaffected with the whole political system. It may have been partly for this reason that even former supporters of the president concluded he should leave. By early July 1974 (before the Judiciary Committee vote and the most damaging revelations), nearly half the business executives polled in a *New York Times* survey favored Nixon's impeachment.

A related reason businessmen began to welcome the prospect of impeachment was that the president became so preoccupied with his personal defense that he neglected the major functions of government. Just as an automobile needs a driver to keep it going, so the corporate complex needs a full-time manager. Four-fifths of the businessmen surveyed felt that Nixon's handling of economic matters was seriously impaired by Watergate.[43]

If the causes of Nixon's downfall are manifold, what about its significance? Many argued that the Watergate affair served to purify American politics and demonstrated that even the highest political officials cannot transgress the law with impunity. In the words of a *New York Times* editorial of July 28, 1974, Watergate showed that elected representatives could insure "the restoration

[43] *New York Times*, July 12, 1974.

of lawfulness and moral responsibility in the highest office in the land." Henry Steele Commager declared that the affair

> demonstrated to the world and, let us hope, to future generations that the Constitution is alive and well, that it can be adapted to the exigencies of governance, and that in an emergency an enlightened and determined democracy can protect and defend its principles, its honor, and its heritage. [44]

In his inaugural address, President Ford echoed the prevailing mood when he proudly stated, "our Constitution works, our great Republic is a Government of laws and not of men."

Watergate may have slowed the drift of power to the presidency, narrowed the use of executive privilege, limited the use of federal agencies for partisan purposes, updated procedures for dealing with abuses of power by elected officials, and strengthened confidence in the legitimacy, responsiveness, and efficacy of American democracy.

Yet there was something bizarre in regarding Watergate as "a triumph for the system."[45] *New York Times* columnist Russell Baker was among those who replied, "It really didn't work."

> The outcome produced by the system is a political absurdity in a nation boastful of its democracy. What do we have as the logical, legal product of the system's working? A President who has never run for national office and who, when his party last worried about going to the people, was not even considered a useful candidate for the dim office of vice-president.
>
> The system left the choosing of this new president to his predecessor, a man driven from office by bipartisan suspicion of felonious conduct, a man whose previous selection at the vice-president shop had earlier been driven from office for taking cash under the desk and cheating on his income tax. . . .
>
> Under the system, we have been cheated in a presidential election, submitted to nearly two years of government by men of criminal productivity and encouraged to feel delighted with the prospect of two more years of government by men we have not elected.
>
> If your car worked as well as the system, you would have had it in the shop ages ago, if not on the used car lot.[46]

Rather than taking pride in the fact that the abuses of Watergate

---

[44]Henry Steele Commager, "The Constitution is Alive and Well," *New York Times*, August 11, 1974.

[45]*Time*, August 19, 1974, p. 3.

[46]Russell Baker, "It Really Didn't Work," *New York Times*, August 19, 1974.

were finally checked, one might ask why they were allowed to occur in the first place—and to go unchecked for so long. Rather than extolling the massive effort to remedy Watergate, one might ask why so much less effort is directed to remedy inequality, poverty, and other injustices in America.

There are a number of reasons for skepticism about the long-range benefits accruing from Watergate. Although the excesses represented by Watergate were put to a stop, the routine political activities that made Watergate possible were not. While illegal surveillance of the Democratic National Committee was condemned, no comparable outcry ever greeted the wiretapping of new left and black militant organizations, and little stands in the way of their continued surveillance and repression. Political money continues to play a leading role in elections. Government agencies continue to favor dominant interests. Future presidents will take care to act legally—or at least to leave no incriminating evidence of their misdeeds. But the imperial president remains a key feature of the corporate complex.

Watergate represented a crisis of procedural, not substantive, democracy. The Watergate investigations were concerned with the legality of political contributions from ITT and the milk lobby in return for favors, not with the routine exchange of favors and benefits between giant corporations and the government; with the abuse of IRS tax audits and confidential information, not with the gross inequities of the entire tax system; with the secrecy and deceit involved in Nixon's order to bomb Cambodia, not with the destruction of innocent people. (Indeed, the House Judiciary Committee rejected recommending the ITT and milk cases and Nixon's bombing of Cambodia as grounds for impeachment.) Political theorist Sheldon Wolin points out:

> The system was successful because it kept the issue of Nixon's removal within the narrowest possible legal bounds. Beginning with the investigations of the Ervin committee, continuing through the House [Judiciary] committee's debates on the articles of impeachment, and persisting in the present efforts to protect Nixon from prosecution, there has been an unrelenting pressure to confine the issues to legal categories, the hearings to courtroom norms, and the abuses to the standards of the criminal law. The pressures came not only from the President's lawyers but from congressmen and senators as well. They worked to prevent a broad political debate about our recent past and the continuing crisis in our national life. . . . It would be foolish to contend that this

system has stage-managed the recent spectacle of Watergate; but it is correct to say that it succeeded in establishing limits to the controversy and controlling its effects. [47]

Thus, Watergate may have strengthened the established system and weakened the prospects for democratic change. Nixon's resignation and the criminal penalties meted out to his associates conveyed the comforting illusion that America had put its political house in order. A call frequently heard in the period following Watergate was the need for unity. (The cover of *Time* magazine's post-resignation issue carried the headline, "The Healing Begins.") But unity and "healing" in this context mean supporting the corporate complex—for change requires division and struggle. Watergate illustrates the resilience of the system and its ability to tolerate and absorb criticism and yet emerge unscathed.

That Watergate partly served to bolster established political institutions should not obscure its role in demystifying American politics. The late Earl Warren, former chief justice, commented on Watergate, "The scandal has shaken the faith of people, not only in the individuals involved, but also [in] the procedures which brought them to their high places."[48]

The televised Ervin Committee hearings and the House Judiciary Committee deliberations, the constant revelations by the media of official wrongdoing, and the publication of the White House tapes provided a unique education in the seamy side of American politics. Americans were allowed backstage and witnessed a president who used profanity, plotted how to mislead the people, and was cynical, shallow, and corrupt. The pardon granted Mr. Nixon suggested a double standard of justice: one for the few in high places, another for most Americans. In an editorial of May 12, 1974, the *New York Times* lamented, "The full damage that [the tapes] have done to the Office of the Presidency . . . is incalculable." It will be difficult in the future to package the president in sacred garb.

The reverberations of Watergate continued long after it had ceased to be the major news of the day; its ultimate signficance will not be known for many years. At least three possible

[47]Sheldon S. Wolin, "From Jamestown to San Clemente," *New York Review of Books*, September 19, 1974, p. 6.
[48]*New York Times*, May 22, 1974.

outcomes can be discerned. The effect of Watergate may be to strengthen popular support for established political institutions; it may heighten popular cynicism, apathy, and despair regarding the prospects for political change; or it may facilitate a movement to attack the deeper problems that barely surfaced in the discussions about Watergate by the media and political officials.

patterns
of
representation

8

competition without representation: political parties and elections

Presidential elections are reported more extensively than virtually any other event in the entire gamut of American politics. Television coverage begins years before the nominating conventions, with endless speculation about the prospects of rivals for the nomination in the two major parties. The conventions and the presidential campaigns are televised in exhaustive detail. Yet the publicity given a presidential campaign is out of all proportion to the election's importance. In terms of structural stability and change, little rides on the outcome of American elections.

One of the central features of American politics this book is attempting to analyze concerns the coexistence of legal equality and procedural democracy in the political sphere, and substantive inequality of resources—economic, political, and social—possessed by different groups of Americans. Elections are the foremost institution of procedural democracy. Citizens are presumably able to elect representatives who would attempt to democratize structural arrangements. Yet they do not do so. Instead, voters regularly elect representatives who tolerate the persistence of deep-rooted inequality.

In order to understand why, an examination of the American electoral process must be broadened to include political parties. The significance of elections depends on the nature and the extent of the alternatives offered to voters and how the alternatives get organized. This in turn requires analyzing the central role of political parties in nominating candidates for office, developing policies, and thereby organizing electoral choice.

One reason for the failure of procedural democracy to alter (or even challenge) structural inequality is that political parties do not offer viable alternatives to the status quo. The two parties are more similar in their policies than they are different. In the twentieth century, with the partial exception of the New Deal, both parties have been united in their support for overall structural arrangements built around corporate capitalism. Conflict between the parties has concerned relatively minor matters, including the rivalry of candidates for office, the differing tactics each party advocates to achieve the same objective of maintaining and stabilizing conditions favorable to corporate dominance, and the marginal benefits each party promises its slightly different constituency.

In rare cases, rival presidential candidates may advocate quite different policies. In 1972, Democratic presidential candidate George McGovern proposed reducing military spending by 25 percent and providing a guaranteed income to all Americans. These goals, although hardly radical, represented a departure from traditional government policies.

The differences between candidates should not be exaggerated, however. Once elected, presidents usually moderate their campaign pledges; hence their election stands are but an imperfect guide to their later actions. One of the sharpest contrasts between candidates occurred in 1964, in regard to the Vietnam policies of Lyndon B. Johnson and Barry Goldwater. Johnson urged moderation and restraint and sharply attacked Goldwater's proposal to escalate the war by aerial attack of North Vietnam. Yet, as the Pentagon Papers later revealed, at the very moment Johnson was criticizing Goldwater, he was planning to escalate the war precisely as Goldwater proposed.

However, even in cases where candidates are virtually indistinguishable from each other, elections are not trivial. Their significance lies in the fact that they encourage the belief (part truth mixed with a good dose of illusion) that established arrangements are freely chosen by the American people and serve their interests. A vote for a candidate represents more than an expression of confidence in a person: it symbolizes an expression of confidence in the *system* of parties, elections, and, ultimately, the American political structure. As political scientist Murray Edelman points out, political parties and elections "quiet resentments and doubts about particular political acts, reaffirm belief in the fundamental rationality and democratic character of the system, and fix conforming habits of future behavior."[1]

As described in earlier chapters, there is a fundamental class cleavage in American society. But this cleavage is not reflected within the party system. Only about 55 to 60 percent of the adult population go to the polls in a typical presidential election. Even fewer vote in off-year elections, when there is no presidential contest. Many of those who do not vote represent the subordinate groups in American society. Among the ranks of nonvoters are found a disproportionate number of blacks, surplus labor, elderly, uneducated, and poor. Political scientist E. E. Schattschneider has called nonvoting

> by a wide margin the most important feature of the whole system, the key to understanding the composition of American politics. . . . It is profoundly characteristic of the behavior of the more fortunate strata of the community that responsibility for widespread nonparticipation is attributed wholly to the ignorance, indifference and shiftlessness of the people. This has always been the rationalization used to justify the exclusion of the lower classes from any political system. There is a better explanation. Abstention reflects the suppression of the options and alternatives that reflect the needs of the nonparticipants.[2]

We suggest that the minor differences separating one party from the other are less significant than the cleavage that pits the voters of *both* parties against nonvoters.

Because of the way political parties are organized and financed, their influence is usually exerted to anchor the political support and loyalty of those Americans who participate. Two

[1]Murray Edelman, *The Symbolic Uses of Politics* (Urbana, Ill., 1964), p. 17.
[2]E. E. Schattschneider, *The Semi-Sovereign People* (New York, 1960), pp. 103–05.

political scientists observe that the long-range effect of elections in the United States "is to stabilize the political order."[3] Yet, since there are growing tensions and conflicts among political participants, the parties' success is by no means certain. In fact, there are signs that the parties are increasingly less effective in maintaining a faithful following among the electorate.

POLITICAL PARTIES AS DEMOCRATIC FORCES

Parties were once a democratizing force in the United States. During the late eighteenth century, when other nations were governed by narrowly-based oligarchies, political parties originated in the United States and contributed four democratizing elements that leavened traditional political arrangements.

American political parties expanded political *participation,* both in the choosing of government officials and in the ruling process itself. Parties first mobilized eligible voters in the period before the Civil War, when restrictions on the suffrage were (compared to other countries) few; and they helped break down the deferential system of politics in which only the socially privileged and wealthy could participate.

This does not mean to suggest that America started out as a pure democracy. For several decades after the Constitution was ratified, the suffrage extended only to white male landowners. In most states, the poor were excluded from participation by a property qualification until the 1820s, and slaves, Indians, and women were excluded even longer. Moreover, the sphere of electoral politics was limited. Within the new federal government, the only officials chosen by popular elections were members of the House of Representatives. Senators and the president were indirectly elected: senators, by state legislatures, which were themselves chosen by popular election; the president, by members of the electoral college, who were also chosen by state legislatures.

And yet, despite numerous qualifications, the United States had the first popular government in the world, and popular

[3]Kenneth Prewitt and Alan Stone, *The Ruling Elites: Elite Theory, Power, and American Democracy* (New York, 1973), p. 179.

interest in politics ran high.[4] In the presidential election of 1840 (which by then was an election where the outcome in the electoral college directly reflected the popular vote), 80 percent of the eligible voters turned out to vote, a figure far higher than current turnout rates.[5]

Political parties represented *contending social and political forces*. By linking groups that were geographically separated, parties made it possible for people to organize and defend their interests within the new national arena. This did not happen overnight. The first national governments were physically and functionally remote from popular forces. It was not until political parties extended their organization to the grass roots—beginning in Andrew Jackson's time (1820s to 1840s)—that one can begin to speak of a national constituency.

American political parties institutionalized *opposition* to the government. In other countries, the men holding public office might organize themselves into a group. But what made the American party system unique was that officeholders were organized into *several* groups, that these groups developed links to popular forces outside the government, and that one of these early groups (the Republicans under Jefferson's leadership) represented an open, organized opposition to the government's policies.

However, neither of the first two party groupings accepted the legitimacy of opposing parties. As historian Richard Hofstadter notes, "the creators of the first American party system on both sides, Federalists and Republicans, were men who looked upon parties as sores on the body politic."[6] In fact, the Federalists, the first party to rule, tried to destroy Republican opposition by passing the Alien and Sedition laws. The Sedition Act made it a crime to express criticism of the government, and the Federalists used it to indict the editors or publishers of fourteen major Republican newspapers. (Their humorless approach can be inferred from their indicting, convicting, and fining one editor "for

---

[4]The French Revolution of 1789 ushered in universal manhood suffrage earlier than in the United States. But Napoleon's coup d'état and the Restoration ended France's brief democratic experiment.

[5]William Nisbet Chambers, "Party Development and the American Mainstream," in William Nisbet Chambers and Walter Dean Burnham, eds., *The American Party Systems: Stages of Political Development* (New York, 1967), p. 12.

[6]Richard Hofstadter, *The Idea of a Party System: The Rise of Legitimate Opposition in the United States, 1780–1840* (Berkeley, Calif., 1969), p. 2.

expressing the wish that the wad of a cannon discharged as a salute to President Adams had hit the broadest part of the President's breeches."[7]) The Federalists not only failed to destroy the Republicans, however, but the attempt cost them office—they were turned out in 1800 when Jefferson was elected president—and was influential in leading to their ultimate disappearance from the political scene.

Parties facilitated *alternation* in office. The replacement of Federalist President John Adams by Thomas Jefferson, a Republican, was the first case of peaceful transference of power from one party to another as a result of election returns. Parties thus made it possible for the principle of majority rule to determine the composition of the government.

On the whole, American political parties and elections in the early years represented a substantial advance in democratic practice over other countries. But what was a democratic—and even influential—system in one epoch may not be equally so in another. During the last century, political parties became both less democratic and less influential as forces affecting the course of American politics.

THE DOMINANT LIBERAL TRADITION

During the course of American history, the party system has rarely been the only forum for the expression of political conflict, nor has it always been the major forum. As political scientist Robert Dahl points out, "From the very first years under the new Constitution American political life has undergone, about once every generation, a conflict over national politics of extreme severity."[8] In addition to the Civil War, when there was outright warfare between opponents, conflict in the United States has found expression through protest activity, political violence, demonstrations, and strikes. Clashes have occurred among or-

[7]Henry Jones Ford, *The Rise and Growth of American Politics* (New York, 1898), p. 112, cited in V. O. Key, Jr., *Politics, Parties, & Pressure Groups* (New York, 1964), p. 205.
[8]Robert A. Dahl, *Political Oppositions in Western Democracies* (New Haven, Conn., 1966), p. 50.

ganized agencies, such as interest groups, business organizations, and labor unions; and among regional, ideological, and ethnic groups. A more violent form of conflict has been the official repression of Indians and the generations of subjugation of blacks.

Yet the extremes of conflict that characterize other countries have been less apparent in the United States. With the important exception of the Civil War, the United States has not experienced the violence of coups d'état, such as frequently occur in Latin America and Africa; or the bitter clash of aristocracy, urban proletariat, bourgeoisie, and Church, such as Europe has undergone.

In contrast to Europe, certain conditions in early America fostered relative equality, discouraged class consciousness, reduced the need for violent disruptions, and provided a framework for a democratic party system. Foremost was the lack of a powerful hereditary aristocracy. Alexis de Tocqueville, a French visitor to the United States in the 1830s, observed in his classic *Democracy in America* that Americans were born equal rather than having to fight a revolution to achieve equality. Men were not frozen into a fixed station, in which they grew up, lived, and expected to die; what counted was individual effort. According to sociologist Seymour M. Lipset, in *The First New Nation,* the leading cultural values in America came to be individualism, equality, and achievement. A second condition that differentiated the United States from Europe was the pluralism of American society, which embraced a gamut of occupational, regional, ethnic, and religious subcultures; encouraged toleration; and splintered power. Third, unlike most Europeans, Americans had a way of escaping from the old life and finding a new one: they could move. Land was plentiful and cheap, and the lure of the frontier was strong.

Lastly was the fact that suffrage requirements were minimal. In eighteenth-century Europe, workers, merchants, and entrepreneurs were legally excluded from political power. As a result, they organized their own political parties, which were illegal and revolutionary, operating against (not within) the political system. In America, where universal male suffrage was achieved before the industrial revolution, political parties were less class oriented and represented coalitions of social, economic, and regional interests. Groups did not have to struggle to gain admission to the system: because of procedural democracy, they were already inside the political arena. At that time, parties were a reasonably accurate reflection of the country's social structure. However, as class divisions hardened after the industrial revolution, American parties became less and less representative of the existing social structure.

The same conditions that acted to moderate conflict in the United States contributed to the acceptance of a basic ideology, which political theorist Louis Hartz has called the liberal tradition.[9] This ideology was based on the views of English philosopher John Locke, whose writings strongly influenced America's early political leaders. Locke believed that individual freedom flourished through private property and limited government, a view ideally suited to the simple conditions of early America. The new order was capitalist and, for Locke (and for Marx, too, when he described the break from feudalism) it represented a radical new step in history: a means of freeing men from restrictive feudal ties and unleashing a burst of individual creative energy.

Capitalism was not seriously challenged in the United States, as it was by socialists and anarchists in Europe and Chartists in England. Nor—again in contrast to Europe—was there a powerful preexisting conservative establishment consisting of the Church, the army, and the aristocracy to stand in capitalism's way.

Procedural democracy came early in the United States in part because of the triumph of capitalism. From its origins, capitalism went hand in hand with legal equality. The framers of the Constitution used procedural democracy to protect the interests of private property. In contrast to the feudal system of fixed status and obligations, capitalism required legal equality and freedom: the freedom of citizens to acquire private property, choose an occupation, and sell their labor for a wage; to enter the market, produce whatever was demanded, and buy and sell the commodities thereby produced. But freedom under capitalism was based on acquisitive, individualistic, and negative values: the freedom to work—not the freedom from hunger. (Indeed, if people in a capitalist system were not hungry, they would not choose to accept arduous work.) The freedom to acquire material goods was limited to those who could afford to pay. In the

[9]Louis Hartz, *The Liberal Tradition in America* (New York, 1955).

political realm, freedom meant the right to participate—so long as capitalist production was not threatened. When some state and municipal governments sponsored anticapitalist reforms in the late nineteenth century, the reforms were declared unconstitutional by the Supreme Court on the grounds that they infringed on the freedom of contract and the rights of private property. In the nineteenth century, government power was used to restrict the freedom of workers to organize and challenge capitalism. Thus, freedom was defined by popular ideology and government in capitalist terms. Freedom and equality in the political sphere were linked to a lack of freedom and to inequality in the economic sphere.

· So long as agriculture predominated, manufacturing was rudimentary, and there were relatively few extremes of wealth, capitalism and procedural democracy could be defended as having expanded freedom in comparison with the feudal system. But when conditions changed toward the end of the nineteenth century—the end of the frontier, an increase in population, technological innovations, and the development of corporate capitalism—procedural democracy and capitalism became the means to justify not freedom but a new oppression.

THE EVOLUTION OF POLITICAL CLEAVAGES

As the United States changed, one can distinguish several periods, each characterized by the dominance of a particular cluster of economic and regional forces. Such forces are usually grouped within a ruling political party and opposed by a minority party containing groups and regions on the defensive. The cleavage between parties both shaped and reflected the major conflicts within the society at that time.

Most periods are characterized by stable party competition. But, as one scholar points out, " 'Politics as usual' in the United States is not politics as always."[10] At periodic intervals, drastic

---

[10]Walter Dean Burnham, "The End of American Party Politics," in Joseph Fiszman and Gene S. Poschman, eds., *The American Political Arena: Selected Readings*, 3d ed., (Boston, 1972), p. 250.

realignments have occurred within the constellation of social, ideological, economic, and regional forces.

When a major new crisis—such as a depression—arises, it pushes older, established political issues into the background and creates new political alignments. The realignment ushers in a new period, dominated by new social forces that are polarized around the issue. Often a new majority party comes into power. However, the ruling party in one period may succeed in dominating a realignment by "capturing" the new social forces and issues. This happened to the Republican party in 1896 and may be occurring under Democratic direction at the present time.

This model provides a useful way to organize the discussion of changing political cleavages in the United States, if one keeps in mind that, like other mediations, the party system does not reflect structural interests accurately because it overrepresents dominant social groups and underrepresents subordinate groups. To summarize what follows: the history of the American party system consists of the early defeat of the Federalists, followed by the dominance of Jefferson's Republican party (the forerunner of today's Democratic party), whose support rested on Southern and agrarian interests. Following the Civil War, control shifted back to the North and, with greater velocity during the industrial revolution at the end of the nineteenth century, to commercial and then corporate power. The Republican party (as it is still known today) held office nearly without interruption from the Civil War to the New Deal by making itself the spokesman for ascendant industrialism and corporate capitalism.

The New Deal represented another major shift, with the formation of a majority coalition within the Democratic party consisting of organized labor, ethnic and urban groups, and the South. Currently, this coalition has been torn by new social tensions, and there is evidence both of the emergence of a new constellation of forces and of a general decline in the parties' control over the electorate.

The Founding Period Until the Civil War

The first broad cleavage pitted mercantile, financial, and manufacturing interests, which were centered in the North and formed the backbone of the Federalist party under Alexander Hamilton's leadership, against agrarian, planter, and small landowning interests, which were concentrated in the South and West and grouped in the Republican party led by Jefferson.

The two parties had different views of government, in line with their different constituencies. The Federalists favored a strong national government acting to develop the country's economy. They sponsored tariffs (beneficial to industry), public roads and canals (which increased commerce), and the creation of a national bank (helpful for financial interests). The Republicans, responsive to their agrarian constituents, favored low taxes and simple frugal government, and they were distrustful of a strong national government as potentially tyrannical.

Yet party differences should not be magnified. Both parties were true to the Lockean liberal tradition described earlier in this chapter. And, once in office, Jefferson's actions belied his earlier philosophy. In keeping with the Republican belief in limited government, he proposed only a few measures; but the effect was to leave in operation the elaborate commercial system erected by his Federalist predecessors. The single most important achievement of his administration—the Louisiana Purchase—opened up vast new commercial possibilities (as well as providing land for small farmers who supported the Republicans).

Despite George Washington's fear, as expressed in his farewell address, that the spirit of party "agitates the community with ill-founded jealousies and false alarms, kindles the animosity of one part against another, foments occasionally riots and insurrection," political parties soon came to have just the opposite effects. They proved a powerful instrument for moderating differences, reducing conflict among groups, and preventing riots and insurrection.

Washington dreamed of government being conducted in a quiet dignified manner among gentlemen. In fact, the Federalist attempt to weaken their opponents and reduce political participation soon ended with their defeat, followed by their virtual extinction by 1812.

Federalist dominance ended with Jefferson's election in 1800. In large part, this was preordained: a party resting mostly on commercial and mercantile interests was bound to fail in a country with few cities and a large agricultural population. Moreover, the Federalists did not conceal their disdain for the lower orders, a mistake in a country where the spirit of egalitarianism ran high and an aristocratic political approach was sure to unleash widespread opposition. Jefferson's success rested on the fact that, unlike the Federalists, he (and the Republicans) accepted popular government.

Parties languished in the Era of Good Feeling that followed Jefferson's presidency. Then, in 1828, Andrew Jackson's election created a fresh impetus to party organization. Jackson was the first president to be nominated by a national convention, rather than by a congressional caucus in which congressmen selected a candidate and lobbied in the states to get him elected. Furthermore, in most states during this period, popular election of pledged presidential electors replaced their election by state legislators. Jackson popularized politics. He revitalized Jefferson's party, creating a party organization that reached throughout the country. He provided a vital link between government and the people and offered voters a sense of participation that had largely been lacking in Jefferson's day and virtually absent in the years following. The number of voters soared from one-half million in 1824 to five million by the time of the Civil War. Voting turnout (the proportion of eligible voters who turn out to vote) jumped from 27 percent in 1824 to 78 percent in 1840.[11]

Jackson's presidency called into existence an opposition party, the Whigs, which, if it inherited the Federalists' constituency of manufacturing interests, was careful not to make the Federalists' mistake of ignoring popular sentiment. In fact, the Whigs (and their successors, the present Republican party) demonstrated how successful a conservative business-oriented party could be in currying popular favor. The Whigs' stress on the image of the common man was symbolized by their nomination of popular military heroes for president: four of their six candidates after 1832 were generals. In similar fashion, the Republicans' only success in presidential elections between 1932 and 1968 was the eight years of General Eisenhower's presidency between 1952 and 1960.

By the end of the Jacksonian period, the party system was formed in a mold that, in many respects, persists to this day. The two parties then in existence are the direct ancestors of the present two major parties. During Jackson's time, the two

[11]Everett Carll Ladd, Jr., *American Political Parties: Social Change and Political Response* (New York, 1970), p. 96; Chambers, "Party Development," p. 32.

became more competitive, with the average difference between their vote declining from 36 percent in 1828 to 9 percent in 1844.[12]

Republicans in Power: 1860 to 1932

As the early party system became more competitive and national in scope, it was torn apart by the bitter sectional rivalry revolving around slavery, opposing Northern commercial interests to Southern planter interests. The party system was too weak to contain the conflict between two economic systems, one based on free labor, the other based on slave labor. The slavery issue destroyed the Whig party, which tried to straddle the fence. A new party was formed, which called itself the Republican party (not because it resembled Jefferson's Republicans, but because it wanted to evoke his popularity). Based in the North, it was created to serve as the vehicle for antislavery commercial interests and abolitionists. When the Republican candidate, Abraham Lincoln, was elected president in 1860, the South seceded from the union and war began.

The Civil War ended in a victory for Northern urban industrial business, which used free labor, over Southern commercial agriculture, which was based on slave labor. The end of slavery did not usher in a social revolution in the South. The efforts of the Radical Republicans (a splinter group) to break up plantations and distribute land to the former slaves failed—thus creating the conditions for the tenant-farming system that kept blacks in a state of semiservitude.[13] For the United States as a whole, the Civil War ended in a victory for procedural democracy and industrial capitalism and put the Republicans in firm control of the federal government. The Democratic party, the dominant party of the previous period, was in no position to challenge the Republicans after the defeat of the South.

Perhaps more important, the Republicans presented themselves as the guardians of rising urban and industrial interests, and in the post-Civil War period the economic balance of power swiftly tipped toward industry. Whereas in 1850, two-thirds of the work force was engaged in agriculture, by 1870 a majority of the

[12]Richard P. McCormick, "Political Development and the Second Party System," in Chambers and Burnham, *The American Party Systems*, p. 99.
[13]Barrington Moore, Jr., *Social Origins of Dictatorship and Democracy* (Boston, 1966), chapter 3.

working class was in nonagricultural occupations. Between 1860 and 1930, the number of industrial workers swelled from one million to eight million. From 1860 to 1920, the urban population doubled every two decades; it took the entire period for the rural population to double. Cities grew especially fast. Before the Civil War, only New York had over 250,000 inhabitants. By the First World War, twenty-three other cities had reached this size.

At this critical turning point in the nation's history, when an urban and industrial revolution was occurring that marked a fundamental transition from the earlier era, the Republican party was able to represent the thrust to industrialization and insure that it was carried out under the guidance of private business interests. Thanks to their control of the Republican party, rising industrial and manufacturing interests were able to resist the protest of agrarian groups against exploitation by railroads, financiers, and middlemen, and prevent political challenge from the growing urban proletariat.[14] Thus, although the Republican party did not advertise itself as a class-based party, it reflected a major regional and historical cleavage that served class interests. After 1896, the Republican party was alone in enthusiastically embracing the industrial boom. Corporate and financial leaders in the Northeast used the party as a vehicle for gaining legitimacy and government acceptance for the expansion of big business. The Republicans' success—they were virtually unchallenged during the entire period from the Civil War until well after the First World War—meant that the industrial revolution in the United States was carried out by private interests relatively unrestrained by opposition from within the party system. Neither the Democratic party nor a series of protest parties (Greenback, Farmers' Alliance, Populist) were successful in their attempts to overturn Republican and business dominance.

In a feeble attempt to rival the Republicans, the Democratic party first tried to emulate them. However, only Grover Cleveland, a conservative Democrat whose probusiness policies were indistinguishable from the Republicans', was successful in winning presidential elections (in 1884 and 1892). Until 1896, "on the fundamental question of the time—the role of government in a modern industrial society—the two national parties had no quarrel. Both saw an identity of interest between the government

---

[14]James L. Sundquist, *Dynamics of the Party System: Alignment and Realignment of Political Parties in the United States* (Washington, D.C., 1973), chapters 6–7.

and the great banking, manufacturing, and railroad corporations."[15] Beginning in 1896, the Democrats tried to forge a rival coalition based on Western and Southern agrarian interests, but the party failed dismally in three electoral defeats (in 1896, 1900, and 1908) under the banner of William Jennings Bryan. Bryan's case summed up the weakness of the party. His major proposal was for monetary policies favoring farmers and debtor interests. He represented the fundamentalist Protestant values of the declining rural areas; as such, he held little appeal for the Northern workers and immigrants (mostly Catholics) whose ranks were swelling in the late nineteenth century.

Rather than attempting to challenge the *manner* in which the Northeastern industrial and financial elite was directing industrial expansion, the Democrats, under Bryan, evoked a nostalgic but outmoded rural past. In a critical election in 1896, Northern workers and immigrants gave their support to Bryan's conservative and victorious opponent, William McKinley. Thus, during a crucial period in its expansion and consolidation, the American working class became organized within rather than against the existing party system.

During the critical years of industrialization, the costs of industrial expansion were financed mostly by the working class: between 1890 and 1914 wages hardly rose, despite a huge industrial boom and massive increases in productivity, total output, profits, and capital investments. As late as 1920, some steelworkers worked a twelve-hour day, 363 days per year.[16] Well into the twentieth century, children worked long hours under hazardous factory conditions for a pittance. The party system failed to reflect the cleavage between those benefiting and those being harmed by industrialization. The system ignored the plight of industrial workers in the North, where the Republicans were dominant; and it ignored poor whites and blacks in the South, where the Democratic party became an instrument for the defense of regional and often racial interests in a way that split blacks from poor whites.

The party system performed a conservative function by its influence over the millions of immigrants pouring into the country. As many immigrants arrived between 1890 and the First World War as had come during the whole preceding century.

---

[15]*Ibid.*, p. 140.
[16]Ladd, *American Political Parties*, p. 125; J. David Greenstone, *Labor in American Politics* (New York, 1969), p. 19.

Given universal suffrage, the new immigrants potentially posed an immense threat to established structural arrangements. However, the urban political machine proved an efficient device for socializing immigrants to accept established arrangements.

When reform efforts were launched by the Progressives in the early twentieth century, they addressed the symptom and not the cause. The Progressives identified corruption as the primary problem and attacked the party machine as the primary cause. Their reforms aimed to end the purchase of votes, political patronage, and graft. By raising barriers to political participation and reducing the material rewards it provided, the Progressives hoped to clean up politics and restrict participation to the "better sort." Yet, corrupt as the urban machine was, it was a far lesser evil than the brutal conditions of industrial production. (Indeed, the machine flourished on graft it received from the industrial sector.) Nonetheless, instead of attacking corporate capitalism, the Progressives accepted the trend toward corporate concentration. Progressive reforms did little to improve conditions for those suffering from industrial expansion; instead of democratizing electoral participation, they served mainly to cripple political parties. The nonpartisan ballot in municipal elections, direct primary, and personal voter registration requirements resulted in a weaker and depoliticized party system. Voting turnout, one measure of political vitality, was far higher before the Progressive reforms than it has ever been since (although other factors contributed to the decline). The party system was permanently undermined by the reforms of the Progressive era, not only as an instrument of manipulation and control but also as a potential agency for mobilizing popular majorities against corporate dominance.[17]

The New Deal and Its Legacy

The first major sign that the Democratic party was no longer acting simply as a spokesman for the rural past was the nomination of Alfred E. Smith for president in 1928. Smith was as different from Bryan as could be imagined. He was a Catholic New Yorker, a big-city immigrant, and a world away from

[17]Walter Dean Burnham, *Critical Elections and the Mainsprings of American Politics* (New York, 1970), *passim.* But see Philip E. Converse, "Change in the American Electorate," in Angus Campbell and Philip E. Converse, eds., *The Human Meaning of Social Change* (New York, 1973), pp. 263–337, for a critique of Burnham's position.

Bryan's rural fundamentalism. Smith proved as unappealing to rural areas and the South as Bryan had been to cities. Able to win only the deep South (pro-Democratic for generations), Massachusetts, and Rhode Island, he lost the election to Herbert Hoover.

Franklin D. Roosevelt, an urbane patrician, was better able to bridge the gap between rural and urban interests in 1932. He was helped by the fact that the Republicans were saddled with responsibility for the Great Depression, which began in 1929. A whole generation identified the GOP (Grand Old Party) as the party of the depression and viewed the Democrats as the party that took power confidently proclaiming, in the words of Roosevelt's first inaugural address, "The only thing we have to fear is fear itself." Generations after the industrial revolution occurred in the United States, the Democrats reached for the constituency that had been the victims of industrial growth—labor, and ethnic and urban groups.

In his recruiting efforts, Roosevelt worked with the fast-rising labor unions in the Congress of Industrial Organizations (CIO). In return for Roosevelt's support, organized labor—officially nonpartisan until the 1930s—came to play a role within the Democratic party comparable to the role played by large labor unions in Western Europe: unions provided funds, personnel, organization, and research for the party. During elections, unions often proved "a valued and integral part of the Democrats' normal campaign apparatus."[18]

Yet the realignment beginning with Smith's candidacy in 1928 and stretching through Roosevelt's election campaigns of 1932 and 1936 was far from forging a class-based party system. Although parties did begin to divide more along class lines, the representation of class divisions was blurred by historical traces persisting from the Civil War. Both New England and the South remained true to past tradition: New England, to the party of Lincoln; the South, to the Democrats. Since both parties formed quite diverse coalitions, each party compromised its stand to avoid antagonizing the different segments of its constituency.

The New Deal softened the edges of industrialism, repaired its worst damage, and used the government's power to stabilize economic conditions and provide benefits to the urban and rural poor hit hardest by the depression. This was a program that the

---

[18]Greenstone, *Labor in American Politics,* p. 9.

Republican party, a backward-looking captive of business interests, could not match. Yet, in part because of the powerful role conservative Southern Democrats played within the party, in part because Roosevelt "never entertained any idea of a fundamental alteration of the structure of ownership and control of business enterprises," the New Deal did not represent a frontal assault on corporate capitalism—regardless of what many outraged business executives thought at the time.[19] Quite the contrary. It was under the liberal auspices of the New Deal (and successive programs sponsored by Democratic presidents since Roosevelt) that the corporate complex experienced its greatest expansion, prosperity, and power. The benefits provided by the New Deal to the disadvantaged, such as Social Security, unemployment insurance, workmen's compensation, and legal recognition for labor unions, helped maintain and stabilize an interdependent system of industrial production. In addition, the government provided lavish benefits to industry in the form of political protection, regulation, tax benefits, grants, and military spending.

In the long run, despite the innovations it sponsored, the New Deal did not challenge the dominance of corporate capitalism any more than its Republican predecessors had; what changed was the rhetoric and the way that corporate interests were protected by government. Nor did the New Deal coalition spell the triumph of the disadvantaged; instead, it further integrated them into the political and economic system. Although corporate capitalism was forced to share power with the burgeoning federal government in Washington, the new alliance did not threaten corporate interests so long as the government remained under the control of "cooperative" forces. Before discussing present-day political cleavages, it is useful to explore how party compliance with the corporate complex has been assured.

MONEY AND POLITICS

If political parties accurately represented the interests of voters, elections would usually pose a threat to established structural arrangements. Given the large proportion of Americans whose interest lies in structural change, one party or the other would find it electorally profitable to attempt to gain these groups' votes.

[19]Ladd, *American Political Parties*, p. 188.

Yet the routine pattern is for parties to differ in only minor respects and not to advocate far-reaching changes.

An important reason is that parties need more than votes to succeed; they also need money. Especially today, elections are costly. The 1972 elections cost well over $400 million. Of this amount, $110 million was spent to nominate and elect candidates for president, most of the money going for media and advertising costs. President Nixon spent $60 million in his election campaign. Democratic candidates for the nomination spent $26 million in the preconvention campaign, and George McGovern spent $27 million in the election campaign itself. Another $100 million went to elect congressmen and senators; about $100 million went to elect state officials, such as governors and state legislators; and the remaining $100 million was spent in local elections.[20]

Election costs have spiraled in recent years: the 1972 election represented a 300 percent increase from the 1960 election. And election costs are high in nonpresidential years as well: $58 million was spent in the 1970 congressional elections.[21]

Who gives political contributions? According to Senator Russell Long, chairman of the Senate Finance Committee, "It would be my guess that about ninety-five percent of campaign funds at the congressional level are derived from businessmen."[22] Although some money is raised through small contributions, a substantial proportion comes from large gifts. In 1968, nearly half the publicly-reported funds raised by the major presidential candidates came from contributions of $500 or more.[23] Political scientist David Nichols found that, in Cleveland, nearly all large political contributors were affluent businessmen, usually corporate executives or lawyers.[24] In recent years, it has become common for gifts to be reported in the hundreds of thousands of dollars and even over $1 million. In 1968 and 1972, Clement Stone, a Chicago insurance executive, contributed $4 million to the Nixon campaigns.[25]

Much political money is corporate money. Corporations are forbidden by law from making direct contributions to political

[20]Unpublished data kindly made available by Herbert Alexander.
[21]Congressional Quarterly, *Dollar Politics* (Washington, D.C., 1971), p. 27.
[22]Philip Stern, *The Rape of the Taxpayer* (New York, 1973), p. 388.
[23]Herbert E. Alexander, *Financing the 1968 Election* (Lexington, Mass., 1971), p. 167.
[24]David Nichols, *Financing Elections: The Politics of an American Ruling Class* (New York, 1974), pp. 77–78.
[25]*The Washington Star,* November 17, 1972.

parties. But this prohibition can be evaded. The two parties net about $2 million from corporate advertising in the convention programs they publish. Highly-paid corporate executives are expected to make personal political contributions, and they are often given bonuses for this purpose. And, when corporations believe the stakes warrant it, they may break the law. The Watergate investigations revealed the means corporations use to hide their tracks: corporate funds "laundered" through foreign bank accounts, gifts secretly made in cash, and free services performed by corporations for political parties. (Executives from fifteen corporations, including Gulf Oil Corporation, American Airlines, and Goodyear Tire and Rubber, were convicted of campaign-finance illegalities following the 1972 election.) While Watergate doubtless represents an exception because of the large amounts of cash involved—and because of the publicity surrounding presidential involvement in the cover-up of the events—it should dispel any illusions about the purity of American political parties and elections.

Contributions are sometimes made to purchase political favors directly. A Senate Watergate Committee staff report revealed that men and women eager to be appointed ambassador contributed over one million dollars to the 1972 Nixon campaign.

Yet the distinction is far from sharp between an outright bribe and a contribution given to elect candidates who will support the donor's interests. Even when no laws are broken, gift-giving is directly or indirectly related to expected returns. In the area of campaign finance as in other areas of American politics, legal equality (in this case the equal right to contribute to one's preferred candidate or party) leads to substantive inequality because of the unequal distribution of resources among different groups in the society. Every group that gives money expects that elected officials will be more responsive to its interests. But those possessing greater financial resources end up with greater influence in the political sphere.

Many directors and officers of the largest corporations, military firms with government contracts, and other members of the business establishment make handsome political contributions. Officers of the 100 largest defense contractors, for example, gave $5 million to President Nixon's reelection campaign. Petroleum-company officials contributed another $6 million. Banking executives gave $4 million, and real-estate men and officials from the pharmaceutical industry each contributed $1 million.[26] All these industries are heavily dependent on government co-operation.

Small-scale capital makes its influence felt through contributions to the campaigns of congressmen, governors, state legislators, mayors, and other local officials. Local interests seeking government help and friendly access—lawyers hoping to be appointed to judgeships, highway contractors, construction companies, real-estate interests—are especially generous. Corporate capital also exerts influence on local and congressional elections through selective contributions at critical leverage points. For example, petroleum companies, the banking industry, and farm interests contribute handsomely to the reelection campaigns of cooperative members of key congressional committees. What should be stressed is that political money is generally used in a routine, usually legal, fashion to maintain a political structure friendly to corporate capitalism. The party system is shaped far less by the occasional bribe or campaign-law violation than by political parties' permanent dependence on private funds. Political contributions are a means by which corporate capitalism offsets the influence of the large numbers of less well-off people who might otherwise pose a threat through shaping and electing parties responsive to their interests.

Wealthy donors support both parties, although most of their gifts go to the Republicans. The result is that, despite the financial support given to the Democrats by labor unions (about half the Democrats' funds come from organized labor), the Democratic party raises less than the Republicans. In the 1968 and 1972 presidential campaigns, the Democratic party ran up deficits and was heavily outspent by the Republican party. Campaign finance specialist Herbert Alexander found that nearly all large contributions by top corporation executives in 1972 went to Republican candidates.

The major consequence of the high costs of campaigning, however, is not to favor one party over the other but to maintain the dominance of *both* parties. The parties' dependence on private contributions means that political conflict takes place within limits acceptable to wealthy donors.

Parties and candidates must prove their "reliability" before

[26]*New York Times*, September 30, 1973; December 10, 1973; January 2, 1974.

they can attract sizeable donations. Since candidates need money before they can even attempt to gain the nomination, political gifts influence the selection of who is to run, long before the election campaign itself. As Will Rogers remarked, "It takes a lot of money to even get beat with."[27] While having lavish campaign funds does not guarantee nomination or election—there are numerous examples of candidates who outspent their rivals and still lost—political aspirants who cannot recruit affluent patrons are pursuing a nearly impossible dream. The role played by money in party politics goes a long way toward nullifying any possible challenge parties might pose to established arrangements.

As a result of public outrage over Watergate-related revelations of abuses made possible by private contributions (including the exchange of ambassadorships for campaign contributions, illegal corporate gifts, and campaign malpractices paid for by large private gifts), Congress enacted a fundamental reform of political finance in 1974. The law provided for partial public financing of presidential primaries and general elections; prohibited private donors from contributing more than $25,000 in an election year to presidential and congressional candidates; and set a ceiling on the amount politicians can spend in presidential and congressional campaigns.

While the 1974 campaign-finance law may well signify a major change, previous campaign-finance reforms have promised much and delivered relatively little. In the past, regulation of campaign spending resembled other aspects of the government regulatory process: the effects were often more symbolic than real. Moreover, the new law gave a boost to the faltering two party system by providing public funds for Democratic and Republican campaign coffers.

REALIGNMENT OR DECAY OF POLITICAL PARTIES?
THE 1970s

A party's electoral following tends to remain stable through time. Most voters develop a sense of psychological attachment with a party when they are young, and this identification persists despite changes in the parties' candidates and stands on particular issues.

[27]Congressional Quarterly, *Dollar Politics,* p. 3.

A sense of partisan identification is thus transmitted from one generation to the next. Electoral studies carried out by the Survey Research Center of the University of Michigan find that this affective attachment of voters to one party or the other acts as an important influence on the voting decision. It can be distinguished from voters' perceptions of the candidates nominated by each party and the stands the parties take on campaign issues. Unless voters strongly prefer the opposite party's candidates or issue position, they will probably vote for the party with which they identify, especially if their sense of party identification is strong. The parties' ability to develop a sense of partisan identification among the electorate is an indication of their strength, or "reach."

One result of the New Deal realignment was that the Democratic party attracted a majority of party identifiers. In election after election since 1932, the Democrats had only to mobilize their natural majority to win. After nearly forty years in which the Democratic party and the New Deal coalition dominated presidential elections (save for the presidency of Eisenhower, a soldier-hero not closely associated with the Republican party) and most congressional elections, the 1970s may represent another period of upheaval and transition. The New Deal coalition has been shaken by the rise of new social issues that are related to fundamental demographic changes in American society, in particular the movement of blacks to the North, the suburbanization of American politics, and the growth of a new middle class. Structural tensions and contradictions may form the basis for new alignments. Yet it is an open question whether the outcome will be a consolidation and continuation of a Democratic majority, a new Republican majority, or a disintegration of party politics in America.

As a result of the industrialization and the fading of Civil War memories in the South, black migration to the North, and the national media's dominance over communications, regional differences in the United States have declined and political life has become nationalized.

Take the movement of Southern blacks northward. Between 1940 and 1970, a total of five million blacks moved to Northern cities. One result was to force into the open the racial issue that the Democratic party had submerged and contained during the New Deal. Before the 1960s, Southern Democrats had succeeded in preventing Northern liberals from using the Democratic party to press for racial justice. When President Truman was nominated for reelection in 1948 on a mild civil-rights plank, Southern Democrats bolted the convention and sponsored their own candidate. Although Truman won reelection, Southern Democrats and conservative Republicans in Congress blocked attempts to pass civil-rights legislation.

But after a sizeable number of blacks had achieved the vote in Northern cities, the race issue came into prominence. Seeking to attract black and liberal votes in the North, Presidents Kennedy and Johnson (especially Johnson) sponsored far-reaching civil-rights legislation. For the first time in recent American history, federal legislation was used to reduce racial discrimination in education, voting, and public accommodations. These policies set in motion the South's swing away from the Democratic party. During the Johnson landslide of 1964, the South abandoned its historic Democratic affiliation, and conservative Southern whites proved a major source of support for Barry Goldwater. The trend continued under President Nixon, whose opposition to school busing, nomination of Southern judges to the Supreme Court, and general conservatism all contributed to the Southern shift toward the Republican party.

The increase in Republican strength in the South is more pronounced in presidential than in local elections. Southern politicians are unwilling to lose the benefits that come from staying within the Democratic party, such as committee chairmanships in Congress deriving from the seniority system. Nonetheless, by 1974, there were Republican senators from Florida, North Carolina, South Carolina, Tennessee, Texas, and Virginia. Between 1964 and 1970, the proportion of Southern voters identifying themselves as Democrats dropped sharply from 58 percent to 38 percent.

Republican gains in the South are matched by their gains among Northern groups that were traditionally Democratic. George Wallace's success in 1968 as a third-party candidate and a general decline in support for the Democratic party among Catholics and workers suggest the wisdom of political analyst Samuel Lubell's observation: "Always in the past the assumption has been that the South, as it changed, would come to resemble the North more and more. . . . [Instead], the North as it changes, may be southernized."[28] Catholic support for the Democratic party has steadily declined from a high of 82 percent in 1960

[28]Samuel Lubell, *The Hidden Crisis in American Politics* (New York, 1971), p. 86.

(when John F. Kennedy, a Catholic, was the Democratic candidate) to 53 percent in 1972. Organized labor's support has also declined: from 75 percent in the 1930s and 1940s, to 46 percent in 1972.[29] Switching to the Republican party is a form of protest for many Catholic, white ethnic, and unionized workers. These groups have become increasingly restive as they experience the brunt of racial strife and urban dislocation and decay. Workers who had achieved a decent but difficult existence saw their new gains threatened by rising taxes, inflation, and the deterioration of property values when neighborhoods became racially mixed; they saw their way of life threatened by radical political movements, the free life styles adopted by youth, the rising incidence of violence in American society, and black insurrection.

Although the Democratic party has lost some of its traditional sources of support, it has gained others, and the net result may well be an increase in Democratic strength. The Northeast has moved toward the Democratic party; New England is no longer a one-party (Republican) region. Black migration to Northern cities has created additional support for the Democratic party. Although the suburban vote has increased by 37 percent between 1952 and 1968, those with Democratic loyalties who have moved to the suburbs have not shifted to the Republican party. A new middle class of pro-Democratic, college-educated professionals has emerged. Youth, particularly college students (who represent nearly half of those in the college-age bracket) are strongly pro-Democratic: among college students identifying with a political party in 1970, 65 percent identified with the Democrats.

For their part, the Democrats have been quick to adopt policies aimed at assuaging the prevailing fears and anxieties of society: they proclaim themselves as vigilant as the Republicans on upholding law and order, oppose the liberalization of drug laws, and are reducing their support for welfare programs.

The Republican party's attempt to forge a new majority may thus have failed: its economic policies when in power have been inept and social changes have not uniformly worked in its favor. Despite the fact that the Republicans have enjoyed the financial support of corporate capitalism and have won four of the six presidential elections between 1952 and 1972, the Democrats

---

[29]Richard Rubin, "The Democratic Coalition in Decline: Changing Support by Key Groups in Critical Regions and Consequences for Intra-Party Dynamics," Ph.D dissertation, Columbia University, 1973, pp. 75–76, 128–29.

Table 8-1

Changes in political affiliation of various population groups, 1960 and 1970

Identification of group	1960			1970			Change		
	D	R	Ind.	D	R	Ind.	D	R	Ind.
1. Gross shift in party identification									
All voters	46	30	23	44	25	31	-2	-5	8
2. All voters, by race									
Whites	46	31	23	40	27	33	-6	-4	10
Blacks	50	19	31	78	4	18	28	-15	-13
3. Whites, by region									
South	61	21	18	44	18	38	-17	-3	20
Rest of country	39	36	25	39	31	30	0	-5	5
Northeast	(37)	(39)	(24)	(35)	(31)	(34)	(-2)	(-8)	(10)
Midwest	(36)	(38)	(26)	(38)	(33)	(29)	(2)	(-5)	(3)
West	(47)	(28)	(25)	(46)	(26)	(28)	(-1)	(-2)	(3)
4. Whites, by religious affiliation									
Protestants	39	38	23	37	32	31	-2	-6	8
Catholics	64	18	18	52	18	30	-12	0	12
Jews	61	9	30	55	5	40	-6	-4	10

5. Whites, by age group

20–29	45	29	26	36	19	45	−9	−10	19
30–39	49	27	24	33	27	40	−16	0	16
40–49	46	29	25	42	24	34	−4	−5	9
50 and over	45	36	19	45	32	23	0	−4	4

6. Whites, by place of residence

Central cities in 12 largest metropolitan areas	54	22	24	52	25	23	−2	3	−1
Suburbs of 12 largest metropolitan areas	32	44	24	39	26	35	7	−18	11
Other cities (over 2,500)	48	31	21	38	28	34	−10	−3	13
Rural	49	28	23	41	27	32	−8	−1	9

7. Whites, by education

Some college	33	46	21	32	34	34	−1	−12	13
No college	50	27	23	43	24	33	−7	−3	10

8. Whites, by social class

Working class	51	26	23	44	22	34	−7	−4	11
Middle class	37	42	21	37	31	32	0	−11	11

Source: James L. Sundquist, *Dynamics of the Party System: Alignment and Realignment of Political Parties in the United States* (Washington, D.C., 1973), pp. 348–49; © 1973 by the Brookings Institution, Washington, D.C.; based on data from University of Michigan, Survey Research Center, 1960 and 1970 polls. Percentages may not add to 100 because of rounding.

have controlled Congress through most of the period since the 1930s, and nearly two-thirds of *voters identifying with a political party* continue to favor the Democrats.

A final blow to Republican efforts to dislodge the Democratic party was the Watergate affair and Nixon's near-impeachment. In the 1974 congressional elections, the Democrats substantially increased their already sizeable lead over the Republicans in both houses of Congress.

Their margin over the Republicans in the Senate went up by three, resulting in a sixty-one to thirty-nine majority. In the House of Representatives, the Democrats added forty-three, with a new majority of 291 to 144. In contrast to its predecessor, the Congress elected in 1974 was younger, less conservative, and even more heavily Democratic. The relatively large turnover resulted from voter opposition to Watergate (four of the Republicans on the House Judiciary Committee who opposed impeachment were defeated for reelection) as well as anger over inflation, economic stagnation, and unemployment. The Democratic sweep was evident at all levels: Democratic gubernatorial candidates replaced Republican incumbents in five states—including the two biggest, New York and California.

But equally as significant as the Democratic tide was voter disgust with established politicians and processes. There was little evidence in the electoral campaign that politicians could propose solutions to the deep-rooted problems facing the country. Voter discontent was evident from the extraordinarily low rate of voter turnout. Fewer than 40 percent of voting-age Americans bothered to go to the polls. What this means is that few of the victorious candidates received the support of an absolute majority.

Thus, the new issues have probably not produced a realignment under Republican control.

However, the Democratic coalition is bitterly divided. Traditional sources of Democratic support clash with blacks and younger, more educated, reform groups. Neither faction can elect a president without the support of the other. Hubert Humphrey had labor's support in 1968, but lost when he failed to attract Democratic reform groups. The opposite situation occurred in 1972, when George McGovern was nominated with the help of "new politics" forces (minorities, the young, women), but alienated organized labor.

Yet, even if the Democrats succeed in conciliating rival factions in the party, they will not be much more able than the Republicans to attack the root cause of present problems: structural inequality. For, as political scientist Everett Ladd and his associates point out, "We cannot escape the conclusion that the Democrats are the majority party in large measure because they are no longer the 'old New Deal coalition;' they have successfully transformed themselves from a party of *have nots* to a party of *haves*."[30] Problems of race, class, and corporate capitalism are becoming more pressing, and it is doubtful whether either party can deal with the new tensions, regardless of a party realignment. As this realization begins to spread, what may be occurring is not a realignment of parties but a loss of support for both parties and a long-run decline of the party system.

American political parties have rarely played a role in innovating or proposing political changes. They have usually *reflected*, not *changed*, structural arrangements. Rather than expressing cleavages with sharpness and clarity, parties have muffled conflict, slowed change, and suppressed tensions. They have generally blown with the winds of power and change, accepting the structural context as given. They have adapted, legitimized, and adjusted; the initiative for change has usually originated outside the party system—from the business and corporate sector, from outraged minorities working outside the party system, and (increasingly in the present era) from the federal government.

That parties do not inscribe a program of structural reform on their banner might be interpreted merely as a response to the opinions of voters—hardly an undemocratic tendency. However, note the consequence: parties thereby abdicate the task of educating voters to possible alternatives to established arrangements. The voters' opinions are taken as given. But this does not mean that voters exercise sovereignty in making up their mind. It means that parties leave to *others*, such as the media, schools, and political officials, the role of defining alternatives. By taking voters as they find them, parties allow other powerful agencies—often controlled by conservative forces—greater latitude in influencing voters.

---

[30]Everett Carll Ladd, Jr., *et al.,* "A New Political Realignment," *The Public Interest* 23 (Spring 1971): 46–63.

There is already evidence that the power of parties to attract political loyalties and provide a means of social control is weakening. For example, at the turn of the century, parties were able to socialize and integrate millions of immigrants into the electorate in a way that did not disrupt political institutions; in recent years, they have been less successful in capturing the loyalties of other new arrivals into the electorate, including youth and disadvantaged groups. Other institutions, particularly government, television, and schools, are more effective as agents of political socialization and integration. Political parties have also become less useful as devices to blur conflict, defuse discontent, and conciliate society's losers. Their role here has been preempted by government's increasing involvement in the social and economic affairs of the country.

The last arena in which political parties have often played a major role is elections: both in the designation of candidates and election campaigns. Yet even in this last remaining stronghold of party activity, the party system has lost its monopoly of control. Moreover, parties have been increasingly less able to convince the public that elections matter.

To simplify our examination of elections, attention will be centered on the office of president. However, about 500,000 public officials are elected in the United States, and voting also takes place on bond issues, referenda, and the like. Thus, while important, presidential elections are only one example of the American electoral process.

Nominating and Electing a President

The closest American parties come to the annual congresses held by major European parties is the national convention held every four years to nominate a president and a vice president and draft a party platform. Since Jackson's time, the national convention has represented the sovereign party, meeting in all its majesty. That picture is changing, however; the convention as a television special has supplanted the convention as a decision-making body.

The party platform is the authoritative guide to the party's policies. Try designating which two of the following planks were in the Democratic platform of 1968, and which two in the Republican:

The forty-hour week adopted 30 years ago needs re-examination to determine whether or not a shorter work week, without a loss of wages, would produce more jobs, increase productivity and stabilize prices.

Use the defense dollar more effectively through simplification of cumbersome, overcentralized administration of the Defense Department, expanded competitive bidding on defense contracts, and improved safeguards against excessive profits.

Our aim is to strengthen state and local law enforcement agencies so that they can do their jobs.

In this endeavor [to eliminate poverty], the resources of private enterprise—not only its economic power but its leadership and ingenuity—must be mobilized.

If you guessed that the first two were from the Democratic platform and the second two from the Republican, your grand score is zero: the order was the opposite. This little exercise tells something about platform writing. Each party tries to court the opposite party's electorate, with the result that they both usually drive toward the center. While on the one hand, parties attempt to attract distinctive constituencies, in an election they will take votes wherever they can find them, without regard to ideology.

Public opinion polls repeatedly show that the broad electorate is unable to distinguish between the policy stands of opposing candidates. Yet responsibility for the electorate's ignorance lies in good measure with the candidates themselves, who take pains to minimize their policy differences and maximize ambiguity. For example, in 1968 the country was wracked by the Vietnam war. To what extent did the Democratic and Republican presidential candidates offer alternative policies toward the war? Not much, according to political scientists Benjamin Page and Richard Brody.

It is possible for scholars, after reading all their [the candidates'] speeches and statements, to arrive at judgments about what their "real" positions were; but the ordinary citizen may be forgiven if he failed to penetrate the haze of vague hints which alternated with total silence about Vietnam in most of the candidates' rhetoric.[31]

[31]Benjamin I. Page and Richard A. Brody, "The Vietnam War Issue," *The American Political Science Review* 66 (December 1972): 987. Also see Stanley Kelley, *Political Campaigning* (Washington, D.C., 1960), pp. 50–84.

Yet voters did correctly perceive the positions of George Wallace and Eugene McCarthy, candidates for the presidential nomination who took clear stands on the war; and voters' attitudes toward Wallace and McCarthy were highly correlated with their own policy position. Page and Brody conclude that "when the American people are presented with a clear choice, they are able and willing to bring their policy preferences to bear."[32]

Their lack of a distinctive program led political scientist Otto Kirchheimer to characterize American parties as "catch-all" parties. Catch-all parties are more concerned with gaining office than with putting policies into effect once they get there. They claim that anything the other party can do, they can do better— but they refuse to engage in an analysis of what needs to be done. That is not only a waste of time but might alienate those who disagree with their reasoning.[33] Thus, although convention disputes over the party platform provide some indication of the strength of various factions, the drafting of a platform has become largely a meaningless ritual.

Political conventions are also losing control over the choice of a presidential candidate. The use of public-opinion polls competes with the expert judgment of local politicians and convention delegates regarding the grass-roots popularity of different candidates. The candidates themselves have begun to develop elaborate preconvention campaigns, such as those of John F. Kennedy in 1960, Barry Goldwater in 1964, Richard M. Nixon in 1968, and George McGovern in 1972. The result is that the choice of a candidate has usually been made even before the convention meets. The convention merely ratifies the results of the informal preconvention selection process, puts on a show for television (the convention is staged to have the maximum nationwide impact on prime time), and disperses. In every presidential convention from 1956 to 1972, both parties nominated a presidential candidate on the first ballot; in previous years, except when there was an incumbent president, a first-ballot nomination was a rarity.

Who gets nominated? An analysis of the candidates illuminates the general significance of political parties and elec-

---

[32]Page and Brody, "The Vietnam War Issue," p. 993.
[33]Otto Kirchheimer, "The Transformation of the Western European Party Systems," in Joseph La Palombara and Myron Weiner, eds., *Political Parties and Political Development* (Princeton, N.J., 1966), pp. 177–200.

tions. To begin with, potential nominees are usually confined to the vice president, senators, and governors; and all but two major candidates in the past half century have been white, male, Protestant, and married with a family. The exceptions are John F. Kennedy, a Catholic, and Adlai Stevenson, who was divorced (both were probably hurt by having these "deviant" characteristics). Put another way, any one of the following characteristics has (until now) been sufficient to disqualify one from consideration: female, black, Jewish, known to have had psychiatric treatment, poor, or atheist. The list could be extended but the point is clear: presidential candidates are chosen out of a small pool from which the vast majority of Americans are excluded. In terms of the criteria of representation described in Chapter 2, the nominating process recruits from a socially unrepresentative segment of the electorate.

Political scientist Donald Matthews has stressed the need for a presidential aspirant to be widely regarded as a possible candidate. If one has not been included in the Gallup poll of possible nominees years before the election—and near the top of the list—his chance of getting the nomination is slight. In the mysterious preselection screening process, a key factor is to be mentioned as presidential timber by leading television and newspaper commentators.[34]

Another important consideration is the ability of a candidate to attract large contributions at the prenomination stage. It is probably at this point, that political money makes its influence felt most—for "unreliable" candidates are not apt to be considered a wise investment. Potential candidates are particularly sensitive to the wishes of wealthy donors at this early stage—for without this initial support a candidate cannot even wage a decent fight for the nominations. The advice Sam Rayburn, a powerful Speaker of the House of Representatives, gave freshmen congressmen puts the point more bluntly: "To get along, go along."

Occasionally, candidates do make proposals that antagonize the business community, with results that serve to prove the rule. In 1964, Barry Goldwater was a frank throwback to an earlier era: he speculated about abolishing the social-security program, turning over TVA to private interests, and rolling back government

[34]Donald R. Matthews, "Presidential Nominations: Process and Outcomes," in James David Barber, ed., *Choosing the President* (Englewood Cliffs, N.J., 1974), pp. 35–70.

regulations. Goldwater claimed that he represented "a choice not an echo" in relation to the New Deal tradition. He was promptly abandoned by a traditional bastion of Republican support—businessmen—who did not want the clock turned back. In 1972, George McGovern was made to appear a "radical" (a term Hubert H. Humphrey pinned on him in the California primary—and virtually the kiss of death in American politics). When McGovern proposed a liberalization of welfare benefits, his fear of adverse business reaction was so great that he sponsored a full-page advertisement in the *Wall Street Journal* (a leading business newspaper) to defend himself against the charge of being antibusiness. Yet McGovern represented at most a moderate challenge to established institutions. His proposal to cut the military budget would still have left the United States with the largest military budget in the world. His "radical" welfare proposals were more modest than programs *already* existing in European countries with *conservative* governments (including England, France, and Italy). [35]

The decline of the parties' power can be seen from their diminished role in the campaign itself. Three mechanisms have replaced parties as the dominant instruments in election campaigns: the candidate's own campaign organization, the media, and professional consulting firms.

Candidates for offices at all levels—from president to town alderman—prefer to develop their own campaign organizations, manned by their personal supporters, separate from the official party and working in uneasy alliance with it. A bewildering array of groups may be formed to work for the candidate's election (there were 222 national-level committees in the 1968 presidential race—many created simply to evade campaign finance laws).[36] Within the overall campaign organization, the regular party apparatus ranks low, for candidates have more trust in, and control over, organizations staffed by their personal associates.

An extreme case was provided by President Nixon's reelection campaign. According to political analyst Theodore H. White,

[35]For example, these countries require that employers provide workers with several weeks annually of paid vacations, and all three have virtually free cradle-to-the-grave medical service for all citizens. Far from being ahead of his time or radical, McGovern would have been regarded as a conservative in most European countries.
[36]Alexander, *Financing the 1968 Election,* p. 117.

the Republican party "was simply allowed to decay so completely that it played no role whatsoever as a national party in the election of 1972."[37] Nixon's campaign organization, the Committee for the Reelection of the President, was staffed by the President's hand-picked personal associates. It was within the CRP organization that the acts of political espionage originated that became known as Watergate.

Although professional party organizations may be on the wane, political activism in the electoral process may be on the rise, as witnessed by the large number of volunteers in recent election campaigns. In contrast to the professional politician or member of a party machine, who entered politics in search of a job, the new (often youthful and educated) amateurs are motivated to participate because of enthusiasm for a candidate's personality or policies. They participate irregularly—mostly at election time, both in the prenomination drive and the election campaign. Their enthusiasm motivates them to perform without pay the tedious but necessary jobs of getting names for a nomination petition, ringing doorbells, manning telephones, and stuffing envelopes. That dedicated volunteers can make a difference is shown by the nomination of Barry Goldwater in 1964, the rapid rise of Eugene McCarthy in 1968 (after thousands of college students poured into New Hampshire to campaign for him in the primary), and the nomination of George McGovern in 1972. The continuing tendency of many political activists to channel their energies through the party and electoral system checks the decline of parties.

The media, especially radio and television, play a fundamental role in political campaigning. It has become commonplace that a candidate can reach more people in one television "spot" than in weeks of arduous campaigning. Reliance on the media reduces the need for elaborate grass-roots party machinery. Assuming the candidate has the money—no small matter as we have seen—the media make possible a campaign blitz, and under conditions of the candidate's own choosing. He need not contend with hostile audiences or be effective in rough and tumble debate. By purchasing television time, the candidate can rehearse and

[37]Theodore H. White, *The Making of the President—1972* (New York, 1973), p. xviii.

"retake" his message until he has caught just the right inflection and appearance of sincerity and spontaneity. He can benefit from the wizardry of modern techniques: makeup artistry, sound and lighting effects, and edited film clips. Television makes the "selling of the president" possible as no other medium can.[38]

Another recent development helping make the party organization obsolete is professional campaign consultants. According to political scientist Frank Sorauf, the parties' "fairly primitive campaign skills have been superseded by a new campaign technology, and more and more they are finding themselves among the technologically unemployed."[39] There have always been specialists in the art of political organizing: people who knew how to get a press conference scheduled, prepare campaign literature, set up a public rally, and resolve the numerous crises that arise in a political campaign. In the past, these people were connected with a party organization and they always worked with only one party.

But in recent years, there has developed whole campaign organizations for hire: the rent-a-car principle applied to politics. The new industry of professional campaign consulting has boomed and now numbers around three hundred firms. In contrast to the former free-lance campaign specialist, the consulting firm handles the entire political campaign: speechwriting, polling, data processing, organizing rallies, and on and on.

Some observers are so impressed that they claim the techniques "constitute one of the most important agents of change in the political system."[40] We have our doubts. For these techniques transform elections into advertising campaigns, with each candidate, like rival brands of soap or cat food, packaged and marketed to gain maximum support. Thus, they simply accelerate the trend toward catch-all parties noted previously.

On balance, indeed, the net effect of the new election mechanisms is to shift even more power into the hands of those who have been dominant in the past. The new style campaigning costs money—lots of it—which, as we saw earlier in the chapter, makes parties dependent on wealthy donors.

[38]Joe McGinnis, *The Selling of the President, 1968* (New York, 1969).
[39]Frank J. Sorauf, *Party Politics in America,* 2d ed., (Boston, 1972), p. 411.
[40]John S. Saloma, III, and Frederick H. Sontag, *Parties: The Real Opportunity for Effective Citizen Politics* (New York, 1973), p. 283.

Decline of the Parties' Electoral Reach

One of the primary activities of American parties has been to mobilize and control the electorate. Yet a number of trends suggest that here, too, the party system is coming apart.

Through the end of the nineteenth century, voting turnout sometimes exceeded 80 percent of the eligible voters. Only 55 percent of voting-age citizens voted in the 1972 presidential election (and turnout in off years is even lower).

One reason for the sharp drop in voting turnout after the turn of the century was the Progressive reform requiring people to register in order to vote, defended by the Progressives as a way to end election malpractices and improve the quality of the electorate. The emergence of personal registration requirements "coincided with the mass immigration of foreign-born newcomers in American cities and the move to disenfranchise Blacks in the South."[41] The registration requirement proved an effective technique, then and now, for reducing the number of voters. Professor of journalism Penn Kimball observes that registration "discriminates most particularly against the poor. . . . Voter registration operates as an effective system of political control."[42]

Who are the nonvoters? Not surprisingly, those who do not vote are among the less advantaged. The largest groups of nonvoters are found among the rural and urban poor, blacks, Mexican-Americans, Puerto Ricans, and the elderly. Another large group includes youth and those who have recently changed residence (and are therefore not eligible to register). As Frank Sorauf points out, "the parties find it easier to be moderate and pragmatic because the electorate to which they respond is largely settled in and committed to the present basic social arrangements."[43]

In the past few years, there has also been a sharp drop in the proportion of Americans who identify with one of the two major parties. As recently as the early 1960s, a large majority of the electorate displayed stable identifications with the Democratic or Republican party. Since then, there has been a rapid rise in the number of those who rate themselves as independents. The proportion of self-identified independents rose from 23 percent in

---

[41]Penn Kimball, *The Disconnected* (New York, 1972), p. 4.
[42]*Ibid.*, pp. 3–4.
[43]Sorauf, *Party Politics*, p. 203.

1960 to 31 percent in 1970. (See Table 8–1, pp. 266–67.) By the mid-1970s, ten million more voters than a decade before declared themselves independents.[44]

Particularly significant is that young people, particularly educated youth, are less apt to identify with one of the two parties. In 1969, 28 percent of college students said they did not identify with either the Democrats or Republicans; two years later, this figure had shot up to 43 percent. Judging from these trends, the party system may be even less able to organize the electorate and get out the vote in the future.

Whereas in the 1950s, voters tended to vote mainly according to their party identification, in the 1960s and 1970s voters have been paying more attention to issues. The increased salience of issues helps explain why split-ticket voting and vote switching between parties have increased. In the 1950s, about one-quarter of those voting reported splitting their vote between candidates of different parties for different offices (for example, voting for a Republican for president and a Democrat for senator). In recent years, that figure has doubled. In 1970, all six of the largest Northern states electing a governor and a senator elected candidates from different parties to the two offices.

Switching parties from one election to the next is also on the rise. One-third of the whites voting in both the 1964 and 1968 presidential elections shifted between the parties. (Blacks voted more consistently for the Democratic party.) Forty percent of Nixon's vote in 1968 came from those who had voted for Lyndon Johnson in 1964. Samuel Lubell has observed, "No other period in American history has been marked by such wild trapeze swingings between the major parties."[45]

Another significant trend is the rise of a third-party vote. In 1968, George Wallace's American Independent party polled over 13 percent of the popular vote, among the highest percentages ever polled by a third-party candidate. Only Wallace's physical disability (caused by an assassination attempt) prevented him from running again in 1972. The surge in support for Wallace indicated personal support that made him a powerful figure in the Democratic party. It may also represent one step in a process of party realignment—the many traditionally Democratic Northern workers and Southern voters who switched to Wallace in 1968

[44]Sundquist, *Dynamics of the Party System*, p. 343.
[45]Lubell, *The Hidden Crisis*, p. 42.

may have found it easier to support the Republican presidential candidate in 1972. On the other hand, the Wallace vote may represent a further breakdown of support for the party system altogether; Wallace may have served to consolidate and strengthen people's feelings of frustration and rage at established parties and political arrangements.

Finally, the decline of the party as an instrument for capturing loyalties can be measured by the rise of new organizations, which originate outside the party arena and mobilize citizens. The civil-rights movement, black protest in Northern cities, and the antiwar movement, all broadly-based activist groups, were directed *against* parties as well as against other established political institutions. In the 1960s and 1970s, middle-class–based protest organizations have raised issues and sponsored activity that at other times might have been conducted within the party system. Such organizations include environmental groups (like the Sierra Club), Ralph Nader's consumer-activist organizations, and John Gardner's Common Cause.

THE FUTURE OF AMERICAN POLITICAL PARTIES

Overall, parties have served as mechanisms for muffling protest, blurring differences, and supporting "moderate" solutions—in brief, they have been conservative agents for sustaining structural arrangements. Parties have had their greatest influence as instruments for binding citizens to the established political system. In a lesser fashion, they have sought to adjust conflicts among dominant groups and accommodate pressures from the disadvantaged. Yet, not only have parties failed to represent constituents' interests by offering an alternative to existing arrangements but they have not even faithfully represented their constituents' wishes. Sociologist Richard Hamilton has shown that a large minority, or even a majority, of the population favored liberal reforms in the 1950s not advocated by the parties, including public health insurance, government-guaranteed employment, and a guaranteed minimum income. Hamilton observes, "Contrary to common belief, majority sentiment in the

United States is solidly liberal with respect to domestic economic welfare issues."[46]

As a result, less and less organized political activity is taking place within the party system. A large minority of Americans have either been ignored by political parties or have decided to turn their backs on the party system altogether, implicitly judging that parties offer little hope for change. Others have engaged in volatile voting behavior, reflecting their anger at not getting what they want from the parties. Political candidates find that other instruments are more efficient than parties in manipulating voters. And groups that do challenge established institutions work through channels outside the two major parties. Parties are increasingly old-fashioned and outmoded. They have proved to be blunt, multipurpose, unwieldy instruments slow to change and adapt. Even within their remaining area of dominance—the nomination and election of public officials—parties are being pushed aside by professional polling agencies, the media, campaign consulting firms, and the personal organizations of the candidates.

Paradoxically, although parties have been conservative instruments of political control, their decline may signify an additional step away from democratic participation. French political scientist Maurice Duverger suggests that "a regime without parties is of necessity a conservative regime."[47] A leading sociologist, Robert Michels, wrote in *Political Parties,* "Organization is the weapon of the weak against the strong." Michels meant that if some means can be devised to harness and organize the energies of the large number of powerless individuals, they are in a stronger position to challenge the small number of those who dominate. However undemocratic and unresponsive, parties offer a potential for organizing opposition to established arrangements.

But, as political scientists Sidney Verba and Norman Nie point out, those needing government help most participate in party politics the least and "those who need governmental assistance the least participate the most."[48] For most Americans,

---

[46]Richard F. Hamilton, *Class and Politics in the United States* (New York, 1972), p. 87.
[47]Maurice Duverger, *Political Parties* (New York, 1963), p. 426.
[48]Sidney Verba and Norman H. Nie, *Participation in America: Political Democracy and Social Equality* (New York, 1972), p. 12.

political participation does not go beyond the act of voting. Verba and Nie report that fewer than one-third of the electorate participates in three or more political activities beside voting, while nearly half is politically inactive.[49]

Granted there is a socioeconomic cleavage between participants and nonparticipants. But are there differences in political perceptions and attitudes as well? For, if such differences do not exist, it might be argued that the preferences of nonparticipants are being represented despite their lack of participation. Nonparticipation might stem not from dissatisfaction but from contentment. However, many studies find that participants and nonparticipants differ in their political attitudes. The reason for lack of participation is not agreement with existing arrangements and shared views with those who participate.

"Our data show," Verba and Nie conclude, "that participants are less aware of serious welfare problems than the population as a whole, less concerned about the income gap between rich and poor, less interested in government support for welfare problems, and less concerned with equal opportunities for black Americans."[50]

But, why then, do not nonparticipants use the vote to get parties working in their interests? The answer is that it is not so simple. The disadvantaged lack the necessary resources: education, money, skills, time, and influence. Voter-registration requirements, complicated and obscure rules for choosing party officials, the entrenched position of powerful leaders, and the looseness of party organizations make it difficult, if not impossible, for opposition groups to act with political effectiveness. Political scientist Michael Parenti sums up the situation:

> If I were to offer any one explanation for non-participation it would be the profound and widespread belief of so many ghetto residents that there exists no means of taking effective action against long-standing grievances, and that investments of scarce time, energy, money, and, perhaps most of all, hope serve for nought except to aggravate one's sense of affliction and impotence."[51]

[49]*Ibid.*, p. 79.
[50]*Ibid.*, p. 298. Also see Austin Ranney, "Turnout and Representation in Presidential Primary Elections," *American Political Science Review* 66 (March 1972): 21–37.
[51]Michael Parenti, "Power and Pluralism: A View from the Bottom," *Journal of Politics* 32 (August 1970): 523–24.

The decline of parties does not signify a decline in political control. To repeat, the new technology of politics is even more firmly in the hands of the dominant than was the traditional style of party politics. Walter Dean Burnham, among the first to describe broad historical changes in the evolution of the party system, has speculated:

> American electoral politics is undergoing a long-term transition into routines designed only to fill offices and symbolically reaffirm "the American way." There also seems to be tendencies for our political parties gradually to evaporate as broad and active intermediaries between the people and their rulers, even as they may well continue to maintain enough organizational strength to screen out the unacceptable or the radical at the nominating stage. . . . Their disappearance as active intermediaries, if not as preliminary screening devices, would only entail the unchallenged ascendancy of the already powerful, unless new structures of collective power were somehow developed to replace them.[52]

American party competition can be likened to professional sports contests with now one team winning and now the other. In both cases, the stakes are high and the competition is tough—and sometimes dirty.

Watergate represented an extreme case of party competition. The Nixon campaign organization financed informers and saboteurs who infiltrated the Democratic party and the campaign organizations of Democratic candidates. Among the dirty tricks were the circulation of scurrilous campaign literature charging Democratic candidates with sexual misconduct, disrupting Democratic telephone banks, and spying on Democratic candidates and organizations. It was the chance discovery of the attempt to "bug" Democratic party headquarters at the Watergate building, in Washington, D.C., that set in motion the series of events leading to the forced resignation of President Nixon. CRP activities were aimed, first, at knocking out Edmund Muskie, the leading Democratic contender, and assuring the nomination of a less threatening candidate. A second aim was to create division and bitterness among Democratic candidates for the nomination, making it difficult for them to unite behind the party's choice. Both purposes were accomplished, in part as a result of illegal acts.

[52]Burnham, "The End of American Party Politics," p. 257.

However, as with the rivalry of professional sports teams, dirty competition is rare; conflict between American political parties usually takes place within a context of shared interests. Underlying the particular interest of each contender in winning the game is a deeper interest in seeing the game continue. In this sense, as noted earlier, the real contest is not between Democrats and Republicans, but between those who are represented by the party system and those who are not.

This chapter has studied why the potential conflict between procedural democracy and structural inequality does not emerge more openly. Elections hold out the possibility of democratizing the social structure. Since procedural democracy provides for legal equality, with every citizen entitled to vote, an electoral majority might be fashioned uniting subordinate groups, in order to challenge dominant interests. In practice, elections have had an opposite effect: most of the time they have stabilized existing arrangements.

Among the reasons for the conservative bias of the electoral system are the lack of alternatives presented by parties to the electorate, the organization and financing of parties, and the higher rate of participation by the well-to-do. Other factors, analyzed in other chapters, include the operation of political institutions (the presidency, Congress, local government, and the courts) and ideological attitudes in America.

Yet as structural tensions intensify, political parties may be losing their capacity to control and limit political choice. To some extent other agencies, including government, the media, and private campaign firms, may be picking up the slack. However, the voters' growing attention to issues, increasing political independence, and rising dissatisfaction with limited political choices suggest the potential for an opposite development. If the party system continues to decay, the possibility expands for either increased control by dominant groups or, alternatively, popular mobilization by subordinate groups to change structural arrangements.

9
formal representation: congress

Because the United States is a sprawling, complex society, it is not possible for all citizens to participate directly in political decision making. Instead, political democracy depends on representative institutions. The House of Representatives and the Senate are the basic formal representative links between the American people and the national government. Congress makes laws, shapes and constrains the actions of the president and the federal bureaucracy, conducts investigations, certifies appointments, and can remove officials from office.

Utilizing the standard of representative democracy developed in Chapter 2, this chapter examines the vitality of congressional representation. The relative decline of Congress as a powerful political force in this century is not in doubt. The causes, features, and implications of the decline are terribly important, not only because they reveal the state of American democracy but because Congress is the institution that most directly legitimizes the political system as an open, responsive democracy.

THE PLACE OF CONGRESS

Even before the Watergate events put Congress in the national limelight, increasing numbers of Americans had begun to lament the decay of Congress as a representative institution. "That branch of government," one press account noted, "that most closely represents the people is not yet broken, but it is bent and in danger of snapping."[1] Although Congress exercised its constitutional responsibilities in the Watergate affair by holding investigative hearings and conducting the impeachment process until Richard Nixon resigned, the pattern of decline has not been reversed. This decline has been occurring for a long time. The story of the changing place of Congress in the American political landscape, we shall see, is to a large extent a tale of the contradictions between the imperatives of corporate capitalism and those of substantive, representative democracy.

The Constitutional Convention of 1787 raised and resolved basic institutional questions of representation. It was widely assumed at the Convention, political scientist Robert Dahl has written, that a popularly elected House of Representatives "would be the driving force in the system; that the people's representatives would be turbulent and insistent; that they would represent majorities and would be indifferent to the rights of [elite] minorities; that the people would be the winds driving the ship of state and their representatives would be the sails, swelling with every gust."[2]

The delegates were divided on the questions of whether, and how, this popular force should be modified and checked. James Madison, in particular, pointed to the dangers of class conflict and popular sovereignty in a strikingly modern statement that put issues of social control on the delegates' agenda:

> In all civilized Countries the people fall into different classes having a real or supposed difference of interests. There will be creditors and debtors, farmers, merchants, and manufacturers. There will be particularly the distinction of rich and poor. . . . An

[1] *Time,* January 15, 1973, p. 12.
[2] Robert Dahl, *Democracy in the United States: Promise and Performance,* 2d. ed. (Chicago, 1972), p. 151.

increase in population will of necessity increase the proportion of those who labour under all the hardships of life and secretly sign for a more equal distribution of its blessings. These may in time outnumber those who are placed above the feelings of indigence. According to the equal laws of suffrage, the power will slide into the hands of the former. . . . How is the danger in all cases of interested coalitions to oppress the minority to be guarded against?[3]

The Convention's answer was a Senate whose principle of representation was very different from that of the House. There were to be two senators from each state, irrespective of its size, and they were to be chosen by the state legislatures, which were presumed to be more favorable to mercantile, financial, and business interests than the electorate as a whole.[4]

Together, the House and the Senate were given substantial responsibilities by the Constitution. Article I, section 8 enumerates Congress' power to levy taxes, borrow and spend money, regulate interstate and foreign commerce, declare war, support the armed forces, create courts inferior to the Supreme Court, and, most generally, "to make all laws which shall be necessary and proper for carrying into execution the foregoing powers, and all other powers vested by this Constitution in the government of the United States, or in any department or officer thereof." In addition, the House of Representatives was granted the power to impeach—that is, to bring charges against—members of the executive and judiciary branches; and the Senate, the power to try all impeachments (conviction requires a two-thirds majority of those voting).

In the early nineteenth century, the Convention's conception of the House as the popular driving force of government was borne out. Indeed, under the leadership of Henry Clay, the House of Representatives dominated the government. When President Madison called for a declaration of war in 1812 (which was approved by both houses), he was largely bowing to pressure from the House. Supreme Court Justice Joseph Storey aptly remarked in 1818, "The House of Representatives has absorbed all the popular feelings and all the effective power of the country."

[3]Charles Tansill, ed., *Documents Illustrative of the Formation of the Union of the American States* (Washington, 1927), pp. 180–81.
[4]Senators were not popularly elected until the passage of the 17th Amendment to the Constitution in 1912.

A transition that heralded future changes in the position of Congress was the presidency of Andrew Jackson (1828 to 1836) who claimed to represent *all* the people—an assertion echoed by most twentieth-century presidents—and attempted to place the presidency at the center of national decision making. In spite of his success in augmenting the power of the Executive Branch, Congress remained preeminent. Even the nineteenth century's most domineering president, Abraham Lincoln, conceded that "Congress should originate as well as perfect its measures without external bias." If anything, the position of Congress was strengthened after the Civil War. In the late nineteenth century, the House, in particular, increased its power under the leadership of strong Speakers who centralized the powers of the chamber in their hands.

Congress reached the height of its powers in the early years of this century. In the opinion of some observers at the time, the Speaker of the House from 1903 to 1911, Joe Cannon, was even more powerful than the president. Like other strong Speakers before him, Cannon made skillful use of his wide congressional powers as presiding member: to make committee assignments; to control floor debates by recognizing only those congressmen he wished to allow to speak; and to chair the Rules Committee, which determined which legislation would be allowed to come up for debate on the House floor. In the utilization of these powers, Cannon and his late nineteenth-century predecessors functioned much like a British prime minister; they led the party caucuses that adopted formal legislative agendas, which were passed by disciplined party majorities.

Under Cannon, the power of the Speaker and the House grew tremendously, but the power of the individual representative was reduced to near impotence. In 1910, the rank and file of the House rebelled. Cannon was disqualified from serving on the Rules Committee; he lost his absolute power to make committee appointments and his arbitrary authority to decide who should speak. No subsequent Speaker has regained these powers.

Paradoxically, the strengthening of the individual congressman's hand vis-à-vis the Speaker weakened the power of the House and made it easier for the president to exercise legislative authority. After his election in 1912, Woodrow Wilson fundamentally transformed the president's legislative role. The shift in the congressional-presidential balance in his administration "was to alter permanently the relationship between Congress and the President." Whereas formerly, strong Speakers like Joe Cannon had been able to function like a British prime minister, now it was the president who assumed the role of party leader and legislative initiator:

> Wilson laid out to Congress a fully formulated legislative program and then used the full powers of his office to induce Congress to enact it. He signalled this major political alteration of the President's role in American politics by dramatically going before Congress in person to address the members. It was the first such appearance of a President before Congress since Jefferson gave up the practice in 1801.[5]

With ups and downs to be sure, the relationship between Congress and the executive has remained much the same since Wilson's presidency. And the most basic changes and crises in twentieth-century American society have further widened the gap in power between these two branches of government. During the depression, Franklin Roosevelt called Congress into special session, presented a presidential program to meet the crisis, and virtually ran over Congress as the Senate and House passed legislation they barely had time to read. In his administrations, the leaders of both houses became the president's men on Capitol Hill. And when Congress balked at presidential legislation, Roosevelt went over the head of Congress and appealed directly to the general public through press conferences and radio "fireside chats." Much of the legislation he proposed, and many bills proposed since then by Presidents Truman, Eisenhower, Kennedy, Johnson, and Nixon, have been rejected by Congress. Yet the shift in the initiation of domestic legislation to the executive has gone unchallenged. The president proposes, Congress disposes.

Roughly 80 percent of the bills enacted into law today originate in the executive branch. No one expects the most important bills to originate in Congress. Indeed, not only has Congress lost the initiative in proposing important bills but it has lost its power to shape the content of legislation as well. Lawrence Chamberlain has noted that between 1882 and 1909 Congress was responsible for intially drafting 55 percent of the

[5]Neil MacNeil, *Forge of Democracy* (New York, 1963), p. 32.

major laws passed in the period; between 1910 and 1932, 46 percent; and in the New Deal, between 1933 and 1940, only 8 percent of the major bills passed were the wholly original work of Congress.[6] The proportion of important bills on which Congress has a major impact has continued to be low since then.

In foreign affairs, the decline of congressional power has been dramatic. In 1918, under the leadership of Henry Cabot Lodge, the Senate rejected Wilson's Versailles treaty and dashed the president's hopes for American participation in the League of Nations. Since then, as the United States has become the dominant power in world politics, the role of Congress has diminished almost to the point of nonexistence. The war in Vietnam was fought without a declaration of war and continued after Congress withdrew its 1964 Tonkin Gulf resolution, which had authorized the president to use armed force to help South Vietnam. The definition and pursuit of foreign-policy objectives —even if they include subversion, terror, and wanton destruction of other countries—take place without substantive intervention by Congress. The president's capacity to act globally is unimpeded by legislative checks and balances.

The decline in the position of the United States Congress is not unique. As a French journalist recently noted, "representative democracy in every industrially advanced country is in a state of profound crisis." But, he added, "we have been accustomed for so long to accept democracy in the form of its outward appearances and parliamentary institutions that its decay often does not become apparent to us until those institutions have either been brushed aside or reduced to a purely decorative role."[7] Though Congress has not as yet become merely decorative, like other parliaments it has been reduced to a position of relatively minor importance in American politics.

The fundamental explanation for the decline of representative democracy can be traced to a development common to advanced capitalism in the United States and other Western democracies: the growth of a vast corporate complex, in which a powerful executive government and powerful economic interests act in concert. However, the erosion of representative democracy

---

[6]Lawrence Chamberlain, *The President, Congress, and Legislation* (New York, 1946), pp. 450–52.

[7]André Gorz, *Socialism and Revolution* (New York, 1973), p. 73.

is perhaps most striking in America, where executive power was initially most circumscribed by congressional prerogatives.

The turning point in the history of the place of Congress vis-à-vis the executive branch—when President Wilson assumed the role of party leader and legislative initiator—took place at the end of the formative period of the corporate complex. The new political and economic configurations of the corporate complex required long-term investment planning, political and administrative stability, and the rationalization of bureaucratic administration. From the vantage point of those who directed the complex, congressional intiative and intervention in these matters were potentially threatening. A far safer solution was provided by the creation of a bureaucracy of regulatory agencies. These agencies, not Congress, set the ground rules for future interactions between corporate capitalism and government, and in so doing, they also presaged and contributed to the decline of Congress.

THE NATURE OF CONGRESSIONAL REPRESENTATION

The functions that Congress does carry out, though they do not infringe on the powers of the corporate complex, are nevertheless important. They provide the potential for checking presidential abuses, as in Watergate, supervising the federal bureaucracy, defining budgetary and tax alternatives, leading public discussion of fundamental issues, providing an additional access to government, and furnishing tangible services to constituents. Whether or not these potential activities are taken up by members of Congress depends in large measure on the nature of congressional representation. Given the possible scope of congressional action, *whose* legislature is the Congress of the United States?

The answer, we suggest, can best be approached by applying the four criteria of representation discussed in Chapter 2. In that chapter, we distinguished between procedures, especially elections, by which representatives are selected; personnel, or the social background characteristics of representatives; consciousness, their substantive orientations; and effectiveness, the ability of representatives to produce the results they desire. Let us examine each in turn.

Elections: Who Cares? Who Wins?

Elections are the centerpiece of procedural democracy. They forge the link between representatives and their constituents. They provide a mechanism not only for choosing between candidates (and between different public policies) but also for keeping elected representatives attentive to the needs and demands of the represented. The Constitution requires the election of the entire House of Representatives and one-third of the Senate every two years. This is intended to insure that the members of Congress will be strongly influenced by the wishes of their constituents as a whole. To the extent that this pattern of influence is attenuated, Congress' claim to be a substantively representative institution diminishes.

But this ability of voters to influence representatives is predicated on an electorate that is politically interested, informed, and involved, and the evidence is increasingly to the contrary. In a classic article on constituents' awareness of congressional candidates, political scientists Donald Stokes and Warren Miller found that the public's knowledge about those competing for office was meager: "Of the people who lived in districts where the House seat was contested in 1958, 59 percent—well over half—said they had neither read nor heard anything about either candidate for Congress, and less than 1 in 5 felt they knew something about both candidates."[8]

More recent findings not only confirm the general lack of public awareness but also indicate that the indifference of constituents to their representatives is on the increase. A Gallup poll conducted in 1970 found that 53 percent of Americans did not know their congressman's name; 75 percent had no idea how their congressman had voted on even one bill in the past year; 76 percent admitted knowing nothing about the activities of their congressman on behalf of the district; 67 percent had given little or no thought to the coming congressional elections; 38 percent did not even know whether their congressman was a Republican or Democrat.[9]

As a result, in spite of the need for representatives and senators to renew their electoral mandate with regularity (every

[8]Donald Stokes and Warren Miller, "Party Government and the Saliency of Congress," in Theodore Lowi and Randall Ripley, eds., *Legislative Politics USA* (Boston, 1973), p. 170.
[9]*Gallup Opinion Index* 64 (October 1970): 9–14.

two and six years respectively), the typical congressman finds himself remarkably free on most matters from broad constituency pressures, or even from constituency knowledge. This near absence of a give-and-take relationship between congressmen and the public may be thought somewhat surprising since enormous sums are spent on election campaigns, and a very large proportion of a congressman's time is spent on cultivating ties to constituents. It is often said—especially about members of the House—that they must begin to run for reelection the day they are elected. What accounts for the failure of congressional elections to develop a reciprocal interchange between representatives and represented?

One part of the explanation has to do with the changing role of the congressman within his district. As one student of politics has argued:

> Fifty years ago, in his district or state, the campaigning Congressman did not have to compete in a world of synthetic celebrities with the mass means of entertainment and distraction. The politician making a speech was looked to for an hour's talk about what was going on in a larger world, and in debates he had neither occasion nor opportunity to consult a ghost writer. He was, after all, one of the best paid men in his locality, and a big man there.[10]

Today, by contrast, there are a multitude of diversions competing for the public's attention, the television set has supplanted the public meeting as a means of campaigning, and the congressman is no longer a leading celebrity in his community. Moreover, other occupations—corporate management, national law firms—offer talented local figures equivalent prestige and rewards.

Even more important in accounting for the lack of public knowledgeability about Congress is the declining place of Congress itself. Since the character of their jobs, neighborhoods, and the wars they are asked to fight are not much affected in a tangible way by congressional actions, most Americans find little reason to take an interest in congressional affairs. The decline of Congress as an effective representative body has produced widespread feelings of disillusionment. When President Nixon's popularity rating dipped to only 25 percent of the electorate in the spring of 1974, Congress was rated positively by only 21 percent. A year earlier, a cross section of Americans told pollster Louis

[10]C. Wright Mills, *The Power Elite* (New York, 1959), p. 250.

Harris "that they felt abandoned and cheated: 69 percent said they felt that 'large corporations have a great deal of influence' in Washington, but only 7 percent said they thought 'the average citizen' had much clout in federal decision-making."[11]

Paradoxically, a major impact of these weakened ties has been a massive increase in spending on political campaigns. As candidates find it harder to command public attention, they must spend more in an effort to get it. Some of the expenditures are staggering. When Abraham Lincoln ran for Congress in 1846, he had one campaign expense—a barrel of cider. Today, a typical House race will cost $75,000 to $100,000. In 1970, a New York congressional aspirant spent $1.8 million in a successful *primary* campaign. Most of his expenditures, like those of other candidates who spend far less, were for media time.

Funds to finance congressional campaigns can be raised from three sources: the candidate's personal wealth, local economic interests, and national economic interests. Personal wealth may be especially important in Senate races. In 1970, there were fifteen major candidates for the Senate in the country's seven largest states. Eleven were millionaires. All four who were not lost. In New York State, the incumbent Republican was the only nonmillionaire in a three-way race. He spent $1.3 million, his opponents' campaigns cost $2 million and $4 million.

But, of course, not all successful candidates are personally wealthy. As discussed in Chapter 7, most campaign funds come from business interests. And one analyst has estimated that in some metropolitan areas, from 10 to 15 percent of Democratic campaign funds come from gangsters and racketeers.[12]

One consequence of the decline of Congress, rising indifference on the part of the electorate, and large-scale, well-financed media campaigns is the clear trend for members of Congress to serve in office longer and longer. Little as citizens know about their representatives, their knowledge about candidates is even scantier. Unlike new candidates, incumbents have had a chance to make a record in office, access to free trips back to the district and free mailing privileges, the ability to provide tangible services to many constituents, and more opportunities to be seen, heard,

---

[11]*Gallup Opinion Index* 107 (May, 1974): 2ff; Robert Sherrill, *Why They Call It Politics* (New York, 1974), p. xii.

[12]William Domhoff, *Fat Cats and Democrats* (New York, 1972), in Mark Green, James Fallows, and David Zwick, *Who Runs Congress?* (New York, 1972), p. 12.

or read about in the mass media. Cumulatively, these advantages result "in a much higher degree of voter recognition for the incumbent than a challenger can hope to obtain except by extraordinarily high spending. Though only half the voters know the name of their congressman, far fewer have ever heard of his opponent."[13] As a result, the average congressman gains 5 percent more of the vote the second time he runs; a senator gains 3 percent. Voter recognition, not substantive representation, has become the key factor in a congressman's effort to get reelected.

In 1787, George Washington endorsed the two-year term for congressmen. Power, he wrote, "is entrusted for certain defined purposes, and for a certain limited period . . . and, whenever it is executed contrary to [the public] interest, or not agreeable to their wishes, their servants can and undoubtably will be recalled." The House would rapidly turn over in membership, it was expected, thereby giving the people a hold on the actions of their representatives.

This expectation has not been borne out. In the nineteenth century, congressional turnover was very high; in 1870, more than half of the representatives sent to the House were newly elected. By 1900, fewer than one-third; and by 1970, fully 88 percent of the members of the House of Representatives and 66 percent of the members of the Senate had been elected to office more than once. The average congressman in 1970 had served for over seven two-year terms; the average senator for over 10 years.[14] Who are these representatives?

The Representatives

In the representative ideal, a representative body mirrors the population as a whole. But no legislature in the world measures up to this standard. It can be argued, moreover, that not only is perfect symmetry between representatives and represented unlikely but that even without it the interests of the population as a whole can be substantively represented. Fair enough—but a disproportionately unrepresentative legislature on the other hand is likely to leave many members of the population without

---

[13]*Ibid.*, p. 241.
[14]Samuel Huntington, "Congressional Responses to the Twentieth Century," in David Truman, ed., *The Congress and America's Future* (Englewood Cliffs, N.J., 1965), pp. 8–9; Green *et al.*, pp. 226–27.

representatives who even minimally comprehend their life situations and needs; while others, who are overrepresented, are likely to have their views taken into account as a matter of course, sometimes without the representatives even being aware of their own predispositions.

These considerations are important in the case of Congress, since the average social background of congressmen differs so strikingly from the population as a whole. In the words of a recent comprehensive study:

> Against the background of the great cultural, religious and ethnic diversity that is America, a close focus upon the Congress reveals it as predominantly an elite club for aging, white Protestant men from the upper levels of the income ladder. Those who represent America in its national legislative bodies are, as a group, a narrow slice of the American pie. Large segments of the population— especially women, working people, and non-whites—are minimally, if at all, represented in Congress.[15]

More than half of Americans are female. In 1972, of the 435 House members, 11 were women (up from 9 in 1942); and of 100 senators, 2 were women (neither serves today). One in nine Americans is black. One member of the Senate and 16 members of the House were black. In the United States, 58 percent of the people are Protestant, 37 percent Catholic, and 5 percent Jewish. In the Senate, 86 percent are Protestants, 12 percent Catholics, and 2 percent Jewish; in the House 73 percent are Protestants, 23 percent Catholics, 3 percent Jewish.

Class patterns of representation are even more skewed. A student of Congress, Richard Zweigenhaft, found that "the fathers of Congressmen are likely to be businessmen or professionals as are the fathers of corporate executives, corporate lawyers, or Ivy League college professors. Apparently the 10 percent of the male population engaged in business or professional careers are highly overrepresented in the number of sons they have who assume leadership in several arenas of American society," including the Congress.[16] Just over half of congressmen, and two-thirds of senators have been trained as lawyers.

---

[15]Richard Zweigenhaft, "Who Are Our Representatives?" unpublished manuscript, p. 15.
[16]*Ibid.*, pp. 10–11.

Other frequent occupations are business, teaching, banking, and farming. One American in three thousand is a millionaire; at least one in five senators is a millionaire. A few members of Congress come from working-class backgrounds. Senator Mike Mansfield's father was a miner, Edmund Muskie's father is a tailor, and Hiram Fong's parents were indentured servants. But in 1972 there were *no* former manual workers in the Senate, and only three former union officials in the House.

Congressmen are unrepresentative in terms of geography as well. Although more and more Americans have come to live in urban and suburban areas, well over half of all senators and congressmen are from rural areas or small towns. Less than one-tenth of American families live on the farm, yet almost one-third of all senators come from farm families. Moreover, compared to political leaders in the executive branch and business executives, congressmen are relatively immobile geographically. A study that compared corporate presidents and senators in 1959 found that 41 percent of senators still lived in their hometowns, compared to only 12 percent of excutives. And a striking 77 percent of congressional leaders were still living in the state of their birth.[17]

The average member of Congress is very much a local notable:

> The typical Congressman may have gone away to college, but he then returned to his home state to pursue an electoral career, working his way up through local office, the state legislature, and eventually to Congress. The typical political executive in the executive branch on the other hand, like the typical corporation executive, went away to college and then did not return home but instead pursued a career in a metropolitan center or worked in one or more national organizations with frequent changes of residence. . . .
>
> Among the sixty-six lawyers in the Senate in 1963, for instance, only two . . . had been "prominent" corporation counsels before going into politics. Administration leaders, in contrast, are far more likely to be affiliated with large national and industrial corporations, with Wall Street or State Street law firms, and with New York banks.[18]

Thus most congressmen come from and represent an overwhelmingly white, male, Protestant, small-town elite that is distinct from the more cosmopolitan (but not more representa-

[17]Huntington, p. 13.
[18]*Ibid.*, pp. 14, 15.

tive) dominant national elite. Big-city congressmen are more likely to be nonwhite, female, Catholic, or Jewish. But like their small-town counterparts, their orientation is predominantly local (urban congressmen with seniority are likely to be local party-machine stalwarts), and their campaigns are largely financed by local capital (especially the real estate, banking, and insurance firms in the district). Both rural and urban congressmen tend to be "part of a local consensus of local politicians, local businessmen, local bankers, local trade union leaders, and local newspaper editors who constitute the opinion-making elite of their districts."[19] They are likely to be part of the group at the weekly lunchtime Rotary Club meeting.

Representation on Whose Behalf?

The dimension of representation we have called "consciousness" is concerned with how representatives see the interests they represent and how they act on behalf of those interests. Given the absence of an effective, broadly-based electorate, the nature of campaign financing, and the social background of the representatives, Congress has become a principal spokesman for locally-based business and political elites—the people who support congressional campaigns, make party nominations, and join the congressman at the local Rotary Club.

Support for programs that advance the interests of small capital, including agricultural interests, is the price the corporate complex must pay for the continued lack of congressional interference in its basic affairs. As O'Connor has noted:

> Corporate capital must forge alliances with traditional agricultural interests (especially those of the southern oligarchy) and small scale capital. The votes of southern and midwestern farm congressmen and other representatives bound to local and regional economic interests (e.g., shipping, soft coal mining, fishing) are indispensible for the legislative victories of corporate liberal policies.[20]

The cost of this support has been high. The loan program of the Small Business Administration, which includes the underwriting of small banks, capital grants to the fishing industry for new boats; stockpiling of textiles by the government at favorable

---

[19]*Ibid.*
[20]James O'Connor, *The Fiscal Crisis of the State* (New York, 1973), p. 168.

prices; and other subsidy programs to local builders and developers, is an example of the effective representation of these interests by congressmen and senators. No local or regional group has used the mechanism of congressional representation more effectively than America's farmers. The following is a typical example.

In the spring of 1974, the federal government ordered the destruction of millions of chickens on Mississippi farms because the chickens had eaten feed that contained traces of a powerful pesticide that has been linked to cancer. Rather than accept the loss or sue the companies that produced the feed, a delegation of farmers and processors from Scott County visited Washington to convince the Department of Agriculture to allow the contaminated chickens to be marketed. Rebuffed there, they sought to get Congress to agree to have their loss covered by the government.

A few days after their arrival, Senator Eastland of Mississippi introduced a bill to pay "a fair value" for the chickens and the cost of destroying them, estimated at $10 million, or about a dollar a chicken. The bill passed through the Senate Agriculture Committee in one day without any public hearings and passed the Senate by a 2 to 1 margin.

Scott County, Mississippi, is overwhelmingly rural. Many of its farmers are black and poor. They are politically unorganized and have little bargaining power, since they must sell their chickens to one of five county processors, who all pay the farmer about two cents a pound. The processors, who owned the nine million chickens, are the dominant economic force in the county and the largest source of political campaign financing. The bill Eastland directed through the Senate was heavily weighted in their favor. "Out of a total of the $10 million indemnification, 785 farmers will divide about $585,000; 1100 workers will divide about $450,000. Five integrated processors will divide nine million dollars, which covers not only their total investment and the cost of killing the birds, but their profits!"[21]

In the past century, Congress has consistently been the most effective spokesman for local farming interests in Washington. As the corporate complex developed, small farmers found themselves out of step with economic developments and at the mercy

[21]James Hightower, "Mississippi Saga of the Chicken-Fried Taxpayer," *The New Republic,* May 4, 1974, p. 13.

of the new large corporations and banks for machinery, financing, and transportation. Farmers used their democratic access to Congress as a counterweight. Since the 1930s, farmers have captured control of federal agricultural programs and have successfully used Congress to defend their position.

Large farmers who control agricultural policy making in Congress often pass legislation that works in their own interests. In the 1960s, the chairman of the House Agriculture Committee pushed a controversial tobacco subsidy through Congress; he owned two vast tobacco farms. Two members of the Senate Agriculture Committee, Senators Talmadge and Byrd, Jr., are huge landholders; Byrd is the owner of the most extensive apple orchards in the world. When Byrd, Sr., served in the Senate he pushed through a subsidy to an unprofitable shipping line that carried his apples to Europe. Columnists Drew Pearson and Jack Anderson argue:

> The farmer legislators . . . pretend to protect the farmer through legislation that actually increases their own profits and gouges the consumers. Their legislative efforts have produced little to improve the lot of the impoverished farm worker or to aid the small farmer. In a very real sense, their Congressional power enables them to wage class warfare upon the poor.[22]

Potentially, the electorate has a check on congressional behavior of this sort. But in practice, the six-year and two-year terms have become a device to hold congressmen accountable to the wealthier segment of the small-capital sector that finances elections and that, unlike many voters, not only knows the congressman's name but how he acts in minute detail. A reciprocal relationship has developed between powerful local interests and members of Congress, who shape policies that are essential for small capital.

By contrast, senators and congressmen do not make the fundamental decisions about the organization or running of the corporate complex. They are, however, in a position to delay, block, or veto policies the corporate complex wishes to implement. As a result, corporate capital attempts to establish working relationships with those members of Congress who occupy strategic locations in the congressional hierarchy. As a congress-

---

[22]Drew Pearson and Jack Anderson, *The Case Against Congress* (New York, 1968), p. 162.

man or senator gets reelected, he becomes less dependent on local capital for campaign financing and more able to hinder or facilitate the passage of legislation favored by national corporate interests. The most obvious of these strategic locations that members of Congress with seniority come to occupy "include elective leadership posts, memberships on party policy (agenda) and steering (committee assignment) committees, committee chairmanships (or in the case of the minority, 'shadow' chairmanships), chairmanships of subcommittees, membership on more than two regular legislative committees, and membership on the Appropriations Committee."[23]

The relationship between corporate capital influential congressmen is reflected in campaign contributions. Committee chairmen in particular often attract money from those whose profits their committee's legislation might affect. Thus, for example, Congressman Wayne Aspinall, who was chairman of the House Interior Committee in 1970, received 79 percent of his $50,000 reelection campaign fund from outside his district. His committee's actions significantly affect profit rates in the oil, mining, and timber industries.

> Aware of this, Kennecott Copper sent Aspinall nine separate checks in 1970; Humble Oil mailed seven checks from Texas; and Shell Oil, Martin Marietta, and American Metal Climax and Oil Shale Corporation also chipped in. From Washington, D.C., help came from lobbyists and executives of Union Oil, Atlantic Richfield, Dow Chemical, Burlington Northern Railroad, and the Southern tobacco industry. . . . The Southwest Forest Industries of Phoenix and the Western Wood Products Association of Portland, Oregon also sent funds.[24]

As a trucking lobbyist put it, after the industry had spent $30,000 to support campaigns of members of the Public Works and Rules committees who had jurisdiction over a pending bill to permit bigger trucks on interstate highways, "We do what we can for those on the committees who might help us. It's as simple as that."[25]

Perhaps the close connection between corporate interests and congressmen in strategic locations, and the narrow nature of

[23]Nelson Polsby, *Congress and the Presidency* (Englewood Cliffs, N.J., 1964), pp. 38–39.
[24]Green *et. al.*, p. 21.
[25]*Ibid.*, p. 231.

the substantive representation congressmen provide, are most apparent in the area of military spending. The Pentagon budget is regularly approved with relatively little examination. Given the lack of pressure from the electorate in general, the most tangible publicly-funded project a congressman can get for his district is a military installation or a defense contract for local firms. Hence the defense budget is characterized by a great deal of logrolling; it is implicitly understood that Congressman A will not question defense spending in Congressman B's district so long as the favor is reciprocated. Not surprisingly, the most vigorous advocates of military retrenchment come from areas with no military installations or defense contractors. Congressman Jamie Whitten, a Mississippi Democrat who serves on the House Appropriations Committee, Subcommittee on Defense, was candid on this point:

> I am convinced that defense is only one of the factors that enter into our determinations for defense spending. The others are pump priming, spreading the immediate benefits of defense spending, taking care of all services, giving military bases to include all sections. . . . There is no state in the Union, and hardly a district in a state which doesn't have defense spending, contracting, or a defense establishment.[26]

Quite often, congressmen who occupy strategic positions engage in business activities in industries that benefit from their institutional position. In 1968, four members of the House Armed Services Committee owned stock in companies that are leading defense contractors; three members of the Interior and Insular Affairs Committee owned stock in oil or gas companies; and twelve members of the House Banking and Currency Committee had an interest in banks, savings and loan associations, or bank holding companies. Many of the senators and congressmen who are lawyers are attached to firms that represent clients in litigation before federal agencies.[27] For example, during George Smathers' service in the Senate, clients of his law practice included Pan American Airlines, Standard Oil, and the Home

---

[26]Testimony before the Joint Economic Committee's Defense Procurement Subcommittee, January 29, 1960.

[27]The law stipulates that members of Congress may not collect legal fees in federal cases; their firms typically find legal dodges such as creating two juridically separate firms, one listing the congressman, the other omitting his name from the roster of partners.

Insurance Agency, a combination that aptly coincided with Smathers' membership on such committees as Finance, Small Business, Judiciary, and Joint Internal Revenue Taxation.[28]

Given the shift in the locus of national political power in this century from the Congress to the executive branch, most of the efforts of corporate interests to influence Congress are essentially *defensive*. As David Truman, a leading analyst of Congress, has noted, organized interest group activity does not seek to convince members of Congress to initiate new policies. Rather, most such activity, especially that of lobbyists in the corporate sector, is "dedicated to preventing any change in the existing order of things. Where there are groups whose claims involve a change, there are as likely to be others . . . vigorously defending the *status quo.*"[29] After studying the relative success or failure of congressional interest-group activity, he concluded that "the business corporation has been such a favored group in the United States . . . it normally enjoys defensive advantages."

An important factor in accounting for corporate "veto power" in Congress is the corporate lobby. The most influential corporate lobbies—including those of the oil, armaments, tobacco, sugar, and automobile industries—are well financed and staffed, often by former congressmen or members of the executive branch who had worked with members of Congress. The American Petroleum Institute, the most powerful—but not the only—trade association, has an annual budget of close to $10 million and a permanent Washington staff of over 200. Its Washington office has been directed in the past decade by Frank Ikard, a Texas congressman from 1952 to 1961. This is a common pattern. Former Senator Earle Clements of Kentucky was an influential tobacco lobbyist in the 1960s; Harold Cooley, a former House Agriculture Committee chairman, has served recently as a lobbyist for sugar interests in Liberia and Thailand; and at least five active members of the banking lobby in 1970 had served on the staff of the Senate Banking and Currency Committee and a subcommittee on housing and urban affairs.[30]

An atmosphere of easy, comradely interchange is developed by lobbyists with members of Congress. Senators, congressmen, and members of their staffs are routinely treated to favors by

[28]Martin Tolchin and Susan Tolchin, *To the Victor* (New York, 1971), pp. 242–43.
[29]David Truman, *The Governmental Process* (New York, 1951), p. 353.
[30]Green *et. al.,* pp. 44–45.

lobbyists who have lavish expense accounts. A committee aide said, "You begin to look forward to those three or four good lunches a week with the lobbyists at the good restaurants, to the $25 bottles of scotch, the football tickets, the occasional junkets, and if you don't watch out, you get pulled into the lobbyist's frame of reference." A former senator has explained the experience:

> The enticer does not generally pay money directly to the public representative. He tries instead, by a series of favors, to put the public official under such a feeling of personal obligation that the latter gradually loses his sense of mission to the public and comes to feel that his first loyalties are to his private benefactors and patrons.[31]

The effect of lobbying on a congressman is thus a subtle and gradual process, with the result that the typical congressman is often sincerely convinced that there is no direct causal connection between these favors and his legislative actions.

Indeed, most members of Congress believe that lobbyists are indispensable to the legislative process. A Brookings Institution study argued that "becuase of the publicity given to early, blatantly improper attempts to influence legislators, the general public views with suspicion anyone classified as a lobbyist. The constructive services that are provided by today's professionals are often little known." A congressman whose views were typical had this to say:

> A lot of people seem to think that lobbying is a bad thing. I think that is one misconception which still needs to be corrected as far as the general public is concerned. Lobbying is an essential part of representative government, and it needs to be encouraged and appreciated. Lobbyists are frequently a source of information. If they come to your offices and explain a program or factors contributing to the need for legislation, you get a better understanding of the problems and answers to them. If you have your independence, and I think we all do, they can teach you what an issue is all about, and you can make your own decision.[32]

But what this perspective fails to see is that lobbying activity systematically injects a powerful bias into the legislative system on behalf of those who command specialized information (such

[31]*Ibid.*, p. 41.
[32]Charles Clapp, *The Congressman* (New York, 1964), pp. 183, 184.

information is never neutral), staff, and money, and who enmesh congressmen in a web of favors ranging from an early evening drink to substantial campaign contributions.

But the success of the corporate sector in developing a built-in veto over congressional action is not merely the result of weak constituency pressures, campaign contributions, or effective lobbying. Congress is not merely a sounding board or "passive registering device . . . for the demands of organized political interest groups."[33] As an institution, Congress has an autonomy and life of its own. Hence we turn to an examination of Congress as an institution and of the ways in which its institutional life affects the character of congressional representation.

Limitations and Controls on Effective Action

The last criterion of representation is effectiveness, a measure of how the procedures and institutional life of representative bodies affect both the orientations of the representatives and their capacity to achieve their aims. Four features of the institutional life of Congress are especially important: its clublike atmosphere, the norm of professionalism, the committee structure, and the nature of the legislative hurdles a bill must leap before it can become a law.

We have seen earlier how the social backgrounds of congressmen separate them from direct contact with and understanding of the relatively subordinate and how the general disinterest of constituents creates a vacuum that is filled by congressmen's own predispositions, reelection needs, and an elaborate network of favored relationships with powerful interests. Congress as an institution further isolates representatives from the general public by providing a comfortable clublike setting for the interaction of members with each other and with noncongressional political participants.

Congress functions as a full-service club for its members. The Senate alone has a dozen restaurants and a barbershop where the senators may get their hair cut for nothing. There are two swimming pools, steam baths, and a shop that sells stationery supplies at discount prices. In addition to their annual salary of $42,500, members of the House and Senate receive generous

[33]Truman, p. 350.

pensions (if they last at least five years in office), inexpensive life insurance, tax breaks if they own two homes, a stationery allowance, a large telephone allowance, almost unlimited mailing privileges, nearly free medical care, and free underground parking. Each year many congressmen travel abroad at government expense, sometimes with little apparent governmental purpose. All this plus continual deference, ease of contact with the powerful both in and out of government, and access to a hectic social life both make the congressman's job desirable indeed—and cut off the representatives even further from the represented. Though the scope of congressional power is limited, the congressman can enjoy a life style similar to those at the top.

This comfortable club, like most clubs, has an elaborate set of norms to regulate the interpersonal behavior of its members. Collectively, these norms dampen conflict among members, restrict their scope of action, and reinforce their general parochialism. As one influential senator put it, "There is great pressure for conformity in the Senate. It's just like living in a small town."[34]

In December 1956, newly elected Senator Joseph Clark of Pennsylvania had lunch with an old friend, Senator Hubert Humphrey. Clark reports that he asked Humphrey, "Tell me how to behave when I get to the Senate."

> He did—for an hour and a half. I left the luncheon I hope a wiser man, as well briefed as a neophyte seeking admission to a new order can be. In essence he said, "Keep your mouth shut and your eyes open. It's a friendly, courteous place. You will have no trouble getting along. . . . You will clash on the filibuster rule with Dick Russell and the Southerners as soon as you take the oath of office. Don't let your ideology embitter your personal relationships. It won't if you behave with maturity. . . . And above all keep your mouth shut for awhile."[35]

This advice encapsulates many of the norms that shape members' actions. Freshman senators and members of the House are expected to serve an apprenticeship. "The new senator," political scientist Donald Matthews has written, "is expected . . . not to take the lead in floor fights. . . . The freshman senator's status is impressed upon him in many ways. He receives the committee

---

[34]Donald Matthews, *U.S. Senators and Their World* (New York, 1960), p. 92.
[35]Joseph Clark, *Congress: The Sapless Branch* (New York, 1964), p. 2.

assignments the other senators do not want. The same is true of his office suite and his seat in the chamber. In committee rooms he is assigned to the end of the table."[36] Although this norm of apprenticeship has been modified in the past decade, especially in the senate, the new member still learns quickly that seniority is the necessary, if not always sufficient, condition of major congressional influence.

He also learns that the normative system discourages independence, dissension, and innovation.[37] When substantive disagreements emerge in debates, conflict is blunted by an elaborate, often hypocritical, code of courtesy. "A cardinal rule of Senate behavior is that political disagreements should not influence personal feelings. . . . The rules prohibit the questioning of a colleague's motives or the criticism of another state."[38] The behavior of members of the Senate and House is further constricted by two other widely shared norms—those of reciprocity and institutional chauvinism. Even congressmen who differ with each other on policy matters are expected to help out a colleague with votes and other favors when not directly affected, and they can expect to be paid back in kind. They are expected as well to develop an unquestioning commitment to Congress and to defend it against detractors. Members of Congress come to feel that whatever differences they have are largely internal matters; to the outside world they present a largely united front. In this enclosed world, those who raise nettlesome issues do so at the cost of influence, friendship, and esteem.

Institutional arrangements are not neutral. As political scientists Wallace Sayre and Herbert Kaufman indicated, procedural matters "are not merely abstract exercises in political architecture and processes. The kinds of decisions that emerge are directly related to the participants favored or disadvantaged by such rules."[39]

The most important congressional procedures are committee organization and seniority. Almost a century ago, Woodrow Wilson observed that "Congress, in its Committee rooms, is Congress at work."[40] The same observation could be made today.

[36]Matthews, p. 93.
[37]See Clapp, pp. 9ff.
[38]Matthews, p. 97.
[39]Wallace Sayre and Herbert Kaufman, *Governing New York City* (New York, 1965), p. 106.
[40]Woodrow Wilson, *Congressional Government* (New York, 1956), p. 83.

Although there are only 21 House and 17 Senate committees, in 1970 there were 267 subcommittees, a number that indicates the extent to which congressional work is specialized and decentralized.

Each party in each chamber has a Committee of the Committees to appoint members. The committee assignments of new congressmen and senators are critical to their careers; if they are to make a substantive impact, it is likely to be through their committee work. But since not all committees are equal in stature or importance, appointment to committees is marked by keen competition. Freshmen rarely get put on the most important committees (the three most significant are the House Ways and Means Committee and the Senate Finance Committee, which have jurisdication over the country's tax structure, and the House Appropriations Committee, which oversees the federal budget and is more important than its Senate counterpart). As an experienced congressman put it, "It would be too risky to put on a person whose views and nature the leadership has no opportunity to assess."[41] Those who show themselves to be nonconformists are screened out in favor of members who have proved that they will act in accordance with prevailing standards of behavior.

Committees are the places where legislation is shaped, promoted, or buried. In his study of the Senate, Donald Matthews found that if a proposal was supported by over 80 percent of the members of the relevant committee, it passed on the floor every time; if from 60 to 79 percent supported the bill in committee, it passed 90 percent of the time. In accordance with the norms of reciprocity and courtesy, most legislators will follow the decision of the committees unless they have a basic reason to doubt it. For almost all legislation, the committee actions are the decisive factor.

Congressional committees work on specialized subject areas, such as labor, education, defense, and agriculture. In theory, they are major battlegrounds where different interests compete in the making of public policy. Individuals and groups who are affected by proposed legislation are usually granted the chance in public hearings to argue their positions, transmit information, and attempt to generate congressional and public

[41]Green *et al.*, p. 55.

support for their point of view. In practice, the routine operation of congressional committees *limits* controversy and buttresses prevailing patterns of dominance in the following ways.[42]

Limited participation and close interaction   The number of people who work on bills in congressional committees is small. Much of the day-to-day work is accomplished in subcommittees of about five legislators. The largest committees are those dealing with appropriations. Yet even their membership totals only 13 percent of the House and 26 percent of the Senate. "Limited participation in a conflict," political scientist Philip Brenner observes, "engenders quick resolution because there are fewer positions to reconcile." Further limiting the range of options explored is the fact that small committees engender close interaction and friendships.

> Over many years members do come to see each other as friends with common problems, rather than as representatives of a position. . . . Close interaction thus encourages members to avoid intense conflict in order to maintain cordial relations with their "friends." It further discourages the congressman who might fight for a position which is antagonistic to prevailing interests from continuing his fight, because in doing so he tends to alienate himself from the people with whom we works closely.[43]

Thus, committees duplicate the clublike atmosphere of congress as a whole and take on an integrated life of their own that often cuts across party lines. Richard Fenno's study of the House Appropriations Committee, for example, found a deeply rooted committee consensus on goals. Members were recruited to produce "a group of individuals with an orientation especially conducive to Committee integration. . . . Key selectors speak of wanting, for the Appropriations Committee, 'the kind of man you can deal with,' or 'a fellow who is well-balanced and won't go off half-cocked on things.' "[44]

Secrecy   Given the wide range of specialization and the sheer number of subcommittees, they cannot adequately be covered by the press. Moreover, much committee work is held in

---

[42]Philip Brenner, "Committee Conflict in the Congressional Arena," *The Annals* 411 (January 1974): 98–100.

[43]*Ibid.*, p. 99.

[44]Richard Fenno, Jr., "The Appropriations Committee as a Political System," in Robert Peabody and Nelson Polsby, eds., *New Perspectives on the House of Representatives* (Chicago, 1963), p. 85.

secret. In the Senate in 1968, according to the *Congressional Quarterly Almanac,* 93 percent of the hearings of the Rules and Administration Committee were held behind closed doors; 46 percent of the Foreign Relations Committee meetings; 30 percent of the Public Works Committee sessions; 67 percent of the Armed Services Committee hearings; and 47 percent of the hearings of the Labor and Public Welfare Committee. In the House, *all* of the Appropriations Committee hearings were conducted in secret. The overall figure for committee hearings held in secret was 43 percent.[45] Although the 1970 Legislative Reorganization Act required that all committee sessions be opened to the public unless a majority of the committee voted for a closed session, 36 percent were still secret in 1971. As a consequence, not only is the general public excluded, but most members of Congress must depend on the judgment of the members of the relevant committee. When a bill reaches the Senate and the House for debate, only the committee members have a detailed acquaintance with the legislation, and they usually remain in control of the floor debate.

Seniority Power within the committee system is determined by seniority. The chairmanship of a committee is allocated automatically to the member of the majority party who has served longest on the committee, thereby preventing a potential cause of conflict. Further, as Philip Brenner notes, seniority procedures "take away a focal point for outsiders [who] . . . would be encouraged to pressure members, and for candidates [who] might be 'encouraged' to campaign on the basis of their positions on upcoming issues."[46]

The seniority system puts a premium on specialization. It is widely agreed that effective legislators are those who focus their energy only on matters that either affect their districts directly or come before their committees. The most senior men on the committees have been there a long time. They have been enmeshed in a mutually beneficial relationship with special-interest groups for decades; and they tend to identify with and share the defensive interests of the most powerful lobbies.

As a result, the committee structure based on seniority is substantively biased for the status quo and against fundamental change. This bias is further reinforced by the fact that the

[45]*Congressional Quarterly Almanac* (Washington, 1968), pp. 798–99.
[46]Brenner, p. 100.

seniority system gives the most power to the least representative. The population of the United States as a whole is increasingly young, geographically mobile and urban. Committee chairmen tend to be old, rural, and Southern. In 1970, the average age of chairmen was sixty-seven; thirteen of twenty-one House chairmen came from rural districts; twelve of the twenty-one House chairmen and nine of the seventeen Senate chairmen (including those of all the most important committees) were from the South.

The committee-agency nexus We saw earlier, in Chapter 5, how corporate capitalism and the executive branch of the federal government have formed the interlocking relationship we call the corporate complex. Congress is not an integral part of this complex. Its relative decline is largely accounted for by its exclusion. Congressional committees, however, pose the key legislative hurdle for corporate-complex policies and actions. Committees can oversee the practices of government regulatory agencies, fail to pass legislation initiated by the executive branch, and modify the president's proposed budget.

These checks are not routinely applied. Individual standing committees have fashioned close and stable relationships with their companion executive agencies. The Department of Agriculture and the agriculture committees, the Pentagon and armed services committees, and the Department of Labor and the education and labor committees have become mutually supportive. The agencies are attentive to the wishes of the committees that formally supervise them, and within Congress the agencies are regarded as the substantive property of the relevant committees.

The support of powerful corporate-sector interest groups for members of Congress in strategic locations and the close interaction, secrecy, and seniority system of the committees facilitate the development of an enduring committee-agency nexus that functions in the interests of the corporate complex. Most issues "tend to be decided in accord with agreements reached in close cooperation between key members of Congress (usually senior committee and subcommittee members), key representatives of interest groups, and key bureaucrats."[47] In this way, Congress, though not an integral part of the corporate complex, becomes its predictable ally.

[47]Lowi and Ripley, p. 161.

The committee-agency nexus is reinforced by congressional budget-making procedures, which have not changed for decades. The budget is never dealt with as a whole. Instead, the parts of the budget proposed by the executive branch are parcelled out to the subcommittees of the House or Senate Appropriations Committee, each of which deals with a specific set of executive agency requests. The subcommittees' recommendations, which are usually supportive of its sister executive agency, are rarely studied or debated in detail either by the committees as a whole or by the full House.

Programs authorized by the Senate and House in specific appropriations bills are never considered in relationship to each other. Consequently, the overall shape of the budget is out of the hands of the representative branch of government. Congress may from time to time alter parts of the whole, but what expenditures are given priority is determined by the executive branch.

For a bill to become a law, it must pass through a labyrinth of procedural hurdles. The nature of this legislative course reinforces the status-quo orientation of most representatives.

Although a bill must be formally introduced by a congressman or senator, major legislation is rarely the work of an individual or even initiated in the Congress. Proposals that lack presidential support usually are doomed. Most major bills are drafted in the executive agencies and are put on the president's legislative program, which becomes the basic legislative agenda. Major legislation is almost always introduced by a leading member, often the chairman, of the standing committee to which the bill is referred. Once the bill is introduced, its fate is largely in the hands of senior committee members, who guard their committee's prerogatives.

Committee procedures in the Senate and the House are essentially similar. Most of the bills referred to committees are never taken up. After they have been introduced on the floor—often by congressmen seeking to build political capital with their constituency—they die a quick death. Public hearings are held on the majority of bills that survive. At their conclusion, the real legislative work begins. The committee goes into closed executive session, where the bill is read line by line. This is called the mark-up stage. At this critical point, the bill is amended, rewritten, or, if no version can be worked out that is acceptable to the majority of the committee, the legislative process ends and the proposal dies. The relatively few bills that emerge successfully from this procedure have the support of a large majority of committee members and are the product of the closed committee process that puts a premium on interpersonal relationships and a broad substantive consensus. Thus, controversial proposals rarely survive.

Once a bill is passed by the relevant committee in the House or the Senate, it is placed on the chamber's calendar. In the Senate, major bills are usually taken up for consideration from the calendar by the majority leader. In the House, bills must be reported out by the Rules Committee, which schedules House business, before they can reach the floor. As one of the more traditionally conservative committees, the Rules Committee has been a major barrier to the consideration of legislation that challenges patterns of dominance.

By now, before the legislation is debated on the Senate and House floors, the bill's substance and possibilities for passage have largely been determined. Though the floor debates seem to the observer to be the most important phase of the legislative process, in fact, the debates rarely influence any votes.

When the House Rules Committee schedules debate on legislation, the congressmen meet as a Committee of the Whole House (identical to the membership of the House of Representatives) to consider the bill and proposed amendments. At this stage, no recorded votes are taken, debating procedures are relaxed, and a quorum of only 100, instead of the usual 218, is required for business. Like the mark-up, this procedure takes place behind closed doors. The Committee of the Whole then reports the bill to the House with any new amendments that have been added. These changes may be voted on again. Then the entire bill as amended is put to a vote.

By contrast to the House, where the Rules Committee usually sets time limits to the floor discussion, debate in the Senate is unlimited. More frequently than not, the majority leader, in agreement with the minority leader, fixes time limits for debate. But this schedule requires unanimous consent. Should one senator object, debate continues.

The Senate provision for unlimited debate can lead to a filibuster, in which one or a group of senators attempt to defeat a measure by holding the floor for hours, or even days, and thus preventing the bill from coming to a vote. If they succeed in holding up Senate business for a long period, the bill is usually dropped. This tactic has been used successfully in the past, principally by Southerners opposed to civil-rights legislation. Cloture, a vote to limit debate, needs support by two-thirds of those voting, not just a majority. Many senators who support a bill are reluctant to vote for cloture for fear of weakening a device that they might wish to use in the future. Like the House Rules Committee barrier, the filibuster is another device used to quash controversial legislation.

If a bill is one of the lucky few to be approved by both the House and Senate, it has still not become law. If, as in most cases, there are differences between the versions passed by the House and the Senate, the bills are sent to a conference committee charged to iron out the discrepancies. Usually composed of five or six members from each house, these *ad hoc* bodies operate in total secrecy; no record is kept of their proceedings. They may alter provisions, insert new amendments, or even write a whole new bill.

The members, or managers, of these committees are not selected at random from the House and Senate. Rather, the conference committee's membership is chosen on the recommendation of the chairman of the standing committee that had jurisdiction over the bill in the first place. Normally, he proposes senior members from his own committee. In this way, the legislative process comes full circle, as the same senior committee specialists who marked-up the bill in private once again have a critical private task—producing the final legislation.

Conference committee reports are the privileged business of each house, since other floor business must be put aside to consider the reports. They may be approved, voted down, or returned to the conference committee. Typically, they are approved, and the bill, now passed in identical form by the Senate and House of Representatives, goes to the president for his approval or veto. Should he sign the bill, it becomes law; should he veto, a vote of two-thirds of the House and Senate is needed to override the president's action and pass the bill into law.

As the most important representative institution in the United States, Congress in action provides a key test for American democracy. Its very existence confers the mantle of democracy on the actions of the national government, yet, in fact, it is a limited representative body. Its scope of action has diminished in this century as the corporate complex has developed. The influence exerted on representatives by their constituents is weak; members' social backgrounds are very different from those of the population as a whole; congressmen tend mainly to represent the interests of small capital and the defensive goals of the corporate complex; and the procedures of the institution reduce conflict and reinforce prevailing structural arrangements.

From time to time, Congress initiates policy and keeps the executive in check. The Clean Air Act of 1970 set federal pollution standards; the Senate Select Committee on Campaign Practices, chaired by Senator Ervin of North Carolina, revealed the details of Watergate to the American people in 1973 and indicated that, however much presidential power had grown, Congress could still play a major political role through its constitutional power to investigate. But these are the exceptions, not the rule. As a result, popular government has become a set of formal procedures, not an open arena of substantive representation.

10

the quality
of
justice

The American justice system of the police, prisons, and courts is the largest in the world. Jails run by local governments alone confined at least 1.5 million Americans in 1970 at a cost of over $300 million. Roughly one of every two hundred citizens in the country's largest cities is a policeman or court officer. More than 300,000 Americans are lawyers. Each state has dozens of different types of courts that conduct trials, hear lawsuits, and provide chances to appeal decisions. Federal courts also hear both criminal and civil cases.

This immense justice system has a large number of tasks. It interpenetrates the society from local neighborhoods to the White House. It determines who the lawbreakers are and how they shall be punished, interprets a written Constitution, legitimizes executive and congressional decisions, provides possibilities for citizens to press their claims, and enables authorities to curb political opposition. How does the justice system manage these tasks? On behalf of which interests?

FORMAL JUSTICE, SUBSTANTIVE INJUSTICE

Formally, the justice system is a nonpolitical system of written laws, legal procedures, and institutions that are the means of securing justice for all Americans. In appearances, trappings, and stated principles and procedures, the justice system is committed to upholding the equality of all citizens before the law. Policemen wear uniforms and judges robes to signify that they are performing their duties in the interest of justice, not for their personal gain. Policemen are protected from partisan political pressures by civil service regulations; judges, by long tenures of office. And all participants in the courtroom process are bound by deference to the authority of the law. In its substantive performance, however, the justice system often acts inconsistently, unfairly, and partially.

The development of a formally nonpolitical legal system was intimately bound up with the development of capitalism in Western Europe. The assertion of parliamentary prerogatives in England after 1688 and the toppling of the Old Regime by the French Revolution of 1789 paved the way for the elaboration of modern legal codes and institutions that adhered to predictable, publicly articulated sets of regulations and procedures. The new capitalist enterprises in these countries were not based on the traditional authority of the lord-serf relationship, and they needed the new legal systems to legitimize their existence and to provide a calculable context within which capitalists could make contracts and exchange goods for money. The law thus provided capitalist enterprises with the legal stability and security they required.

America's legal system, from the colonial period to the present, has had its roots in British law. After the American Revolution, however, key legal questions remained unresolved, the most important being the relationship between the individual states and the national government. The Articles of Confederation, the country's first constitution that went into effect in 1781, allowed each state to retain "its sovreignty, freedom and independence" and declared that every power not "expressly delegated" to the national government was reserved to the states. In the national Congress, each state had one vote.

The new national government could neither tax nor regulate commerce. As a result, it failed to prevent costly economic disputes between states and provide the kind of stable climate necessary for economic development. The Constitutional Convention of 1787 was largely the result of the dissatisfaction of financial and commercial groups with existing legal arrangements.

The Founding Fathers drafted a Constitution that provided for truly revolutionary democratic procedures and liberties. But they also acted to protect their economic interests. Many provisions of the Constitution were drafted to protect property rights. By creating a national government that had powers of taxation, sole control over a national monetary system, and the right to regulate interstate and foreign commerce, the Constitution developed the legal framework for the nineteenth- and twentieth-century growth of American capitalism.

Formal legal equality of citizens is another key feature of capitalist economic development. Unlike feudal relationships that tied serfs to particular fiefs, capitalist relationships are contractual. Workers sell their labor for a wage to those who contract to buy it. This exchange relationship is an exchange between legal equals: wages for work. But, under capitalism, legally free and equal citizens are substantively unequal. Indeed, as we saw in Chapter 2, this contrast between legal equality and substantive inequality is the central problem of democratic theory.

The contrast between formal legal equality and substantive inequality is mirrored in the routine operation of the American justice system. Since the law has no official political or economic ends or goals, it cannot act against the inequalities caused by corporate capitalism. As a result, the law, which safeguards the rights of both capital and labor in apparently neutral fashion, buttresses the social structure and supports existing patterns of dominance.

But if the most important consequence of the justice system is its contribution to the maintenance of the corporate-capitalist order, formal legal equality has also considerably widened the average citizen's freedom by granting basic rights, including free speech, freedom from unreasonable search and seizure, and religious choice.

Even political elites may be penalized for violating the norms and procedures of the justice system—at least when the violations are so flagrant as to arouse public indignation. When the Watergate grand jury indicted President Nixon's closest political associates in March 1974 (H. R. Haldeman, John Ehrlichman, John Mitchell, and Charles Colson, as well as three lesser figures), charging them with conspiracy to obstruct justice and perjury, it acted according to the formal standards of the system irrespective of the former high positions of the defendants. When public officials are brought to justice, one of the side effects is the perpetuation of the ideological claim that all citizens are equal before the law, that the norms and procedures of the justice system are binding on all members of the polity.

Thus, although we shall see that the justice system of the police, prisons, and courts is one of the key bulwarks of the social order and a central agency of social control, it also sets a formal framework of rights and procedures that give citizens tangible resources and acts to restrain the power of the dominant. The two basic contradictions built into the justice system are that it both upholds equality and perpetuates inequality; it enlarges and protects freedom at the same time that it acts as an instrument of social control.

We shall examine the operations and contradictions of the justice system in four areas: the Supreme Court, civil courts, criminal justice, and the legal machinery used to repress political opposition and dissent.

THE ROLE AND POWERS OF THE SUPREME COURT

The United States Supreme Court bestrides the entire justice system. It is the court of last resort; there is none higher. Indeed, it is the only court mentioned in the Constitution: "The Judicial power of the United States shall be vested in one Supreme Court, and in such inferior courts as the Congress may from time to time ordain and establish."

Historically, the Supreme Court has performed four basic functions:

First, The Court has legitimized the political and economic actions of the most powerful. With the exception of transitional periods like the mid-nineteenth century and the 1930s, the Court almost without fail has supported the policies of the dominant national, as opposed to regional, interests of the time.

Second, the Court has provided an arena where conflicts can be settled between those in positions of economic and political power: between unions and corporations, state and federal governments, Congress and the executive branch. The Court thus provides an extra political means of resolving intraelite conflicts.

The third function of the Supreme Court has been to take decisions that may be too difficult or unpopular for the president or Congress to take. The May 1954 *Brown* v. *Board of Education* decision, which held segregation in public schools unconstitutional, was fundamental in challenging the quasi-feudal, precapitalist pattern of social relations in the South. But at the time, neither the president nor Congress would have been prepared to take this step because of the electoral perils involved. Thus, through the Court, elites can satisfy some of the needs and demands of subordinates without taking responsibility for these actions.

Fourth, the Court, more than any other part of the justice system, has acted to protect and extend the system's formal legal protections. Hence the Supreme Court has been the pivotal arena for the expansion of the rights of criminal defendants and the protection of civil liberties and civil rights. In this respect, the Court has at least partial institutional autonomy, since it takes these decisions according to the logic of formal legal justice, often over the opposition of important members of the corporate and political elite. Let us examine how the Court has carried out these four functions.

The United States has a dual court system. Both the states and the federal government maintain trial courts. State courts far outnumber federal courts: there are only eighty-nine federal district courts for the entire country (with 333 federal district court judges in all), but there are thousands of state courts, reaching into every governmental jurisdiction. Federal courts hear criminal matters that concern federal law; they hear non-criminal, or civil, matters that involve either citizens of more than one state or complaints filed by the federal government. State courts hear the rest.

Today, both state and federal courts have their own appeals procedures. Decisions of city, county, and state trial courts may be appealed to state appellate courts; decisions of United States district courts may be appealed to one of eleven federal courts of appeal, and then to the Supreme Court. In a few cases, decisions of district courts may be appealed directly to the Supreme Court.

This dual structure dates only from 1891. For the first century of American independence, the basic structure of the federal courts was a subject of struggle between competing regional and national interests. By mentioning only the Supreme Court, the Constitution left two basic issues unresolved: "(1) Should lower federal courts be created at all, or should adjudication of claims of a federal nature be adjudicated in the first instance by state courts?; and (2) if lower federal courts were created, what limitations should Congress place over their jurisdiction?"[1]

The Judiciary Act of 1789 represented a compromise between those who saw federal courts as a threat to state interests and those who viewed a system of state courts as inevitably parochial, and thus unable to dispense justice fairly to out-of-state citizens. The Act established lower federal courts, but limited them to a state focus: their jurisdictions were drawn along state lines, the federal district judge was required to be a resident of his district, and the major task of the new lower federal courts was the preparation of materials for Supreme Court justices who traveled to the localities to hear cases.

Institutional federal supremacy was finally established with the creation of a federal court of appeals in 1891. The new court detached the appeals procedure from the pressures of the states and districts, diminished the possibilities of interpretations of the law varying too widely from area to area, and freed the Supreme Court from routine duties so that it could concentrate on more substantive matters.

The Supreme Court caps the dual court system, whose basic organization has remained virtually unchanged since 1891. The Court receives the vast majority of its cases from the federal district and appellate courts and from the state courts. Whereas review of lower federal court decisions has been widely accepted as logical and necessary, the Court's power to review state court decisions, as we shall see, has been the source of much dispute.

In addition, in a very small number of cases involving foreign diplomats or a state as a party, the Court has original jurisdiction and gets the cases directly. Though often ignored by students of the Supreme Court, these cases are usually extremely important and politically controversial. Recent examples have included

[1]Richard Richardson and Kenneth Vines, *The Politics of Federal Courts* (Boston, 1970), p. 19.

disputes between the federal government and California, Louisiana, Texas, and Florida concerning title to rich oil deposits just off the coast; and *South Carolina* v. *Katzenbach* (1966), in which the Court sustained the constitutionality of the 1965 Voting Rights Act, whose purpose was to guarantee Southern blacks the right to vote in the face of restrictive state practices.

Many more cases are filed with the court each year than it has time or inclination to hear. Hence the Court carefully chooses which cases to hear, following principles expressed by Justice Fred Vinson in 1949:

> The Supreme Court is not, and never has been, primarily concerned with the correction of errors in lower court decisions. In almost all cases within the Court's appellate jurisdiction, the petitioner has already received an appellate review of his case. . . . The function of the Supreme Court is, therefore, to resolve conflicts of opinion on federal questions that have arisen among lower courts, to pass upon questions of wide import under the Constitution, laws and treaties of the United States, and to exercise supervisory power over lower federal courts. If we took every case in which an interesting legal question is raised, or our *prima facie* impression is that the decision below is erroneous, we could not fill the Constitutional and statutory responsibilities placed upon the Court. To remain effective, *the Supreme Court must continue to decide only those cases which present questions whose resolution will have immediate importance far beyond the particular facts and parties involved.* [2]

Supreme Court decisions have frequently been the result of legal battles that mirrored the basic cleavages between different economic and political interests expressed in different periods of American history. Broadly, the Court has passed through four ideological periods: until the Civil War it was preeminently concerned with protecting national economic and political interests at the expense of state and regional interests (there were important countercurrents within the court to be sure). From the Civil War to the New Deal, the Court was largely the spokesman for both small capital and emerging corporate capital, who more often than not resisted the extension of federal intervention in the market (again, with countercurrents). From the New Deal to the

---

[2]Fred Vinson, "Work of the Federal Courts," *Supreme Court Reporter*, 1949, cited in Emmette S. Redford *et al.*, *Politics and Government in the United States* (New York, 1968), p. 474. Emphasis added.

late 1960s, the Court functioned largely in the interests of the corporate complex and made decisions that were necessary for its expansion and stability, but could not easily have been made by the president or Congress. Since the late 1960s, with the legal foundations of corporate capitalism secured, the Court has been used more explicitly than in the past as an element in a strategy to secure a fundamental electoral realignment favorable to the Republican party.

The Marshall Court: Two Landmark Decisions

Up to the Civil War, the basic issues to confront the Court concerned the scope of national, as opposed to state, powers. The earliest broad cleavage in the country was that between the largely Southern and Western agrarian, planter, and small landowning interests in the Republican party led by Thomas Jefferson; and the largely Northern manufacturing, finance, and mercantile interests who dominated the Federalist party led by Alexander Hamilton. Two key decisions taken by the Supreme Court in this period under the leadership of Chief Justice John Marshall (who served from 1801 to 1835) established the national supremacy of the federal government and the principle of judicial review by the Supreme Court of acts of Congress. Each marked the triumph of national, industrial interests over agrarian, local interests.

In 1791, the Congress established a United States Bank. The issue found Hamilton and Jefferson sharply divided. Hamilton argued that the Bank was necessary for the national fiscal well-being of the country and that the authorization of the bank was constitutional because Congress had the power "to make all laws necessary and proper for carrying into execution" the powers of the national government (Article I, Section 8). Jefferson, who hoped America's future would be one of a small landowning agrarian democracy, opposed the Bank. He argued that Congress did not have the power to establish a national bank: Congress had the right to pass only those laws that were *indispensably* necessary to carry out governmental powers. By passing the Bank bill, the Federalist-dominated Congress opted for the more liberal interpretation of its powers.

The issue came to the Supreme Court in 1819, after the state of Maryland had taxed the bank and the bank had refused to pay.

In a far-reaching decision in the case of *McCulloch* v. *Maryland*, the Court supported the bank. "Let the end be legitimate, let it be within the scope of the Constitution," Marshall wrote, "and all means which are appropriate, which are plainly adapted to that end, which are not prohibited, but consist within the letter and spirit of the Constitution, are Constitutional."

The decision not only supported Hamilton's broad reading of the "implied powers" clause of the Constitution but it made clear that where state and national laws conflicted, the state law would be declared unconstitutional by the Court. The Court has never wavered from this principle since, but it has been a recurring point of controversy as many state regulations and programs, including provisions for racial segregation, have been struck down.

Earlier, in the case of *Marbury* v. *Madison* (1803), the Marshall court first asserted the Supreme Court's right to declare acts of Congress or the president unconstitutional. This power, called *judicial review*, authorizes the Court "to hold unconstitutional and hence unenforceable any law, any official action based upon it, and any illegal action by a public official that it deems to be in conflict with the Basic Law, in the United States its Constitution."[3]

The case itself is fascinating. Thomas Jefferson defeated President John Adams' reelection bid in 1800. Adams feared for the survival of his Federalist party and decided to pack the federal judiciary before leaving office with as many Federalists as possible. Early in 1801, at Adams' suggestion, the outgoing Federalist-dominated Congress passed two court acts providing for the appointment of forty-eight new federal judges. Adams also appointed his secretary of state, John Marshall, chief justice of the Supreme Court.

As secretary of state, Marshall was given the task of delivering the commissions to the new judges. But on the eve of the inauguration of Thomas Jefferson, and of his own assumption of the duties of chief justice, Marshall ran out of time and was unable to deliver seventeen of the commissions. He left them to be delivered by his successor as secretary of state, James Madison.

Jefferson and Madison decided not to carry out Adams'

[3]Henry J. Abraham, *The Judicial Process* (New York, 1965), p. 251.

appointments. A number of the disappointed prospective judges hired Adams' former attorney general, Charles Lee, to seek redress in the courts. Lee petitioned to the Supreme Court on behalf of William Marbury, basing his case on an article of the Judiciary Act of 1789 that gave the Supreme Court the power to issue a writ (called a *writ of mandamus*) ordering public officials to perform their official duties.

It was probably expected that Marshall would rule on behalf of Marbury in order to get more Federalists on the bench and to use the full powers granted to the Court by Congress. Indeed, in his opinion, Marshall stated that he thought Marbury had a just complaint based on the law. But instead of upholding Marbury's case, he used the opportunity to make a landmark decision that widened the power of the Court more than any other before or since.

He argued that the article of the Judiciary Act of 1789 was *unconstitutional* because Congress had by law added to the original constitutional jurisdiction of the Supreme Court, something that the Constitution does not permit. By rejecting the claims of a Federalist petitioner and overturning a law passed by a Federalist congress, Marshall succeeded in securing a basic Federalist objective—the doctrine of judicial review, which at the time was seen as a protection to the propertied against the dangers of congressional democracy.[4] He wrote, echoing almost exactly Alexander Hamilton's arguments in *The Federalist* No. 78: "It is emphatically the province and duty of the judicial department to say what the law is. . . . A law repugnant to the Constitution is void; . . . courts as well as other departments are bound by that instrument." As a result of this decision, Federalist principles triumphed, even though the Federalist party soon disintegrated. The Supreme Court had asserted the right of judicial review and had strongly reinforced the Constitution's declaration that it is the supreme law of the land.

After Marshall's death in 1835, President Andrew Jackson appointed Roger Taney, a Maryland Democrat, to the post of chief justice. In contrast to the Marshall Court, Taney's faithfully represented the opposing side of the dominant national cleavage of the period. As one scholar notes, Taney, in his decisions

---

[4]Wallace Mendelson, *Capitalism, Democracy and the Supreme Court* (New York, 1960), p. 20.

favored "states rights" and *agrarian* property, that is, land and slaves. From a totally different milieu than the great constitutional nationalist who preceded him, Taney, and with him a majority of his court, demonstrated a faithful attachment to the economic interests of the South and the rapidly developing frontier of the West.[5]

The end of this antiindustrial interlude of the Court can be dated from the Taney Court's best-known decision, *Dred Scott* v. *Sanford* (1857). By a 7 to 2 vote, the Court, now dominated by the South, decided that no black could be an American citizen; that a black was "a person of an inferior order"; that no individual of African descent was "a portion of this American people"; and that blacks were slaves and possessions of their owners no matter whether they were in a slave or a free area of the country. This decision, historians agree, hastened the onset of the Civil War.

It also speeded the demise of the Taney Court. Taney continued to serve until 1864, but he was stripped of effective power by the outbreak of the Civil War; during the Civil War (1861 to 1865), President Lincoln acted as a near-dictator, ignoring constitutional niceties where he thought appropriate, and in 1863 Congress increased the size of the court from nine to ten.[6] By 1864, with the appointment of Salmon Chase as chief justice, the Court was securely in the hands of Northern Republicans, who were chiefly concerned with safeguarding property and providing a legal climate for the development of competitive industrial capitalism.

The Court as Protector of Corporate Capitalism

The Marshall Court in two landmark cases—*Gibbons* v. *Ogden* (1824) and *Dartmouth College* v. *Woodward* (1819)—had provided the legal framework for the protection of incipient industrialization by ruling in favor of federal control of interstate commerce (thus laying the groundwork for national capitalism) and by declaring that contracts were inviolable. The predominantly Republican-dominated Courts of the late nineteenth and early twentieth century further extended the legal infrastructure

---

[5]Abraham, p. 303.
[6]Congress altered the size of the Court two more times in this decade; from ten to seven in 1866, and from seven to nine in 1869.

of capitalism. Most notably, corporations were given legal status as persons in 1888; they now had a charter of civil liberties, which would be used to declare unconstitutional state and federal laws that restricted their operations as well as labor-union activities of organizing and strikes. In 1895 alone, other Court decisions dismissed prosecutions against the sugar trust, declared the income tax unconstitutional, and upheld the contempt conviction of Eugene Debs, a socialist who was president of the American Railway Union.

After the turn of the century, with the development of an increasingly dominant corporate sector, the Court's continued probusiness orientation was no longer as clear-cut. In attempting to curb attacks on the unbridled power of business by labor unions and Progressive reformers, the Court often struck down or delayed measures that the immense new corporations wanted. For example, workmen's compensation bills, which the corporations wanted to limit their liability for workers' accidents, were declared unconstitutional by the Supreme Court in 1920 and 1924; it struck down child-labor legislation from 1916 to the late 1930s (unlike small-capital farms and family farms, the larger corporations did not need to employ children).

Yet, on balance, the zealous protection of property, the shackling of unions, and the limitations on corporate legal vulnerability won for the Supreme Court the enthusiastic support of America's capitalists. In 1895, a New York bank president told an audience of businessmen: "I give you, gentlemen, the Supreme Court of the United States—guardian of the dollar, defender of private property, enemy of spoliation, sheet anchor of the Republic!" Sixteen years later, a Standard Oil executive praised a Court decision limiting the scope of the Sherman Antitrust Act: "I am for the Supreme Court every time. For more than a hundred years it has been at work and it has never made a mistake."[7]

This kind of direct, often blatant defense of the capitalist order that the Supreme Court provided, however, stood in the way of the New Deal effort to save corporate capitalism during the depression of the 1930s. The Court continued to rule narrowly on behalf of laissez faire by striking down legislation regulating agriculture, the railroads, and setting minimum wages. In 1937, President Roosevelt sought to smash this roadblock to modern-

[7]Redford, pp. 498–99.

ized capitalism by proposing "whenever a Judge or Justice of any Federal Court has reached the age of seventy and does not avail himself of the opportunity to retire on a pension, a new member shall be appointed by the President then in office, and with the approval, as required by the Constitution, of the Senate of the United States."[8] Since six of the nine justices then serving were over seventy, Roosevelt was in effect proposing to add up to six new members to give the New Deal a majority.

Though Congress refused to go along (an alliance of those opposed to the New Deal and those who favored the change but thought it should be done by constitutional amendment, rather than legislation, prevented the bill's passage), two of the justices now began to vote with the New Deal. By 1941, the turnabout was complete. Roosevelt was able to make four new appointments in four years, cementing his majority.

The Warren and Burger Courts

From the late 1930s to the present, the relationship between the Court and the corporate complex has generally been much more indirect than it was before and during the New Deal. Since 1937, the justices have consistently held themselves aloof from the management of the economy. Instead, they have let the corporate complex manage and regulate the economy without Court interference. In this respect, the Court has served the interests of corporate capital, since its hands-off policy has made it possible for the elaborate interpenetration of government and corporate capitalism to continue to develop.

Thus, while almost all of the Court's pre-1937 rulings were in the field of property controls, including taxation, regulation of commerce, antitrust cases, and labor relations, today the Supreme Court's economy-related rulings are largely confined to settling conflicts between authorities: they turn largely on interpretations of actions by federal regulatory commissions, of tax laws, and of the federal regulation of labor relations. In all these areas of decision, however contentious they may be at times, the existence of corporate capitalism is never questioned.

The Court increasingly came to spend the bulk of its time on cases dealing with criminal procedures, civil liberties, and civil rights, especially under Chief Justice Earl Warren, who was

[8]Theodore Becker and Malcolm Feeley, eds., *The Impact of Supreme Court Decisions* (New York, 1973), p. 41.

appointed by President Eisenhower in 1953 and served through the Eisenhower, Kennedy, and Johnson administrations. The Warren Court consistently acted to protect and extend the legal system's commitment to formal equality. Among its landmark decisions were *Baker* v. *Carr* (1962), in which the Court held that the federal courts could act to ensure that the drawing of election district lines by state legislatures give each vote equal meaning (thus each district had to have roughly the same population); *Miranda* v. *Arizona* (1966), which stated that confessions obtained under interrogation from criminal suspects were not admissable as courtroom evidence unless the accused person had been informed of his rights to remain silent and be represented by a lawyer; and *Harper* v. *Virginia State Board of Elections* (1966), in which the Court determined that requiring voters pay a poll tax (a device to keep blacks from voting) violated the guarantees of equal protection of the Fourteenth Amendment. Desegregation and voting rights have consistently been upheld, defendants' pretrial rights have been made more explicit, and one man, one vote has become the national standard.

In all of these decisions, the same principle operated: citizens have a right to legal, but not substantive, economic equality. Hence the outcome of these decisions has been to widen the political community and make more and more citizens legal equals; but in not challenging the dominance of corporate capitalism, the Court has indirectly served to perpetuate citizens' economic inequality.

The Court has been well fitted for its four main tasks of authenticating the actions and securing the goals of the corporate complex; of providing an arena for settling conflicts between authorities; of furnishing an alternative channel for taking difficult or unpopular decisions; and of protecting and extending the formal legal equality of American jurisprudence. The lifetime tenure of justices, their private deliberations, the majesty of their surroundings—all promote the myth that the Supreme Court is a strictly legal institution, detached from and impartial to political and economic interests. Their social backgrounds, moreover, have set them apart from the average American: they have overwhelmingly been wealthy, successful white Protestant lawyers, from the same milieu as the leaders of the corporate complex.

Like almost every other president before him, Richard Nixon made appointments to the Court (Chief Justice Burger, and justices Blackmun, Powell, and Rehnquist) to change its ideological complexion. What is different is that Nixon's transformation in the Court's composition and perspectives did not reflect fundamental economic interests. As a candidate in 1968, Nixon attacked the libertarian decisions of the Warren Court and pledged to rectify the Court's shortcomings by appointing conservative justices. His four appointments in his first term were calculated to win the votes of "middle America" to the Republican party.

The Burger Court has behaved much as President Nixon expected. It has reversed many of the protections the Warren Court extended to criminal defendants and has ruled in favor of allowing communities to decide their own standards of obscenity (subject to court review). Most dramatically, the Court has supported the Nixon Administration's stand against busing to achieve racial integration of the schools. In July 1974, the Court overturned a lower court ruling that had mandated busing across city lines in the Detroit metropolitan area to integrate the region's public schools. All of Nixon's appointees voted with the majority, and all of the dissenters had served on the Warren Court.

But like its predecessors, the Burger Court has been unwilling to forego the Court's role as the protector of the legal process. When President Nixon sought to withhold tape-recorded conversations (on the grounds of executive privilege) that the special prosecutor had requested as evidence for the Watergate trials of the president's closest political allies, the Court ruled unanimously that the tapes had to be turned over. In this case, *United States* v. *Nixon* (1974), the Court reaffirmed the principle laid down by the Marshall Court in the early nineteenth century that the Supreme Court is the ultimate interpreter of the Constitution.

WHOSE CIVIL COURTS?

The judicial system is composed of both criminal and civil courts. As opposed to criminal courts, which try alleged law-breakers, civil courts settle disputes of varied kinds *within* the law, including disputes between insurers and claimants, tenants and landlords, debtors and creditors. Civil courts also legitimate private agreements, such as marriage and child adoption. In both of these categories, the courts lend the government's power to private citizens. If the court finds that the plaintiff's grievance is justified, it issues either a judgment or an injunction.

Both judgments and injunctions involve the state's police powers. A judgment authorizes the plaintiff to call on the police "to oust a tenant, to reclaim some property, to sell property belonging to a defendant, or to seize the defendant's wages or property. An injunction, on the other hand, is an order directed to the defendant and prohibits him from engaging in an activity about which the plaintiff complained."[9] Should the defendant not comply, he may be arrested.

Civil courts thus have wide powers to use government authority and sanctions to advance or deter the objectives of private citizens. Like the Supreme Court, civil courts operate according to formal rules that specify the kind of evidence needed to win a case and the nature of penalties and sanctions that the court may impose. In this respect, the court appears as a neutral formal arbiter of conflict; and, as many surveys indicate, most Americans place great trust in the equity of civil courts.[10]

Yet within this formal system of civil justice, there is a persistent pattern of substantive inequality. Because relatively poor defendants have little knowledge of the civil courts and lack the resources to use them effectively, landlords consistently do better than tenants, creditors than debtors. Even small claims courts, which usually hear financial disputes involving less than $500 and which were officially created to make justice more accessible to the poor, "have become the instruments of businessmen who are their most regular clients."[11] As political scientist Craig Wanner noted, "Civil courts, like other governmental regulatory agencies, develop informal patterns of interaction with their regulated clientele. As interactions become regularized, the more powerful clientele groups are able to extract concessions from the courts in return for becoming a loyal and vocal ally."[12]

[9]Herbert Jacob, *Debtors in Court* (Chicago, 1969), p. 17.
[10]For a useful discussion of civil courts, see Herbert Jacob, *Urban Justice* (Englewood Cliffs, N.J., 1973), chapter seven.
[11]Herbert Jacob, "Small Claims Courts as Collection Agencies," *Stanford Law Review* 4 (1952).
[12]Craig Wanner, "A Harvest of Profits: Exploring the Symbiotic Relationship Between Urban Civil Trial Courts and the Business Community," unpublished manuscript, p. 1.

Civil courts have thus become adjuncts of small, local capital. An examination of the routine operation of the courts in the area of debt collection gives an indication of how legal equality may not only underpin but also promote substantive inequalities.[13] There are many incentives for businessmen to use the civil courts to collect debts. The biggest incentive is probably an excellent chance of success. Almost three-quarters of all cases are decided for the plaintiff. In only 1 percent of the cases studied by Wanner did the judge rule in favor of the defendant (other cases were dismissed for a variety of reasons, such as the defendant could not be found or was not properly named in the complaint). Another incentive is that, for businessmen, the initiation of civil-court claims is a relatively cheap process. Since many firms have lawyers on retainer (whose fees are tax deductible), and since the burden of the expense of prosecution, court costs, and marshal's fees may be passed along to the debtor if he loses the case (as he almost always does), civil-court claims are a strikingly good investment. Moreover, courts often award business plaintiffs a higher amount than the original debt; the only limits on interest charges, handling charges and so on are the size of the plaintiff's request and what the trial judge thinks reasonable.

The defendant, on the other hand, is not so well placed. The very threat of a lawsuit and the possibility of having to appear in court impel many to settle on unfavorable terms out of court. Defendants are usually alone in seeking legal advice, and lawyers are expensive. Some defendants do not seek legal help when they feel they owe the debt; as a result, they put their property rights and interests in more jeopardy than necessary, since the terms of paying off a debt are a matter for the court to decide. The defendant who does go to court must take time off from his job and also faces the prospect that, if the judgment is against him, his salary will be garnished (deducted from to pay the debt). And this could even cost him his job, since most employers prefer to discharge debtors rather than do the bookeeping necessary when wages are garnished.

If the defendant ignores the lawsuit, bargains privately once the suit has been filed, or merely procrastinates, "after the

---

[13]The information that follows is drawn from Wanner's recent study of 7900 civil court cases in Baltimore, Milwaukee, and Cleveland between 1965 and 1970, and from Jacob's surveys of debtors and businessmen in four Wisconsin cities.

passage of several days (8 to 28 depending on the jurisdiction) from the filing of the complaint and its service on the debtor, the claim becomes an established fact—even if there has never been a review of the facts by the court."[14] At this point, the judgment is made by a court clerk, not a judge.

CRIMINAL JUSTICE

Civil courts are systematically inclined to favor local business interests and provide them with inexpensive services. But usually their decisions only cost people money. Criminal-court proceedings, on the other hand, involve incarceration; and the criminal-justice system of the police, courts, and prisons affects virtually every member of the population. The 700,000 criminal-case defendants whose cases are heard by major trial courts each year, and the millions of others who are either arrested or are victims of crimes, are involved with at least the police, usually some court officials or prosecutors, and sometimes, even if not convicted, with the prisons. Before examining these elements of the criminal-justice system, let us first briefly examine the nature of crime in the United States.[15]

Crime and Criminals

Almost all of us are criminals at one time or another. In 1965, the President's Crime Commission found that 91 percent of all adult Americans "had committed acts for which they might have received jail or prison sentences." Since most Americans do not go to jail, it is obvious that the criminal-justice system pays *selective* attention to crime, concentrating on the crimes of homicide, rape, assault, robbery, and burglary. Former Attorney General Ramsey Clark noted that almost all of these crimes are committed for the purpose of obtaining money or property; fully seven-eighths of the FBI-Index crimes are crimes against property.

[14]Wanner, p. 9.
[15]Much of what follows in this section is drawn from the suggestive article by David Gordon, "Class and the Economics of Crime," *Review of Radical Political Economics* 3 (Summer 1971).

Yet, he observed, many of the relatively hidden crimes the justice system consistently ignores—most of them white-collar crimes like tax evasion, embezzlement, price-fixing, and consumer fraud—are much more profitable than those that command most police and media attention.

> Illicit gains from white-collar crime far exceed those of all other crime combined. . . . One corporate price-fixing conspiracy criminally converted more money each year than all of the hundreds of thousands of burglaries, larcenies, or thefts in the entire nation during those same years. Reported bank embezzlements cost ten times more than bank robberies each year.[16]

The crimes committed by those who work in the small-capital sector of the economy, which includes the majority of blacks and other minorities, are the chief business of the criminal-justice complex, while, more often than not, white-collar criminals are dealt with by private auspices—"private psychiatric and counselling assistance often supplant prosecution."[17] Even in the "classes of offenses committed by rich and poor equally, it is rarely the rich who end up behind bars."[18]

It is important to recognize that conditions in contemporary America make crime particularly attractive and accessible. Poor blacks confined to the small-capital sector of the economy often find that crime brings higher financial rewards and higher group status than they could ever hope to achieve otherwise and even, as in numbers-running, carries relatively low risks of apprehension and conviction. Many illegal activities run by organized crime—drug traffic, gambling, prostitution—are "consensual crimes . . . desired by the consuming public."[19] The goods and services provided by organized crime are not only desired, they are in great demand; and profits are high. And corporate white-collar crime is consistent with the logic of profit of corporate capitalism.

The basic difference between the kinds of crime people commit is largely due to the opportunities presented them. Ghetto residents do not have easy access to jobs in large corporations, to relatively unobtrusive patterns of communication, or to paper

[16]Ramsey Clark, *Crime in America* (New York, 1970), p. 38.
[17]Gordon, p. 54.
[18]Ronald Goldfarb, "Prison: The National Poorhouse," *The New Republic* (November 1969), p. 312.
[19]Clark, p. 68.

transactions involving large sums of money. Moreover, poor-people's crimes, economist David Gordon notes, are much more apt to be violent because of the selectivity of the criminal-justice complex. He notes that it is only natural

> that those who run the highest risks of arrest and conviction may have to rely on the threat or commission of violence in order to protect themselves. . . . Completely in contrast, corporate crime does not require violence because it is ignored by the police; corporate criminals can safely assume that they do not face the threat of jail, and do not therefore have to cover their tracks with the threat of harming those who betray them.[20]

Of course not all white-collar crime is ignored: when the criminal practices of the relatively well-to-do become egregiously offensive in their violation of the law, they must be punished in order to protect the ideological claim that all are equal under the law. But for the most part, the justice system disregards white-collar crime. In the past, much violent and working-class crime was also ignored by the justice system, since those "crimes rarely impinged on the lives of the more affluent. Gambling, prostitution, dope and robbery seemed to flourish in the slums of the early twentieth century, and the police rarely moved to intervene."[21] As crime has burst out of its traditional slum boundaries, it has become a "crisis." The justice system's concern with crime by subordinates has thus been directly related to the class status of the victims (most crimes, however, are still committed by the poor against the poor).

Indeed, crime and the creation of means to control it have traditionally been problems of boundaries and social control. The origins of modern police forces provide a case in point.

The Police

Modern police forces are only a century and a half old. They were created quite consciously to protect existing structural arrange-ments. London's police force, which was the model for American urban police, was the first to be established. Its founding in 1829 was not a response, as sociologist Allan Silver notes, to criminal-

[20]Gordon, p. 61.
[21]*Ibid.*, p. 62.

ity as such, but to the growth of a destitute underclass in early industrial England that was thought to threaten the social order.

> It was more than a question of annoyance, indignation, or personal insecurity; the social order itself was threatened by an entity whose characteristic name reflects the fears of the time—the "dangerous classes". . . . But even where the term is not explicitly invoked, the image persists—one of an unmanageable, volatile, and convulsively criminal class at the base of society.[22]

Before the creation of the professional, bureaucratic police force, police functions in England were carried out by local property owners who acted as constables. However, as the size of the underclass grew under the impact of industrialization, most large property owners became increasingly vulnerable as direct targets of popular abuse. The agrarian rich responded by attempting to strengthen the private constabulary, but most of the new manufacturers "turned towards a bureaucratic police system that insulated them from popular violence, drew attack and animosity upon itself, and seemed to separate the assertion of 'constitution al' authority from that of social and economic dominance." From the moment of their creation, modern police forces were the officially sanctioned legal enforcers of the prevailing structural arrangements. By their regular presence among all classes, especially the new industrial proletariat, the police permeated society in a way that traditional landed constabularies could not. As one authority noted, "the police penetration of civil society lay not only in its narrow application to crime and violence. In a broader sense, it represented the penetration and continual presence of central political authority throughout daily life."[23]

Individually, the policeman maintains order and tanquility on his beat; collectively, the police act as guardians of the social order as a whole. This structural role is fraught with tension, since, often, the police must *police* a hostile public, and their definition of order and appropriate public behavior may clash with the perspectives of the community. A reporter who spent two years with the Philadelphia police force found that the police

---

[22]Allan Silver, "The Demand for Order in Civil Society: A Review of Some Themes in the History of Urban Crime, Police, and Riot," in David Bordua, ed., *The Police: Six Sociological Essays* (New York, 1967), p. 3.
[23]*Ibid.*, pp. 12–13.

interpenetrated poor neighborhoods so completely that they often produced heightened tension, anxiety, and the disruption of neighborhood life:

> The neighborhoods seem to be overflowing with police cars, which give the police an enlarged presence as they pass. Cars are frequently seen whizzing down the street, their sirens blaring and their emergency lights flashing. It is common to see police cars streak down intersections, breaking red lights, running over sidewalks and into alleys. Every day, many times on some days, people walking on the sidewalk see the police converge, jump from their cars with guns drawn, abandoning their cars in the middle of the street, doors open.[24]

In this context, policemen develop what sociologist Jerome Skolnick calls a working personality. They use a perceptual shorthand of characteristics such as race, dress, language, and gestures to identify in advance those people likely to pose a threat to order on their beat. Thus police often come to see the world as divided between "us" and "them"; anyone identified as one of "them" is likely to be the target of harassment that goes beyond the law. The result is a significant number of what have been called police abuses, a term that is misleading since these "abuses" are an integral part of routine policing.

Police act to preserve their authority even if their actions violate the formal rules under which they operate. After conducting an extensive study into abuses by the New York City police, attorney Paul Chevigny concluded that challenges to police authority are consistently met by "anger and one or more weapons out of the arsenal of legal sanctions from a summons up through summary corporal punishment. Criminal charges, beginning with disorderly conduct and ranging up to felonious assault are commonly laid to cover the actions of the policeman and to punish the offender." Chevigny found that for most policemen, arrest was equivalent to guilt; hence many arrests are followed by false or misleading testimony by policemen in court. "Distortion of the facts becomes the most pervasive and the most significant of abuses. The police ethic justifies any action which is intended to maintain order or to convict any wrongdoer (i.e., anyone actually or potentially guilty of a crime)."[25]

[24]Jonathan Rubenstein, *City Police* (New York, 1973), p. 351.
[25]Paul Chevigny, *Police Power* (New York, 1969), pp. 276–77.

This pattern of routine illegal policing to protect police authority is made possible by the extraordinary discretion police have on the job, by the presumption of innocence their actions carry, and by the protective solidarity of police bureaucracies. The policeman on the beat, despite the hierarchical proto-military characteristics of police organization, operates virtually without supervision. Police selectively enforce the law by deciding which people to suspect and which laws to enforce (white-collar crimes, as we have seen, and the wealthy are rarely police targets).

In a policeman's world of "us" and "them," the only completely trustworthy people are fellow policemen. Socially and organizationally isolated from the communities in which they work, the police develop a sense of solidarity and exclusiveness. Thus corrupt policemen as well as those who violate the legal rights of citizens are usually protected by their colleagues. The overworked, harassed, possibly authoritarian and racist policeman may use unnecessary violence, make illegal arrests, lie in court, and be on the take, but he is more likely than not to escape detection outside his precinct work group.

Criminal Courts

Once arrested, a defendant becomes enmeshed in the other two institutions of the formal justice complex—criminal courts and prisons. Bail is the first step in the process beyond arrest, and bail practices weigh heavily on the poor. Early Anglo-Saxon law provided for bail because the wait between arrest and trial was often lengthy, and the cost of detention to the sheriff was high. When the defendant posted collateral security, he was free pending trial. Virtually the same system operates today, at least in theory.

The Constitution prohibits "excessive bail," yet does not give defendants an absolute right to bail. But it is widely agreed among jurists that since those arrested are formally presumed innocent until proven guilty, the defendant should ordinarily be given his freedom until he is tried. In practice, however, bail is often set at levels higher than defendants can afford. A 1960 study in New York found that of all defendants charged with criminal assault, burglary, forgery, larceny, narcotics possession, robbery, and sex crimes, 29 percent were denied bail, and fewer than

Table 10–1
Eventual sentence for those freed on bail or parole and those detained in jail while awaiting trial, New York City, 1960

Charge on which guilt was determined	Freed on bail or parole			Detained while awaiting trial		
	Suspended sentence (percent)	Prison (percent)	Total cases	Suspended sentence (percent)	Prison (percent)	Total cases
Assault	42	58	26	6	94	73
Dangerous weapons	30	70	10	9	91	11
Larceny	42	58	40	7	93	107
Narcotics	41	59	17	—	100	16
Robbery	22	78	18	3	97	59
Others	43	57	14	12	88	17

Source: Charles Ares, Anne Rankin, and Herbert Sturz, "The Manhattan Bail Project: An Interim Report on the Use of Pre-Trial Parole," 38 *New York University Law Review* (1963), p. 85.

one-third were granted bail under $1000.[26] Of those whose bail exceeded $1000, only about half were able to post bond. As a result of such practices, of the prisoners in local and county jails in the United States in 1970, *fully 52 percent had not been convicted of a crime.* Most of these were poor and black.[27] The wide discretion available to judges in setting bail is thus routinely used to segregate and punish those whom the police identified as guilty and who are too poor to raise bail.

Those who are put in jail because they are unable to make bail are treated exactly like convicted prisoners and for no inconsiderable period of time: a wait of up to six months is common. Perhaps most importantly, they are placed at a great disadvantage in terms of their defense, as it is much more difficult to prepare a defense in jail than out. As political scientist Herbert Jacob notes, "Even if one receives assigned counsel or is defended by a public defender, one cannot personally round up witnesses and assist the attorney in interviewing them."[28] As the classic study on bail in New York City revealed, there is a demonstrable relationship between being detained in jail awaiting trial and the likelihood of having to go to prison after the trial.

[26]Charles Ares *et al.*, "The Manhattan Bail Project: An Interim Report on the Use of Pre-Trial Parole," in James Klonoski *et al.*, eds., *The Politics of Local Justice* (Boston, 1970), pp. 79, 80, 86.
[27]Jacob, *Urban Justice*, p.103.
[28]Herbert Jacob, *Justice in America* (Boston, 1972), p. 170.

Almost half of those freed pending trial were either found innocent or spared prison sentences, while over 90 percent of those detained while awaiting trial were found guilty and sentenced to prison. The latter group not only was more likely to be convicted but they automatically forfeited their chance of probation after conviction. One of the basic conditions of probation is that the individual be employed; but it was hardly likely that those imprisoned pending trial could have kept their jobs. The class bias of policing procedures is thus reinforced by the administration of bail and parole.

The vast majority of criminal cases never come to trial. A recent analysis of the disposition of felony cases averaged the available figures for 1965 to 1969 to give a rough indication of how cases are settled in a typical year in different cities. Of 22,000 felony arrests made in Chicago, only 900 came to trial with the defendant entering a not-guilty plea; in Houston, only 360 of 16,000 arrests; in Detroit, 900 of 20,000 arrests; in Brooklyn, New York, 300 of 15,000; and in Los Angeles, 10,400 of 69,000.[29] Most of the other cases are resolved by the defendant pleading guilty, often as the outcome of a process known as plea bargaining.

Defendants are often charged with multiple crimes, some involving much more serious penalties than others. As a result, prosecutors have the leeway to negotiate with defendants: in exchange for a plea of guilty on the lesser charge, the others are dropped. Where there is only one charge against the defendant, the prosecutor offers to argue for a reduced sentence in exchange for a guilty plea. The extent of discretion available to prosecutors is not specified by law; hence they are free to act as *de facto* judges who make the critical decisions about innocence, guilt, and length of sentences.

A recent spectacular case of plea bargaining involved former Vice President Spiro Agnew. In October 1973, Agnew resigned his office and, in a Baltimore courtroom, pleaded "no contest" to a government charge of income-tax evasion. This plea was the outcome of elaborate bargaining between the vice president and the Justice Department, which had uncovered evidence that Agnew, a former Baltimore County executive and Maryland governor, had extorted bribes from state contractors for almost a decade. Had he been charged and convicted of all the crimes the

[29]Donald McIntyre and David Lippman, Prosecutors and Early Disposition of Felony Cases," *American Bar Association Journal* 56 (1970): 1156–57.

prosecutors alleged he committed (Agnew has consistently maintained his innocence) he might have gone to prison for many years; instead, in exchange for his plea, the government settled for a sentence of three years of unsupervised probation and a $10,000 fine.

Most defendants are not nearly as well known, of course, and plea bargaining for them is much more routine. Generally, the formal adversary confrontation between prosecutor and the defendant's lawyer is a meeting of unequals. Most defendants in urban criminal courts are represented by court-employed public defenders or lawyers from private agencies like the Legal Aid Society. Many of these lawyers are well intentioned, but have little experience in criminal law. They are usually just out of law school and have had virtually no courtroom experience. They lack funds to investigate the police-prosecutor version of events; since most cases do not even get to court, it is this version that serves as the basis for the terms of the bargain. Counsel may be assigned to the defendant many days after his arrest and pretrial imprisonment; by then, the defendant may have made an incriminating statement to the police or prosecutor that may be inadmissable as courtroom evidence but is damaging in the plea-bargaining process. And the public defender's or Legal Aid lawyer's caseload may be so heavy that there is almost no time to prepare for the confrontation with the prosecutor.

Plea bargaining has considerable advantages for the permanent members of the criminal-justice system. It permits an extraordinarily high rate of conviction (sometimes even in cases where the evidence would be insufficient for a jury-trial conviction), which enhances prosecutors' law-and-order reelection appeals and helps policemen win promotions. It relieves prosecutors from having to prepare cases for trial, and it lightens and simplifies the judges' workload, since all they need do is ratify decisions reached by prosecutors and defendants' lawyers. In short, although some defendants may gain lighter sentences from the plea-bargaining process, the arrangement is much more likely to benefit the justice establishment.

Without the cooperation of criminal-court judges, plea bargaining could not exist. Judges who are supposed to be neutral arbiters of courtroom proceedings become accomplices in the inequitable dispensation of justice by permitting their courtrooms to be used at critical junctures. They "cooperate by imposing harsher sentences on defendants convicted after a trial than on those who plead guilty, by maintaining predictable decision patterns according to which defense and prosecutor can calculate their own actions, and by supporting requests for delay, plea and sentence made by prosecutors."[30]

It is often rightly observed that the behavior of criminal-court judges is limited by the actions of police, the size of their caseloads, deals worked out between prosecutors and defense lawyers, and administrative procedures beyond their control. Nevertheless, judges are the gatekeepers of the system of formal criminal justice. They not only legitimate plea bargaining but they also have the power to schedule cases, set bail, dismiss charges, admit evidence, influence juries (in the small proportion of cases that come to trial), and sentence with wide discretion.

Criminal-court judges are selected by a wide array of differing procedures. These include a "merit" procedure by which a governor appoints from a list of nominees compiled by a nonpartisan committee and selection by either the state legislature or local city councils. In most states, however, judges are chosen either through judicial elections or by governors and mayors. In both cases, public information is limited, and devotion to a political party is a more important test than legal competence.

Judicial elections rarely evoke much public controversy or attention. Since it is against judicial ethics to campaign with great vigor, the candidates' campaigns usually lack issues or colorful personalities. As a result, the candidate nominated by the area's majority party is overwhelmingly likely to win. Securing the party's nomination is tantamount to election.

Appointment to the bench, likewise, is a procedure that is hardly subject to much popular control. Because the population processed by the courts is relatively powerless, and because they are often nonparticipants in the electoral system and thus do not threaten local politicians in any way, criminal-court judgeships give decaying party organizations the opportunity to reward loyal lawyers at almost no political cost. And in return for appointing friends to the bench, local politicians gain privileged access to the courts, opportunities to make more patronage appointments in auxiliary court personnel, and significant sums of money. (Political scientists Wallace Sayre and Herbert Kaufman estimated in

---

[30]Jacob, *Justice in America*, p. 104.

1960 that the typical judicial candidate in New York City contributed $20,000 to the Democratic party.)

For these reasons, undistinguished local lawyers who have been active in party affairs and who have sufficient funds to buy their judgeships are given preference. When the New York State Legislature authorized twenty new criminal-court judgeships in 1968, party leaders broke their agreement to have their nominees cleared by the presiding justice for Manhattan and the Bronx and nominated men who could not have possibly secured approval. One, who was filling an interim appointment, routinely called defendants "idiots." A second was sixty-four years old and had little litigation experience. A third had admitted under oath that he had failed to report a $100,000 narcotics bribe attempt that involved a fellow state legislator.[31] As a result of such nominations, a New York district attorney has noted, the bench is full of lazy judges who keep bankers' hours and a funeral director's pace. "Bestowed as a reward for loyal party service, a place on the bench is seen as the most honorable sort of quasi-retirement."[32]

Appointments of judges like these are not to be deplored merely because they are political—any appointment procedure is political—but because of the way they affect those who are processed through the formal system of criminal justice. The interests of *both* defendants *and* victims of crime (most of whom are poor) are hurt by the charade of most criminal courts.

Thus the criminal courts, through the *form* of legal institutions and assumptions, legitimize the control of the most subordinate. Hence the following description of the criminal courts by a journalist who has been investigating corruption is, on one level, a story of irrational inconsistencies, but, on another, is a description of how one critical institution deals with and controls those without power:

> The problem with the courts is more widespread than just the mere extremities of scandal—it is also the general lack of fairness, reason, and dignity for the mass of defendants . . . in the lower criminal courts . . . the average defendant confronts the average judge. Just sit there any morning and you will see judges who regularly remand 16-year old addicts to jail instead of paroling them to narcotics treatment programs. . . . You will see judges

[31]Martin Tolchin and Susan Tolchin, *To the Victor: Political Patronage From the Clubhouse to the White House* (New York, 1971), p. 133.
[32]Richard Kuh, *New Leader,* January 8, 1973.

who don't listen, judges who insult lawyers and defendants, judges who are not intelligent enough to follow complex or subtle legal argument, judges who are blatantly biased against blacks and Puerto Ricans, judges who call defendants names like "scum" and "animals."

You will see inexperienced Legal Aid Lawyers represent 50 poor defendants in a day, and not have time to ask more than their names beforehand. You will see defendants who have been in jail for nine months without seeing a judge, and who could have been paroled months earlier. You will see pleas and sentences delayed because probation reports are lost in a maze of bureaucracy. You will see heroin dealers in red jump suits post $25,000 bail in cash and addicts locked up for a year because they don't have $50. And a cop convicted of selling heroin be given a suspended sentence.

I have seen judges fine landlords $15 for 200 violations of the housing code, including failure to provide heat and hot water, and then have lunch with the landlord's lawyer. I have seen one judge sentence a Puerto Rican junkie to three years in prison for shoplifting some clothes and another judge give probation to a white defendant who wore a suit, and had a private lawyer, and had been convicted of embezzling $150,000 from a bank.[33]

Jury trials, as we have seen, are rare. But they are important in sustaining the public view that the judicial system is just. But even these most visible, and thus most just, exercises of the formal justice complex are biased in two ways.

The jury The size of juries differs from state to state. In some, only six people serve in minor cases and twelve in major cases; in other states, twelve jurors are required in all cases. But everywhere, the composition of juries is likely to be unrepresentative. Businessmen and professionals tend to be much overrepresented, workers and minority groups much underrepresented. In Baltimore, for example, a study found that "professionals, managers and proprietors constituted only 18.7 percent of the population but contributed 40.2 percent of the jurors. . . . At the same time 41.4 percent of the population were working-class people but only 13.4 percent of the jurors were blue-collared."[34]

Procedures for the selection of juries make equal representation nearly impossible. In almost all cases, jurors are selected

[33]Jack Newfield, "Mindlessly, Randomly, Hurriedly, Blindly," *The Village Voice*, February, 1973, pp. 8, 24.
[34]Edwin S. Mills, "Statistical Study of Occupations of Jurors in a U.S. District Court," *Maryland Law Review* XXII (1962): 205–16, cited in Jacob, *Justice in America*, p. 124.

from lists of registered voters; but, as we discussed in Chapter 8, the poorer a man is, the less likely he is to register to vote. Many states excuse women from jury duty. Since jurors get paid for service, commissioners in small localities often use jury duty as a focus of patronage and choose friends and acquaintances to serve. On the other hand, a juror's pay is usually lower than a typical worker can earn in a day's work; hence many blue-collar workers who would lose wages ask to be excused on grounds of financial hardship. White-collar workers, by contrast, often continue to be paid while they serve. Class bias is thus built into the jury system. Finally, those previously convicted of a crime are ineligible for jury duty.

Sentencing   Conviction by a jury may result in vastly different consequences for different defendants, depending on the sentence handed out by the presiding judge. Here too the most subordinate are likely to fare least well. Numerous investigations have documented that blacks in both the North and South receive significantly longer prison sentences than whites convicted in the same jurisdiction for the same crime.[35] Small drug users of heroin and cocaine are often given long prison terms, but large drug dealers often go free; a state senate committee in New York found that of all those "*convicted* (not arrested) for possession of more than one pound of heroin or cocaine between January 1969 and October 1971, 40 percent received no jail sentence at all, and 26 percent received less than one year in jail."[36] Yet the crime of possession of more than one pound of hard drugs in New York carried a maximum penalty of *life imprisonment.* Not surprisingly, many observers have concluded that the temptations open to criminal-court judges because of the discretion they have in sentencing leads some to corruption.

Judges also look out for the interests of other members of the formal justice complex. Of the 80 policemen convicted for corruption in New York City between 1968 and July 1972, "49 were either set free or given suspended sentences, and 31 received jail terms, 14 for less than one year."[37]

---

[35]Henry Bullock, "Significance of the Racial Factor in the Length of Prison Sentences," *Journal of Criminal Law, Criminology, and Police Science* 52 (1961): 411–17; and United States Commission on Civil Rights, *Report Number Five: Justice* (Washington, 1961).
[36]Newfield, p. 25.
[37]*Ibid.*

Prisons

In 1970, there were 4,037 local and county jails in the United States holding a population of 160,000 on an average day, a population equivalent to the state of North Dakota; state and federal prisons hold 200,000 Americans. But since there is a continuous turnover, the number of Americans who are imprisoned each year is far greater: at least 1.5 million—and some estimates put the figure as high as 5.5 million.[38] The cost of running this incarceration system is staggering: in 1970, a total of $324,278,000 was spent on American jails, or about $2,000 per inmate per year.

These jails and prisons house America's most graphic losers, the most subordinate in a system of corporate capitalism. They are dependent on the decisions of others for the basic amenities of their lives and if convicted of a crime, stripped of political rights to vote and hold office. Most have not been convicted of a crime. Many are mentally ill, alcoholic, or addicted to hard drugs. Virtually all are poor, unemployed, ill-educated, and either black or Hispanic. About two-thirds have been in jail before. They are often despised by their fellow citizens.

Their condition of social, economic, and political subordination is reflected in the custodial brutality of American jails. Most rural jails hold inmates convicted of misdemeanors, transients awaiting transfer to other facilities, and people being detained before trial who cannot raise bail. These prisons are usually governed by local county boards and directly controlled by locally elected sheriffs who are also principally responsible for police duties. "The majority of county jails suffer from a perennial lack of funding, from physical neglect, from the absence of any kind of program. Frequently, they fail to meet even the most rudimentary safety and health standards."[39]

At a polar extreme is the large urban jail, such as the Tombs in New York, Los Angeles' massive jail system, and Chicago's notorious Cook County Jail. More than half of the country's prisoners are held in jails of this type. Most often they are under the control of the chief of police; in some cities they are run by autonomous departments of correction. The overwhelming num-

[38]Edith Elizabeth Flynn, "Jails and Criminal Justice," in Lloyd Ohlin, ed., *Prisoners in America* (New York, 1973), p. 55.
[39]*Ibid.*, p. 59.

ber of inmates in these jails are pretrial prisoners; 80 percent of the prisoners in Philadelphia have not been convicted of a crime. Without exception, these jails are characterized by overcrowding, brutality, and dehumanizing conditions.

Most jails as well as state and federal prisons in which most convicted felons are housed cage their prisoners in cells. Conditions are unsanitary: many cells lack toilets and sinks and most prisons smell of human excrement. These institutions are understaffed and fail to provide even minimal supervision to guarantee the safety of inmates. Indeed, dormitory conditions in most prisons, overcrowding, and the lack of useful activities and recreational facilities turn prisoners against each other, and inmates develop their own means of control. Robbery, homosexual rape, extortion, and other physical violence are not only tolerated but they are made inevitable by the institution's physical and human organization. For these reasons, when subordinates leave the prisons, they are even more ill-prepared than when they entered to challenge and overcome their subordination effectively. Hence most remain or become criminals. Once arrested, they enter the system of formal criminal justice again, and the cycle comes full circle.

LEGAL REPRESSION AND THE POLITICAL TRIAL

In the criminal-justice system, legal procedures have clearly been adopted for the substantive purpose of social control. Its institutions routinely police and process the least well-off members of society in order to maintain the present social order. Earlier, we saw how existing patterns of dominance are reinforced by the civil courts and, largely though not exclusively through the exercise of its power of judicial review, by the Supreme Court.

The myth that the judicial system is nonpolitical is most clearly punctured when we examine the ways in which its institutions have been used to quash articulate, organized political opposition that has operated *outside* of the structural limits of party politics, elections, and interest-group competition. When challenges have been mounted against the prevailing social order, authorities have moved to use the formal justice system to eliminate foes from political competition and to establish the outer limits of safe, acceptable dissent.

The most important legal basis for recent political prosecutions is conspiracy. Conspiracy laws make it a crime to conspire to commit certain acts, whether or not the acts are carried out. Conspiracy, legal scholar Herbert Packer has noted, is the "shabbiest weapon in the prosecutor's arsenal" because "it is what is referred to as an 'inchoate crime.' It does not require proof that anyone did anything illegal, but only that he intended to commit a crime, or . . . that he 'agreed' to commit a crime."[40]

Throughout the nineteenth century, conspiracy laws were routinely used to prevent workers from organizing unions. In the landmark cases of the *Boot and Shoemakers of Philadelphia* in 1806 and the *Journeymen Cordwainers of New York* in 1811, workers were convicted of the charge of criminal conspiracy for trying to organize a union. Today, union activity is seen as basically supportive of the corporate complex and is protected by law. But conspiracy laws are still being used. In the past decade, antiwar activists and black militants have been prosecuted by the government for conspiracy.

To name only some of the more celebrated cases: In 1968, five well-known antiwar spokesmen, including Dr. Benjamin Spock and the Reverend William Sloane Coffin, were tried for conspiracy to counsel, aid, and abet violations of the Selective Service law and to hinder administration of the draft. Only one defendant (Marcus Raskin) was acquitted. In 1969, eight radical activists were tried for conspiracy under an amendment to the Civil Rights Act of 1968 that made it a crime to cross state lines with the *intent* to incite a riot. They were charged with conspiring to create disorder at the 1968 Democratic party convention in Chicago. Six (including Black Panther Bobby Seale, Tom Hayden, and Abbie Hoffman) were convicted. And in 1970, Manhattan's district attorney charged twenty one members of the Panthers with conspiracy to blow up department stores, the Statue of Liberty, and other public tragets. They were acquitted; eventually the convictions of the draft and Chicago cases were reversed on appeal.

The Justice Department knew that most of its cases were weak. In this respect, the 1973 trial, held in Gainesville, Florida,

[40]Noam Chomsky *et al.*, eds., *Trials of the Resistance* (New York, 1970), p. 173.

of seven antiwar veterans (and an eighth supporter) on charges of having conspired to assault the 1972 Republican national convention with automatic weapons, slingshots, and crowbows was typical. After a month-long trial, the jury took only three hours to bring in its verdict of not guilty. "They had nothing on those boys," a juror remarked afterwards.[41] The prosecution of this conspiracy case and others was not aimed primarily at conviction, but at disrupting and harassing radical activity. Conspiracy trials take a long time; they keep radicals away from their activities; they cost a good deal of money; and they provide others with a symbolic warning of what might be in store for them. The cases were brought not to uphold the conspiracy laws, but to crush opposition through legal means.

In virtually all of these trials, moreover, evidence revealed how thoroughly the government had sought to use its police powers to infiltrate radical organizations. The Gainesville veterans' group had been infiltrated by undercover policemen; in one case, where five priests were accused of raiding the offices of a New Jersey draft board, the judge told the jury it could acquit because "of overreaching participation by government agents or informers."[42]

Conspiracy laws and trials, of course, are not the only means of overt political repression. Some laws are explicitly directed at political opposition.[43] In 1940, Congress passed the Alien Registration Act (Smith Act), which made it illegal to teach or advocate the overthrow of the government of the United States by force, or to organize groups or publish materials for that purpose. Conspiring to commit these acts was also made a crime. A decade later, the Internal Security Act (McCarran Act) was passed. This act established a Subversive Activities Control Board that was to hold hearings to determine whether certain organizations were "Communist." If they were found to be, they were required to register with the attorney general, disclose their sources of funding and expenditures, and give the names and addresses of their officers. Members of organizations identified by the board as

[41]*New York Times,* September 9, 1973.
[42]*Ibid.*
[43]Much of the following discussion is drawn from Alan Wolfe, *The Seamy Side of Democracy: Repression in America* (New York, 1973).

Communist were forbidden to work in defense plants, apply for or use a passport, or hold nonelective federal jobs. These acts and numerous others passed by the federal and state governments were aimed to suppress not the actions of individuals or groups, but the expression of their opinions and their ability to organize.

These laws were passed in the heyday of the cold war. Up to the early 1960s, the Supreme Court consistently held that the anti-Communist legislation was constitutional; in 1961, for example, the Court found in favor of the government, which had prosecuted individuals under the Smith Act for "knowing membership" in the Communist party. But as the cold war began to ease, as the Kennedy, Johnson, and Nixon administrations pursued a policy of détente with the Soviet Union, the Supreme Court began to find many aspects of these laws unconstitutional. As one judicial scholar noted, "The dominant lesson of our history in the relation of the judiciary to repression is that courts love liberty most when it is under pressure least."[44]

Very few laws are overtly repressive. But a great many can be used for repressive purposes. For example, immigration and deportation laws, which define the attributes of citizenship, were often used in the past to exclude and deport political activists. In the case of *Fong Yue Ting* v. *The United States* (1893), the Supreme Court found that the federal government's right to expel foreigners who had not become naturalized citizens "is as absolute and unqualified as the right to prohibit their entrance into the country." Leaders of the radical trade union, Industrial Workers of the World, were deported in the early 1920s as undesirables. Deportation has since been used retroactively; people who had joined the Communist party when membership was legal were deported after passage of the Smith Act in 1950.

Indeed, virtually any law, however innocuous, can provide the basis for the repression of political opposition. In the late 1960s, the police in Oakland, California, enforced traffic regulations much more strictly against members of the Black Panthers, a radical nationalist organization, than the general public in order to keep Panthers off the streets and to make them conscious that they were likely to be stopped and searched regularly. A fund-raising party for the Marxist W. E. B. DuBois Club held in

---

[44]John P. Frank, cited in Redford, *et al.*, p. 554.

Manhattan in 1966 was raided by narcotics police who claimed to be searching for drugs:

> All the young people were held for fifteen hours by the police,then charged and cleared for arraignment. As there were no narcotics present (the DuBois Club, the group's infiltrator must have informed the police, was opposed to the use of drugs), the charges were eventually dismissed. No convictions were seriously entertained. The purpose of the raid was just one of nuisance.[45]

The existence of many laws prohibiting certain forms of conduct, in short, makes it possible for police and prosecutors to use their wide enforcement discretion to establish limits of legitimate political action. As an analysis of legal repression concluded, "Laws exist in a political context. . . . The existence of a government of laws and not men is sometimes praised, but when the laws are used by the men to preserve their own power, the law itself becomes the problem."[46]

CONTRADICTIONS

Legally, every American citizen is entitled to equal protection under the law. In actuality, only a small minority receive it. Within the bounds of present arrangements, the contradiction between formal equality and substantive inequality cannot be overcome. As political scientist Isaac Balbus has noted, at the core of the legal system are "the umbilical connections between formal legal rationality and capitalism; indeed . . . it is precisely the combination of formal legal equality and extreme economic inequality which is the distinctive character of the liberal state."[47]

Although the contradiction cannot be overcome within corporate capitalist America, it has been managed differently in different contexts. One set of circumstances may require the legal system to uphold formal equality even in an area where it does not usually intervene. Conversely, in a different situation, the

---

[45]Wolfe, p. 96.
[46]*Ibid.*, pp. 101–02.
[47]Isaac Balbus, *The Dialectics of Legal Repression: Black Rebels Before the American Criminal Courts* (New York, 1973), p. 5.

justice system may abandon the principle of legal equality altogether. Consider the response of the criminal courts to the ghetto rebellions of the 1960s as a case in point.

The rebellions were seen at the time as profoundly threatening to authorities, since their targets of white-owned property and the police were the most visible symbols of economic legitimacy and public authority. It thus appeared that a *structural* challenge was being mounted against existing patterns of dominance. The justice system reacted by defending those arrangements *at the expense of formal legal protections.*

The police acted to contain and subdue the disorders, often quite ruthlessly and with unnecessary brutality. In New Jersey, the Governor's Select Commission on Civil Disorder, for example, concluded that "the amount of ammunition expended by police forces was out of all proportion to the mission assigned them . . . this reflects a pattern of police action for which there is no possible justification."[48] This behavior was quite consistent with the more routine pattern of police abuses, which, as we have seen, usually stem from what police see as direct threats to their authority. The greater the threat, the greater the likelihood that the police will act without reference to formal legal restraints.

The same proved true of the criminal courts, whose behavior unmistakeably betrayed a commitment to civil order first and to formal standards of legality only secondarily.

Jerome Skolnick studied the judicial response to racial violence in Detroit, Newark, Washington, D.C., Baltimore, and Chicago. In all these cities, the "constitutional right to bail was almost invariably replaced by what in effect was a policy of preventive detention." In Detroit, the twelve judges who heard the rebellion cases agreed at a meeting on the second day of the violence to set bonds averaging $10,000, a sum very much higher than most of the defendants could afford. In violation of routine legal procedure, the high bail policy in all of the cities was "applied uniformly—ignoring the nature of the charge, family and job status of those arrested, the prior record, and all other factors usually considered in the setting of bail."[49]

---

[48]Governor's Select Commission on Civil Disorder of New Jersey, *Report for Action,* in Theodore Becker and Vernon Murray, eds., *Government Lawlessness in America* (New York, 1971), p. 4.
[49]Jerome Skolnik, "Judicial Response in Crisis," in *ibid.,* pp. 161–62.

The judges thus deliberately put aside the canons of formal legality to keep their prisoners incarcerated until structural stability was restored. The imperatives of social control overrode their commitment to legality and justice. In reply to a reporter who questioned the constitutionality of high bail, Chicago's chief judge said, "What do you want me to do—cry crocodile tears for people who take advantage of their city?" In Detroit, a criminal-court judge justified his actions by arguing, "We had no way of knowing whether there was a revolution in progress or whether the city was going to be burned down or what."[50]

But if the justice system is used both routinely and in "emergencies" to maintain social order, the contradiction between formal justice and substantive injustice provides possibilities—as the decisions of the Warren Court indicated—for enlarging the range of choice available to subordinates. Whether or not these opportunities will be taken up largely depends on the actions of movements for basic change, which can force the courts to rule on major issues in accordance with the principles of formal justice. Without the National Association for the Advancement of Colored People, there would have been no *Brown* v. *Board of Education;* and without the women's movement, there would have been no *Roe* v. *Wade* (1973) and *Doe* v. *Bolton* (1973), which upheld a woman's right to abortion. The formal legality that the justice system cannot do without can thus be turned back on substantive inequities. But much depends, as we shall see, on the ideological tools people have to make sense of reality. Hence we now turn to a discussion of ideology and the creation of consciousness.

[50]*Ibid.*, pp. 164, 162.

managing
political
struggle

11

ideology and the creation of consciousness

"Our behavior is a function of our experience. We act according to the way we see things."

R. D. LAING, *The Politics of Experience.*[1]

"The ideas of the ruling class are, in every age, the ruling ideas."

K. MARX and F. ENGELS, *The German Ideology.*[2]

What people think strongly influences what they do. Their perceptions are shaped by their cultural environment, a swirling mix of ideas, symbols, attitudes, opinions, and entertainment. In the United States, there appears to be a particularly rapid flux and whirl of experimentation and change—what H. L. Nieburg has called "culture storm"—as fads and fashions succeed each other with bewildering rapidity.[3] How can the political significance of culture be studied? How do people come to believe what they do? Who controls how people define reality, how they perceive the world, and what they believe is right and wrong?

The proposition by Marx and Engels cited above provides a trenchant (if oversimplified) analysis of the political relevance of

---

[1]R. D. Laing, *The Politics of Experience* (New York, 1967), p. 28.
[2]Karl Marx and Frederick Engels, *The German Ideology* (New York, 1947), p. 39.
[3]H. L. Nieburg, *Culture Storm: Politics and the Ritual Order* (New York, 1973).

culture. As a general rule, they suggest, most people's ideas, and thus the way they see reality, are controlled by those who also control the means of production and occupy powerful political positions. According to Marx, the power to define reality, just as economic and political power, is unequally distributed. The ideas held by rulers—what they pronounce to be accurate and right—will generally be the prevailing ideas of society at large. British scholar Frank Parkin suggests that Marx's proposition

> rests on the plausible assumption that those groups in society which occupy positions of the greatest power and privilege will also tend to have the greatest access to the means of legitimation. . . . Dominant values are in a sense a representation of the perceptions and interests of the relatively privileged; yet by virtue of the institutional backing they receive such values often form the basis of moral judgments of underprivileged groups. In a way, dominant values tend to set the standards for what is considered to be objectively "right."[4]

DOMINANT, ACCOMMODATIONIST, AND OPPOSITION IDEOLOGY

Parkin has suggested a way to classify the political relevance of ideas and culture. (We are adapting his scheme for present purposes.) He identifies three main ideologies: dominant, accommodationist and opposition. The dominant ideology is what Marx meant by the term *ruling ideas.* Put forward by established authorities, the dominant ideology praises traditional arrangements, denies the existence of conflicts of interest between authorities and subordinates, and opposes political change.

The paradox of American politics is that dominant values stressed liberty and democracy from the beginning. In other countries, dominant values were conservative and upheld inherited aristocratic privilege; democracy and liberty were part of the opposition ideology. However, democratic values in the United States have been confined to the narrow sphere of elections for political office; they have not undermined established arrange-

[4]Frank Parkin, *Class Inequality and Political Order* (New York, 1971), pp. 82–83.

ments, and they did not prevent the rise of corporate capitalism. The requirement of democracy has not extended to the sphere of production. Liberty has been defined in the United States as private ownership of property and freedom to pursue wealth—an individualistic and materialistic notion of liberty that is closely connected with capitalism. Consequently, democratic values of equality in the political sphere (procedural democracy) coexist with capitalist values of inequality in the sphere of production.

When landholding was widespread and many Americans were independent entrepreneurs and small property holders, the contradiction between democracy in the political sphere and capitalism in the productive sphere was less apparent. However, as the ranks of corporate labor (both manual and white collar) and government employment have increased, fewer and fewer Americans have an independent economic position. Because of the structural inequality between owners of capital and wage earners, democratic procedures in the political sphere have come to have little significance. Sociologist C. Wright Mills has observed:

> Over the last hundred years, the United States has been transformed from a nation of small capitalists into a nation of hired employees; but the ideology suitable for the nation of small capitalists persists, as if that small-propertied world were still a going concern.[5]

In the present day, dominant values accept corporate capitalism as the ideal arrangement and brand any questioning of the corporate complex within the United States (as well as American dominance abroad) as irresponsible, radical, and even subversive. The dominant ideology "educates" Americans to accept as natural both the basic capital-labor division and their place in the hierarchy of production and politics. Those who fail to get good jobs and who have little control over their lives are led to believe that it is no one's fault but their own.

What makes the dominant ideology influential is not so much that it is believed—while many Americans accept its tenets, many others do not. Its major significance lies in its influence over how alternatives are defined. E. E. Schattschneider points out that the "definition of alternatives is the supreme instrument of power."[6]

---

[5]C. Wright Mills, *White Collar: The American Middle Classes* (New York, 1951), p. 34.

[6]E. E. Schattschneider, *The Semi-Sovereign People* (New York, 1960), p. 68.

The dominant ideology makes alternatives to established arrangements appear risky and irresponsible and thus undercuts dissent. People who are unhappy about the status quo are persuaded that any other system would be worse.

In contrast to the dominant ideology, the accommodative ideology questions prevailing arrangements. It perceives a host of problems, deficiencies, and evils in America, ranging from low wages, poverty, unemployment, bad housing, poor health, and racial and sexual discrimination, to excessive spending for military purposes, political corruption, inflation, high taxes, the squandering of natural resources, and pollution. Far from being satisfied with things as they are, the accommodative ideology seeks improvement in these diverse areas. It advocates bringing pressure to bear on authorities in order to remedy the deficiencies in American society. Taken together, the problems identified by the accommodative ideology add up to a powerful indictment.

The weakness of the accommodative perspective, however, is that it does not add these problems together. The various difficulties are perceived as separate and unrelated, each requiring its own solution. Therefore, demands by different groups within the accommodative framework are not coordinated and often clash. Thus workers in the corporate sector seek higher wages at the same time that consumer movements seek lower prices. Neither group recognizes that the two demands clash within a system of corporate price-fixing. In such a framework, there is no way to assign priority to the various evils and to plan an effective strategy of change. Particular changes may be made—the Truth in Lending Law, the Highway Safety Act, civil-rights legislation, the Environmental Protection Act, and improvements in particular cities or in the situation of particular groups (women, homosexuals, blacks)—but continued control by the corporate complex goes unchallenged.

The accommodative ideology accepts the basic structure of inequality as natural and inevitable. At the same time, it offers an acceptable way for the discontented to express grievances.

Thus, although the accommodative ideology may raise issues that prove unsettling to established arrangements, it does so in a way that permits adjustments to be made and discontent to be defused without structural change.

The third ideology—what Parkin calls the opposition ideology—shares with the accommodative ideology a stress on the problems that exist in the United States. But the opposition critique reaches much further: it regards them not merely as evils in themselves but as a manifestation of systematic structural inequality. From the opposition perspective, not only are problems linked but they are cumulative—those who have little education are unable to obtain good jobs and their children have less chance to get adequate education. Low-paying jobs go along with poor housing, poor health, and a lack of other resources; these problems in turn are linked to a system of corporate capitalism in which inequality is inherent in the capital-labor division.

How can this situation be changed? The opposition ideology believes that piecemeal reforms do not address the basic problem of inequality and that a strategy of structural change must be devised to overcome the contradictions of corporate capitalism. (Chapter 14 will discuss what form this strategy might take.)

Poverty: Contrasting Views

To illustrate the differing perspectives, let us examine attitudes toward poverty in America. In the dominant American ideology, poverty hardly exists. The United States is the richest country in the world and has a far higher per capita income than any other country. Even the poor in America live better than much of the world's population. Those who express concern about poverty are thus merely meddlesome troublemakers. In 1973, the government ordered all federal agencies to eliminate the term *poverty* from official documents and replace it with *low income*—as if banishing the word would make the condition go away.[7] Further, the poor have only themselves to blame. America is a land of wealth and opportunity and anyone who does not get ahead doubtless lacks determination, motivation, and the willingness to work. Even admitting that many Americans live far from well, it is doubtful whether government action can be helpful in alleviating poverty. Since public programs may only make matters worse (for example, by causing inflation and the growth of government), the best policy is to do nothing unless political challenge from the poor makes a response by government absolutely necessary. But if political action is needed, those in government and other leadership positions are best qualified to diagnose the problem and sponsor a solution.

[7] *New York Times,* December 12, 1973.

The accommodative ideology argues that not only does poverty exist but it is widespread. It specifies that a certain proportion of the population—too large a proportion in its view—does not share in the affluence of American society and that government help should be given to those falling below the poverty line. It is a disgrace that some Americans should go hungry in a country that produces well over one trillion dollars of goods and services per year. However, from the accommodative perspective, poverty is an isolated social ailment that can be engineered away through government programs, such as food stamps, public housing, welfare payments, and coordinated anti-poverty attacks. In the accommodationist view, poverty can be handled without basic change in the organization of production or the political sphere. Adequate remedies will come as a result of careful study of the problem, enlightened public opinion, and pressure directed to government through publicity, pressure-group activity, and the election of responsive legislators.

The opposition critique refuses to define the problem as one of poverty per se, for this implies that poverty is amenable to treatment as a separate problem from corporate capitalism and inequality of wealth and power. In the opposition view, accommodationist attacks on poverty will at most alleviate only the worst manifestations of poverty without resolving the larger problem of inequality. And, since addressing the more fundamental issue would require broader structural change, programs tailored to the specific problem of poverty will probably fail. The arsenal of innovations in the antipoverty programs of the 1960s did little to diminish inequalities of income in the United States, and these programs were abolished (and inequality increased) when the political threat that produced them had subsided. In the opposition view, the lesson to be drawn is that what needs to be confronted is not poverty, but the power of the corporate complex and structural inequality.[8]

It appears that, in the competition among the three ideolo-

[8]Labelling an ideology as dominant, accommodative, or opposition does not determine its accuracy or validity. Some established arrangements may be worth preserving, and the dominant ideology may accurately describe them. On the other hand, adopting an opposition ideology emphasizing structure is no guarantee of accuracy. A structural analysis that "explained" contemporary America by reference to a Communist conspiracy would be nonsense. But we believe that the opposition analysis potentially provides the best tool for understanding contemporary America. The other two modes have built-in limitations both because they ignore some of the largest features of politics and because they defend inequity.

gies, most Americans have chosen the dominant and accommodative ideologies. The democratic verdict seems to be for the continuation of present arrangements. At least until recently, the observation by V. O. Key was quite accurate: "The great political triumph of large-scale enterprise has been the manufacture of a public opinion favorably disposed toward, or at least tolerant of, gigantic corporations."[9] However, as we saw in Chapter 8 (on political parties), alternatives to the dominant ideology rarely gain a fair hearing. In the competition among the three ideologies, the dominant ideology has the decided advantage, the accommodationist has some chance of being heard, and the opposition ideology is usually suppressed. Institutions that shape consciousness and ideological attitudes are biased in favor of the dominant ideology. Culture in the United States thus acts as a mediation to distort the debate among competing alternatives. Despite formal guarantees of freedom of speech, the "marketplace of ideas" is controlled to a considerable extent.

SOCIALIZATION TO DOMINANT VALUES

The dominant values can be considered the "official" creed; they are what most of the people hear most of the time. Dominant ideas are taught in elementary school, high school, and college; they are presented over television and in newspapers and are proclaimed at presidential press conferences and during congressional elections by candidates of both parties. To understand how dominant values are disseminated, it is useful to focus on the three institutional mechanisms of schools, media, and government.

Schools and Domination

Schools have been called a "model of society," and, along with television, they constitute a child's first sustained contact with the wider society outside the home.[10]

---

[9]V. O. Key, Jr., *Politics, Parties, & Pressure Groups*, 5th ed., (New York, 1964), p. 96.
[10]Joseph Grannis, "The School as a Model of Society," in Norman Adler and Charles Harrington, eds., *The Learning of Political Behavior* (Glenview, Ill., 1970), pp. 137–48.

The hidden curriculum   Since there is little formal instruction in American history, politics, or civics until the later grades of elementary school, one might suppose that it is not until this point that schools affect children's political beliefs. Yet what children learn is not confined to the content of their courses. Indeed, some scholars argue that school may exercise its greatest political influence in the earliest years, before children have even the haziest conception of American politics.[11]

Two aspects of schooling need to be distinguished. On the one hand, there is the formal curriculum: the three R's, civics, science, and the like. Most school boards and teachers consider that formal subject teaching is what school is all about. To be sure, students do spend time grappling with the mysteries of multiplication and division. Much of their school day, however, is spent in ways that are irrelevant to the formal curriculum. Philip Jackson, a professor of education who carried out extended case studies of several elementary-school classrooms, points out that, in the typical school, relatively large numbers of children are brought together into a relatively small room and confined there most of the school day. Academic learning in such a situation is difficult at best. Children spend an inordinate amount of time in "noneducational" activities—lining up, waiting to get the teacher's attention, pledging allegiance to the flag, taking tests, pretending to study, lunch period, play, and listening to the teacher scold.[12]

Yet these activities are probably politically more influential than any formal instruction in civics. They form part of what can be labelled the "hidden curriculum," whose symbolic message pervades the educational system from the early grades. According to Professor Jackson, "From kindergarten onward, the student begins to learn what life is really like in the company."[13] Let us delve into this hidden curriculum to understand its message.

The first political lesson of school is that attendance is compulsory. Jackson notes, "There is an important fact about a student's life that teachers and parents often prefer not to talk about, at least not in front of students. This is the fact that young

---

[11]David Easton and Jack Dennis, *Children in the Political System* (New York, 1969), chapters 4–6.
[12]Philip Jackson, *Life in Classrooms* (New York, 1968).
[13]*Ibid.*, p. 73.

people have to be in schools, whether they want to be or not."[14]

Once in school, children learn that they are subject to the teacher's well-nigh absolute authority. Underlying the hidden curriculum is the importance of obedience and hierarchy. Teachers rarely get angry, Jackson notes, when a child does not know the right answer. But they can, and do, lose their temper when they consider that a child is breaking the rules of proper classroom conduct. Jackson points out, "The several rules of order that characterize most elementary school classrooms all share a single goal: the prevention of 'disturbances.' "[15]

Children soon learn that success in the classroom comes from playing the game the teacher's way and thereby gaining the teacher's approval. Teachers reward children who obey instructions, display initiative (but not too much and in an acceptable form), and appear interested in the designated subject matter— but are adept at switching to a new subject at the teacher's request. Children are encouraged to compete with each other, rather than cooperate to find the right answer. (At the extreme, trying to help others is called cheating and brings severe penalties.) The hidden curriculum thus teaches lessons that are far more important for living in the world of politics and corporate capitalism than knowledge of reading and writing; it teaches "the importance of identification papers, records, tardy slips, no whispering to your neighbor, the acceptable dress, signatures, forms, and tests."[16] Success in school, as in later life, comes from performing well in a situation of hierarchical control.

Coming closer to formal political indoctrination, the ritual of school is permeated by respect for government. Most classrooms display the American flag, and in most schools the pledge of allegiance is recited daily. One study found that patriotic songs are sung every day in a majority of classrooms in the lower grades.[17]

The formal curriculum   The political instruction that children receive is consistent with the message of the hidden curriculum. Children are schooled in the dominant ideology as a matter of course. A greater proportion of elementary-school time

---

[14]*Ibid.*, p. 9.

[15]*Ibid.*, p. 104.

[16]Marcus G. Raskin, *Being and Doing* (New York, 1971), p. 112.

[17]David D. Hess and Judith V. Torney, *The Development of Political Attitudes in Children* (Garden City, 1968), p. 123.

is devoted to political indoctrination in American than in Soviet schools.[18] In civics courses, the dominant mythology is presented as if it were an accurate description of reality. America is a democracy in which the people rule. Government exists to help people solve their problems. The good citizen supports his government and acts through established institutions. Little is said about poverty, conflict, violence, militarism, corporate power, or racism in America. When particular minority groups are mentioned, their "good" leaders are praised: Dr. Martin Luther King, Jr., and Jackie Robinson, not Malcolm X or Eldridge Cleaver.

As a result

> the small child sees a vision of holiness when he chances to glance toward government—a sanctity and rightness of the demigoddess who dispenses the milk of human kindness. The government protects us, helps us, is good, and cares for us when we are in need, answer most children. . . . From the earliest grade the child sees the President as on a commanding height, far above adults as well as children. The President flies in on angel's wings, smiling, beneficent, powerful, almost beyond the realm of mere mortals.[19]

The drastic decline of respect for political institutions among American adults beginning in the mid-1960s doubtless has affected children. Young Americans growing up in an era where presidential illegality has been widely publicized probably have quite different attitudes than their predecessors. Yet interviews with children directed by political scientist Fred Greenstein in June 1973, when President Nixon's popularity was plummeting, suggest that children continue to retain highly positive attitudes toward authority.[20]

Although children may become disenchanted in later life, a strong residue of patriotism remains that reinforces the dominant ideology.[21] In a study of political attitudes in five nations, the United States had the highest proportion of citizens who ex-

---

[18]G. Z. F. Bereday and B. B. Stretch, "Political Education in the U.S.A. and the U.S.S.R.," *Comparative Education Review* 7 (1963): 9–16.

[19]Easton and Dennis, pp. 137, 171.

[20]Fred I. Greenstein, "What the President Means to Americans: Presidential 'Choice' Between Elections," in James David Barber, ed., *Choosing a President* (Englewood Cliffs, N.J., 1974), p. 134.

[21]It should be noted that most studies of children's political attitudes derive from studies of white middle-class children. The few studies based on children from other backgrounds are not conclusive.

pressed pride in their country's political institutions.[22] This finding has been interpreted as evidence of the excellence of American institutions, but it might with equal validity be used as evidence of the effectiveness of American political indoctrination.

In part, children are deceived in schools because teachers themselves believe the dominant myths. One study found that most elementary-school teachers believe that Congress and voting are the most significant elements in American government.[23] When teachers are misinformed, the result is "compulsory miseducation."[24]

Reproducing the social structure: differential socialization While the dominant ideology recognizes that children are born into wealthy or poor homes, it argues that the road to social advancement in our technological society is through educational attainment. And, since access to education is presumably open to all as a result of equal educational opportunity, it follows that schools serve as an equalizing and democratizing instrument in America.

In fact, however, a review of education suggests that access to education is heavily influenced by a student's social origins. Students from different classes receive a different symbolic message, different amounts of education, and, in fact, a different kind of education. As a result, schools act as a mechanism to reproduce existing social inequalities in the next generation. Economist Samuel Bowles observes:

> In modern America the school has replaced the frontier and the Horatio Alger type as the ultimate repository of that "equality of opportunity" which was promised to all. Yet the educational system does not and cannot lead to much greater equality of opportunity or of income under capitalism. The American school system is in fact instrumental in the legitimation of inequality and its transmission from one generation to the next.[25]

Middle-class and lower-class children receive a different symbolic message in school. Middle-class suburban children

[22]Gabriel Almond and Sidney Verba, *The Civic Culture* (Boston, 1965), p. 64.
[23]Hess and Torney, p. 41.
[24]Paul Goodman, *Compulsory Miseducation* (New York, 1964).
[25]Samuel Bowles, "Unequal Education and the Reproduction of the Hierarchical Division of Labor," in Richard C. Edwards, Michael Reich, and Thomas E. Weisskopf, eds., *The Capitalist System* (Englewood Cliffs, N.J., 1972), pp. 218–19.

attend school in new buildings with good facilities. Their teachers are motivated and interested in getting students into the best colleges. Discipline is relaxed and students are treated with respect. By contrast, lower-class children get the opposite symbolic message. Whereas middle-class children are taught to exercise initiative and compete, lower-class children are taught to trust and accept authority. Most schools in lower-class neighborhoods are shoddy, inadequate, overcrowded, and dirty. Rich states spend twice as much per capita on education as poor ones, and, within states, a similar pattern prevails among rich and poor school districts.[26]

Differential treatment of middle- and lower-class children intrudes into individual classrooms as well. One study found that teachers in the Southwest with Mexican-American and Anglo students called on Anglo students more frequently, praised and encouraged them more, and devoted more time to them. Mexican-American students received extra attention from teachers in only one respect: they were scolded more.[27]

The amount of education that lower- and middle-class children get differs sharply. On the average, children from relatively well-to-do backgrounds receive four more years of education than do children from poor backgrounds. Since a person's occupation and future income usually depend on the length of time he or she has stayed in school, the additional education middle-class children receive assures that they will get the better positions in the future. Thus, the class structure is reproduced from one generation to the next.

Particularly important is the question of higher education. The expansion of college enrollment has been dramatic. In 1935, 12 percent of all college-age youths were in college; in 1970, the comparable figure was 40 percent.[28] Ten million youths are presently attending institutions of higher education.[29] Yet this expansion and the upgrading of employer's educational requirements may not signify an upgrading of jobs. Many jobs that

[26]John D. Owen, "Inequality and Discrimination in the Public School System," in David Mermelstein, ed., *Economics: Mainstream Readings and Radical Critiques* (New York, 1970), pp. 137–45.

[27]U. S. Commission on Civil Rights, *Teachers and Students: Differences in Teacher Interaction with Mexican-American and Anglo Students, Report V: Mexican-American Education Study* (Washington, D.C., 1973), p. 17.

[28]Daniel Bell, *The Coming of Post-Industrial Society* (New York, 1973), p. 318.

[29]*New York Times,* January 13, 1974.

Table 11-1
College attendance of high-school graduates by income, 1966

Family income in 1965	Percentage of 1966 high-school graduates who started college by February, 1967
Under $3,000	19.8
$3,000–$4,000	32.3
$4,000–$6,000	36.9
$6,000–$7,000	41.1
$7,500–$10,000	51.0
$10,000–$15,000	61.3
Over $15,000	86.7
Total, all incomes	46.9%

Source: Frank Ackerman, Howard Birnbaum, James Wetzler, and Andrew Zimbalist, "The Extent of Income Inequality in the United States," in Richard C. Edwards, Michael Reich, and Thomas E. Weisskopf, eds., *The Capitalist System: A Radical Analysis of American Society* (Englewood Cliffs, N.J., 1972), p. 216. Reprinted by permission of the authors.

formerly required only a high-school diploma now demand a college degree. Many students graduating from college face an uncertain future due to the lack of sufficient jobs requiring advanced training.

Moreover, college attendance still depends less on ability than on parental income. In 1967, only 20 percent of high-school graduates from poor economic backgrounds enrolled in college compared to 87 percent of graduates from well-to-do backgrounds.[30] Among children of equal IQ or academic achievements, those from well-to-do backgrounds stand a far better chance of attending college. Statistical analyses by Samuel Bowles and Herbert Gintis suggest that social-class background and the number of years spent in school (which is also related to social class) count for more than IQ in explaining later economic success.[31]

Nor, despite the rise in the average amount of schooling, is access to education becoming more egalitarian. The amount of

[30]Bowles, p. 224.
[31]This section draws on the pioneering research of Samuel Bowles and Herbert Gintis. See Bowles, *ibid.*; Herbert Gintis, "The New Working Class and Revolutionary Youth," *Socialist Revolution* 1 (May–June 1970); and Bowles and Gintis, "I.Q. in the U.S. Class Structure," *Social Policy* 3 (November–December 1972 and January–February 1973).

schooling a student obtains in the present period is as closely tied to his or her social background as was the case a half century ago. The generalization that emerges from the research conducted by Bowles and Gintis is that it is better to be born rich than smart. Equal opportunity in education is largely a myth.

Children from affluent backgrounds also get better quality education. Already mentioned are the superior conditions in well-to-do suburban schools. In addition, many schools use a tracking system that supposedly separates students on the basis of ability ("fast" versus "slow" learners) but, in fact, separates them on the basis of social class. Tracking maximizes the educational opportunities of middle- and upper-class students and limits the educational opportunities of poor students. The "better" students (who are usually white and well-off) are channeled into an academic course of studies at an early age, encouraged to compete for honors, and oriented toward entrance into college. Nonwhite and other poor students are usually shunted into vocational areas—in effect relegating them to jobs as manual workers in the corporate sector, low-paying jobs in the small-capital sector, or unemployment in the ranks of surplus labor.

The case of New York City is instructive. In 1967, 40 percent of the public high-school population was nonwhite, but nonwhites represented 60 percent of the student body at New York's vocational high schools and only 10 percent of the students at Bronx High School of Science and Brooklyn Tech (two of the city's elite public high schools). Within New York's academic high schools, nonwhites represented 36 percent of the graduating class—but only 7 percent of the graduates who went to college. [32]

That children from privileged backgrounds attend better schools, perform better in school, stay longer in school, and are more likely to attend college partly results from the cultural context of education. For example, educational authorities—teachers, school boards, principals, and college admissions committees—are mostly middle class and white. IQ tests ask questions that middle-class children (given their home backgrounds and quite irrespective of intelligence) have a better chance of answering. Middle-class children can study in better home condi-

---

[32]Florence Howe and Paul Lauter, "How the School System Is Rigged for Failure," in Edwards, Reich, and Weisskopf, pp. 232–33.

tions, have more chance of getting help from parents, and are continually exposed to the kind of knowledge and behavior that is the mark of the superior student. Thus, factors linked to structural inequality stack the deck against the possibility of lower-class children using the educational system to advance their interests. The general rule is not disproved by the few minority-group students who obtain a good education despite the odds— and whom college recruiters beat the bushes to find. The conclusion drawn by one study is hardly excessive: "In the light of tracking [and the other factors reviewed here] schools become . . . not the means of democratization and liberation, but of oppression."[33]

Yet the myth of equal educational opportunity serves an important political purpose within the dominant ideology: it "demonstrates" to those who do not secure good positions that they do not deserve them. Political theorist John Schaar has suggested that the belief in equal educational opportunity

> breaks up solidaristic opposition to existing conditions of inequality by holding out to the ablest and most ambitious members of the disadvantaged groups the enticing prospect of rising from their lowly state into a more prosperous condition. The rules of the game remain the same: the fundamental character of the social-economic system is unaltered. All that happens is that individuals are given the chance to struggle up the social ladder, change their position on it, and step on the fingers of those beneath them.[34]

College Although the process is less apparent at the college level, political indoctrination of the dominant ideology continues to be common. Two factors may be singled out as illustrations. Most textbooks assigned to introductory college courses in American government accept the dominant ideology as fact. The average textbook emphasizes such traditional elements of American politics as political parties, Congress, elections, and presidential leadership. What gets left out, however, are important aspects of American political life—for example, the organization of production, the relationship between big business and big government, and the interaction between the police, prisons, and courts.

---

[33]*Ibid.*, p. 234.
[34]John H. Schaar, "Equality and Opportunity, and Beyond," in Herbert G. Reid, *Up the Mainstream: A Critique of Ideology in American Politics and Everyday Life* (New York, 1974), p. 240.

A widely read textbook concludes by describing opportunities for college graduates to engage in politics. It urges students to join one of the two major political parties and to help register new voters. The authors advise students with deeper interests in politics to apply for positions in the government, Foreign Service, Peace Corps, or VISTA.[35] For these authors, political activity means reinforcing established arrangements. In another textbook, a picture of President Johnson bears the caption: "The President represents the American consensus. He speaks for the entire nation and represents the entire political community: e pluribus unum."[36] The authors ignore the fact that Johnson spoke for only part of the community, could not possibly represent the American consensus because it did not exist (the nation was bitterly divided during his presidency), and decided not to run for a second full term precisely because he had antagonized so many.

In an indirect way, colleges also transmit different messages to students of different class backgrounds. Few children from poor backgrounds see the inside of a college at all—unless it is as a janitor, cook, or maid. To these young people, college represents the insurmountable barriers between the rich and the poor. Those who do make it to college cannot afford the expensive tuition of prestigious private universities (over $3,000 per year) and generally attend large state universities, junior colleges, or community colleges. The "market value" of degrees from these latter institutions—measured by the ability to obtain a well-paying job or a position of influence—is less than that of a degree from a private university, especially an Ivy League or other prestigious college. A sizeable proportion of the highest positions in the public and corporate sectors are held by those who have attended a handful of private universities. At the other end of the class spectrum, most junior colleges and community colleges offer primarily vocational training to those destined for lower-middle positions in the corporate hierarchy.

Overall, the most important political influence of schools is to reproduce the contours of American social structure. The

[35]James MacGregor Burns and Jack Peltason, *Government by the People*, 8th ed., (Englewood Cliffs, N.J., 1972), Epilogue.
[36]Dan Nimmo and Thomas D. Ungs, *American Political Patterns*, 3d. ed., (Boston, 1973), p. 38.

lowest positions in society are occupied by "dropouts" from school, usually from poor backgrounds. Middle-level positions are held by the offspring of those in the corporate-labor sector or small-scale capital. And future authorities are recruited from the sons and daughters of the advantaged.

The second important influence schools have is to purvey dominant values and secure political compliance. Despite a rhetoric of personal development and equal opportunity, schools at all levels perpetuate the myths about America and mold cultural attitudes of obedience and respect for established political and economic institutions.

The Consciousness Industry

The media are an influential means of communicating dominant ideology among adults: nine American homes in ten have at least one television receiver. The daily circulation of American newspapers is sixty-seven million. Each night over fifty million American families watch television network news. Television often presents images that cast discredit on prevailing institutions and thus apparently contradicts the dominant ideology. The sight of Police Chief Bull Connor's police dogs attacking unarmed black children in Montgomery, Alabama, galvanized public opinion throughout the country and created support for the civil-rights struggles of the early 1960s. The televised hearings of the Senate Watergate Committee and the House Judiciary Committee (when it recommended President Nixon's impeachment) shook Americans' confidence in their leaders. Yet the politically unstabilizing effect of television should not be exaggerated. On the whole, television is quite timid in its criticism of prevailing arrangements and reluctant to question the official ideology. One reason lies in the fact that, through government licensing, control over most of the air waves—a community resource as public as air and water—is granted to private business to use for a profit.

Television and radio networks and local stations are important members of the corporate complex. NBC is owned by the Radio Corporation of America, the twentieth largest industrial corporation in the United States. CBS and ABC, which also rank among the few hundred largest corporations, are immense communications empires; each controls record companies, motion picture studios, movie theaters, and publishing companies. All three networks have major Pentagon contracts for radar, electronics, and communication equipment. As one student of television has pointed out:

> Since the controllers of the broadcast media, generally, represent corporate and business orientations, and find the present broadcasting and economic systems profitable, they have a special stake in the continuation of the present situation. They therefore view as disruptive, radical, subversive, or even unpatriotic, forces, materials and programs which might, however indirectly, disrupt the present arrangement. It is natural that the voices of the media should speak the language of business, for their masters are big business.[37]

Television is first and foremost a big prosperous business. The television stations in the fifty most populous markets average 36 percent profit on gross revenues and a rate of return on capital as high as 200 to 300 percent. Thus, each year a television station may earn several times what its broadcasting equipment and other capital are worth.[38]

Not only is television big business but it is also dependent on the advertising dollar of big business for its profits. Well over $1 billion each year is paid by corporate advertisers to the three networks.[39] Television stations generally follow the adage: don't bite the hand that feeds you. In 1970, NBC presented a documentary, "The Migrant," describing the miserable conditions of farm workers on a Florida citrus-fruit farm owned by a subsidiary of Coca-Cola. The next year, ads for Coke no longer appeared on NBC—and the message was not lost on the broadcasting industry.[40] Economic factors make for a system of informal private censorship.

Newspapers are slightly more courageous than television, in part because they derive their revenue from readers as well as from advertisers. But newspapers are also business enterprises whose publishers represent business interests. For example,

---

[37]Harry J. Skornia, *Television and the News: A Critical Appraisal* (Palo Alto, Calif., 1968), p. 70.

[38]Ronald H. Coase, "The Economics of Broadcasting and Public Policy," in Paul W. MacAvry, ed., *The Crisis of the Regulatory Commissions: An Introduction to a Current Issue of Public Policy* (New York, 1970), p. 95.

[39]Les Brown, *Television: The Business Behind the Box* (New York, 1971), p. 49.

[40]*Ibid.,* pp. 196–203.

small-town newspapers (of which there are fifteen hundred in the United States) contribute to dominant values by ardently supporting local business and commerce. Local papers have a particularly influential position because there is generally only one newspaper per city, and thus they have a monopoly on what local news is printed. Often, all the local newspapers and radio and television stations in an area are owned by one business group. In Topeka, Kansas, for example, Stauffer Publications owns Topeka's only morning, evening, and Sunday newspapers, as well as the city's only commercial television station, the city's highest powered AM radio station, and five other newspapers in Kansas. Similar ties between newspapers and broadcasting exist in Milwaukee, St. Louis, Des Moines, Minneapolis, Washington, D.C., Philadelphia, Dallas, Atlanta, and San Francisco.[41]

Local newspapers and broadcast media are firmly anchored in the small-capital sector. Their owners aim to make a profit and to preserve arrangements favorable to local business interests. They employ few investigative reporters, report mostly "human interest" news and crime, provide little critical political analysis, and blanket their pages with advertising and low-quality entertainment.

Television news The media present a hidden message very different from their official attitude of "let the chips fall where they may." The point can be illustrated by an analysis of television news, which, according to polls, is the news medium attracting the widest following and greatest confidence. Television news presents distant activities with a clarity and drama no scholarly analysis or newspaper can match. But television news also has characteristics that inhibit reflection and analysis. First, the quantity of information that can be presented is limited: fewer words are spoken during a half-hour news telecast than are printed on one page of a daily newspaper. Television compresses items, presents them in rapid-fire thirty-second sequences, and thus is forced to oversimplify.

Second, television news is superficial. News items focus on the unusual, anecdotal, and photogenic, no amount of which is sufficient to provide a basis for public awareness or knowledge of critical issues. "In the news land of television," communications

[41]Walter Pincus, "Quality News," *The New Republic*, May 18, 1974, pp. 15–17. The Justice Department has challenged some of these monopolies.

specialist Harry Skornia notes, "where the showman is king, the news is expected to entertain rather than primarily to inform."[42] A spectacular mine disaster, airplane crash, or traffic accident gets prominent coverage; but the day-to-day conditions that make work unrewarding, difficult, and dangerous go unreported. When television network news was lengthened in the 1960s from fifteen to thirty minutes nightly, it is doubtful that Americans became significantly better informed about their country's politics. Listening to radio stations that broadcast news twenty-four hours per day produces headaches, not political understanding.

Television wields tremendous power through its ability to decide what is newsworthy. Radical activist Jerry Rubin suggests, "An event *happens* when it goes on TV."[43] Indeed, much television news is what historian Daniel Boorstin calls pseudo-images—events staged for their symbolic impact rather than because of any intrinsic importance. News conferences, public speeches and ceremonies, even protest demonstrations may be of this kind.[44]

The media thus shape reality as much as they reflect it. Journalist Edward Epstein asks, "Why, a couple of years ago, did ecology stories come into favor while black-militant stories seemed to die out?" It is impossible to say how new categories of news emerge.[45] It is a commonplace that bias in news presentation is unavoidable. Among the myriad of events that occur each day, only a few items will be selected for presentation in a newscast. Moreover, the same event can be presented in as many different ways as there are points of view. What kind of bias shapes television news in America?

The major bias that underlies television newscasts is that of the dominant ideology. One reason is that, among all the news media, television engages least in investigative reporting. The television networks spend millions for election-night coverage, but they employ fewer reporters for investigative journalism than a large daily newspaper. (It was reporters for the *Washington Post* who presisted in digging out the story of official corruption behind the Watergate break-in and cover-up.) Television com-

---

[42]Skornia, p. 29.
[43]Jerry Rubin, *Do It! Scenarios of the Revolution* (New York, 1970), p. 107.
[44]Daniel Boorstin, *The Image* (New York, 1961).
[45]Edward Jay Epstein, "The Selection of Reality," *The New Yorker,* March 3, 1973, p. 52.

mentators (like most newspaper reporters) rely on those in authority for much of their news. After the massacre of prisoners at Attica by state troopers in 1971, the media accepted at face value the official accounts that falsely placed responsibility for the killings on the prisoners.

Television news does not put events in perspective. Commentators uniformly share a witty, bland, detached approach. The rapid juxtaposition of news items of grave importance, "human interest" stories, and advertising helps reduce any critical sting. If the rituals of student and black confrontations with the police are presented, the analysis needed to understand the structural cleavage underlying these conflicts is not. Political scientist Robert Dahl points out, "The amount of time and space devoted by the mass media to views openly hostile to the prevailing ideology is negligible. . . . Hence the general effect of the mass media is to reinforce the existing institutions and ideology."[46]

Governmental pressure also influences networks and stations to stay within the dominant ideology. The government has a potent weapon to brandish against radio and television broadcasters through the authority of the Federal Communications Commission (FCC) to grant, renew, or refuse to renew broadcast franchises and issue broadcast regulations. Although the FCC is prohibited from exercising censorship of news broadcasts, the government's life-and-death hold over television and radio broadcasters makes them especially careful not to antagonize the government. Self-censorship has the same effect as official censorship.

Television's search for the sensational often means that it cannot avoid being visual dynamite. During the 1960s, the media portrayed dramatic instances of protest activity and police repression, including urban rebellions and antiwar rallies, the 1968 Democratic National Convention in Chicago (where television coverage alternated between convention proceedings and a police riot occurring outside the convention hall), and police killings on the campuses of Kent State and Jackson State.

But government officials soon counterattacked. In a manner reminiscent of the ancient custom of killing a messenger who

---

[46]Robert Dahl, *Political Opposition in Western Democracies* (New Haven, Conn., 1966), pp. 47–48.

bore unwelcome tidings, the government blamed television for the seething antiwar and black-militant protest movements. The government also tried to reduce coverage of political activists. In 1969, Vice President Spiro Agnew pointedly reminded the networks that they were licensed by the government, yet, he complained, the news fraternity did not "represent the views of America" (implying that only news items welcome to the majority should be represented). In 1972, Clay T. Whitehead, White House director of telecommunications policy, escalated the attack by charging that network news consisted of "ideological plugola" peddled by "so-called professionals who confuse sensationalism with sense and who dispense elitist gossip in the guise of news analysis." Whitehead threatened that the government would not renew television-station franchises if the critical bite of news was not muted. Documents made public in the Watergate affair showed that government attacks were carefully organized. They included attempts, in the words of White House aides, to "tear down the institution" of broadcast journalism.[47] A transcript of presidential conversations revealed that President Nixon considered retaliating against the *Washington Post* for breaking the Watergate story by challenging the *Post's* control over two television stations.

Government attacks have two purposes: to intimidate the networks and to discredit television news. The *New York Times* commented: "The White House message to American broadcasters . . . is blunt: Stay away from controversial subjects."[48]

The government's attack on network news in the past few years has been part of a broader assault on all the news media. Government measures included attempting to use the courts to prevent publication of material embarrassing to the government (the Pentagon Papers); undercutting public broadcasting by appointing politically reliable officials to head the Public Broadcasting System; tapping journalists' telephones; and weakening investigative reporting by compelling reporters to divulge confidential notes and sources of information (at least four reporters have been jailed for refusing to cooperate).

Government attacks at the top are felt all along the line. Robert J. Boyle, editor of a newspaper in Pottstown, Penn-

---

[47]*New York Times,* November 2, 1973.
[48]*Ibid.,* December 23, 1972.

sylvania, reports: "The bee stings in Washington and the pain is felt in Pottstown, too. . . . Censorship, government controls and secrecy are not limited to people like [Jack] Anderson. The small-town newsman is also feeling the sting."[49] Boyle describes how police and other local officials, following Washington's lead, have clammed up and refuse to cooperate with newspaper reporters.

The government has been quite successful in getting the news media to toe the dominant ideological line. The president of the Associated Press commented that "newsgathering in 1972 was more difficult than at any time since World War II, because of censorship, [government] harrassment of reporters and a 'spreading cloak of secrecy.' "[50]

Entertainment: the hidden political message In terms of prime time, total hours of programming, and (probably) the impact of television on political attitudes, entertainment far outweighs news in importance. Entertainment programming provides even greater support to dominant values. The political impact of entertainment is heightened because the distinction between fact and fiction is often masked in television: much entertainment consists of "real life" serials purportedly based on "actual cases from the files of" the New York City or Los Angeles police departments, or a particular hospital or law firm. No effort is spared to make the presentation appear true to life—uniforms, surroundings, and professional jargon all convey the impression that the program is an accurate reflection of reality.

In fact, entertainment programs glamorize and slant reality. Authorities are usually warm, concerned, and sincere people attempting to help the community. Although facing manifold difficulties, they usually manage to come out on top. In the strange world of television, crimes never go unsolved, patients rarely die, and defendants are almost never convicted of crimes they did not commit. As for those at the bottom, they are beset by problems, but none so great that—thanks to the good will of authorities—they cannot be solved within their half hour of allotted television time. The possibility of rebellion against the status quo is never evoked, except by a radical, a hippy, or a

---

[49] *Ibid.*, March 23, 1973.
[50] *Ibid.*, February 13, 1972.

militant black—whose harebrained schemes are proved wrong by the patient efforts of wise moderate authorities. Even more than in news broadcasts, the message of entertainment programs is that there is no reason for fundamental change, since dominant institutions are responsive to individual grievances—and serious group grievances of class and race do not exist.

Advertising   Perhaps television's greatest impact is through advertising—the reason why commercial broadcasters are in business in the first place. Like entertainment, advertising describes a world that does not exist. Automobile ads portray their wares in the tranquil setting of country lanes and green fields. One would never know that automobiles cause traffic jams, fatal accidents, and pollution. Airplane rides are relaxed, smooth, and efficient, with fine meals and attractive friendly stewardesses. Not shown is the difficulty of reaching the airport, the long waits for planes that are often late, the overbooking that systematically occurs—and the large proportion of the population that cannot afford to utilize the "wings of man."

Advertising oversimplifies and stereotypes the world. A woman's chief cares are dirty dishes, floors, and shirt collars; preparing meals for her children and husband; and looking like a model. Blacks are smiling, cheerful, and middle class—just like white Americans. True, many television ads are replete with anxiety—pharmaceutical companies see to that. But sleeplessness, indigestion, headaches, nervous tension, anger—the difficulties that afflict Americans living in the stressful conditions of corporate capitalism—soon vanish after swallowing pills thoughtfully provided (at exorbitant prices) by the American drug industry. One reason for high prices, incidentally, is the enormous expense of television advertising: Alka-Seltzer spends $23 million annually on advertising to generate sales of $60 million, which means that thirty-eight cents of every dollar a customer pays for Alka-Seltzer goes to underwrite the company's advertising campaign.[51]

Television advertising suggests that the answer to one's problems is to be found in material goods—political change is never the answer. Thus, you have no friends? Use our mouthwash or deodorant. Fed up with your job? Sneak a week in the

---

[51]Barry Weisberg, *Beyond Repair: The Ecology of Capitalism* (Boston, 1971), p. 55.

Caribbean. Unable to pay your bills? "Consolidate" your debts with a loan or a credit card. The advertising political parties sponsor at election time provides an exact parallel to this approach. Want to solve the country's problems? Vote for our party and everything will be fine.

Television advertising begins to have an impact early in life—children no longer sing nursery rhymes, they sing Kellogg's Frosted Flakes jingles. Children log more time watching television than they spend in school. An average child sees seventy television commercials a day—25,000 each year.[52]

Corporate advertising on television can be quite explicitly political, as when Johnny Cash tells viewers how Exxon is cleaning up America, G.E. pours forth progress, and Ma Bell brings joy into the wretched lives of separated Americans. More generally, the constant barrage of television advertising can be considered political propaganda that infects American culture with materialism, competitiveness, a manipulative attitude toward one's own body and toward others, and an acceptance of corporate capitalism.

The Government as Socializer

Government officials at all levels—from the president to the local policeman—represent an important socializing influence. Government does not simply reflect and respond to public opinion, as the dominant imagery of procedural democracy suggests. Instead, government is constantly concerned with shaping and manipulating public opinion. A presidential press conference is better understood as an attempt to build support for the president's policies than an exercise in clarification. A screaming police car is delivering a symbolic message: opposition to authorities brings quick reprisal.

Among the government's major concerns are how to package its image, manage the news, subdue political opinion, and suppress dissent. For government officials, according to one observer, "Public opinion is simply one more problem that demands skillful management."[53] To this end, the federal government earmarks about $400 million each year to cover public informa-

[52]*New York Times*, May 12, 1974.
[53]Richard J. Barnet, *Roots of War* (New York, 1972), p. 267.

tion activities—double the entire amount spent for newsgathering by the two major wire services (AP and UPI), the ten largest newspapers in the country, and the three major television networks.[54]

The government's disdain for truth is amply documented whenever private government deliberations are made public. One example is the Pentagon Papers, a secret government study of the Vietnam war leaked to the press by Daniel Ellsberg in 1971. The Pentagon Papers revealed that at the time President Kennedy was publicly arguing that the Soviet Union and China inspired and directed the North Vietnamese, he was privately being told the opposite by his advisers. The Pentagon Papers describe how the "domino theory" (which held that if South Vietnam turned Communist, this would act as a falling domino and force other Asian countries to go Communist) was privately rejected by the president at the same time that he used it as official public justification for American intervention. Government officials may lie to others within the government: President Johnson fabricated details of an attack by North Vietnam on American ships in the Gulf of Tonkin in 1964 to convince Congress to grant him authority to expand the war. The resolution that he submitted to Congress, supposedly drafted as a result of the attack, had been prepared months earlier. More recently, President Nixon announced to the American people in April 1970 (when he ordered an invasion of Cambodia) that the United States had never previously violated the neutrality of Cambodia; the president subsequently admitted that a systematic bombing campaign deep within Cambodian territory had been going on for a year before his announcement.

The transcripts of taped conversations in the White House relating to the Watergate break-in reveal that what dominated discussions was the question, as Mr. Nixon says at one point, "how do you handle that PR-wise?" On March 21, 1973, the president discussed in detail the options available to keep the truth from coming out. He suggested that a White House statement be issued, saying that the initial payments made to the Watergate defendants (which were, in fact, supplied by presidential aides as hush money to buy silence) had come from a Cuban defense committee.

[54]William Rivers and Wilbur Schramm, *Responsibility in Mass Communications* (New York, 1969), p. 97.

Presidential adviser John Dean III replied, "Well, yeah. We can put it together. That isn't of course quite the way it happened, but—."

"I know," said Mr. Nixon, "but that's the way it is going to have to happen."

By changing people's perception of reality rather than the reality itself, the actual adjustments that might erode authorities' power need not be carried out. Thus, government action resembles an elaborate minuet in which promises and symbolic activity play a larger role than the redistribution of power. When a mine caves in, the government expresses sympathy for the victims and sponsors an "investigation"—which soothes public distress but does not require owners to improve safety conditions. When a group's discontent boils over into actual protest, the president appoints a "blue ribbon" study commission of "distinguished citizens"—a symbolic gesture that takes the place of meeting the group's demands. In recent years, official commissions have been appointed to study problems of youth, campus disorders, aging, urban discontent, and violence. The recommendations of these commissions are either politically "safe" (which is to be expected, given the composition of the panels) or, in the rare event they require substantial reform, are ignored by the government.

The extent of the government's attempt to harness symbols to its own ends can be savored merely by enumerating terms used in official parlance: *urban renewal, the war on poverty, Office of Economic Opportunity, the independent regulatory commissions, and the Department of Defense.* Their reality is very different from the implied meaning. For example, the war on poverty mainly benefited not the poor but professional welfare bureaucrats, scholars carrying out urban research, and (above all) local businessmen— physicians benefiting from medicare and medicaid, slum landlords who end up with a high proportion of welfare money, and road contractors who received much of the appropriations for Appalachia. And one could never tell from its title that the Department of Defense is among the foremost forces for militarism in the world.[55]

The lawmaking process socializes to dominant values. Automobile-safety laws add a few safety features to automobiles, but

---

[55]See Murray Edelman, *The Symbolic Uses of Politics* (Urbana, Ill., 1964), and *Politics as Symbolic Action* (Chicago, 1971).

they do not require a basic redesign of automobiles or provide incentives to reduce reliance on automobile transportion. As political scientist Murray Edelman notes, because laws "function as reassurances that threats in the economic environment are under control, their indirect effect is to permit greater exploitation of tangible resources by the organized groups concerned than would be possible if the legal symbols were absent."[56]

The institutions and procedures of democracy, notably political parties and elections, deliver the dominant ideological message that established arrangements are freely chosen by American citizens. Political scientist Dan Nimmo suggests that election "campaigns are a significant form of symbolic reassurance contributing to the stability of democratic regimes. . . . By voting we acquire the feeling that we as citizens are participating in governing the political system."[57] Thus, the normal functioning of democratic institutions is probably more influential in strengthening dominant values than any possible conspiracy by political authorities.

Schools, the media, and government have been analyzed in detail because they are the most important institutions through which dominant values are communicated to the population. However, *all* institutions in the United States that do not challenge existing structural arrangements can be considered as socializing instruments of dominant values. Socialization occurs on the job and in the armed forces, where hierarchy and authoritarian values predominate.

The ability of schools, media, and government to shape people's political consciousness should not be exaggerated. The complex process by which individuals and groups develop political attitudes cannot be reduced to a simple formula. People are not passive agents, easily manipulated. Children display a healthy suspicion of schools and teachers. Citizens distrust or ignore what they are told by politicans and television. The effect of socializing institutions is often quite different from what might be expected. To illustrate, political scientist John Mueller found that, despite the greater degree of antiwar protest and the wider television coverage of the Vietnam war compared to the Korean war (which led many observers to conclude that antiwar opinion

[56]Murray Edelman, "Symbols and Political Quiescence," in Reid, pp. 42–43.
[57]Dan Nimmo, *The Political Persuaders* (Englewood Cliffs, N.J., 1970), pp. 5–7.

was more widespread during the Vietnam war), Americans reacted, on the whole, in similar ways to the two wars.[58]

The Decline of the Dominant Ideology

A convergence of social, economic, and political problems has weakened the hold of the dominant ideology in recent years. As economic growth has slowed down, American corporate capitalism, which requires constant expansion both to provide benefits for capital and to hold out the promise of social mobility to workers, becomes less able to attract support. Institutional mediations, such as parties and Congress, have lost their hold. Revelations by crusading journalists, public-interest lawyers, and critical scholars concerning injustice and the illegal activities of political officials, from the president down, have further weakened the dominant ideology. It is becoming clear to increasing numbers of Americans that the procedures of democracy, which the dominant ideology uses to legitimize present arrangements, can also be used by discontented groups to air grievances.

The result has been a sharp rise recently in the number of people who have lost faith in the dominant ideology. Even the dry statistics of public-opinion polls are eloquent. Between 1966 and 1972, the proportion of Americans agreeing with the statement: "People who run the country don't care what happens to people such as myself," went from 26 percent to 50 percent.[59] In 1964, one-fifth of the population said that government could not be trusted to do what is right all the time; in 1972, the proportion of the population expressing this opinion doubled.[60] In 1964, 28 percent of the electorate felt government helped special interests more than general interests; by 1972, 58 percent of the electorate were in this category.[61] Among college youth, 37 percent agreed in 1969 that "big business needs reform or elimination"; four years later, 54 percent agreed with this statement.[62] A Gallup poll reported that the proportion of Americans "dissatisfied with the

[58]John E. Mueller, *Wars, Presidents and Public Opinion* (New York, 1973), pp. 62, 167.
[59]Louis Harris, *The Anguish of Change* (New York, 1973), p. 10, and unpublished data from Harris.
[60]Arthur H. Miller *et al.*, "A Majority Party in Disarray: Policy Polarization in the 1972 Election," unpublished paper, University of Michigan, p. 46.
[61]*Ibid.*, pp. 46–47.
[62]Daniel Yankelovich, Inc., poll reported in *New York Times*, May 26, 1974.

Table 11–2
Drop in confidence for leadership groups

Have "great deal" of confidence in:	1966 %	1973 %	CHANGE %
Doctors	72	48	−24
Financial leaders	67	39	−28
Scientists	56	37	−19
Military leaders	62	35	−27
Educators	61	33	−28
Psychiatrists	51	31	−20
Religious leaders	41	30	−11
Retail store operators	48	28	−20
U.S. Supreme Court	51	28	−23
Executive branch of government	41	27	−14
Business leaders	55	27	−28
Congress	42	21	−21
Press leaders	29	18	−11
People running TV	25	17	− 8
Labor leaders	22	15	− 7
Advertising leaders	21	12	− 9

Source: Reprinted from *The Anguish of Change* by Louis Harris (p. 12). By permission of W. W. Norton & Company, Inc. Copyright © 1973 by W. W. Norton & Company, Inc.

way this nation is being governed" went from 54 to 66 percent between 1971 and 1973.[63]

The general drop in confidence accorded established leaders can be seen from the following trend: whereas in 1966, a majority of Americans expressed high confidence in eight out of sixteen leadership groups; by 1972 not one of the sixteen groups attracted the confidence of a majority of Americans.[64] (See Table 11–2.)

That Americans are not blindly trustful of their leaders can also be seen from the fact that nearly half of those who were questioned in a poll agreed that "most political parties care only about winning elections and nothing more," and a majority agreed that "most politicians are looking out for themselves above all else" and that "most politicians are bought off by some private interests."[65] Such feelings have led to an increased sense

[63]*New York Times*, October 14, 1973.
[64]Harris, p. 12.
[65]Herbert McClosky, "Consensus and Ideology in American Politics," *American Political Science Review* 58 (June, 1964): 361–82.

of alienation from government. According to a scale devised by public-opinion analyst Louis Harris, the proportion of those who felt alienated increased from 34 to 46 percent between 1966 and 1972. As one might expect, satisfaction is highly correlated with income: in 1972, only 30 percent of those with incomes of $15,000 or more felt alienated compared to 63 percent of those with incomes below $5,000.[66]

SOCIALIZING TO THE ACCOMMODATIVE IDEOLOGY

Although dominant values have the edge in the United States, the existence of discontented groups and democratic procedures of free speech, press, and elections provide some opportunities for the airing of accommodationist values.

To some extent, schools and universities help foster accommodative ideology. Teachers may stress the importance of critical analyses, and there is official dedication to academic freedom and free inquiry. School provides a means of liberation from parental influences; and peer group socialization—the influence of students on each other—is often directed against dominant institutions. Particularly in college, students may become critical of established arrangements.

As with schools, so with the media—if the major message is dominant values, an accommodative note often creeps in. As mentioned earlier, in the realm of civil rights, Watergate, and presidential misconduct, the media's investigations and publicity served to sharpen discontent. While the media do not provide a neutral forum, they do offer limited possibilities for groups that otherwise might encounter a stone wall of silence. As a result of their protest activities, blacks, American Indians, and other disadvantaged groups have gained access to the media. Especially noteworthy is the role of newspapers, particularly influential newspapers like the *New York Times* and *Washington Post;* weekly news magazines; and, above all, weekly and monthly journals like the *New Republic, New York Review of Books, Ramparts,* the *Nation,* and the *Progressive,* which often expose official misconduct and criticize government policies.

[66]Harris, p. 130.

Although television entertainment rarely questions dominant values, it may implicitly portray alternatives to the dominant ideology. For example, television programs may depict the hardships of working-class life or show blacks in situations where they are equal or superior to whites ("Mod Squad"). Entertainment and advertising may unintentionally feed accommodationist protest and ideology by holding out to the deprived the glamor of the "good life" and implying that everyone is entitled to partake. The consequence may be for people to take the message seriously and break into a neighborhood appliance store for the color television that they have been told no home should be without.

A few government officials may act as spokesmen for the accommodationist mode, such as the handful of senators who were early opponents of the American invasion of Vietnam (including Senators Gruening, Morse, and McGovern). Another example was the pressure Stanley Pottinger, former head of the Civil Rights division of the Department of Health, Education, and Welfare, directed at colleges and universities to hire qualified black and female professors.

Most foundations provide financial support for politically safe activities, including cultural affairs (orchestras, museums, opera companies), medical research, and education. However, some foundation support goes for accommodative activity. Notable in this regard is the Ford Foundation, the country's largest foundation, which has sponsored voter-registration drives aimed at expanding the number of black voters in the South, and school decentralization and preschool programs that provide benefits for racial minorities and the poor. The Ford Foundation illustrates the thin line that separates the dominant and accommodative ideologies. By attempting to anticipate and identify problems, publicize them, and propose new alternatives, the Ford Foundation has sometimes been criticized for engaging in controversial activities. Yet the aim of this accommodative activity is to devise reforms to make the system work better. Far from undermining established arrangements, the ultimate effect is probably to strengthen them.

Groups such as the American Civil Liberties Union, the National Association for the Advancement of Colored People, the Americans for Democratic Action, Ralph Nader's various organizations, Friends of the Earth, Common Cause, and organized labor (the AFL–CIO) often focus criticism on particular problems. These organizations voice specific grievances and educate many to question the dominant ideology. Yet these groups stop short of an opposition stance.

Protest directed at particular issues and criticism of prevailing arrangements within the United States are mostly within the accommodative mode. Newspaper and television accounts question specific wrongdoing, but the private ownership of the media makes an opposition critique unlikely. Universities permit students and faculty to enjoy freedom of thought—so long as it remains "responsible" and does not threaten to spill over into disruptive action. Foundations and public-interest groups mute their criticism for fear of jeopardizing their financial support and tax status. A series of segmented protests by individual groups provides the seeds for an opposition movement, but it does not by itself constitute such a movement. Unless the accommodative ideology enlarges its perspective to include a structural critique, dominant values and institutions are not likely to be shaken.

THE OPPOSITION IDEOLOGY IN
HISTORICAL PERSPECTIVE

Compared to countries in Western Europe, a strongly-based opposition movement and ideology are weakly represented in the United States. Some of the reasons were discussed in Chapter 8. The lack of a feudal past and the widespread distribution of property in the United States made for a more fluid social structure. With the notable exception of a permanently suppressed black minority, Americans generally calculated that social betterment could come through efforts to change their individual situation rather than the whole political and economic system.

But opposition ideology and movements have not been absent from the American past. Three recent periods can be identified when active opposition movements flourished. In all three cases, authorities reacted by using repression at variance with procedural democracy. Although the dominant ideology holds that differences of opinion are tolerated in the United States and points to the lack of opposition movements as evidence of American democracy, there are clear limits to official tolerance (regardless of what First Amendment guarantees of free speech and assembly may say). Authorities may tolerate dissent within the accommodative perspective (although even this is far from certain: witness government attacks on the media); but when criticism of prevailing arrangements takes on an opposition hue, authorities have acted to crush the emerging movement.

The Populist and Socialist movements prior to the First World War presented radical critiques of the growing power of corporations. Both movements represented viable challenges to the status quo. They offered intelligent analyses and feasible alternatives. Both attracted widespread support and elected candidates to political office. (In the first decades of the twentieth century, the Socialist party elected eighty state legislators and mayors in a number of cities, including Milwaukee, Wisconsin; Schenectady, New York; and Butte, Montana.) Moreover, the Socialist party opposed United States entry into the First World War in the name of pacifism, antimilitarism, and anticapitalism. As the only organized opposition to the war, it attracted further support.

The Socialist party was soon made the target of government retaliation under the Espionage Act of 1917. The government declared many Socialist publications illegal and refused them the use of the mails. It illegally tapped the telephones of Socialist party leaders, expelled from the country aliens who were party members, and imprisoned Socialist editors and party leaders (most notably Eugene Debs, the party's candidate for president). As with later attacks on opposition movements, the government used an arsenal of illegal procedures: police surveillance and violence, judicial repression, and the passage of laws designed to "get" opposition members (in violation of the constitutional prohibition on bills of attainder). The government's counterattack was successful and, at a critical juncture—during the period of corporate consolidation—a potentially effective opposition to the corporate complex was shattered.[67]

During the depression of the 1930s, when the country was plagued by economic stagnation, widespread unemployment, and poverty, a number of opposition movements again began to

---

[67]James Weinstein, *The Decline of Socialism in America, 1912–1925* (New York, 1967).

develop, including the Socialist party, the Communist party, and others. The threat was met first by New Deal welfare programs for the poor, which undercut the opposition and helped save capitalism. Later, during the Second World War and the 1940s and 1950s, nationalism, patriotism, and loyalty were used against the left. A "red scare" was instituted in schools, government, media, and industry, partly at the instigation in the late 1940s of Senator Joseph McCarthy of Wisconsin (hence the term *McCarthyism* often used to characterize the period). Government and private "loyalty" programs were established for the purpose of denying jobs to suspected critics of American institutions. The threat of bolshevism and the Soviet Union was used to suppress opposition within the United States, and, for generations, dissent in America was equated with a lack of patriotism.

The 1960s represent the third period containing an opposition movement. During that time, a host of accommodationist demands were expressed—and many were apparently accepted by the federal government. Spurred by the youthful call of President John F. Kennedy for exploration of a "new frontier," reform became the order of the day. The 1960s saw the launching of antipoverty programs, expanded welfare programs, civil-rights legislation, and environmental-protection measures. Yet, in retrospect, the multitude of reforms frequently amounted to little more than the symbolic sops that Murray Edelman describes as government's characteristic response to demands for change. The Kennedy and Johnson reforms were often more style than substance. Despite the "civil-rights revolution," most nonwhites continue to occupy subordinate positions and constitute a disproportionate percentage of the prison population. The American welfare system continues to be far less adequate than those of European countries possessing a fraction of America's resources. Moreover, at the very time Presidents Kennedy and Johnson were accepting accommodationist demands and sponsoring the Great Society in the United States (President Johnson's label for his programs), these same presidents were ordering the destruction of societies in Southeast Asia.

However, the accommodationist demands of the 1960s contained the seeds of a mass-based opposition movement and ideology. For many individuals and groups, there was a wavering between an accommodative critique of particular problems and an opposition challenge to the entire structure of patterned inequality. Many subordinate groups engaged in protest—blacks, chicanos and other Spanish-speaking groups, American Indians, women, homosexuals, and students. The demands voiced by a host of individual groups often remained within the accommodationist ideology. Groups attempted to improve their own status without confronting more generalized patterns of inequality.

Yet a particular group's criticism can take an opposition turn if the focus of discontent broadens to include analysis of wider political arrangements. The antiwar movement began by criticizing the American invasion of Vietnam; but accommodationist analysis became opposition when it began to be argued that the causes of the war were not simply the result of mistakes and miscalculations by American political leaders, but were rooted in basic internal arrangements in America (the military-industrial complex) and America's self-appointed position abroad as guardian of the status quo.

The new left was the first major American opposition movement in America since the 1930s, and, according to journalist Kirkpatrick Sale, it was "the first really *homegrown* left in America."[68] It emerged from two angry accommodationist protests of the 1960s: the civil-rights movement in the beginning of the decade and the antiwar protest beginning in the mid-1960s. Among its organizational antecedents were the Student Nonviolent Coordinating Committee (SNCC), founded in 1960, which played a leading role in the civil-rights protest and organized freedom rides and sit-ins in the South; and Students for a Democratic Society (SDS), also founded in 1960, which supported teach-ins, antiwar rallies, draft resistance, campus opposition to the Vietnam war, and community control. (A related movement—black militancy—is described in Chapter 12.)

The opposition movement was far more widespread in the late 1960s than is often realized. Two hundred and forty-nine civil disturbances occurred throughout the United States in 1967. In April 1968 alone, following the assassination of Martin Luther King, Jr., there were 237.[69] In addition to black rebellion, antiwar protest reached nationwide proportions. The peace movement went far beyond the few universities that received much of the media's attention. Occupation of campuses and large-scale demonstrations occurred not only at Berkeley, Chicago, Colum-

68Kirkpatrick Sale, *SDS* (New York, 1973), p. 8.
69Adam Yarmolinsky, *The Military Establishment* (New York, 1970), p. 189.

bia, Cornell, and Wisconsin but also at the University of Colorado, University of Kentucky, Vanderbilt, Duke, Missouri, and the University of Washington. More than half the large American universities experienced demonstrations against corporate and military recruiters on campus during the fall of 1967.[70] One million students boycotted classes during an antiwar moratorium on April 26, 1968. In 1969 alone, the police were called in at over one hundred colleges.

The peak of antiwar protest occurred after the United States invasion of Cambodia in April 1970, when four-fifths of all American colleges and universities had demonstrations and five hundred universities and colleges were closed down.[71] In two campus demonstrations during May 1970—Kent State, Ohio, and Jackson State, Mississippi—police and National Guard opened fire on striking demonstrators, killing and wounding students. According to Sale, the "May insurrection was one of the great unreported stories of the decade."[72] (It might be noted that throughout the 1960s, one person died as the result of student actions, when the Army Mathematics Research Center at the University of Wisconsin was bombed in 1970. During the same period, police violence took the lives of seventeen students.)

The new left of the 1960s was quite different from the "old left" of the 1930s. Members of the new left aimed to achieve large-scale changes—the end of the Vietnam war, the elimination of racist practices in America, and the overturn of corporate dominance at home and abroad. But members of the new left also sought ways to transform their own lives in the present, rather than waiting for overall changes in society. They rejected the organized, regimented, hierarchical life of corporate capitalism and many experimented with drugs, sex, and communal living styles. They sought to regain control over their own lives by stressing personal responsibility and demanding to participate in decisions that affected their everyday lives. They attempted to democratize institutions like the school, family, and local community.

In their zeal to transform the present, members of the new left had an important impact on values and political practice. The new left encouraged a freedom in personal relations and life

---

[70]Sale, p. 380.
[71]Harris, p. 219; Sale, p. 636.
[72]Sale, p. 639.

styles. It succeeded in applying massive pressure to reduce American involvement in the Vietnam war. University links to the military-industrial complex were weakened: classified research became prohibited on many campuses, military training units were dissolved, and military recruiting was ended. President Johnson's decision not to seek a second full term in 1968 was in good part a result of the opposition to his war policies mounted by the new left and the peace movement. The new left (along with the woman's movement and black militancy) was responsible for a cultural upheaval in America and a questioning of long-established values. The new left demonstrated that changes could be effected through the dedicated efforts of an opposition.

But the new left also had serious weaknesses, which sprang partly from its strength. As a result of its opposition to strong, internal leadership and organization, and because it feared that a national organization would produce a new bureaucracy and would stifle decentralized direct democracy, it failed to mobilize many people outside college campuses who potentially supported its goals. ("There was . . . something very deep in us that drove us away from leadership," comments Todd Gitlin, a former president of SDS.[73]) It failed to reach groups such as workers and racial minorities, who were often skeptical of how new-left goals would improve their particular situation. The new left's insistence on spontaneity and its opposition to leadership provided the opening wedge for the officially sponsored counterattack of the late 1960s.

After initially being caught off guard by the success of the opposition movement (both the antiwar movement and black militancy), authorities soon responded to the opposition challenge. In *Counterrevolution and Revolt,* critical theorist Herbert Marcuse has described what he calls a preventive counterrevolution, waged by the government against a revolution that never occurred.[74] Official repression took a variety of forms.

Much of the anticipatory counterrevolution consisted of an attempt to smash the credibility of the opposition ideology and demonstrate the superiority of the dominant ideology. Dominant institutions, including government and universities, participated in the crackdown. Government harrassment of the media has already been reviewed, and the use of political trials by the

---

[73]Todd Gitlin, "Maybe you need a Weatherman after all," *Village Voice,* October 18, 1973, p. 29.
[74]Herbert Marcuse, *Counterrevolution and Revolt* (Boston, 1972), chapter 1.

government to suppress dissent has been described in Chapter 10. In addition, government agencies were directed to root out opposition organizations. In May 1968, the director of the FBI directed all FBI offices to attack organizations and individuals "who spout revolution and unlawfully challenge society to obtain their demands."[75] The FBI wiretapped the telephones of those suspected of opposition beliefs and activities, infiltrated opposition groups, and planted agents provocateurs who suggested that the group use violent means. (This could be used to justify police intervention on the grounds that the group was considering using illegal means!) In 1969, the Internal Revenue Service appointed a special group whose mission was to examine tax records and harrass radical individuals and organizations. The unit collected files on ten thousand individuals before it was disbanded in 1973.[76] Government agencies, including the FBI and intelligence units of the armed forces, compiled computerized files on fifteen million Americans. The Pentagon alone had one thousand agents assigned to domestic surveillance in the fall of 1967.[77] The FBI assigned two thousand agents to the new left, and by 1970 every college campus in the country had its own undercover FBI agent (usually posing as a student). University officials expelled student leaders who organized student protest movements. On the local level, municipal authorities created their own "red squads," with their personnel numbering 14 in Columbus, Ohio, 40 in Boston, 70 in Detroit, 84 in Los Angeles, 123 in New York, and 500 in Chicago.[78]

A bizarre example of government "vigilance" in 1973 suggests the degree to which everyday political activity was under government surveillance. The FBI admitted it had conducted a criminal investigation of a high-school student who wrote to the Socialist Workers party as part of a class project. The agency had become suspicious of the student as a result of its mail check of all letters addressed to the party.

Police brutality was common during nonviolent demonstrations, occupations, and acts of civil disobedience. Tear gas, beatings, and mass arrests were frequently used to suppress dissent.

The military also participated in the crackdown on opposi-

[75]*New York Times*, December 7, 1973.
[76]*Ibid.*, April 9, 1974.
[77]Sale, p. 406.
[78]*Ibid.*, p. 544.

tion. Former Deputy Assistant Secretary of Defense Adam Yarmolinsky has described the elaborate arrangements developed by the military to deal with opposition challenges. After the riots that followed the assassination of Martin Luther King, Jr., in 1968, the Pentagon established a Directorate for Civil Disturbance Planning and Operations, manned by 180 employees, which was responsible for supervising military activity during domestic political challenge. The directorate also trained 2,700 military personnel and police officers in methods of riot control and community relations. As Yarmolinsky comments, "The directorate and the [training] course . . . are both striking illustrations of the growing use of military power in domestic affairs, the developing paramilitary character of local law enforcement services, and the increased interconnection through training, joint research, and shared styles of the civilian and military authority."[79] National Guard units were used 139 times in civil, political, and racial disturbances between 1965 and 1968.

As a result of these measures, dissent was crushed in the United States. There was an apparent return to the easygoing apathetic ways of the 1950s—illustrated on college campuses by the revival of proms, fraternities, and beer drinking. University officials encouraged these harmless practices—for the harried college president, they were infinitely preferable to a campus takeover. Other evidence that the political challenge had been quelled included the decrease in funding of government programs for the poor, the decline of black enrollments in college after their expansion in the 1960s due to black protest, and a reduction of corporate contributions to "responsible" black organizations (like the Urban League), which had been supported in the 1960s as a counterweight to radical black organizations.[80]

We can sum up and simplify what occurred in the recent past as follows: political conflict in the United States normally takes the form of competition between dominant interests and accommodative protest. However, during the unusual period of the 1960s, a more basic cleavage developed between dominant interests and an emergent opposition movement to the corporate complex. Whereas authorities may accept or reject accommodationist demands, they always seek to destroy an opposition movement.

[79]Yarmolinsky, p. 171.
[80]*New York Times*, February 3, 1974.

The least costly way is through symbol manipulation—appointing a commission, controlling the media, or adopting the form but not the substance of reform (as when black lingo became popular in the media, or when Lyndon Johnson vowed that "we shall overcome"). The next step is the adoption of accommodative reforms—those that do not pose a basic threat to the corporate complex. In practice, authorities rarely accept even these demands—they are often diluted when applied and thus transformed into merely symbolic concessions. Nonetheless, accepting accommodative demands provides a safety valve for discontent, enlarges the constituency of the dominant, and puts authorities in a favorable light—by making them appear receptive to criticism and generous to the disadvantaged. If these gestures do not disarm the opposition, authorities take the further step of active repression—the dark side of authorities' responsiveness to accommodationist demands.

By the middle 1970s, aided by the withdrawal of United States combat troops from Vietnam, the weakness of the opposition, and a harsh crackdown on dissent, those in authority appear to have regained control. Yet the breakdown of control by institutions like political parties, the failure of corporate capitalism, and popular disillusionment with political and corporate leaders suggest that a potential exists for a new opposition movement. We shall examine this question in the last chapter.

IDEOLOGY AND DEMOCRACY

A number of studies by political scientists suggest that the political beliefs of most Americans are diffuse and inadequately thought out. On the basis of public-opinion surveys, political scientist Philip Converse has concluded that of all Americans only 3 percent (most of whom are wealthy and educated) can be said to adhere to a political ideology. (Converse defines ideology as a logically coherent set of principles explaining political reality and justifying political preferences.) The opinions of the average citizen appear shifting and inconsistent. When asked a series of questions about attitudes toward government, few people display stable attitudes over a period of time.[81] Thus, Converse finds a large gap between the educated elite and the general public. When political scientist Robert Lane interviewed New Haven workers, he found that they did not have a firm sense of justice and an articulate set of principles that could be considered an ideology.[82]

Findings such as these, combined with other studies showing that most Americans are politically uninformed, have led scholars to conclude that the mass public is poorly equipped to participate in politics and that the American people cannot be trusted to rule themselves. Hence, these scholars argue, it is just as well that voting turnout rates are low and that few people are politically active.

The assertion that Americans do not have a clear conception of ideology implies that most Americans do not rationally perceive their interests. In part this is correct. Recall Marx's proposition that the prevailing ideas of a society are those of the ruling class. The general electorate is constantly barraged with messages reinforcing the dominant ideology. Most Americans get fragmented, low-quality information. They are misled about their interests by schools, media, and government. Since they lack the resources, education, and time to analyze their interests in depth, they are often misinformed. An important consequence of the dominant ideology is to mask the connection between people's problems and the actions of government. For example, most Americans know they want lower prices, but they do not have the political or economic expertise or power to defend their interests through political activity. Politics seems remote from their personal situation.

By contrast, those with greater resources consistently receive superior information—not only do they listen to television news broadcasts but they read one or several newspapers, subscribe to specialized journals, and hire experts to provide additional information and watch over their interests. The wealthy and powerful are better equipped to perceive and defend their interests. They utilize political activity and government help as a matter of course. There is thus more likely to be a divergence between the subjective and objective interests of the majority of

[81]Philip E. Converse, "The Nature of Belief Systems in Mass Publics," in David E. Apter, ed., *Ideology and Discontent* (New York, 1964), pp. 206–61.
[82]Robert Lane, *Political Ideology* (New York, 1962).

Americans compared to the privileged. Again it appears logical that the mass electorate is not capable of engaging in articulate political analysis and effective political action.

However, other evidence suggests that the broad spectrum of Americans are quite aware of their interests and are neither as witless nor as nonideological as leading studies suggest. When ideology is defined in terms meaningful to average Americans, they display attitudes that are rational in terms of their particular situation. Political scientist Lewis Lipsitz argues:

> Ideology must be thought of in a manner more subtle than either Lane or Converse allowed for. First, grievances and issues must be distinguished. Significant portions of a population may have grievances without those grievances being shaped into issues by political activists.[83]

When Lipsitz interviewed the poor in Durham, North Carolina, he found:

> The dominant theme is the sense of being cheated: one's government is not concerned enough with one's well-being; one's government is willing to spend money on what appears to many of these men as frivolous or illegitimate enterprises [military spending] while it fails to meet their own deeply felt day-to-day needs.[84]

These opinions are hardly irrational—they may, in fact, be judged more compelling than the argument of cold-war strategists that more money should be spent on military and other nonproductive ends. What is missing is the link between these perceptions and political action. But this, too, is reasonable in light of the slender resources many people have (time, wealth, skill) and the lack of viable alternatives available.

Studies showing that Americans lack a firm ideology are often construed to mean that people are basically content with existing public policies. But in a study based on public-opinion data, Richard Hamilton concludes that this belief is a myth. As discussed in Chapter 8, a large proportion of Americans favor measures for redistributing income and providing public support to low-income groups. Years before these issues were discussed by political officials as serious possibilities, many Americans

[83]Lewis Lipsitz, "On Political Belief: The Grievances of the Poor," in Philip Green and Sanford Levinson, eds., *Power and Community: Dissenting Essays in Political Science* (New York, 1970), p. 167.
[84]*Ibid.*, p. 165.

favored public health insurance, guaranteed employment, and a minimum annual wage.[85] Another study showed that 71 percent of Americans want the tax laws rewritten to raise taxes for the wealthy and reduce them for Americans with lower incomes.[86] Hamilton suggests that important political alternatives do not reach the political agenda because the real state of public opinion is concealed from most people. While a large proportion, often a majority, favors liberal measures, this is not widely known because of the distorting lenses of the media, organizations, and political parties, which are controlled by more conservative interests.

Discontent is widespread in the United States. When questioned about their cares, many Americans express anxiety about economic problems, health, and family matters.[87] On the basis of interviews with corporate-sector workers, sociologists Richard Sennett and Jonathan Cobb find that most workers are unhappy and feel personally defeated. Although they have achieved some success in American society, they blame themselves for not having climbed even higher—into a middle-class professional position. They share a common feeling of being mistreated, of not having control over their lives. Yet the grievances workers feel, based in large part on accurate perceptions of their situation, do not lead to an opposition ideology and movement, or even to an accommodationist outlook.[88]

In the absence of political movements that articulate workers' grievances, the tendency is to internalize and privatize problems. Americans are troubled, but they keep their worries to themselves and do not see the political relevance of their unhappiness. Or they take individual action borne from despair—America has the highest crime rate among industrialized nations, surely a sign of political discontent, as well as the highest rate of divorce and mental illness.

The result is that the grievances of the disadvantaged remain segmented and segregated within the different sectors of the social structure. Anger is not based on an opposition analysis linking the various inequalities to a structure of exploitation and

[85]Richard Hamilton, *Class and Politics in the United States* (New York, 1972), pp. 89–93.

[86]Harris, p. 10.

[87]Hamilton, p. 85.

[88]Richard Sennett and Jonathan Cobb, *The Hidden Injuries of Class* (New York, 1972). Also see Studs Terkel, *Working* (New York, 1974).

is not integrated into a mass-based movement. It is often turned against others at the bottom, not those in positions of dominance. Hard-hat workers feel aggrieved at their working conditions— but blame their difficulties on black workers competing for jobs or "welfare chisellers" who require tax support. Rebellious blacks break into a small retail outlet and grab a color television, but they do not unite in an attack against corporations or government. "Social inequality is maintained by creating a morality of anxiety. . . . The logic of discontent leads people to turn on each other rather than on the 'system.' "[89] Murray Edelman has described the general process as follows:

> In their political behavior [and ideologies] since at least the Civil War the American poor have offered a revealing example of the potency of myth in creating a particular identity and thereby promoting submissiveness and docility in the face of deprivation. Americans are taught at home, in the schools, and in pervasive political rhetoric that America is the land of equal opportunity; that there is equality before the law; that government accurately reflects the voice of the people, but does not shape it; that political and economic values are allocated fairly. Given such opportunity, those who are poor are inclined to attribute their unhappy condition to their own failings and inadequacies. . . . In consequence the poor have typically been meek, acquiescent in their role and status, and grateful for the welfare benefits they receive: benefits whose very meagerness further defines the worth of the recipients. The American poor have required less coercion and less in social security guarantees to maintain their quiescence than has been true in other developed countries.[90]

Democratic Attitudes: The Few Versus the Many

Another leading finding about American political attitudes is that the political elite is more likely than the general electorate to defend democratic practices. In one frequently-cited study, political scientist Herbert McClosky questioned delegates to the two parties' 1956 national conventions (he termed them political influentials) and compared their responses with responses to the same questions posed to a random sample of the general population. McClosky found that both political influentials and the general population were likely to approve of democratic rules of

[89]Sennett and Cobb, p. 173.
[90]Edelman, *Politics as Symbolic Action*, pp. 55–56.

the game and general principles of freedom of speech and opinion, with influentials especially apt to display approval. Neither group showed as much support for democracy when asked to apply these general principles to specific cases, although influentials were again more democratic than noninfluentials. (For example, three times more noninfluentials than influentials agreed with the proposition: "A book that contains wrong political views cannot be a good book and does not deserve to be published.") McClosky observed, "Democratic ideology and consensus are poorly developed among the electorate and only imperfectly realized among the political influentials."[91] The conclusion drawn by many political scientists is that democracy in the United States is a slender reed—protected by influentials in America against the undemocratically inclined mass population.

Yet the argument is inaccurate in two important respects. First, it fails to distinguish attitudes from behavior. The educated have learned at school that support for civil liberties is good, and it is hardly surprising that they should demonstrate verbal support for these procedures when questioned. But in terms of their actions, the record of influentials and the institutions they control (government, the media, industry, schools) is bleak. During Senator Joseph McCarthy's virulent redbaiting attacks on "pinkos" and Communists during the 1950s, most influentials stood by passively. Moreover, while surveys showed that lower-status, poorly-educated Americans were sympathetic to McCarthy, his voting support in Wisconsin (the state he represented in the Senate) came from upper-middle-class traditional Republican areas.[92] Similarly, influential white Southerners have often used white racist sentiment and practices to divide blacks from the white working class. In recent years, corporations, political parties, law enforcement agencies, cabinet officials, presidential advisers, and the president himself have violated democratic procedures—hardly a sign that influentials have a strong commitment to democracy. (The prosecution of high government officials in the Watergate affair and President Nixon's forced resignation may temporarily curb the worst excesses of official wrongdoing—but will probably not prove a durable influence in purifying American politics.) If we look at what people *do* rather than only at what they *say*, we find that the powerful act in

[91]McClosky, p. 376.
[92]Hamilton, p. 115. Also see Michael P. Rogin, *Intellectuals and McCarthy* (Cambridge, Mass., 1969).

undemocratic ways all the time—by running dominant institutions in an undermocratic fashion.

The argument that influentials are more democratic than the general electorate is also deficient because it defines democracy in terms of procedural equality (civil rights and liberties) but neglects substantive equality (power and wealth). When it comes to attitudes about the redistribution of money and power McClosky found the electorate espousing *more* democratic beliefs (for example, a government-guaranteed job and minimum living standards).[93] The powerful apparently support only those elements of democracy that do not reduce their privilege.

Thus, the idea that the privileged are the best friends of democracy is largely part of the dominant ideology, not an accurate description of their behavior. If actions speak louder than words, the privileged prove to be poor defenders of democracy. To entrust democracy to the safekeeping of authorities is like entrusting the sheep to the wolves.

[93]McClosky, p. 369. Lipsitz makes this point in the article cited above.

12

urban politics
and social control

Newark, New Jersey, is a city of 400,000 people. It does not have a single first-run movie theater. In the 1960s, half of its doctors moved out of the city to practice in the suburbs. Since 1940, the city's largely impoverished black population has quadrupled and is now a majority. For the most part they live in substandard homes, many beyond repair. One in five of Newark's houses has no central heating; 8,000 have no toilets. The decay and abandonment of old housing is proceeding at a much faster rate than new construction. Yet, downtown, two new office towers of eighteen and thirty floors have been built with urban renewal funds as headquarters for locally-based corporations. Newark's former mayor is in prison for extortion. In the summer of 1967, racial violence rocked the city; as a result, twenty-three people were killed, $10,500,000 worth of property was destroyed.

Newark is not a typical American city. Many cities, especially in parts of the South, Southwest, and West, whose economies are based on corporate expansion and new technology industries, such as aerospace, are prospering. But Newark, at the other extreme, as one observer has noted, is "a foretaste of things to come . . . the probable future that faces many of our older cities."[1] These older cities include the country's largest cities,

[1]George Sternlieb, "The City as Sandbox, " *The Public Interest* 25 (Fall 1971): 14.

which have been the focal point of American economic growth and international trade since the Civil War. Virtually all the major corporations are headquartered there. These cities are also home to most of the country's poor, and to a great variety of small-capital businesses. They are cultural and ideological centers.

An examination of the nature of politics in the major, older cities allows us to explore basic social and economic processes of American life. Thus, on his visit to the United States in 1904, the German sociologist Max Weber noted that America's cities resemble a "man whose skin has been peeled off and whose entrails one sees at work."[2] Moreover, since the politics of these cities involve increasingly harsh competition for scarce resources, their study concretely illustrates the issues of mediations and social control that are central to this book. To use the metaphor of the coiled spring adopted at the outset, in these cities the tensions caused by class and racial inequalities are forcing the coil apart; at the same time, urban political elites are attempting to keep the coil locked. Such tensions characterize American politics as a whole. But their expression is perhaps most apparent in cities like Boston, Chicago, New York, Philadelphia, and Detroit.

DEPENDENT CITIES: THE CITY AS COLONY?

These older cities are caught up in a complex web of political and economic relationships with the wider society. They are not autonomous entities, not even legally. Changes in municipal tax laws, forms of government, jurisdictional boundaries, and local civil-service regulations usually require approval by state governments.

This juridical dependency is symptomatic of the broader substantive dependency of most cities. Their significant problems of housing, crime, transportation, welfare, and finance—commonly lumped together as "the urban crisis"—are generated by causes relating to class and race that are inherent in the society, and over which cities have little control.

Welfare is an example of this. In New York City, with a

[2]Hans Gerth and C. Wright Mills, eds., *From Max Weber* (New York, 1958), p. 15.

population of almost 8 million people, about 1.2 million are presently receiving some form of welfare assistance. This represents more than double the number on welfare five years ago. As late as 1965, 20 percent of the city's budget was allocated to secondary and elementary education, and only 12 percent to welfare programs. By 1970, only 18 percent of the budget was appropriated for education, compared to a staggering 23 percent for welfare. In September 1968, 60 percent of the persons under eighteen in New York were receiving public assistance.

Although, as we shall see later in this chapter, other factors are involved, the root causes of the growth of urban welfare rolls are economic. After studying welfare in New York, the economist David Gordon concluded that the "cause of the welfare 'crisis' is simply the widespread poverty in the city—not chiseling or welfare rights organizations or liberal administrative practices."[3] Indeed, in any given year in the past decade, only about 60 percent of the potentially eligible recipients have actually been on the welfare rolls.

The conditions that lead to widespread poverty are not "caused" by the cities, nor can they be significantly affected at that level. An individual's earning power and employability are dependent on many factors. These factors include characteristics of the local labor market, such as its rate of growth and the nature of the demand for labor; characteristics of the industry in which the individual is employed, such as profit rates, technology, unionization, and the industry's relationship to government; and individual characteristics, such as age, sex, and race.

The poverty in a given city also reflects migration patterns over which the receiving city has virtually no control. The increasing concentration of Southern agriculture, for example, has resulted in fewer jobs and has driven blacks off the land. Similarly, high unemployment rates in Puerto Rico and other Caribbean economies have impelled people to look for economic opportunities in the major urban centers of the United States. Like welfare, other poverty-related problems such as crime, drug abuse, ineffective schools, and severe health problems—all of which have to be dealt with by city governments—are caused by

---

[3]David Gordon, "Income and Welfare in New York City," *The Public Interest* 16 (Summer 1969): 87.

factors external to the cities where their impact is ultimately felt.

The cities' lack of control over the origins of the basic problems that beset them has been complemented by the changing economic functions of cities, growing class and racial divisions between cities and suburbs, and an increasing dependence of cities on external resources.

From the outset, the growth of industrial capitalism depended on the massive growth of cities. Factories demanded an available work force, detached from the land. Industries needed to be spatially concentrated to facilitate the exchange of goods and to insure the ready availability of banking and legal services. Not surprisingly, therefore, America's older cities grew most rapidly in the last third of the nineteenth and first third of the twentieth centuries. (Chicago's population doubled between 1900 and 1930; New York's almost quadrupled between 1890 and 1930, only partially as a result of the extension of the city's boundaries.) In these decades, the United States was transformed from a largely agrarian, landholding society into an increasingly urbanized corporate capitalist society. The burgeoning cities were the repository of cheap unskilled labor, largely immigrant, that filled the menial positions at the lower levels of the expanding corporate economy. Hence, by the middle of this century, the following description of the urban economy was appropriate:

> The urban areas of this nation are the setting for the most powerful and complex industrialization in the world. Cities are the center of commerce and of the transportation and communications infrastructure which underpins the economy. Modern cities are central administration points for large corporations and the financial centers of America. They are also the central marketplaces for every conceivable kind of commercial good and service. The urban economy contains not only most of the productive capacity of the nation, but also most of its capacity to consume.[4]

The cities still maintain a strategic economic position today. Virtually all the headquarters of America's one hundred largest industrial corporations are in the large cities. The central business districts of these cities have continued to grow (often with the help of urban renewal funds) because corporate offices need to be

---

[4]Roger Friedland, "Corporations and Urban Renewal," unpublished manuscript.

in a location that maximizes their access to branch managers, sales executives, and buyers; because they need a large number of clerical workers to staff their headquarters; and because they need to be near the "business services which the corporation cannot internally provide. These often include: financing agents for investment and stock transfer, banks to service operating capital needs, advertising, printing, data processing, consulting firms in various managerial and technical areas, etc."[5] In the past two decades, most new private-sector urban jobs have been created by corporate headquarters expansion.

But this trend has been offset by the loss of jobs in corporate manufacturing, which is expanding in the suburbs and has declined sharply in almost every major city. New York City alone has lost almost 200,000 such jobs in the 1970s. In some cities they hardly exist any longer. As a result, the growth of the older cities has stopped. Major cities today are *losing* population, and a growing proportion of wages and subsistence payments are being provided by jobs in small-capital businesses, government employment, and welfare.

Although the older city business centers remain important to large industrial and financial corporations, increasing numbers of their employees—from top-level executives to shopfloor workers—have moved to the suburbs. The majority of small-capital workers, by contrast, have been left behind in the inner cities. Most are black and many poor. High rent and property value levels and exclusionary zoning laws make it very difficult for these workers to leave the cities. As a result, the relationship between city and suburb largely reflects the relationship between the small-capital and corporate sectors of American capitalism.

This division between cities and suburbs is a relatively new development. Class, ethnic, and racial distinctions, of course, historically have been expressed within American cities. The largest cities in particular have long been divided into relatively homogeneous neighborhoods. But since the Second World War, these traditional urban divisions have been jumbled and reorganized under the impact of massive suburban growth.

Much like the dynamic discussed in Chapter 4 that insures that the corporate sector grows and profits at the expense of small capital, the suburbs have prospered at the expense of the cities.

[5]*Ibid.*

Relatively affluent, largely white, suburban residents come into the cities in the morning to work, utilize the cities' resources and services during the day, and go home at night without paying city taxes. They are thus subsidized by the taxes relatively poorer city residents pay to maintain police, traffic, and other vital services; and they take back to the suburbs a considerable portion of their incomes and wealth, thus reducing the cities' resources even further.

Historically, American urban growth resembled a process of internal geographic colonization, as corporate-capitalist interests "captured" more and more territory in order to create large mass industrial cities. Present-day neighborhoods in many cities—such as Morrisania in the Bronx, New York, Germantown in Philadelphia, and Roxbury in Boston, which were settled in the seventeenth century—were self-governing entities before they were absorbed into the growing cities in the nineteenth century. Present cities, social analyst Milton Kotler has thus argued, can be seen as urban empires "ruled by a central neighborhood, while the other neighborhoods are political associations under its control. , , , Cities in the nineteenth century abolished the governments of neighboring political units and have since controlled their territories by means of political administration for their central interests."[6] This process of annexation permitted downtown business interests to broaden the cities' tax base, control land use planning over a wider area, and extend the police powers of the city to workers' neighborhoods.

In many respects, this form of colonization *within* cities continues today, but the content of the relationship has changed. Whereas in the late nineteenth century, developing corporate firms sought to gain political control over the areas in which their workers lived, today "downtown" presides over a population that provides only a diminishing tax base and, as we shall see, increasing problems of social control. The growing black and Hispanic populations of the cities especially are seen not as potential corporate-sector laborers, but as groups that threaten a precarious social peace. Since stability and order are necessary for the smooth functioning of downtown headquarters, colonial-like dominance within cities is now directed toward defusing discontent.

[6]Milton Kotler, *Neighborhood Government* (Indianapolis, 1969), chapter one.

THE ROLE OF URBAN POLITICIANS AND OFFICIALS

The fiscal plight of the colonized cities has become acute. Many major city budgets tripled between 1960 and 1970; but since a large proportion of the relatively well-to-do have moved to the suburbs, city tax revenues have suffered accordingly. As a result, the cities are decreasingly in control of their financial houses. About 25 percent of major city revenues were provided by state and federal aid ten years ago. Today, roughly half are raised this way. Consequently, America's older cities are heavily dependent for their most basic services on funding decisions made by state and federal legislators and officials, many whom lack a direct city constituency. The ability of cities to rebuild slums, provide for educational expansion, and construct new transit facilities, for example, depends on actions taken by people who are often not even indirectly responsible to those who live in the cities. Such politicians are more accountable to rural and suburban interests. Hence the cities are continually vulnerable to shifts in allocations and priorities over which they have little control.

Urban politicians and officials must govern in this colonial-like situation. In the context of fundamental changes in the economic functions of cities, the relatively new pattern of city-suburb relationships, and the cities' fiscal dependency, the position of those who govern is exceptionally difficult. Since the cities are recipients of problems they do not generate or control; since American society's basic inequalities of class and race are expressed and experienced directly in the major cities; and since those who rule the cities lack the resources to solve problems of housing, poverty, education, and transportation (yet their constituencies widely expect them to be able to do so), their aim becomes *the management of the consequences of their inability to solve urban problems.*

While many small and medium-size cities are governed quite openly by local business interests, this is rarely the case in the larger cities. Rather, they are managed by "arbiter governments"[7] that perceive their basic task as one of containing and defusing social conflicts, and of maintaining the order necessary for the smooth functioning of the urban economy. Given these basic

[7]Oliver Williams, "A Typology of Comparative Local Government," *Midwest Journal of Political Science* (May 1961): 160.

conditions (and the fact that the bulk of their campaign funds come from local real-estate men, bankers, and small-capital businessmen), local politicians functionally come to serve the interests of local small capital, and rule *indirectly* on behalf of corporate-sector interests.

In this respect, a key feature of classic colonial patterns of social control—indirect rule through native leaders—is replicated in the cities. The potentially unruly local population is not governed directly by headquarters businessmen, but by locally-selected politicians whose scope of action is severely limited. Thus, the politicians can be likened to colonial administrators. Anthropologist Peter Worsley, in his analysis of colonialism, says that in order to communicate with and to control the colonized, the colonial administrators needed authority figures who could provide "a bridge of legitimation," thus enabling "an administration to divide and rule: popular resentments and hatreds could be deflected on to the local officials while the ultimate authority could remain remote, unseen, and 'above the battle.' "[8]

URBAN DISCONTENT AND CHALLENGES TO AUTHORITY

The more people who accept the social structure as just, who consent to their relative subordination, the more secure authorities can be. As urban problems have increased and urban officials have not been able to deal with them successfully, growing numbers of people who live in the cities have come to be discontented not only in an imprecise, accommodationist way, but have developed what we called an opposition perspective in Chapter 11.

In urban America in the 1960s, there was a marked decline in support for prevailing structures of political authority. The most prominent development was the ferment that took place in the urban black communities. The racial violence in New York in 1964, Watts in 1965, Newark and Detroit in 1967, and in hundreds of other cities during the decade, was profoundly political. The targets of attack by blacks, including the police and white-owned property, were visible symbols of public order and a capitalist social structure.

[8]Peter Worsley, *The Third World* (London, 1967), p. 38.

These rebellions reflected the particularly harsh impact the colonized position of the cities has had on ghetto residents. Some observers compared the violence to nationalist anticolonial uprisings against the mother countries. Sociologist Robert Blauner argued that the riots were mass rebellions against a colonial-like status:

> The thrust of the action has been to clear out an alien presence, white men and officials, rather than a drive to kill whites as in a conventional race riot. . . . More accurately the revolts pointed to alienation from this system on the part of many poor and also not so poor blacks. The sacredness of private property, that unconsciously accepted bulwark of our social arrangements, was rejected. . . . Obviously the society's bases of legitimacy and authority have been attacked.[9]

Another analyst saw the riots as an amalgam of reformist and potentially revolutionary tendencies. In identifying the riots as reform movements, he said that the violence "may perhaps be best understood as a kind of wildcat strike" that represented a revolt "of the ghetto rank and file against an established black leadership which . . . has failed to deliver the goods, and a form of direct action intended to communicate grievances and apply pressure on the white 'managers' of the ghetto." The second and more radical aspect of the riots as a potentially revolutionary rebellion "consists of an impulsive, large-scale effort to break the control of the white authorities over the ghetto, to seize territory and property by force, and to replace white authority with indigenous control. . . ."[10]

Widespread black rejection of prevailing authority patterns has not only been expressed in these expressive, bloody rebellions. Movements for community control of school systems and the police emerged in most American cities. Protests and demonstrations became almost daily events, as tenants' organizations and welfare-rights groups developed in nearly every major city. Assaults on visible structures of authority became commonplace. School vandalism increased markedly. Police became the targets

[9]Robert Blauner, "Internal Colonialism and Ghetto Revolt," *Social Problems* 16 (Spring, 1969): 399.
[10]David Boesel, "An Analysis of the Ghetto Riots," in David Boesel and Peter Rossi, eds., *Cities Under Siege: An Anatomy of the Ghetto Riots* (New York, 1971).

of verbal and, occasionally, fatal physical abuse. Street crime moved out of the ghettos into all-white areas that had largely been crime-free. Social analysts Frances Piven and Richard Cloward noted, "The main conclusion to be drawn from an appraisal of the disorder of the 1960s is that the old pattern of servile conformity was shattered: the trauma and anger of an oppressed people not only had been released, but had been turned against the social structure."[11]

Although the apparent rejection of the prevailing order has been most dramatic in the urban black community, there have been signs of parallel developments among other urban groups. The political behavior of white ethnic (largely Catholic) workers has been in flux. As immigrants, and later as native-born citizens, they have been linked to the political system through three separate, yet related institutions: the Democratic party urban political machines, the Catholic Church, and the trade unions of the AFL and CIO. Each of these institutions has undergone considerable change in the past three decades.

The Democratic party organizations, to be discussed more fully later in this chapter, have declined in power in almost every major city (Chicago is the leading exception), and in some have completely disappeared. In the Church, the ecumenicism of Pope John XXIII, the civil disobedience activities of radical priests like Philip and Daniel Berrigan and other members of the Catholic left, and the closing down of many parochial schools are just three of many signs of significant change. And, while party organizations have decayed, and the Church has been in ferment, the unions have settled down to routine collective bargaining— hardly as exhilarating as the economic struggles of the 1930s. Thus, by the beginning of the 1970s, none of these three institutions commanded the legitimacy and emotional support among white ethnic workers that they had previously.

As a result, the high level of discontent that invariably pervades working-class life (the product of such factors as job insecurity, monotonous work, modest wages, and lack of control over the work process) not only appeared to increase but also was no longer necessarily channeled into institutional activities that lent direct support to the status quo. More and more workers

[11]Frances Piven and Richard Cloward, *Regulating the Poor* (New York, 1971), p. 227.

appeared to echo the sentiments of the ironworker who told journalist Pete Hamill:

> I'm going out of my mind. I average about $8,500 a year, pretty good money. I work my ass off. But I can't make it. I come home at the end of the week, I start paying the bills, I give my wife some money for food. And there's nothing left. Maybe if I work overtime I get $15 or $20 to spend on myself. But most of the time, there's nothing.[12]

As traditional outlets for the increasing discontent of workers gave way, they vented their anger both at those beneath and above them in the social structure. Workers' behavior suddenly appeared as a jumble of contradictions: plant sabotage and attacks on welfare; support for quasi-populist candidates of the left and right and a majority vote for Richard Nixon; an assembly-line turnover at automobile factories that approaches 100 percent annually; and participation in drug and crime subcultures whose victims are often other workers.

In addition to blacks and workers, others joined in activities that at least potentially challenged urban structures of authority. Among university students and relatively well-off professionals, anti-Vietnam war protests became vehicles for a wider rejection of the prevailing pattern of structure and choice. In professions like medicine, social work, and education, radical professional groups were founded, and some, such as The Union of Radical Political Economics, flourished. And a burgeoning cultural revolution among young people, who rejected society's dominant sexual and work ethics, also contained the seeds of even more basic transformations.

POLITICAL MACHINES AND SOCIAL CONTROL

These changes in people's political attitudes are significant threats in themselves to those in authority, but since they have occurred in the context of a profound shift in the nature of urban political institutions, they are doubly threatening. In particular,

---

[12]Pete Hamill, "The Revolt of the White Lower-Middle-Class," in Louise Kapp Howe, ed., *The White Majority* (New York, 1970) p. 11.

the events of the 1960s indicated the extent to which the breakdown of urban political machines has threatened both small-capital and corporate interests.

Political machines are party organizations that are basically nonissue oriented and held together by the currency of jobs, favors, and protection. The machines flourished in the late nineteenth and early twentieth centuries—a period of mass migration from Europe. The lowest level of these hierarchical organizations was the precinct; several precincts made up a ward. One of the ward leaders usually was the city boss. The dividing line between party machine and government had a tendency to blur. Richard Croker, the New York Democratic party boss in the 1890s, sought to fuse the two: "All the employees of the city government," he stated, "from the Mayor to the porter who makes the fire in his office should be members of the Tammany organization."[13] One of his ward leaders, George Washington Plunkitt, described how he cemented relationships between his district's population and the party:

> What tells in holdin' your grip on your district is to go right down among the poor families and help them in the different ways they need help. I've got a regular system for this. If there's a fire in Ninth, Tenth, or Eleventh Avenue any hour of the day or night, I'm usually there with some of my election district captains as soon as the fire engines. . . . I just get quarters for them, buy clothes for them if their clothes were burned up, and fix them up till they get things runnin' again. It's philanthropy, but it's good politics too—mighty good politics.[14]

Sociologist Robert Merton suggests that the provision of basic services like these are overlooked by those who criticize the machines as corrupt or inefficient. The party organizations, he argues, were terribly important for the immigrant newcomers. Machines humanized assistance and personalized politics; they provided ethnic businessmen with contacts and contracts; and they offered immigrants a new avenue of economic mobility.[15]

[13]Richard Croker, "Tammany Hall and the Democracy," in *Tammany Hall Souvenir of the Inauguration of Cleveland and Stevenson* (New York, 1893), p. 69.
[14]William Riordan, ed., *Plunkitt of Tammany Hall* (New York, 1963), pp. 27–28.
[15]Robert Merton, "The Latent Functions of the Machine," in Edward Banfield, ed., *Urban Government* (New York, 1969).

But this analysis ignores the role the machines played in protecting economic interests.

From the vantage point of entrenched economic interests, the entry of new groups into politics is unsettling. The very arrival of new groups poses a potential challenge to the system that is keeping the coiled spring of an unequal social structure from uncoiling. Hence the manner in which newcomers are linked to existing political arrangements affects the continuity and stability of the political system.

The development of industrial capitalism in the late nineteenth and early twentieth centuries, and the massive influx of European ethnic groups (and blacks from the South during and after the First World War) posed this kind of challenge to the cities. Yet, as political scientist Michael Rogin notes, although "in Europe industrialization uprooted the peasants from the land and brought them to the cities where they became revolutionary workers . . . the uprooted European peasants who settled in American cities remained conservative."[16] In large measure this can be explained by the conservative nature of the party machines.

Machine politicians acted as buffers between the immigrants and local economic elites. Policial scientist James Scott observed, "Frequently, a three-cornered relationship developed in which the machine politician could be viewed as a broker who, in return for financial assistance from wealthy elites, promoted their policy interests while in office, while passing along a portion of the gain to a particularistic electorate from whom he 'rented' his authority."[17] The machines had a procapitalist ideology, emphasized short-run gains rather than basic change, and reinforced the legitimacy of existing arrangements by providing the immigrant with concrete rewards and thus allying him with the political system.

The machine both stabilized and reinforced existing class and ethnic divisions. In Boston, New York, Philadelphia, Chicago, and other major American cities at the turn of the century, machine organizations utilized these divisions to build electoral coalitions united by common interests. Chicago, for example, was

---

[16]Michael Paul Rogin, *The Intellectuals and McCarthy* (Cambridge, 1967), p. 187.
[17]James Scott, "Corruption, Machine Politics and Political Change," *American Political Science Review* 63 (December 1969): 1155.

described by an English journalist in 1897 as "the most American of cities, and yet the most mongrel; the second American city of the globe, the fifth German city, the third Swedish, the second Polish, the first and only veritable Babel of the age."[18] In 1890, three-quarters of Chicago's population either had been born abroad or had foreign-born parents; in the 1890s new immigration from eastern and southern Europe began to make an additional impact. By 1920, only 642,000 of the city's 2,700,000 residents were of native white parentage. Well over a million whites were the second generation children of immigrants, and nearly a million were themselves foreign-born. They were settled in over twenty-five distinct ethnic communities.

As a result, city political organizations had to put together electoral coalitions composed of blocs of ethnic groups, each of which, *as a group*, functioned as a key unit of political organization. By offering ethnic communities the opportunity to enter the political process, the machines solidified group consciousness and perpetuated the division of the city, demographically and politically, into ethnic components. In his classic analysis of party organizations, M. Ostrogorski, a Russian analyst, captured this point:

> In the popular wards of the large cities the small politician has no need to create the political following which he forms around him; he finds it ready at hand in social life, in which neighborly ties, and above all common tastes and mutual sympathies give rise to small sets, groups of people who regularly meet to enjoy the pleasures of sociability and friendship. The street corner serves them as a rendezvous as long as they are in the youthful stage. Then, when they grow older and have a few cents to spend, they meet in a drinking saloon or in a room hired for the purpose with their modest contribution. Several "gangs" unite to found a sort of club, in which they give small parties, balls, or simply smoke, drink and amuse themselves. This merry crew is a latent political force; when the elections come around it may furnish a compact band of voters. The small politician has but to lay his hand on it. Often he himself has grown up in the gang or with it. . . .[19]

[18]G. W. Steevens, cited in Ira Katznelson, *Black Men, White Cities* (New York, 1973), p. 87.

[19]M. Ostrogorski, *Democracy and the Organization of Political Parties*, vol. 2 (London, 1908), pp. 368–69.

But the machine did not act only as the stabilizer and reinforcer of existing class and ethnic divisions. It acted as the social cement linking relatively poor working-class citizens and the capitalist economic structure on terms that appeared to benefit both. The dominant economic interests in the cities— industrial corporations, real-estate interests, banks, public utilities, merchants—achieved structural protection at the relatively low cost of payoffs to the machine's voters. For business interests, the machines not only provided a relatively passive citizenry but also produced concrete economic gains, including market regulation and stabilization, manipulation of regulations in favor of industry, favoritism in the letting of governmental contracts, exclusive licensing for preferred utilities, and possibilities for tax fraud. Machine voters often received little more than symbolic rewards and palliatives like bags of coal and, occasionally, jobs.

The political machines thus were able, on the whole, to control the discontents of the period and channel them into "safe" political activities because they offered an institutionalized means of participation in government and were distributors of urban political rewards. As long as the political energies of the millions of mostly Catholic and Jewish workers from Europe and blacks from the South were absorbed by the particularistic politics of the machines, the stability of urban America was relatively assured.

THE REFORM IMPULSE:
INSTITUTIONAL CONSEQUENCES

Not all the newcomers to the cities were immigrants or Southern blacks. Many of the new arrivals during the late nineteenth and twentieth centuries came from rural America. For them, especially for the articulate native middle class, a small but growing urban group, the massive migration from Europe and the South was frightening and threatening. "The rural, small town, Protestant American coming face to face with the city for the first time," political scientist Eugene Lewis wrote, "found what must have been to him a complete perversion of American life. The machine, the corruption, the ethnic, and the general conditions of the city itself must have been a profound shock."[20]

From this native American social base, a reform movement emerged that challenged the supremacy of the machines. It counterposed a "nonpartisan" view of the municipal world that stressed the autonomous individual as the key political participant, a fundamental faith in nineteenth-century capitalism, and a fervent belief in the virtues of a science and technology. The reformers advocated the professionalization of social welfare, restrictions on immigration and the Americanization of immigrants, and the depoliticization of urban government in the name of efficiency. If the machine was the key expression of immigrant political action, the development of a civil service based on "objective merit" as opposed to patronage and favoritism is the hallmark of reform activity. Thus, in many middle-size cities (up to 500,000 people), the reform movement succeeded in replacing party government with a nonpartisan system by 1930. Today, roughly half of America's middle-size cities have a council-manager form of government headed by an administrative technician who directs city affairs on a nonparty basis. But in the large cities with massive immigrant populations, the political machines survived the reformers' attacks in the early decades of this century.

The depression of the 1930s marked the turning point in the fortunes of the big-city machines. In this period of material and political crisis, many of the machine functions were nationalized as the machine's isolated, fragmented, localized responses proved inadequate to the task of keeping social order. As the federal government took over the functions of managing the economy and providing social-welfare programs, and as the immigration from Europe and the South slowed to a trickle, the machines' power base eroded. Moreover, machines flourish best in expanding economies that can afford their expensive habits. In the depression period of great scarcity, the machines simply lacked sufficient rewards to compete with the quickly developing professionalized, bureaucratized social-welfare programs that eliminated much of the available patronage. The machines were

[20]Eugene Lewis, *The Urban Political System* (Hinsdale, Illinois, 1973), p. 70.

now less able to secure their followers' means of subsistence, manage economic distress, and provide other services.

With this decline of most party organizations, the locus of political power in urban America has shifted in the past four decades to relatively autonomous, rapidly growing service bureaucracies. As the cities' economic capacities and number of available jobs diminish, the most dynamic growth has taken place in public employment. From 1947 to 1967, municipal government employees in the United States nearly tripled in number to seven million (compared with well under three million civilian federal employees), and city government payrolls increased from $541 million to $3.1 billion.

Public-service bureaucracies are not nearly as well equipped as the machines were to prevent and manage conflict and discontent. Although the bureaucracies (welfare, police, sanitation, housing, education, most prominently) distribute services and benefits and provide jobs they *do not organize or control participation in politics.* Their closed system of promotion, their stress on professional standards and hierarchy, and their specialization make them appear as alien forces to many city residents. As a result, the bureaucracies themselves have become basic targets and causes of urban discontent. "With the expansion of the state," political scientist Margaret Levi notes, "poor people have gained a viable and accessible target of attack."[21] This development is not surprising since the most immediate vivid contacts many citizens have with local government are with service bureaucracies. Almost all citizens at some point in their lives are under the control of school systems and health care organizations; millions of city dwellers are on welfare; most look to the police for some degree of protection; and many are processed through the law enforcement agencies, the courts, and the prisons. Lower-level employees in these bureaucracies—the teachers, social workers, nurses, clerks, policemen, and lower court judges, who have been called street-level bureaucrats— most directly represent government to the governed.[22]

These contacts are often fraught with tension. Street-level bureaucrats are in extremely sensitive positions. They constantly

---

[21]Margaret Levi, "Poor People Against the State," unpublished manuscript.
[22]Michael Lipsky, "Toward a Theory of Street-Level Bureaucracy," unpublished manuscript.

interact with the public, have considerable discretion on the job, and, perhaps most importantly, have great power over the lives of the people with whom they deal. Policemen are authorized to use lethal force if necessary, teachers can affect the future of a student through grading, social workers can cut a family off from its means of subsistence, and judges can dispose of large chunks of people's lives. Moreover, the bureaucrats' clients are captive audiences, to whom the bureaucrats are hardly ever responsible. Rather, they are accountable to their superiors in the bureaucracy.

However, street-level bureaucrats have difficult jobs. Typically, they must operate in an environment that makes it impossible for them to satisfy their professional ideals. Too often, the resources available to them are inadequate—there are too many children in the classroom, too many cases in the courts, not enough policemen in high crime areas. The bureaucrat works in a situation where his authority is challenged regularly, and where there is a higher than average possibility of physical or psychic threat. Policemen may be shot, teachers may have to confront disruptive classes, social workers may be verbally abused.

In dealing with these difficulties, street-level bureaucrats often act in ways that heighten urban conflict. Policemen may come to see and to treat all blacks as potential criminals. Lower court judges often process cases so quickly that justice is hardly a likely outcome. Social workers often penalize clients who rebel against the agency's routines. Health clinic doctors and nurses, under the pressure of their workload, may treat their patients inhumanely. Teachers often typecast and stigmatize nonconformist pupils and parents.

A recent study by sociologist Gerald Levy of a midwestern ghetto school captured this dynamic: "Upon first arriving at Midway School, new teachers are overwhelmed with the rhetoric of control. All the orientation conferences with administrators and bull-sessions with older teachers stress the overriding priority of classroom discipline and order in the halls." The teacher is urged by his superiors not to get too involved with the pupils, "to show as little emotion as possible, detach himself from his own destruction, and act as if it were not happening to him." Routines are set up to fill time safely: "the more the enterprising teacher can involve his children in routines the less likely they are to threaten his control." Skillful disciplinary measures are used to keep order by both teachers and administrative staff. The teachers who apply this controlled terror and who communicate to the children what social and economic claims they can make on the larger society know little of the ghetto area that surrounds the school: " . . . most have never ventured beyond the delicatessen two blocks from the school. For them it is nine to three, a quick drive out . . . or a quick walk to the nearby subway."

The school, Levy concluded, "is a world of harrassed teachers, angry parents and disillusioned children. It is a chaotic, often brutal world in which teachers and children destroy each other." The administration lacks the ability to control the situation; it compensates by adopting a bland language of professionalism that stresses administrative routines. Parents, who are disillusioned by the whole situation and frustrated by the lack of achievement of their children, find that the only access they have to the school is the PTA, a group without any power or control, and that at PTA meetings administrators confine their responses to reassuring comments. Professional convenience and routines conflict directly with the needs of parents and their children.[23]

This kind of interaction is not unique to educational bureaucracies. As a result, the gulf between urban bureaucrat and client inevitably grows, as does popular discontent with an apparently remote, unresponsive, irresponsible government. The process of bureaucratic interaction, in short, is profoundly alienating. Thus, whereas party machines fostered support for existing patterns of dominance, bureaucratic control mechanisms generate heightened discontent.

Finally, as previously discussed, the cities' structural environment makes it impossible for urban authorities to solve the problems that the bureaucracies are charged to address. One consequence, paradoxically, is continued bureaucratic growth. Sociologist Robert Alford has succinctly captured the process:

> Demands for action on a 'problem'—health, poverty, delinquency, decaying central cities, the environment, education, jobs—are followed by responses by political leaders and administrative agencies. New agencies are established, old agencies begin new programs, more staff are hired, budgets are spent. . . . You name a problem and there is a program for it and an agency or ten to handle it.

[23]Gerald Levy, *Ghetto School* (New York, 1970), pp. 79ff.

But the *problem* which generated this flurry of activity is not solved. It may even get worse, the more is done about it. Nevertheless, both publics and politicians have a sense that something has been done because of all the money that has been spent, all the offices that have been set up, all the clients handled, all the staff hired. The programs and agencies continue; the budgets are annually appropriated.

Suddenly, the unsolved problem again becomes a crisis. Some enterprising reporter uncovers a scandal in the FHA-backed housing program, cockroaches in the hospitals, apathy in the classroom, no jobs awaiting graduates of the Job Corps, brutality in the mental hospitals. Or some clients, taxpayers, disinterested citizens' group or aspiring politician blows the whistle. Any one of innumerable horrors awaits those who scratch the surface of almost any public institution. The result: another investigation, another set of hearings, new legislation, administrative rulings, agencies, programs, staff, budgets. And so on and on.[24]

THE POLITICAL CRISIS OF CONTROL

The combination of a shift in attitudes among many urban residents, the decline of party organizations, and the Topsy-like growth of urban bureaucracy with its attendant street-level tensions has produced a political crisis of control for urban authorities. Urban authorities have responded by utilizing, with varying degrees of consciousness and purposefulness, a wide array of available social-control mechanisms. Thus, perhaps most obviously, local police forces were substantially strengthened in many cities after the ghetto revolts of the mid-1960s, and new police intelligence units were established.

Alford argues that the expansion of bureaucratic agencies itself has a control function. Since the problems of the cities are deep-seated and cannot be resolved without a basic shift in the political economy of the urban areas, the heightened degree of dissatisfaction "has led to desperate attempts to create mechanisms which will give groups making demands the illusion of a response without the substance . . . the responses are means of

[24]Robert Alford, "Social Needs, Political Demands, and Administrative Responses," unpublished manuscript.

controlling the demands, of maintaining social stability with as little tangible response as possible."[25] Local politicians possess symbolic power but lack substantive power. And since problems cannot be solved locally, bureaucratic proliferation may be seen as an attempt to manage tensions and demands.

Consider again the case of welfare. Between 1960 and 1970, the percentage of poor families in the major metropolitan areas remained roughly the same (although their composition changed—43 percent of poor families in New York City were black or Hispanic in 1960; 70 percent in 1970), as did the percentage of people eligible for welfare who claimed their benefits—yet welfare rolls more than doubled. Although the root cause of the welfare "crisis" was poverty, that alone cannot explain what happened in New York and other cities in that decade. A critical factor was the change in eligibility standards. Between January 1964 and November 1968, because of a liberalization of grant standards, the number of people eligible for welfare increased by about 170 percent. The implications, economist David Gordon wrote, are clear. "If New York State had not decided to offer people an income at least equal to what the federal government calls the poverty line, there would be no welfare crisis at all. We would, in its place, have a far greater amount of poverty."[26]

Thus the critical issue is why did New York and other states in this period opt, quite consciously, for a welfare "crisis" by lowering eligibility standards rather than maintain a continuation of the old levels that kept more people at depressed income levels? Altruism, perhaps?

Hardly likely, especially since elected officials had a great deal to lose by becoming publicly identified as supporters of expanded welfare programs. Piven and Cloward suggested the most persuasive answer. The rise in welfare rolls was directly related to the rise in black discontent, which was expressed most dramatically in the violent ghetto rebellions:

> If the relief rise in the early 1960s coincided with the rise in disorder, this relationship was even more striking after 1964. As protests, demonstrations, riots, and other forms of disorder reached unprecedented heights between 1965 and 1968, the relief

[25]*Ibid.*
[26]Gordon, p. 86.

rolls climbed 58 percent, having already risen 31 percent in the preceding four years. The 121 urban counties showed an increase of 80 percent after 1964; in the "big five" urban counties, the rolls more than doubled (up to 105 percent).[27]

Historically, they argued, drawing on the English and American experience, there is a cycle of welfare relief: massive dislocations (early industrialization in England, the depression and mass black migration to the North in the United States) produce massive discontents. One response by authorities is to liberalize welfare requirements—a relatively simple, direct way of "buying off" discontent. As overt discontent ebbs, welfare eligibility standards are raised once more, thus channeling more people into low-paid menial work. Although a causal relationship is very difficult to prove, Piven and Cloward's approach to welfare could have been used to accurately predict the welfare contraction of the early 1970s. In almost every American state in 1972, welfare rolls dropped; not coincidentally, by 1972 the period of massive ghetto rebellions had passed—at least for the time being.

This case of an attempt at social control by bureaucratic rewards is hardly unique. The New York City municipal payroll expanded from 240,000 to 380,000 jobs in the 1960s. School expenditures in Boston rose from $35 million in 1961 to $96 million in 1971. "As the turmoil of the 1960s rose," Piven pointed out, "so did city costs. . . . New York now spends half again as much per capita as other cities over a million, and three times as much as the other 288 cities."[28] In Chicago, by contrast, where machine-style politics have survived, garbage collection costs and per-pupil school expenditures are roughly *one-half* of New York's. Thus where party-control mechanisms that organize participation in politics continue to operate, the need for bureaucratic rewards to maintain control is much lower.

Compared to political machines that dispense public goods covertly as private favors, bureaucratic bargaining is public and thus more difficult for authorities. Each concession tends to become the subject of open political conflict and the occasion for a round of escalating demands. For example, when one group of municipal employees is awarded a salary increase, other unions

[27]Piven and Cloward, p. 245.
[28]Frances Piven, "The Urban Crisis: Who Got What and Why," in Robert Paul Wolff, ed., *1984 Revisited* (New York, 1973), pp. 184–85.

can base their salary demands on that settlement. In cities already constrained by their colonial-like status and by the diminution of economic functions, the politics of bureaucratic rewards exacerbates group tensions and discontents, fuels the cities' growing fiscal plight, and, paradoxically, becomes the only political game worth playing in a world of increasingly scarce resources.

NEW INSTITUTIONAL BUFFERS

Urban authorities in cities marked by the advanced atrophy of party organizations have sought in the recent past to augment the bureaucratic tools of social control by creating new urban institutions designed to perform the buffer role once played so effectively by machines. This program of building "new machines" has been sponsored by both national and local political elites. In cities like New York and Boston, reform mayors, who had been elected in spite of the absence of effective party organizations to work on their behalf, developed a new type of urban political organization. This included neighborhood city halls, urban action task forces and pilot programs for neighborhood government. Like similar federal programs (such as the Community Action programs discussed in Chapter 13), the city organizations sought to structure the political participation of angry people and to establish administrative mechainsms that would reach neighborhoods (without disturbing the existing structure of power and resources).

The case of New York, once again, is instructive. Mayor Lindsay, in June 1970, proposed the establishment of sixty-two "neighborhood government" offices, each serving a population of approximately 130,000. The stated aims of the program included the improvement of city services "by making [city] agencies more responsive and accountable at the neighborhood level"; the reduction of "the distance that citizens feel exists between themselves and city government"; and the creation of the "basis for a single coordinated governmental presence in each neighborhood, recognized and supported by the community, the municipal government, and all elected officials."[29]

[29]Ira Katznelson, "Urban Counterrevolution," in *ibid.,* p. 150.

This statement of goals indicated the "new machine" quality of the proposal. The program's organizational roots of neighborhood government (which, since its inception in 1970, has undergone significant changes in the pilot areas) further reveal the relationship of this kind of program to the urban political crisis of control. Running as the Republican-Liberal candidate in 1965, Lindsay lacked even the inadequate organizational support the Democratic party then was capable of providing its candidate. To compensate, his campaign manager organized storefront headquarters in the city's neighborhoods to duplicate the functions of the machines in getting out the vote. After Lindsay's election, these storefronts, in spite of the opposition from the Democratic city council, developed into neighborhood city halls, which served as grievance centers and dispensed services. Writing about one such neighborhood office, Lindsay noted that

> the hall was staffed by three professionals supplemented by volunteers who . . . both as residents and 'ombudsmen' . . . could channel complaints and intelligence directly into the machinery of the city administration. The results were impressive. The number of cases handled jumped from 2,200 in 1967 to more than 8,000 in the first nine months of 1968. More important, however, was the fact that local residents realized that their neighborhood city hall was an effective mechanism for getting grievances resolved.[30]

From his perspective, Lindsay noted, the most pressing racial problem when he assumed office was not primarily one of racism or objective exploitation, but one of black alienation and discontent:

> What we saw in early 1966 was that within the ghetto, discontent and alienation were at the breaking point. We saw that a basic commitment to ending that alienation through greater contact was essential. And we knew that words alone would not do the job. . . . Thus, through the fall of 1966 and into the spring of 1967 *we made plans for a structured, formal link between the neighborhoods and the city.*[31]

The program for neighborhood government thus explicitly sought to create new links between citizens and government that not only closely resembled political machines but also carried out the conservative control functions of the machines.

---

[30]John V. Lindsay, *The City* (New York, 1970), p. 118.
[31]*Ibid.*, pp. 87, 95. Emphasis added.

These local institutional reforms were paralleled by others initiated by national authorities, who were concerned by the rising tide of urban discontent. The hallmark of the Great Society programs of Lyndon Johnson's presidency was "the direct relationship between the national government and the ghettos, a relationship in which both the state and local governments were undercut." It became apparent to some of the more sophisticated members of the national government that at least one cause of the massive discontent of the 1960s was the shift in the locus of political power from the machines to the bureaucracies. Hence an attempt was made to bypass the usual political arrangements that quite clearly were not adequately performing the function of social control. According to Piven and Cloward, the new federally sponsored "machines"

> became the base for new black political organizations whose rhetoric may have been thunderous, but whose activities came to consist mainly of vying for position and patronage within the urban political system. . . . Over a period of time, in other words, federal intervention had the effect of absorbing and directing many of the agitational elements in the black population. . . . Those who regard these federal actions as unintended, as a mistake, will have to account for the reason the mistake was repeated and enlarged from one legislative program to another as the decade wore on.[32]

These new institutional forms, both locally and nationally sponsored, are appropriate buffers for large, heterogeneous (racially and ethnically) cities with atrophied party organizations. In other locales, urban politicians have responded to their political crisis of control by utilizing similar techniques. In Chicago, the one case where a strong Democratic party machine survives, with only minor signs of diminishing success, black and white workers are linked to the political system on traditional-machine terms.

In cities with majority, or near majority black populations (most notably, Cleveland, Gary, Newark, and Atlanta), black mayors have been elected, usually with the financial support of both national and local corporations and foundations. Once in office, irrespective of the degree of their support for fundamental structural change, black mayors usually find it impossible to transform their cities' condition. Like other big-city mayors, they lack political resources and power to solve their cities' most

[32]Piven and Cloward, pp. 274–77.

pressing problems. They often find, moreover, that whatever degree of real local power exists, it is not to be found in city hall. In Newark, a community organizer has noted that

> there are 100 men or so, representing the downtown financial centers and suburban political interests who control land use, planning and money in this urban colony. . . . Since the decision to 'save Newark' there has been a lot of construction and investment in the downtown area financed by urban renewal money, but . . . with a combination of low corporate taxes, urban renewal tax write-offs, and special tax abatements, the large corporations that build themselves headquarters downtown are building the sanctuaries that force white property owners to pay back-breaking taxes, force rents up for everyone else and deny the city enough money to maintain even minimal services and schools.[33]

CONCLUSION: BACK TO NEWARK

The experience of Newark's Mayor Gibson, who was elected in 1970, indicates the limits within which even honest men of good will must operate in governing American cities. "I have promised to work toward that great day in 1970 when we shall have elected a talented, progressive and imaginative black mayor who will be able to give Newark an honest, moral and people-oriented government," a leading supporter of Gibson's proclaimed before his election.[34] In his term of office, Gibson has largely lived up to this advance notice. Yet the city remains plagued by all of the substantive problems he inherited—a changing population base, loss of jobs, abandoned and decaying housing, a troubled educational system, a worsening fiscal crisis, and bureaucracies that remain independent and unresponsive—even to the Mayor. The police, in particular, the most autonomous of the city agencies, have resisted mayoral interventions. Their relationship is symbolized by what happened one night in 1971 when Gibson chose to tour the city's hospitals. When his car broke down, he radioed for police assistance. The reply: "Let the son of a bitch walk."[35]

[33]Alec Grishkevitch, letter to the *New York Times*, September 7, 1971.
[34]Robert Curvin, "Black Power in Newark: Kenneth Gibson's First Year," unpublished manuscript.
[35]*Ibid.*

Like other big-city mayors, Gibson has found that, whether he likes it or not, his job is to keep social peace in the face of overwhelming social inequalities and contradictions he cannot resolve. In the short run, Newark's first black mayor has been able to provide symbolic satisfaction and greater access to municipal jobs for the black majority. But symbolic and bureaucratic rewards will not keep the lid on forever. The situation in Newark and other major American cities is not likely to change in the near future. Big-city politics are thus likely to be played out in a context of ever scarcer resources, heightened class and racial tensions, and increased competition for declining rewards.

13

the welfare state

In a television address in April 1969, President Nixon proposed a Family Assistance Plan (FAP) that, if it had passed, would have guaranteed a minimum income to every American family with children, and would have supplemented the earnings of the working poor. Every family of four, for instance, would have received a minimum of $1600 per year and would have had its income supplemented as long as family earnings were under $4000. It was estimated that the plan would have cost $4 billion in its first year of operation.

Coming from a conservative Republican president who had campaigned against welfare, for the work ethic, for "law and order," and who had been elected without direct black support, this proposal to give federal funds directly to the poor seemed remarkable. *Newsweek* called the proposal "so sweeping that even some of his own Republican Cabinet Officers were left gasping for conservative breath." The liberal Detroit *Free Press* found FAP "more radical than anything done by the Johnson administration," whose actions had included the creation of an Office of Economic Opportunity (OEO) to supervise a multimillion-dollar War on Poverty.[1]

[1] Daniel P. Moynihan, *The Politics of a Guaranteed Income* (New York, 1973), pp. 252–53.

Such comments stressed the apparently radical content of FAP without adequately coming to terms with the program's intent, which was to stabilize the structure of society, not to change it. From the perspective of those who governed the United States in the late 1960s, the social order gave every impression of crumbling. Daniel Moynihan, who served in sub-cabinet and cabinet-level positions under Presidents Kennedy, Johnson, and Nixon, and who was the architect of the welfare reform bill, captured the mood of near panic at the top:

> Nixon shared the anxiety . . . that the spiral of increasing urban racial violence . . . had not ceased. In 1965 there had been four major riots and civil disturbances in the country. In 1966 there were twenty-one major riots and civil disorders. In 1967 there were eighty-three major riots and civil disturbances. In the first seven months of 1968 there were fifty-seven major riots and disturbances. . . . In retrospect the domestic turbulence of the United States in the late 1960s may come to appear something less than cataclysmic. But this was not the view of the men then in office. Mayors, governors—presidents—took it as given that things were in a hell of a shape and that something had to be done.[2]

Moynihan rightly argued that Nixon's FAP proposal can only be understood as an attempt to deal with growing mass black discontent. Indeed, the leaders of the corporate community, who had the most to lose in the face of mass insurgency, largely favored the Nixon initiative. The specific features of the Family Assistance Plan were developed from proposals of a conference Governor Nelson Rockefeller of New York called in March 1967 "to help plan new approaches to public welfare in the United States." The steering committee consisted of some of the most successful members of the corporate complex, including Joseph Block (chairman of the executive committee of Inland Steel), Albert Nickerson (chief executive officer of Mobil Oil), Gustave Levy (head of the New York Stock Exchange), and Joseph Wilson (chairman of the board and chief executive officer of the Xerox corporation).

The conference collectively recommended that the present welfare system be replaced by a program of income maintenance. It argued for the acceptance of the objective that basic economic support at the federally defined poverty level be provided for all

[2]*Ibid.,* pp. 101–02.

Americans. But any such system, the conference cautioned, "should contain strong incentives to work." Moynihan commented that the "governor's inspiration was to turn to the heads of the large capitalist enterprises of the nation, a community with few ties, certainly, to the Social Security system, having bitterly opposed its establishment, but now including among its members men of generous disposition on social issues, *a tendency much accentuated by the onset of urban rioting.*"[3] In other words, rather than the existence of poverty, what concerned many businessmen was the disruption resulting from poverty. (As we shall see, important segments of American business did support the passage of the Social Security Act of 1935. On this point, then, Moynihan's account is partially misleading.)

The contradiction between the seeming radicalism of the proposal and the intent of its formulators highlights the inherent ambiguity of welfare-state reforms. Welfare-state programs hold out the promise of augmented resources to subordinates and of a more stable social structure to the privileged, who seek to insure both the continued and compliant submission of the subordinate. What realities underpin this ambiguous character of the welfare state?

THE DUAL WELFARE SYSTEM:
SOCIAL CAPITAL AND SOCIAL EXPENSES

Before attempting an answer, it is necessary to distinguish two quite different, though related, categories of welfare-state programs. The first provides tangible benefits to better-off workers in the corporate and state sectors. Most of these programs take the form of social insurance. Old-Age and Survivors and Disability Insurance under Social Security are the best known and most inclusive. The second category is directed at the poor in the small-capital sector. The most important of these programs is Aid to Families with Dependent Children (AFDC), the heart of which is commonly referred to as welfare.

[3]*Ibid.*, p. 56. Emphasis added.

As differentiated by economist James O'Connor, the first category, which he calls *social capital,* directly or indirectly serves the interests of private corporations. By using tax money to provide benefits and insurance for workers, social-capital expenditures lower labor costs for corporations and thus increase corporate productivity and profitability. The second category, which O'Connor calls *social expenses,* is not productive or profitable, but is equally necessary to corporate capitalism because it maintains the social order. The routine operation of the economy creates economic dislocations, including unemployment, underemployment, and a high proportion of workers whose wages are at or near subsistence levels. The resulting discontent threatens social stability. Thus, there are programs such as the AFDC that are "designed chiefly to keep social peace among unemployed workers."[4]

As we shall see, there are basic inequities between the two parts of the dual welfare state. Compared with social-insurance programs, social-expense programs provide recipients with lower levels of support; they are called by less legitimate names (relief vs. compensation); they tend to be administered by state and local governments; and they stigmatize the poor. These differences are no accident. The two kinds of programs service the needs of different sectors of American capitalism. Yet they spring from the same historical roots.

HISTORICAL FOUNDATIONS

The history of state involvement in social welfare can be variously interpreted. On the one hand, it can be seen as an account of the growing liberalization of provisions for the poor and of developing attempts to address the causes of poverty. Before 1935, the United States lacked even a basic social-security program of the sort that had long been adopted in the capitalist countries of Western Europe. By 1964, the government's involvement in social welfare had expanded to such an extent that an

[4]James O'Connor, *The Fiscal Crisis of the State* (New York, 1973), p. 7.

American president declared unconditional war on poverty; five years later, a conservative president proposed a guaranteed minimum income for all Americans. But, on the other hand, the growth of the welfare state can be seen as the continuation of basic historical traditions that "include repression, local financing and administration, a minimization of the amount of money spent on the poor, an emphasis on the work ethic, a distinction between the deserving and the undeserving poor, and a stigma attached to those who are dependent on relief."[5] As a result, the major innovations in public-welfare policy in this century have consistently been paternalistic at best, and often punitive to the poor.

Twentieth-century American welfare programs are rooted in the assumptions and practices of the English Poor Law of 1598. The act was passed in response to the social problems created by the shift from feudal to early capitalist patterns of agriculture, which drove many agricultural laborers off the land. Under the provisions of earlier laws, wandering paupers were punished with whipping, branding, enslavement, and even death. Yet these repressive measures became inadequate in controlling the rapidly increasing numbers of dispossessed workers. A British historian captured the mood of the period, which is remarkably similar to that of contemporary America in many respects:

> Wanderers were feared in the sixteenth century as likely to be thieves and rogues, and if in any number to cause more serious trouble, perhaps even political disturbances. . . . mobility of labour was to be feared. As Tawney has said, the sixteenth century lived in terror of the tramp. . . . The combination of fear and feeling can be detected in the preamble to the Elizabethan statute of 1598:
>
> *whereas a good part of the strength of this realm consisteth in the number of good and able subjects . . . and of late years more than in time past there have been sundry towns, parishes and houses of husbandry destroyed and become desolate, whereof a great number of poor people are become wanderers, idle and loose, which is the cause of infinite inconvenience . . .*[6]

[5]Bruno Stein, *On Relief* (New York, 1971), p. 43.
[6]Maurice Bruce, *The Coming of the Welfare State* (New York, 1966), pp. 24, 26.

The Poor Law attempted to deal with this breakdown of social control by mandating that local governments maintain their *own* poor at the smallest level of government, the parish. Local officials were given wide latitude in determining the level of benefits and how they would be disbursed. All able-bodied people, including children, were compelled to work. A refusal to work was a punishable crime.

The principles of the Poor Law, and of the subsequent amendments to it that usually followed periods of mass unrest in Britain, were transplanted to the American colonies and became the basis of American social welfare. The autonomy of localities produced widely different eighteenth- and nineteenth-century welfare policies for the poor. It also enabled localities to reduce their tax burdens by making nonresidents ineligible for welfare (such residency requirements were only ruled unconstitutional by the Supreme Court in 1969). Regulations that made work compulsory provided an ample low-paid work force for developing capitalist enterprises. And like English Poor Law practices, which often segregated the poor in workhouses and poorhouses, American social-welfare policies were administered in such a way as to stigmatize the poor and distinguish between the deserving and undeserving poor.

Local welfare systems could not survive the ravages of the depression, nor were they compatible with the basic shift in the economy from small-scale, largely local or regional capital to corporate capital. As more and more Americans became poor (most of whom had little experience with hard-core poverty), the federal government nationalized welfare policy by funding and setting standards for traditionally autonomous local welfare programs. Nevertheless, many of the system's basic characteristics continued to prevail.

The Social Security Act of 1935 created a countrywide framework for a dual welfare state. It established the basic programs of social capital and social expenses. The social-capital expenditures included Social Security and a federal/state system of unemployment compensation. The bill's most significant program of social expenses was Aid to Dependent Children (ADC), which has developed into today's AFDC. Augmented by programs of public health, food stamps, public housing, and other services, it remains the core of the social-expenses welfare state.

SOCIAL WELFARE AND THE NEW DEAL

The Social Security Act was not passed in an economic or political vacuum. With the election of Franklin D. Roosevelt in 1932, the federal government began to respond more actively to the massive economic upheaval of the depression. The first response to the New Deal to soaring unemployment rates was the substitution of work relief for direct cash relief. By mid-January 1934 the Civil Works Administration (CWA) had put four million Americans to work, thus making the federal government the largest employer in the country.

But by the spring of 1934 the CWA was closed down. It had drawn the widespread opposition of the corporate community, whose members feared the CWA threatened the private-enterprise system. "Work relief raised the specter of government activity in areas hitherto reserved for private enterprise, and CWA minimum wage scales raised the specter of government interference in the conduct of private enterprise."[7] The abolition of the CWA signified that Roosevelt sought to win support from businessmen (albeit unsuccessfully) in the first year of the New Deal and to restore their confidence in American capitalism.

By the congressional elections of 1934, growing business opposition to the Roosevelt regime made it necessary for the president to seek to save capitalism and members of the corporate order in spite of themselves. As *Fortune* magazine noted in 1935, it was "fairly evident to most disinterested critics" that the New Deal had "the preservation of capitalism at all times in view." A small minority of the corporate community agreed with this assessment and played a major role in the administration, but in the main Roosevelt had to build his political constituency of farmers, workers, and homeowners without overt business support.

The defection of much of his minority business support from Roosevelt's political coalition eliminated political cross-pressures in the administration and freed it to deal with mass discontent more directly than might otherwise have been possible. With the end of the CWA in 1934, millions of Americans who had been

[7]Frances Fox Piven and Richard Cloward, *Regulating the Poor: The Functions of Public Welfare* (New York, 1971), p. 82.

given jobs now found themselves again dependent on the largesse of private, local, or state relief agencies. Their restiveness was palpable. Many, at the time, thought the United States was in a prerevolutionary situation:

> For discontent had not evaporated with the elections of 1932; rather, it was stilled for a moment by the promise of a new regime, the confidence a new leader inspired. However, as the Depression wore on, with conditions showing little improvement, unrest surfaced. By 1934, various dissident leaders were drawing upon this unrest, giving it organizational form and coherence, aspiring to build political movements that would change the face of America.[8]

Roosevelt responded by promoting social-welfare legislation that undercut these growing dissident movements and acted to restore stability. In his January 4, 1935, State of the Union message, Roosevelt proposed sweeping reforms, including redistributive tax laws, new labor legislation, the restoration of national work relief, and programs of social insurance. The proposals were largely gutted by the Congress, but the passage of diluted versions had a larger symbolic importance: it convinced many of the discontented that the federal government was acting vigorously on their behalf.

The measure that had the most direct impact on the unemployed was the restoration of massive publicly-funded employment under the Works Progress Administration (WPA). Millions of Americans were once more put to work, a fact that more than anything else eased the threat of civil disorder. But after 1936, as the most important dissident movements of the period (including the Townsend Old People's Movement, the Workers Alliance, and other populist organizations of the left and right) declined in membership and influence, the New Deal quickly reduced its concessions to the poor, and the number of federally-paid jobs was sharply cut. Once the threat of a civil uprising had passed, the government withdrew from the employment picture in order to restore the traditional prerogatives of private capital.

Hence the most enduring welfare innovation of the depression was not work relief, but the Social Security Act. It provided the basic framework for the modern American welfare state, and its provisions meshed with, rather than challenged, the dominant

[8]*Ibid.*, p. 85.

corporate system. Unemployment insurance, social security pensions, and categorical aid to mothers and families with dependent children have been with us ever since. Before analyzing their importance to the smooth functioning of the corporate complex, let us examine the second major period of welfare-state innovation in this century, the middle 1960s.

WAR ON POVERTY: WAR ON DISORDER

The massive expansion of federal involvement in social welfare has puzzled many observers. In 1961, when John F. Kennedy sponsored the appropriation of $10 million for grants to "youth development" under the Juvenile Delinquency and Youth Offenses Control Act; when, two years later, $150 million were authorized for community mental health centers; when, in 1964, Title Two of the Economic Opportunity Act (the antipoverty bill of the War on Poverty) allocated $350 million to community action programs that called for the "maximum feasible participation of residents of the areas and members of the groups served"; and when Congress passed a Model Citizens program to rehabilitate blighted neighborhoods in 1966, there was a marked *absence* of interest groups pressing for the legislation. At the initiative of the White House the bills all passed in an apparent political vacuum. How could this phenomenon be explained?

Moynihan developed a widely accepted explanation that he labeled "the professionalism of reform":

> Increasingly efforts to change the American social system for the better arose from initiatives undertaken by persons whose profession was to do just that. Whereas previously the role of organized society had been largely passive—the machinery would work if someone made it work—now the process began to acquire a self-starting capacity of its own.[9]

Unlike the New Deal programs, he argued, which were generated by long sustained political pressure and discontent, and which in turn defused discontent, the early New Frontier and Great

[9]Daniel P. Moynihan, *Maximum Feasible Misunderstanding* (New York, 1969), p. 23.

Society programs of Presidents Kennedy and Johnson originated in a period when "the American poor, black and white, were surprisingly inert. . . . The war on poverty was not declared at the behest of the poor: it was declared in their interest by persons confident of their own judgement in such matters."[10] The development of these programs thus reflected the rise of a technocratic professional elite and the growth of a knowledge industry based on universities and foundations.

While the professionalism of reform played an important part in the expansion of the welfare state in the 1960s, it is not the whole story. It does not account for the *political* appeals of the professionals' proposals and, hence, the reasons for their adoption by politicians, and it tells us little about the impact of the new programs in dealing with the unprecedented black discontent of the middle and late 1960s.

Kennedy's close election victory in 1960 revealed basic weaknesses in the Democratic coalition. The South in particular was no longer a secure party base. In the Northern cities, many Democratic voters were moving to the suburbs, where their political allegiances were more uncertain. In their place were millions of black migrants from the South—a large number of whom did not vote—who had few established links with urban party organizations.

It was this new constituency that the Kennedy and Johnson administrations needed. Hence they welcomed the programs proposed by the reform professionals:

> Each program singled out the 'inner city' as its main target; each provided a basketful of services; each channeled some portion of its funds more or less directly to new organizations in the 'inner city', circumventing the existing municipal agencies which traditionally controlled services. . . . it was ghetto neighborhoods that these programs were chiefly designed to reach, and by tactics reminiscent of the traditional political machine.[11]

By creating a direct link between the federal government and the ghettos, the Democratic administrations not only bypassed existing service bureaucracies but also left the traditional white ethnic party organizations relatively undisturbed. In short, the new

[10]*Ibid.,* pp. 34–35.
[11]Piven and Cloward, pp. 260–61.

programs promised a high electoral payoff at relatively low risk. Blacks were to be integrated into the predominantly Democratic urban political system by way of social-welfare programs in traditional machine-like fashion.

However, this combination of professional proposals and electoral imperatives provided authorities with effective tools to defuse the black rebellions in the middle years of the decade in two respects. First, the programs created a vehicle for the political integration of the most talented, articulate, militant young blacks of the period. Militant action was now often directed at winning larger shares of urban patronage rather than at working for structural change. In Baltimore, political scientist Peter Bachrach noted that the federally funded programs "provided black groups with . . . decision-making arenas in which the struggle for power could be fought out in the open and within the confines of the political system." Similarly, urbanist John Strange noted that in Durham and other North Carolina cities, "community action, with special emphasis on participation and community organization, has . . . channeled dissatisfaction and unrest into forms and issues which can be dealt with."[12]

Secondly, the expansion of the government's welfare role helped defuse mass discontent by providing tangible, if limited, benefits, including easier access to AFDC welfare, higher welfare payments, and new job opportunities. In short, then, black discontent was not caused by the new programs (the causes were structural, not manufactured by government), nor were the programs originally aimed at defusing discontent (electoral considerations were of primary importance). Nevertheless, with the outbreak of massive civil disorder in the middle 1960s, the state used both traditional welfare programs like AFDC and the newly created programs like Community Action to absorb and canalize the discontent. In this respect, the expansion and operation of welfare-state programs in the 1960s bears a striking resemblance to the programs of the New Deal.

Whether or not they were proposed or passed as the result of mass movements and pressures, all the welfare-state programs, from the Social Security Act of 1935 to Nixon's Family Assistance Plan of 1969, share one basic characteristic: *they are meant to stabilize the social order, not create structural change.* They do

[12]Cited in *ibid.*, p. 274.

not challenge the existence of the corporate complex. Instead, they seek to alleviate—not correct—the basic structural inequalities that are part and parcel of the American corporate-capital system.

This point was stressed by the German sociologist Georg Simmel, who commented at the turn of the century on Bismarck's social-welfare program:

> If we take into consideration this meaning of assistance to the poor, it becomes clear that the fact of taking away from the rich to give to the poor does not aim at equalizing their individual positions, and is not, even in its orientation, directed at suppressing the social difference between the rich and the poor. On the contrary, assistance is based on the structure of society, whatever it may be. . . . The goal of assistance is precisely to mitigate certain extreme manifestations of social differentiation, so that the social structure may continue to be based on this differentiation.

This structure-protecting feature of welfare-state measures, he argued, is apparent because "if assistance were to be based on the interests of the poor person, there would, in principle, be no limit on the transmission of poverty in favor of the poor, a transmission that would lead to the equality of all." But structural transformation is what the dominant want to prevent; as a result, "there is no reason to aid the person more than is required by the maintenance of the *status quo*."[13]

THE DUAL WELFARE SYSTEM AND THE CORPORATE SECTOR

We have seen how welfare-state reforms were utilized to defuse discontent in periods of challenges (or potential challenges) to structural arrangements. But the welfare state also has economic and political functions in more normal periods. Since the welfare state is not an undifferentiated whole, however, it is necessary to explore these functions with reference to local and regional small capital and the dominant corporate sector. Each of these two

[13]Georg Simmel, "The Poor," in Chaim I. Waxman, ed., *Poverty: Power and Politics* (New York, 1968), pp. 3–9.

sectors employs about one-third of the work force, and each is serviced differently by the welfare state. First let us consider the relationship of the welfare state to the corporate sector. The distinction between the two kinds of welfare-state programs dates back to the Social Security Act of 1935. The social-insurance provisions of the bill, which insure against old age, retirement, and unemployment—as well as similar programs adopted in the 1940s, including veteran's life insurance and insurance against work-related accidents—directly support the needs of the corporate complex. Paradoxically, although these insurance payments go to workers, "the fundamental intent and effect of social security is to expand productivity, production, and profits. *Seen in this way, social insurance is not primarily insurance for workers but a kind of insurance for capitalists and corporations.*"[14] What does this statement mean?

Most corporate leaders would probably agree that the relatively better-off workers in large-capital firms will work harder if they are more secure economically. Thus, many industries instituted systems of workmen's compensation well before such insurance was mandated by law. Although the passage of most landmark pieces of social legislation was primarily the result of political activity by powerful organized workers, corporate leaders of the largest, most economically advanced industries have often been in the vanguard of those demanding the expansion of the social-insurance system.

Today, social-insurance programs enjoy the enthusiastic support of both business and labor in the corporate sector. A look at Social Security indicates the reasons. Retired workers in the 1970s share about $45 billion each year in Social Security payments, up from $19 billion in 1964.[15] Workers are taxed to pay for these benefits at the rate of 5.8 percent of the first $13,200 they earn each year. An identical tax is paid by the employer. But most economists believe that, in the case of corporations, the employer's share is passed along to the worker in the form of lower wages. Thus, while corporate employers largely escape having to make a real contribution to the social-security system, corporate workers in effect pay a tax (both direct and indirect) of almost 12

[14]O'Connor, p. 138.
[15]Charles L. Schultze *et al.*, *Setting National Priorities: The 1972 Budget* (Washington, D.C., 1972), p. 21.

percent on their income. Hence the corporation profits at their expense.

In turn, however, corporate-sector workers gain at the expense of the lower-paid workers in small-capital industries. Although all workers are taxed equally up to the first $13,200 they earn (income over this figure is exempt), the more an individual earns while working, the higher his retirement payments. Moreover, millions of people who have been unemployed for long periods do not accumulate the required work-time and receive no benefits at all when they retire, even though they paid taxes when they worked.

In spite of the fact that the social-security tax is America's most regressive tax (exempting interest, profit, rent, capital gains, and all payroll income over $13,200), this and other programs of social insurance, like unemployment insurance and workmen's compensation, favor the corporate worker and thus are supported by organized labor as well as by corporate management. The corporations are enabled to keep wage costs down, and corporate-sector workers gain by what economist Milton Friedman has called "the poor man's welfare payment to the middle class."[16] As O'Connor noted:

> Organized labor is more or less satisfied because the system redistributes income in its favor. Monopoly capital is also relatively happy because the system insures comparative harmony with labor. If monopoly sector workers were compelled to contribute as much as they receive upon retirement, current money wages would have to be slashed sharply. But if retired workers received what they actually paid in, retirement benefits would be impossibly low. In either event, monopoly sector labor-management relations would be seriously impaired. Workers would bitterly resist technological and other changes that threatened their jobs, the ability of unions to maintain discipline would be undermined, and in most industries management would be faced with more uncertainty.[17]

Moreover, as rank-and-file workers have come to agitate for better pensions, labor leaders and corporate managements have moved to resolve their shared dilemma by pressuring the federal government for more liberalized social-insurance programs. The ritual pattern was set in 1949 when Walter Reuther, the president

---

[16]Milton Friedman, "The Poor Man's Welfare Payment to the Middle Class," *The Washington Monthly* (May 1972): 16.
[17]O'Connor, pp. 139–40.

of the United Automobile Workers (UAW), successfully prodded the automobile companies to pressure for liberalized social security by negotiating a contract that included an expensive pension plan. "The effect of the 'Reuther system' is that corporations socialize . . . costs . . . and thus defend their profits, union leaders conserve their hegemony over the rank and file, and labor discipline and morale are maintained."[18]

SMALL CAPITAL AND THE WELFARE STATE

The relationship between small capital and the welfare state is quite different from that between the welfare state and corporate capital. First, although the small-capital sector is increasingly anachronistic, the federal government helps maintain the existence of "surplus capitalists" by providing them with a form of welfare in much the same way it provides foreign aid to "underdeveloped" countries. The cost of this support is billions of dollars in direct and indirect subsidies to farmers (under the direction of the Department of Agriculture) and small businessmen (financed by the Small Business Administration).[19]

Workers in the small-capital sector tend to be lower paid, less unionized, and less economically secure than corporate-sector workers. They are more likely to be unemployed for longer periods. They are often excluded from social-insurance programs, and when included, receive smaller benefits. These sectoral imbalances, historian Eric Hobsbawn noted, constitute "the rhythm of social disruption" of industrial capitalism.[20] Industrial growth increases imbalances between regions of the country (the Southwest is booming, but the older urban cores are stagnating economically) and between different industries (plastics production has increased considerably, while the domestic shoe industry has declined). Whereas corporate workers share somewhat in the gains of corporate growth and technical progress, small-capital workers do not; on the contrary, as we saw in Chapter 4, the wage

---

[18]*Ibid.*, p. 141.
[19]C. Lowell Harriss, "Subsidies in the United States," *Public Finance* 16 (no. 4, 1961): 276.
[20]O'Connor, p. 159.

gap between the two sectors has widened considerably in the past quarter century.

As a result, an increasing proportion of the small-capital sector population has become dependent on welfare programs for subsistence. With the continuing decline in the economic position of small-capital-sector workers, the traditional correlation between unemployment and AFDC welfare rates no longer held by the middle 1960s. Since the depression, the number of new welfare cases rose and fell with the monthly rise and fall of male unemployment. But "with the onset of the 1960s the relationship weakened abruptly, and by 1963 vanished altogether. Or rather, reversed itself. For the next five years the nonwhite male unemployment rate declined steadily and the number of AFDC cases rose steadily."[21]

This shift reflected the growing gap between corporate- and small-capital–sector wages. At the end of the Second World War, small-capital–sector workers earned roughly 75 percent of the wages of corporate-sector workers; in the 1960s, their relative earnings declined to 60 percent.[22] Thus even those in the small-capital sector who had jobs were increasingly unable to adequately support their families. Men deserted their wives and children either out of a sense of shame or because their families would be better off with AFDC payments. The welfare rolls skyrocketed as more and more families became dependent on the state. (This, of course, as we noted in Chapter 12, was hardly the only cause of the welfare explosion of the 1960s.) Low wages and underemployment, as well as unemployment, now contributed directly to the growth of the welfare state. Throughout the 1960s, the number of welfare recipients grew by almost 10 percent per year.[23]

In response to this trend, the federal government has experimented with job-training schemes in an attempt "to transform social expense outlays (welfare) into social capital for the competitive sector."[24] The Manpower Development and Training Act of 1964 provides for on-the-job training that equips workers for small-capital, not corporate, sector jobs. After studying the program, economist Jerome Joffe concluded that it "has primarily

[21]Moynihan, *The Politics of a Guaranteed Income*, p. 82.
[22]Barry Bluestone, "Economic Crisis and the Law of Uneven Development," *Politics and Society* 3 (Fall 1972): 68.
[23]*Wall Street Journal*, April 24, 1969.
[24]O'Connor, p. 166.

provided training for low skill high-turnover jobs in both the rising sectors in the central city, e.g., nurse's aide, and the traditional low-wage industry occupations, e.g., sewing machine operator."[25]

Most importantly of all for the small-capital sector, the operations of the welfare state reinforce the harsh employment market. In periods when the social order is not under stress, the welfare system operates to compel people into low-paid, menial work by following the principle of "less eligibility" proclaimed in England in 1834, which declared that welfare payments should provide a standard of living less desirable than "the situation of the independent laborer of the lowest class." The traditional workhouses that underpinned this principle in England were

designed to spur men to contrive ways of supporting themselves by their own industry, *to offer themselves to any employer on any terms*. It did this by making pariahs of those who could not support themselves; they served as an object lesson, a means of celebrating the virtues of work by the terrible example of their agony.[26]

This principle makes it possible to understand the ritual degradation of the welfare client, a degradation that is no accident. In contrast to the insurance programs O'Connor labelled social capital, one of the main functions of the social-expenses welfare system is to demarcate a boundary between the "deserving" and "undeserving" poor. The boundary is made clear as soon as a person applies for welfare. AFDC welfare centers are typically dingy, forbidding places; long waits for attention and a clinical atmosphere set a dehumanizing tone. Once applicants are called to meet a caseworker, their lives are probed in intimate, exhaustive detail—work, family, and finances are all grist for the welfare workers' mill. One prospective welfare recipient described an early experience with the system:

At the Welfare they got this man they call him the Resources man and sometimes he is also a woman. Whenever you apply for welfare, you must be sent to him because he must ask you a lot of questions. All kinds of questions. Like he may ask you if you belong to a union or are in the Army. Then he will try to do something about that to keep you off welfare.

[25]Jerome Joffe, "The Limits of Urban Policy," *Review of Radical Political Economics* 4 (Summer 1972): 101.
[26]Piven and Cloward, pp. 34, 35.

Finally, after being shunted between four caseworkers who refused to put him on the rolls, "I go away from the welfare center as rich as when I came there." He found a subsistence wage job, but the factory was unionized and the workers went out on strike.

> I have no savings yet, so I must go again to welfare, but this man wants to know when I got my last check. Then he says he can't help me because it is not so long ago that I shouldn't have some money. And he tells me to come back in another week if the strike isn't settled, but today when I went to see him he said, 'Look for work and come back again in another week.' I just don't think he wants to give me the welfare. So that's the way it is again. I have moved out of my room and I am staying with my uncle . . . If the strike ends soon maybe I will save my money and go to another city. I have friends in Philadelphia. They say it is not so cruel about the welfare.[27]

Once they succeed in getting on the welfare rolls, recipients are subjected to further degradation. Routinely they are kept under surveillance, exhorted by welfare workers to "rehabilitate" themselves, and asked to prove that they are not welfare chiselers or frauds. They are underbudgeted by welfare workers who are given incentives to keep costs down. They are defined as useless in a society that values work and production; and from time to time, they are denounced as such by politicians in search of headlines. Most importantly, they are treated as, and become, functionally powerless, dependent on the decisions of others over whom they exercise virtually no control. They come to share the society's image of them as unworthy, and to collaborate in the system that perpetuates their subordination. There are almost no appeals made by welfare recipients on grounds of deprivation either of money or of civil liberties, which are their due under the Social Security Act. "In 1964, when the overall welfare rolls stood at about 500,000 persons in New York City, *a mere fifteen appeals were taken in an entire year.* Even considering that the poor are ill-informed about such procedures and that they have no money for legal assistance, this is still striking evidence of acquiescence."[28]

This process of systematic degradation also works to discourage *potential* welfare clients, who will accept subsistence

[27]Richard M. Elman, *The Poorhouse State* (New York, 1966), pp. 94–96.
[28]Piven and Cloward, p. 173.

wages rather than suffer the consequences of being on welfare. Only 15,000 of the 150,000 families eligible for wage subsidies in New York City in 1968 claimed the benefit. An activist lawyer reported that:

> During a meeting in Brownsville in 1967 with a group of about 120 Puerto Rican strikers, I estimated on the basis of family size and income that more than half of the men present were eligible for supplementary cash assistance. When I suggested that the strikers apply for welfare, the audience responded with some boos and much silence. "Not even when the strike is on?" I said. Visibly annoyed, their leader replied, "No, Mr. Attorney, we don't want welfare even when we have nothing."[29]

But those who refuse welfare are trapped in jobs that simply do not pay enough to support a family decently. In his 1968 economic report, Mayor Lindsay of New York proudly announced that unemployment was down, but he neglected to add that 900,000 of the city's 2.2 million jobholders earned less than $2.25 per hour before taxes (or $4,600 per year).[30]

Active discouragement of qualified relief recipients increases as the threat of mass discontent ebbs. In the late 1960s, for example, after the wave of ghetto rebellions had passed, city after city moved to make it more difficult to get on the welfare rolls. In New York, the Bureau of the Budget recommended to the mayor that a case backlog be deliberately created by consolidating the welfare centers and by cutting welfare personnel. Consolidation of the centers began in 1970. Since then, the rise of the welfare rolls has dramatically stopped—at the cost of much human suffering.

Perhaps the dilemma is most acute in the case of the welfare mother who is given contradictory cues by society. She is told to stay at home with her children, on the one hand, but to work to support herself, on the other. The welfare system also makes it virtually impossible for her to better her situation.

> Mary Thomas' case was typical. She would like to quit her job as a saleswoman in a clothing store, in order to return to school and become a medical technician. Unfortunately, though welfare will subsidize the day care of her five children while she works at the store, it will not do so while she returns to school for four years. Nor will welfare pay her tuition. It is thus difficult, if not

[29]James Graham, *The Enemies of the Poor* (New York, 1970), p. 45.
[30]*Ibid.*, p. 46.

impossible, for her to work in anything except a low-paying, dead-end job. . . . The federal minimum wage of $1.60 an hour means that for all her hard labor, a woman who has several children will still be stuck in poverty. . . . there are ten million jobs that pay less than the minimum wage; if she is a woman, she has a good chance to get one of these. In fact, public officials such as Senator Long and Elliot Richardson have argued that welfare recipients ought to work for less than the minimum wage ($1.20 an hour) if private industry jobs are unavailable.[31]

Welfare thus perpetuates the dependency it claims to find distressing by using wretchedness to reinforce job-market exploitation.

At the extreme, welfare recipients are treated as nonpeople. In Aiken, South Carolina, County Hospital records show that thirteen of thirty-four welfare mothers whose children's births were paid for by government funds in 1972 were sterilized. The doctor who performed the hysterectomies received payments of $60,000 for his hospital work that year. The doctor "defended his policy in the local press and said that he required welfare mothers with three children to receive care. He said he was doing so because of the heavy tax burden they were causing."[32]

The economic benefits for the small-capital sector are obvious. But there are ideological payoffs as well. By segregating and stigmatizing the "productively useless," "the welfare state does not oppose but counterbalances the utilitarian assumptions of the middle class."[33] In terms of the dominant American ideology, the clients of the AFDC system are obvious failures and are punished as such.

TWO KINDS OF WELFARE STATE PROFESSIONALS

As the welfare state has grown since the mid-1930s, so have the numbers of professionals who plan and staff its operations. Since the Second World War, in particular, the rapid growth of the social-science field has provided the welfare state with a cadre of

---

[31]Lynne Iglitzin, "Women and Welfare," unpublished manuscript.
[32]*New York Times,* August 3, 1973.
[33]Alvin Gouldner, *The Coming Crisis of Western Sociology* (New York, 1971), pp. 81–82.

professional planners. Indeed, the expansion of the welfare state and of the social sciences has occurred in tandem. Thus, between 1962 and 1964, boom years for new welfare programs, federal expenditures on social-science research increased by 70 percent to $200,000,000 per year.

These monies were not simply intended to further knowledge in the abstract. As sociologist Alvin Gouldner pointed out, the government expected that "the social sciences will help solve ramifying practical problems. In particular, it is expected that the social sciences will help administrators to design and operate national policies, welfare apparatus, urban settlements, and even industrial establishments."[34] In response to these demands, the social sciences have developed new techniques—including decision-theory, cybernetics, and operations research—that provide policymakers with politically acceptable options.

But, as Gouldner also pointed out, social scientists not only provide the state with a refined capability in developing welfare programs but they also provide the appropriate reformist rhetoric

> to persuade resistant or undecided segments of the society that such problems do, indeed, exist and are of dangerous proportions. Once committed to such intervention, the state acquires a vested interest of its own in "advertising" the social problems for whose solution it seeks financing. In other words, the state requires social researches that can *expose* those social problems with which the state is ready to deal.[35]

A second group of professionals—social workers, nurses, nursery-school teachers—administer the programs directly, and distribute welfare-state rewards, such as they are, to clients. But the interests of this group of professionals, as distributors of desired or necessary goods and services, often clash with the interests of the consumers of those services. These clashes, political scientist Deborah Stone observes, are of three kinds:

(1) The theory of professional work has a middle-class orientation. Service to a client is assumed to be discrete and temporary, on the assumption that all is basically well, but a transient "ailment" needs to be remedied. The result is that professionals "offer help with individual problems, while lower-class people face discrimination as a class." Regressive tax and credit laws,

[34] *Ibid.*, p. 345.
[35] *Ibid.*, p. 35.

slums, and inadequate health care are not individual problems. Hence, professionals, "by treating their clients on an *ad hoc,* short-term, and symptomatic basis, can at the very best only restore them to the *status quo,* and at the worst make their lives more difficult."

(2) The reward structure of service professions, in general, discourages service to a lower-class clientele. New public health nurses, school teachers, social workers, policemen, and child guidance therapists are initially assigned to the poorest neighborhoods and, with time and experience, "promoted" to wealthier districts:

> This kind of reward structure means that the most needy . . . are served, if at all, by the least experienced and least competent members of the profession. It also serves to inculcate class prejudices into individual members of the profession. Thus, the status concerns of a profession lead the profession as a whole to provide its best services to higher-status groups, and lead individual professionals to eschew services to the poor.[36]

(3) Professionals seek to maintain freedom from outside control and an image of competence. One of the hallmarks of a profession is its autonomy—its freedom to set its own standards of behavior. As a result, professionals typically resist any moves toward community control that would jeopardize their authority. This resistance is justified by a claim of superior competence; hence, to safeguard this image, professionals protect even the most incompetent of their members.

THE FRAGMENTATION OF SUBORDINATES

Political scientist Alan Wolfe defined "alienated politics" as "the process through which people in similar positions are separated from each other, forced to compete instead of cooperate."[37] In this fashion, the routine operation of the American welfare state divides different groups of subordinates from each other along sectoral and ethnic lines. Consider the divide between corporate-

[36]Deborah Stone, "Professionals and the Welfare State," unpublished manuscript.
[37]Alan Wolfe, "New Directions in the Marxist Theory of Politics," *Politics and Society* 4 (Winter 1974): 148.

and small-capital–sector workers. As we noted, both sectors' workers are taxed at identical rates for social security, yet the better-paid corporate workers receive higher benefits on retirement. In complementary fashion, welfare programs for small-capital–sector workers are paid for in part by the taxes of corporate-sector workers. Thus, while the real income of corporate-sector workers is increased by social-insurance programs, it is reduced in turn by the taxes they must pay to finance a welfare population created as a consequence of corporate-sector growth. "In this sense," O'Connor concluded, "the state budget can be seen as a complex mechanism that redistributes income backward and forward within the working class—all to maintain industrial and social-political harmony, expand productivity, and accelerate accumulation and profits in the monopoly sector."[38] The divisions thus promoted between workers are further accentuated by a racial divide, since most white workers are in the corporate sector, but a majority of blacks are in the small-capital sector. Thus welfare-state programs exacerbate racial stereotypes and antagonisms by establishing pocketbook conflicts of interest.

In still another way, the Great Society programs of the 1960s, which undoubtedly did provide new resources to the poor, often divided the poor from each other. A recent study of a Community Action Program (CAP) in the Tremont section of the Bronx, New York, for example, found that three-quarters of the people in the area believed that the CAP had intensified antagonism between Puerto Ricans and blacks and had had little effect on the neighborhood's poverty. Black and Puerto Rican leaders focused their energies on relatively nonproductive programs and on fighting each other. For this reason, the study concluded, the program operated primarily as "a social control output, with the community action bureaucracy functioning as a social control agent and as another authority with which the poor must cope."[39] This case is hardly unique.[40] Within the limits of Community

---

[38]O'Connor, p. 162.
[39]Kenneth J. Pollinger and Annette C. Pollinger, *Community Action and the Poor* (New York, 1972), pp. 201ff, 18.
[40]Peter Marris and Martin Rein, *Dilemmas of Social Reform* (Chicago, 1967); and Kenneth Clark and Jeanette Hopkins, *A Relevant War Against Poverty* (New York, 1970).

Action and Model Cities programs and other welfare-state activities that mandate participation by the poor, the following situations develop:

> Key processes and mechanisms 1) blunt and defuse demands; 2) coopt potential opposition; 3) create so *much* participation that effective policy making by representative groups is stalemated; 4) create so *much* representation that a classic veto-group situation is created which allows almost any group to block action, and 5) requires so *much* consensus that decisions which challenge the vital interests of *any* group are impossible.[41]

The consequence is heightened frustration that further divides the victimized from each other.

CONTRADICTIONS

The continued expansion of the welfare state has thus complemented the corporate and small-capital sectors of American capitalism. But the compatibility of the welfare state and the operation of the economy is an uneasy one. The relationship is characterized by a number of contradictions—the most important of which are a growing fiscal crisis, a developing antagonism between welfare distributors and consumers, a political inability to prevent opposition to programs for the poor, and, most broadly, a contradiction between the logic of profit and the logic of need.

The fiscal crisis   The growth of the corporate sector and the maintenance of the small-capital sector, we have seen, require the continued expansion of welfare-state programs. This produces a massive increase in state expenditures, both in grants and services to recipients and in salaries to a growing number of employees. Each aspect of the increase is relatively immune to much limitation. The programs, in routine periods, continue to expand at roughly the same rate in both Democratic and Republican administrations and under liberal and conservative presidents

---

[41]Robert Alford, "Social Needs, Political Demands, and Administrative Responses," unpublished manuscript.

(their rhetoric notwithstanding). The annual wage bill at the federal, state, and local levels continues to rise rapidly because the number of workers has increased and their increased unionization in a period of high inflation has brought about accelerated wage demands. Between 1965 and 1972 in New York City, for example, the annual wage bill for government employees increased at an annual rate of 9.7 percent, from $1.7 to $3.3 billion. Inflation accounted for about half of this increase, real wage gains for one-fourth, and an increase in the size of the work force for the rest.

An increase in costs affects the government very differently from the way it affects private industry. Corporations administer their prices to pass along costs to consumers. Government, by contrast, has three ways it can increase its revenues. First, it can try to step up the economy's rate of growth by deficit spending in order to generate more tax revenues. But this strategy is flawed on two counts—it is inflationary (and hence politically risky), and it often exacerbates inequalities between the corporate and small-capital sectors, thus necessitating the further expansion of welfare expenditures.

Secondly, the government can try to increase the productivity of state employees, but this is inherently difficult since, unlike the corporate sector, the government is a "labor intensive," not a "capital intensive" economic arena. Like most new government activities, new welfare programs require more people to a greater extent than they require or use more hardware.

Thirdly, the government can raise taxes. Politically, this solution is increasingly risky to attempt. Since most corporate taxes are passed on to consumers, and the tax structure as a whole is highly regressive, a disproportionate tax burden falls on corporate-sector workers, who find it difficult to shelter their income from taxation. They have come increasingly to understand, resent, and resist this pattern of disproportionate taxation and bitterly recognize that they are expected to foot the bill for the expansion of the welfare state. Thus, while tax issues have divided workers from each other, all workers are united in opposing higher taxes, thus making it increasingly difficult for the state to fund its programs.

A distributor-consumer antagonism   The conflict of interest between the distributors of welfare-state largesse and the

recipients has resulted in the growth of the welfare-rights movement, which, in part, grew out of the activity of community action
programs. In the spring of 1966, George Wiley, a black professor
of chemistry, opened a Poverty Rights Action Center as a vehicle
for the National Welfare Rights Organization. The NWRO became the umbrella organization of formerly independent, local
protest groups, whose members were mostly black women. By
1969, NWRO had over one hundred thousand dues-paying members in approximately 350 affiliated groups.

Most of the organization's efforts have been directed at
providing collective muscle to back up individual grievances. It
has also staged hundreds of demonstrations aimed at undermining welfare restrictions and punitive regulations, and at obtaining
benefits that are legally mandated, but which local agencies often
withhold. NWRO became a nationally visible pressure group of a
consumer population that traditionally had been intimidated into
mute submission. This development has helped the poor become
important political participants on welfare issues (Moynihan
credits the NWRO, for example, with a key role in defeating
Nixon's FAP), has shifted class patterns of leadership within the
black community, and contains the promise of a new political
base that can raise issues transcending the organization's initial
focus on welfare.[42]

But the recent decline in NWRO membership and activity
(whether permanent or temporary is not yet clear) indicates the
inherent difficulty of organizing relatively subordinate consumers
around the issues of distribution. To attract members who are
rightly cynical of the political process, organizations like NWRO
must demonstrate "that participants will have more than a
marginal effect on anticipated rewards" and must "overcome
generalized disinterest in political activity." To maintain membership, they must continually demonstrate their strength and
command of political skills and adopt tactics that are both
effective and acceptable to the majority of members.[43]

Added to these difficulties are the counterstrategies available
to authorities, who may:

(1) Make concessions that cripple organizational initiatives.

[42]Larry Jackson, "The Black Agenda: What Role for the Popular Strata,"
Afro-American Studies 3 (1972): 67–74.
[43]Michael Lipsky and Margaret Levi "Community Organization as a Political
Resource," *Urban Affairs Annual* 6 (1972): 177–88.

Minor gains may confer responsibilities on the organization that are beyond its capacity to fulfill. A tenant group, for example, when offered the chance to administer buildings whose maintenance it protested, may find it is ill-equipped for this task.

(2) Avoid responsibility for specific action and programs by passing the buck to other government units or by arguing that there is a distinction between those who initiate programs and those who implement them.

(3) Change their procedures, thereby countering a protest organization's productive tactics. The response of welfare agencies to NWRO is a good example. The organization attracted many new members by claiming, and proving, that it could help them obtain the special welfare benefits available under "special needs" and "emergency" categories. In response, many local welfare bureaucracies replaced the emergency special-grants system with a flat-grant system, under which all welfare recipients received money, not just members of NWRO. As a result, a key NWRO organizational tactic was canceled out.[44]

Opposition to programs for the poor As we have seen, welfare-state programs often try to deal directly with the discontented in order to disturb as little as possible the more satisfactory political arrangements with other portions of the population. However, this encapsulation strategy does not always work. The War on Poverty Community Action programs are a good example. The very logic of the programs dictated that they would burst the bounds set by their creators. The programs were designed to mobilize and organize the poor to protest their condition and to direct their protest activity at local authorities. But the targets of these protests, especially big-city mayors, were not prepared to be scapegoats in the "larger" interest of social control. They feared for their political lives, and fought successfully to emasculate such programs. Moreover, although the programs aimed at separating black from white ethnic political activity in order to secure the allegiance of both for the Democratic party, this goal was inherently impossible. As the media began to publicize the visible protests that were an integral part of the program, white ethnics countermobilized for a share of the action. Increased taxes for the support of OEO, the inflation caused by the Vietnam war, and the distribution of symbolic satisfactions to the black community, which they felt were denied

[44]*Ibid.*, 195.

to themselves, impelled white ethnics—most of whom were corporate-sector workers—to become vocal antagonists of the Great Society programs. Once these programs began to threaten other political alignments, they had to be reined in, and Congress began a continuing process of limiting the scope of action available to the Executive branch in administering the War on Poverty.

Profit and need   Although the welfare state complements, and is in fact necessary, for the country's advanced capitalist economy, its logic of need is diametrically opposed to the economy's logic of profit. Welfare-state programs are publicly fought over, defended, and legitimized on the basis of the deprivation of one group or another. Carried to its conclusion, as Simmel argued, this logic of need would be satisfied only when structural inequalities are overcome.

Yet welfare-state programs and debates about them take place within a context of corporate capitalism, which is driven by goals of growth and profit. For this reason, French commentator André Gorz has argued that *logically* the welfare state is in "antagonism to the capitalist system. . . . Collective needs are . . . objectively in contradiction to the logic of capitalist development . . . since the welfare sector is necessarily outside of the criteria of profit."[45]

The tension between the two sectors has existed for some time, but the heightening of the fiscal crisis, the intensification of antagonisms between those who distribute and those who receive welfare services, and growing political conflict over the question of who pays for and who benefits from the welfare state make it likely that the contradiction between need and profit will prove increasingly difficult to manage.

Even more importantly, the expansion of the welfare state requires a large surplus of capital for programs that, by themselves, do not turn over a profit and which are not directly productive. Today, because the economic position of the United States is declining in the world market and the size of the state sector is growing much faster than the corporate sector, the funds needed for state programs are not as readily available as in the past. In the past, there were sufficient funds to provide both social capital (which made corporations more productive and profita-

---

[45]André Gorz, *Strategy for Labor* (Boston, 1968), p. 98.

ble) and social expenses (which defused discontent); today, more choices have to be made between these kinds of programs. Thus, programs of social expenses are challenging the imperatives of growth and profit. For this reason, German political sociologist Claus Offe concluded, "the political-administrative system of late capitalist societies, tailored to satisfy in concrete ways the requirements of maintaining the capitalist order, will reveal itself as an alien element."[46] The resolution of this contradiction, as we argue in the next chapter, is in doubt, but the antagonism between a logic of need and a logic of profit may be a promising basis on which to build movements for structural change.

[46]Claus Offe, "The Abolition of Market Control and the Problem of Legitimacy," *Kapitalistate* 1 (1973): 112.

conclusion

14
capitalism, socialism, and democracy

Travelers to the United States have often remarked on the extraordinary diversity and pace of life. In contrast to other industrialized capitalist countries, the most constant feature of American society is change. One American family in four moves every year. One out of every three couples taking out a marriage license today will divorce. Automobile styles change annually. Technological innovations from Teflon pans to precision laser-guided bombs are produced—and discarded—at a rate unmatched by any other nation.

Political change also appears amazingly rapid and widespread. Roughly four-fifths of American workers voted for the presidential candidate of the Democratic party in 1964; over half voted for the Republican candidate in 1972. Until the passage of the Voting Rights Act of 1965, blacks in most Southern states, indeed a majority of blacks in the United States, were denied the right to vote. Today, some Northern and Southern cities have black mayors. Even strongly held and expressed personal opinions shift dramatically. Some of the chief architects of the Vietnam war were expert witnesses for the defense at the 1971 trial of Daniel Ellsberg, who was accused by the government of damaging national security by leaking the Pentagon Papers to the press.

A recent best seller, entitled *Future Shock,* caught this kaleidoscopic whirl and argued that the pace of change had become so rapid that Americans were suffering from an inability to cope.[1] Yet an undifferentiated focus on change is misleading for two reasons. First, by failing to distinguish which changes are significant, it conveys the impression that no change is significant. The blur of constant change seems to add up to an overall stability. Moreover, an undifferentiated focus on change obscures a deeper structural continuity in which the corporate complex shapes the character of American politics. Most news items stress changes occurring; precisely because of its durability, attention is rarely called to structural continuity. Although a police shootout will make the front page of the local newspaper, a description of the control functions of the police or the racial and class composition of those arrested by the police will not. In this chapter, we examine the political challenge posed by rapid change in the United States, the attempt by those in authority to contain change within "acceptable" structural limits, possible alternative future developments, and appropriate strategic responses for those committed to constructing an authentically democratic America.

CONTRADICTIONS AND CHANGE

The mere fact of change—any change—poses a potential challenge to prevailing patterns of dominance. For many years, automobile companies found it profitable to produce ever larger, more expensive automobiles. Unintentionally, however, this decision produced a number of destabilizing consequences. As cars got longer, city streets became inadequate, gasoline consumption and prices went up, and discontent about traffic jams, lack of parking facilities, and the cost of driving increased. As a result, the sale of small imported cars soared and the demand for large automobiles plummeted. American automobile companies suffered, the American dollar was weakened, and American technological and financial dominance were eroded.

[1] Alvin Toffler, *Future Shock* (New York, 1971).

Two other examples: the mechanization and concentration of farming in the South increased output and profits for white Southern landowners. At the same time, these changes in production impelled five million blacks to migrate to northern and western cities in the last thirty years. This basic demographic change has "Southernized" Northern politics. A different kind of change involved the invention of long-playing phonograph records in the 1940s, which made it possible for musical traditions to develop among a vast young audience. Records, are, of course, predominantly a form of entertainment. But in the 1960s, a number of folk singers, including Bob Dylan, Joan Baez, and Phil Ochs, used recordings both to reflect and create cultural change and political protest.

These examples from diverse areas—the corporate pursuit of profit, rural modernization, and cultural innovation—suggest the unexpected ways that apparently nonpolitical changes may produce challenges that potentially threaten basic arrangements of dominance. Potential threats cannot entirely be eliminated unless change itself is totally suppressed—clearly an impossibility. A priority task for political and corporate authorities is to sort out and deal with those changes that are potentially threatening. Conversely, those who oppose patterns of dominance must utilize changes in order to focus political energies on strategies for weakening dominance and promoting democracy.

In this book we have suggested that the character of American politics is shaped by structural inequality—those Americans with meager material resources, status, and political power have fundamentally different interests from those on top. Structure, thus, generates basic conflicts of interest and produces the seeds of its own transformation. At a given time, the political scene appears static. But like a motion picture, a single frame is incapable of expressing all of reality. Over time, structural change occurs as an outcome of the conflicts pregnant in the social structure. These oppositions, or contradictions, are rooted in inequality and provide the motor force for change.

Structural contradictions furnish the framework for politics. It is in the interest of those on top to prevent the emergence of conflicts based on these contradictions, if possible, and to manage the conflicts if necessary. It is in the interest of the majority, on the other hand, to overcome contradictions by challenging the dominant minority and democratizing the social order. But everyday political reality may not appear to correspond directly to the clash of contradictory structural interests. Actual political behavior depends on the ideological and institutional means that the dominant use to protect their position and others use to challenge authorities. These ideological and institutional mechanisms (such as corporate capitalism, Congress and the presidency, dominant and accommodative ideologies, urban mechanisms of control, and the justice system) are filters that mediate between structure and behavior.

At any given historical moment, therefore, there is no automatic, predetermined outcome. Contradictions contain both the seeds of change and of repression. Which outcome will triumph depends preeminently on the mediations that we have discussed in this book. Most of the analysis has focused on how the dominant use ideology and institutions to control changes that challenge their interests. But these varied mechanisms, we have noted, have been undergoing considerable decay.

For example, political parties command the loyalties of followers less and less, Congress is viewed with increasing cynicism by Americans and has become an institution in search of a purpose, the presidency is losing its sacred aura, and the dominant ideology is losing its hold over public consciousness. As a result, people are becoming less attached to established political institutions and are potentially more available for new modes of action. Many have developed accommodative and even opposition ideologies that call for change.

In periods when mechanisms of social control are strong, stability prevails despite structural contradictions. When mechanisms of control decay, however, citizens may see their interests more clearly, act on them, and begin to make history. This does not mean that structural change will necessarily occur: rulers may develop new mechanisms of control to manage new challenges. On the other hand, rulers may fail to contain the challenge. In a period of decaying ideology and institutions, contradictions sharpen and the future is more open.

In the United States, we are living in such a period. Without trying to make a precise prediction of what the future may hold, we can distinguish three contrasting possible outcomes, which are based on the dominant, accommodative, and opposition ideologies described in Chapter 11.

DOMINANT OUTCOME: SUCCESSFUL REPRESSION

If the dominant ideology prevails and the dominant outcome occurs in the future, the corporate complex will expand its control even further over other sectors of the economy, particularly small business, industry, and agriculture. The top few hundred corporations will control virtually the entire productive apparatus. The interpenetration of corporate capitalism and the state will become even closer. This economic Goliath will be capped by an enormous planning apparatus to coordinate manpower, raw materials, capital, and demand in the interests of the minority controlling the complex. More and more, costs will be socialized (borne by the whole community in terms of taxes, destruction of the environment, and cost of public education to train the work force), while profits will remain in private hands. Within the state, the executive branch will grow larger and more powerful.

The majority of the population will come to depend either on jobs in the corporate sector or on welfare payments from the state. The first group will be a skilled proletariat—engineers, statisticians, professors, electricians, computer programmers, and welfare workers—that will receive benefits and status from the corporate complex without having authority on the job or significant political power. The second group will consist of the productively useless. They will be dependent for their subsistence on government programs: medical aid, food allowances, cash transfer payments, rent subsidies. They will thus represent a politically impotent clientele of the corporate complex. Alongside the large productive sector, therefore, will be a growing social-welfare complex consisting of welfare bureaucrats who dispense government largesse and exercise social control over much of the population. The state will contract out many welfare activities to the corporate sector. As with the lucrative military procurement policies of the government, the corporate sector will benefit lavishly. Thus, this new arrangement will provide a guaranteed demand for corporate output and an additional outlet for the investment of surplus capital.

To replace the decaying instruments of control of the past, rulers will develop forms of repression adapted to a monolithic, rationalized, centralized social structure. Broadly, these will be of two kinds: hard and soft. Physical repression—surveillance techniques, "crowd control," police and military weapons—will become more technologically sophisticated and efficient. Police and military personnel will interpenetrate society, and the distinction between military and police forces will fade. Hints of dissent will be rooted out and crushed. The population, if unruly, will be treated like captives of a conquered province.

Soft measures of institutional repression will consist of increased inauthentic participation and symbolic control. The population will be manipulated to join organizations that will give them the illusion of power without the reality. Rigged by the dominant, these organizations will utilize the paraphernalia of democracy—debate, elections, investigations, petitions, and resolutions—to convince the majority that they are participating in an open, legitimate, democratic political and economic system. These organizations may include neighborhood councils, professional associations, university senates, welfare clients' consultative committees, and shopfloor workers' committees. Despite the appearance, the result will be a further decline of democracy in America.

The corporate complex will become more adept at shaping values that sustain structural arrangements. Schools and media will more loudly proclaim the democratic virtues and material benefits of the corporate order. Culture will increasingly be controlled by the powerful and directed at maintaining happy political conformity. Entertainment and news will be almost indistinguishable, as news becomes mythologized and entertainment holds forth an idealized, perverted picture of reality. The outward forms of civil liberties may remain—free speech, free press, and rights of assembly—but the substance will be eroded. Dominant values will crowd out accommodative and opposition ideologies. Those on top will seek to direct the resentments, frustrations, and grievances inevitably generated by this system of privilege not against the system as a whole or against those in authority but against fellow subordinates: blacks versus whites; welfare recipients versus skilled workers; neighborhoods versus impotent city governments.

A number of factors point to the likelihood of this outcome. The most persuasive piece of evidence is that much of what has been described already exists, and if some present trends continue uninterrupted, the dominant outcome might be the result. In previous chapters, we have described the increase in corporate concentration and control in past decades and the rise of the state in this century as a central economic participant. The presidency has become much more centralized and the executive branch of government increasingly influential. The state-welfare sector is the fastest growing segment of the economy. Police repression is an increasingly familiar feature of American life. New mechanisms of social control have been developed. Political trials and government intimidation of the media have partially succeeded in stifling the emergence of alternative ideologies.

Since the dominant outcome is obviously in the interests of those on top, and given the increasing challenges and the decay of existing mediations, it is not unthinkable that the dominant will try to protect their interests even at the expense of democracy. Moreover, the ability of most Americans to resist the dominant outcome will be limited. There is a continuing wide disparity in institutional and ideological resources available to the dominant and potential challengers. Those mediations that remain powerful as mechanisms of social control—the media, the police, the courts—are largely in the hands of those on top. Most Americans will lack sufficient wealth, organizational resources, and influence to prevent a complete takeover by the dominant.

In the absence of countertrends our analysis could stop here. Fortunately, though, this is not the case. The record of the past few years is by no means simply one of increasing control by the powerful. Alongside the trends discussed above, there is evidence of increasing anger, resistance, and opposition by a growing number of Americans. Important new countermovements have emerged: union insurgencies against both corporate and established union leaders, black-power movements, and consumer- and welfare-rights organizations, to name only a few.

Corporate and state officials are not all-powerful, as witnessed by the decaying of traditional institutional and ideological mediations. Moreover, the new mechanisms that rulers have devised to replace decaying institutions of the past have thus far proven less successful in manipulating the population. Professional bureaucracies at the city level are adept at disbursing state benefits, and professional campaign agencies can package candidates efficiently—but neither is as effective as the former party machine in organizing participation. Thus, the new institutional means of control may not be able to contain structural contradictions.

We have argued that democratic procedures alone are insufficient to assure substantive democracy. But procedural democracy does set limits that, if adhered to, would retard the emergence of the dominant outcome. Watergate and Nixon's forced resignation indicate that public and corporate officials at the highest levels may suffer the consequences of gross violations of the law. The press may reveal details of surveillance, corruption, and physical abuse by those in authority. However manipulated and controlled, elections provide a chance for challenging those in control. Guarantees of free speech and press as well as formal justice may be used to develop alternatives for seeing and understanding reality. In short, the formal democracy that rulers use to legitimize their positions may be turned back against them.

ACCOMMODATIONIST OUTCOME:
PIECEMEAL CHALLENGE AND RESPONSE

In the accommodationist outcome, the corporate complex will remain in control but will face increasing problems and challenges to its power. Small businessmen and farmers, burdened by higher taxes and the administered prices of the corporate sector, will use their available resources (control of local and state governments, the illusion of free enterprise, and access to congressmen and parts of the executive branch) to resist further corporate expansion and state interference. The state will attempt to extend its area of control over other productive sectors both in order to carry out the function of rationalization and coordination more efficiently and to increase the power of state officials. State regulations will proliferate, and state capital will be used to extend the reach of the corporate complex. Small businessmen and farmers will become dependent on state largesse (small business loans, agricultural subsidies).

A host of new groups will clamor for help from the government. Corporate capitalists will need massive inputs of state capital for advanced technological projects. Small capital will need government in order to defend itself from corporate encroachment. The state sector will flourish as government activities expand. Corporate-sector workers will seek help from the state in order to obtain higher wages, better social security programs, and better working conditions. Surplus labor and workers in the small capital sector will become more vulnerable and hence come to depend on government even for basic amenities. As more and more Americans come to be consumers of vital government services and depend on government bureaucracies, citizens will feel powerless, resentful, and angry.

The growing contradictions in the economy will be expressed in a turbulent, issue-oriented ad hoc politics of increasing fragmentation and bitterness. On the one hand, many Americans will be increasingly discontent with the hand they are dealt and increasingly prone to challenge authorities. Within the productive sphere, workers' discontents will burst the bounds of institutionalized class politics. Workers will demonstrate anger toward corporate authorities by high turnover rates, absenteeism, wildcat strikes, and plant sabotage; toward union leaders by challenging them in union elections. Many state and professional employees will use the strike weapon as they never have before. Blacks will use expressive violence, guerrilla tactics, and sustained militant organization to challenge internal colonialism. Tenant associations, welfare-rights groups, and environmental-protection organizations will mount political campaigns. In the electoral sphere, voters will be increasingly frustrated in their efforts to utilize traditional channels of representation. The result may be either a further decline in voting turnout (thus discrediting the idea that the system is democratically chosen) or the emergence of new political movements seeking change.

Throughout the society, then, there will be pressure points where particular groups will strain against the bounds of established arrangements. Yet this protest activity, informed by an accommodative ideology, will direct its anger to particular authorities within particular spheres. It will not add up to a structural critique or structural challenge. Protest will remain fragmented, uncoordinated, and ephemeral, and it will often be directed at other subordinates (for example, white ethnic workers in the corporate sector against small-capital–sector blacks).

In face of these variegated challenges, authorities will improvise tactical and institutional responses. A rent strike may be met by a combination of court-ordered convictions, police har-

rassment, and apparently conciliatory gestures—an offer to negotiate, appointment of a study commission, and a soothing pro-
nouncement by a local city official. Authorities will constantly use
the arsenal of repressive techniques available to them and devise
new responses to fit particular challenges. The effect will be one
resembling the frenetic activity of a fire department—each day
brings new crises. The resulting stalemate will add up neither to a
secure victory for the dominant nor to structural change.

Evidence for the ascendancy of the accommodationist outcome begins with the fact that it is happening already. Merely
open any daily newspaper for confirmation. Within recent years,
the following series of crises have been solemnly proclaimed by
political leaders, only to disappear from sight once the challenging group was disarmed: urban crisis, environment crisis, welfare
crisis, energy crisis, moral crisis, law-and-order crisis, balance-
of-payments crisis, and racial crisis. These crises are definitions
by authorities of the ad hoc politics we described. They are crises
for two reasons: they are manifestations of contradictions rooted
in the social structure; and, from the vantage point of those on
top, they potentially threaten existing patterns of dominance.

The emergence of new bases of inequality increases the
probability of the accommodationist outcome. Welfare programs,
for example, create two antagonistic groups—recipients and
welfare bureaucrats. Similarly, the integration of universities into
the corporate complex sets students and junior faculty against
senior faculty and the administration. But each conflict is relatively self-contained, with its own autonomous set of issues,
actors, institutions, and dynamics.

Although in the long run the accommodationist approach
only patches up holes temporarily, in the short run it is likely to
persist. Once the dynamic of ad hoc politics is set into motion, it
tends to reproduce itself as more and more people become
involved in "irregular politics," develop an accommodationist
ideology, and discover their ability to challenge authorities.
Demands achieved or denied generate new demands; awareness
of grievances in one area may make individuals more aware of
discontents in others. The result is a whirligig of action and
reaction, challenge and repression.

Finally, the accommodationist alternative has been buttressed by the development of a problems-oriented social
science. Prompted in large part by the need of authorities for solu-

tions to particular challenges, economists, sociologists, political scientists, systems analysts, social planners, and policy analysts have churned out studies and technical solutions for each "crisis." Typically, they analyze the problem from authorities' points of view and adopt an apparently neutral, clinical perspective that in fact blurs fundamental structural conflicts.

However, the accommodationist alternative is inherently unstable, both for dominants and subordinates. At multiple pressure points in the system, authorities find themselves challenged by increasingly militant and irate subordinates. They are constantly tempted to abandon democratic procedures, escalate repression, and choose the dominant outcome in an attempt to eliminate challenge once and for all. For subordinates, a contrary dynamic is set in motion: demands and grievances pile up. As they are met by institutional and symbolic repression, authorities become increasingly unmasked. Thus, what begins as fragmented, accommodationist protest can escalate into coherent, broad-based opposition.

As a result, the accommodationist outcome, although a strong possibility in the near future, is not likely to be permanent. The fragile equilibrium of the accommodationist outcome may collapse as a result either of authorities trying to intensify control through the dominant outcome or of an oppositionist movement gaining the strength to achieve structural change.

OPPOSITION OUTCOME:
STRUCTURAL CHANGE AND SOCIALISM

Both the dominant and the accommodationist outcomes are based on the *preservation* of the structural inequalities rooted in American capitalism. By contrast, the opposition outcome represents an elimination of structural inequalities. In this respect, the opposition outcome is not simply "more of the same." Instead, it represents a qualitative change in the social structure and political processes, with a corresponding change in the everyday lives of American citizens. Put another way, the opposition outcome takes democracy seriously. It consists of substantive as well as procedural democracy. It democratizes decisions not only in the sphere of government but in the spheres of the economy and society.

As we have suggested in this book, the key place to begin an analysis of structural transformation is the country's productive apparatus. The way a society produces its goods and the choice of goods it produces fundamentally shape the social and political life of the society.

At present, as we have seen in Chapter 3, basic decisions for the whole American economy regarding what will be produced, the conditions of production, wages, and the setting of prices are largely controlled by a group no larger than the population of a small town. These men, as we have seen, are unrepresentative both of the American population generally and of workers within the productive sector. The direction of movement, then, from present arrangements to the opposition outcome is clear: toward democratization of control over production, distribution, and consumption. The shift from present arrangements to the opposition outcome represents a shift from corporate capitalism to democratic socialism. What might this mean?

Among the critical points at which democratization is necessary in order to overcome present structural contradictions and achieve socialism are the overall allocation of resources to the production of goods and services; the work place of production of goods (for example, factories) and services (universities, hospitals, welfare agencies, banks); the point of consumption of goods and services; and the realm of culture and values.

Presently, the corporate complex—executives of the top corporations, the very wealthy, and top officials of the executive branch of the federal government—decide how resources are allocated. Decisions are made not on the basis of the greatest social needs but on the basis of highest profits. Although all Americans are affected, those who have the greatest needs participate least in decisions and benefits. The opposition outcome (or socialism) would reverse these priorities by democratizing decisions regarding America's productive capacity. In the present arrangement, although the costs of production are socialized, major benefits are appropriated by a minority. In the opposition outcome, costs would be borne more equitably by the whole community and benefits would be socialized—shared by members of the community on the basis of their needs.

Once America's productive capacity is democratized and no longer controlled by the corporate complex, the uses made of that capacity will also be transformed. The actions of the corporate complex have produced socially disastrous results: poverty, militarism, urban squalor, racism, sexism, destruction of resources, and the proliferation of destructive and wasteful products. Under socialism, full importance would be given to the social consequences of production. Instead of the principal criterion being production for profit and the maintenance of inequality between those who own and control capital and those who work for a wage, the principal criterion in the opposition outcome would be production for the purpose of diminishing human misery and serving human need. Scarce resources would be directed where social need—not private profit—is greatest. For example, socialism would radically alter the balance between individual and collective transport. A system of transportation built around the automobile is more wasteful, costly, and dangerous than public transport by train, bus, or (for short distances) bicycle or walking. If the tight grip of the automobile lobby were broken, cities could be wrested away from automobiles and returned to people, and the resources presently squandered on automobiles, highways, and gasoline could be used to maintain a high-quality system of low-cost (or possibly even free) public transport. (The total cost to the community of transporting people by public transport is a small fraction of present transportation costs built around the automobile.)

Another example: in a capitalist economy, technological advances—such as air travel, xerography, computers, television—often become the basis for privately-controlled, profitable new industries. In a socialist economy, technological innovations would be democratically controlled and used to benefit the whole community. As an illustration, cable television could be used to decentralize communication and foster creativity through inexpensive local productions of news, entertainment, and performing arts programs. It would be relatively simple to devise a system of access to cable television whereby technical assistance and broadcasting time would be allotted to community groups. Yet corporate advertisers, television networks, and local broadcasters (in alliance with the Federal Communications Commission) have mostly succeeded until now in limiting the democratic potential of cable television.

What would be the concrete mechanisms for making decisions under socialism? While the precise shape of such arrangements must be developed in practice—socialism is not a ready-made blueprint to be mechanically applied, nor do we want to impose our own view—some guidelines are possible. Various groups whose needs are not presently considered—workers, consumers, women, ethnic minorities—would be represented in democratic decision making. Machinery could be developed at all levels—community, state, and national—to represent groups in the decision-making process. One example is the French planning process.[2] Planning commissions are organized on the basis of the whole nation, of specialized sectors (particular industries, scientific research, and so on), and by regions. The commissions bring together representatives of producers, consumers, workers, and government to recommend goals and suggest how to allocate resources for the French economy.

The shift in procedures for making basic decisions over the allocation of productive resources involves a changed view of government. Presently, many of the most important decisions shaping the society are not regarded as political. Judged by the extent to which their decisions affect our lives, the top management of United States Steel and Minnesota Mining and Manufacturing are no less powerful than the mayor of Atlanta or the governor of Arizona. Yet what the latter do is considered political and what the former do is considered outside the public domain. The opposition outcome would reflect a more accurate view of what is political. Moreover, it would recognize that even what is presently considered public—the activities of government—serve private interests by strengthening corporate capitalism and reproducing structural inequalities. Democratizing decisions over the use of productive resources reflects the recognition of the widened sphere of politics in an advanced industrial age.

The socialist outcome would democratize the work place of production. Presently, control over those who work to produce goods and services is from the top down: managers receive their authority from those who own and control the means of production and exercise that authority in undemocratic fashion over workers. The clearest example is in factories, where workers are rigidly controlled and continuously overseen by foremen. But by and large, all workers, including white-collar and professional

[2]Stephen S. Cohen, *Modern Capitalist Planning: The French Model* (Cambridge, Mass., 1969). The example is limited by the fact that France remains a capitalist society; private business interests remain powerful and often ally with government representatives on the planning commissions to dominate the planning process.

workers, are in basically the same powerless situation. Although their situation may be obscured by higher status, higher pay, and more routine discretion on the job, they do not participate in basic management decisions any more than manual workers.

Socialism would reverse this situation by replacing the top-down principle with the principle of collective democratic decision making by the workers. Such a principle is already in operation in factories in many countries—including Sweden, China, Cuba, and Yugoslavia. For example, in a Volvo automobile plant in Sweden (a country whose political system contains features of both capitalism and socialism), the traditional assembly line is a thing of the past. Labor unions helped develop the overall organization of the factory, and workers helped plan the assembly process. Instead of a worker having to repeat mindlessly the same operation for months, teams of workers, responsible for specified quotas, are free to divide up tasks and determine the pace of work. As a result, workers can vary tasks, exercise ingenuity in the work process, mingle with their co-workers on the job, and alternate work and rest. Each team of workers, numbering from fifteen to twenty five, has a comfortably furnished lounge, equipped with refrigerator and sauna. The result of the radically transformed work process is that workers are relaxed and cheerful at the end of the working day. Yet the cost of the factory is only 10 percent more than the traditional automobile assembly plant, and even this extra investment is offset by low absenteeism and high output.[3] The Volvo example demonstrates that it is not technological obstacles that prevent worker control on the job but resistance by owners and managers in a capitalist economy.

Under existing arrangements, control over consumption is from the top down: regulations regarding eligibility for welfare, the choice of what goods shall be produced and how they shall be advertised, price-setting, tax policies to pay for government services, and the allocation of resources within the society as a whole to various uses—all these decisions are made by those who control the production of goods and services rather than by those who use them. With the exception of the wealthy and powerful, the customer is rarely king. In the socialist outcome, consumers would share in the process of controlling production and distribu-

---

[3]*Le Monde,* June 11, 1974; Tom Wicker, "A Plant Built for Workers," *New York Times,* May 21, 1974, and Tom Wicker, "People vs. Production," *New York Times,* May 24, 1974.

tion. Thus, hospital patients, university students, and shoppers would not be treated as passive recipients but would have the opportunity to participate in decisions regarding the goods and services that these institutions dispense. For example, within the university, students would share responsibility for planning the curriculum, and for hiring and promoting staff members. This system of authentic participation contrasts with the present system of inauthentic student participation in such forums as student government, whose powers are miniscule, or university senates, where students are in a tiny minority

Democratizing consumption also means demystifying specialization. Much of what passes for specialized knowledge is in fact the jealously guarded preserve of "professionals" who privatize knowledge for profit and status. In the opposition outcome, the unnecessary gap between "professionals" and "laymen" would narrow, and consumers would become less dependent on specialists to whom they now look for a host of goods and services. Automobile repairing and health care are two areas where this is true. Most citizens are presently helpless in face of malfunctions of their cars and bodies. Yet many disorders could be diagnosed and repaired by a person of average intelligence with a minimal amount of training. In both fields, to be sure, some disorders require specialized treatment, which only someone with longer training is qualified to dispense. But citizens can also learn the limits of their knowledge and, thus, know when they need to refer to a specialist.

How will citizens become self-reliant rather than hopelessly dependent on the services of others? One effective way would be through a change in socialization. Schools would teach basic skills necessary for dealing with the natural and physical environment. As in the Israeli kibbutz and the Chinese commune, the artificial split between "mind-work" and "physical-work" as well as the cleavage between city and country would diminish. Physical work would not be considered demeaning, and the narrow specialization that produces reliance on experts would decrease. In a more general way, socialism would nurture different motivations and values. Capitalist socialization encourages the search for material acquisition, makes waste a virtue, and emphasizes such values as competitiveness and obedience. Socialist socialization would encourage the search for spiritual fulfillment and stress the values of cooperation and self-reliance.

In the United States today, racial relations are geared to a dual labor market that confines most black workers to the small-capital and surplus-labor sectors: blacks still have the worst jobs, the lowest salaries, the meanest housing, and the least control over their lives and neighborhoods. In addition, they are subject to daily discrimination from sources ranging from neighborhood policemen to the dominant culture that denigrates, trivializes, or ignores the black society.

The opposition outcome would strive to eliminate these expressions of inequality. For example, it would end economic arrangements that confine most blacks to the small-capital and surplus-labor sectors of the economy. In the newly organized economy, they would have equal access to all jobs. This goal cannot be accomplished simply by outlawing racial discrimination in hiring. It will also be necessary to recognize that race has been a fundamental basis of inequality for hundreds of years and that economic equalization requires direct positive measures such as compensatory programs in education, health care, and job placement.

The dominant culture has always had a virulent strain of racism that, in the opposition outcome, would be replaced by authentic cultural diversity. Underpinned by economic equality, this diversity would be reflected in society at large as well as in newspapers, radio and television, schools, and the entertainment industry. Blacks would not lose their cultural identity (unless they so chose) but would become an ethnic group that could take pride in its heritage.

Socialism would strive to overcome sexist practices and attitudes in the United States. As a first step, discrimination in the labor market would cease: women would have the same opportunity as men to attain challenging employment. Publicly-provided day-care centers would enable those who chose to take jobs outside the home. In a far-reaching way, sexist attitudes and conceptions, which presently demean both women and men, would be transformed: American society would deemphasize the "machismo" virtues of domination, acquisition, and "toughness." Although the nuclear family might persist, cooperative living arrangements would be freely available for those who chose. (American communes and the Israeli kibbutz suggest the range of possibilities.)

The opposition outcome would attempt to transform America's relationship to the world. Just as socialism would democratize the control and use of productive resources within the United States, so in the international sphere it would employ America's immense resources to benefit, not control, those in other countries. At the present time, a capitalist America aims at producing or maintaining stable capitalist regimes that are usually repressive and often dependent on American military and economic support. A socialist America would ally with democratic, egalitarian forces abroad rather than with undemocratic forces. Note, however, that the opposition outcome would involve a cutback in wasteful consumption by Americans, who would relinquish privileges that have come with global dominance.

Socialism is not a shopping bag of improvements but a coherent system. Capitalism in America has changed in important respects, but its fundamental features remain the same. In contrast to the dominant and accommodationist outcomes, which retain the capitalist framework, socialism represents a radical break with present arrangements. Whereas capitalism is based on profit, inequality, and the split between capital and labor, socialism is based on human need, equality, a sharing of control over the community's productive capacity, and an equitable distribution of benefits.

This does not mean that socialism would usher in a utopia where "correct" decisions would always be made and all compulsion and injustice eliminated. Some current hardships, such as disagreeable tasks, the social costs of industrial production, and the dehumanizing effects of bureaucracy, would persist—albeit to a lesser degree. New questions would arise, for example, how to allocate resources. Socialism would not signify the end of political conflict—struggle is rooted in the human condition. But the likelihood of meeting basic human needs equitably and reducing compulsion and injustice would be greater under socialism than under corporate capitalism.

At the present time, there is no democratic socialist society in the world to serve as a model. It is necessary to choose selectively from other countries where successful experiments can be identified and to develop new theoretical possibilities appropriate to the unique conditions in the United States. Yet the fact that a prototype does not exist is no cause for despair. As the wealthiest, most powerful, and most technologically advanced society in history, the United States has a rare opportunity to help diminish suffering and domination in the world and to contribute to the liberation of mankind. At an earlier stage in history, the United States delivered a revolutionary message to the world. As the fulfillment of the democratic promise, socialism would represent a rebirth of this message.

It is important to correct some common misconceptions about socialism. Socialism need not be a system of state control, in which large corporations are taken over by government and run pretty much as they were before, nor does it mean that an all-powerful state and party apparatus would regulate every aspect of life and create a drab uniformity of taste, dress, and culture. Instead, democratic socialism would radically enlarge the sphere of citizen participation and decision making at all levels. People would seek individual goals and would not be mere automatons in a totalitarian society. Indeed, under socialism, individuality and privacy could flourish more than under present conditions of apparent cultural freedom, where, in fact, tastes are largely rigged by the advertising, entertainment, popular music, clothing, and communications industries.

Will the opposition outcome benefit all members of the society? Of course not. Precisely because socialism aims at abolishing privilege, it follows that those who presently are privileged will be deprived of their dominance. But by a democratic accounting scheme in which everyone counts equally, most Americans will benefit from structural change.

Let us review here, too, the possibilities for and against socialism in America.

Structural inequality is rooted in corporate capitalism. Fundamental inequalities can be temporarily maintained; they cannot, however, be eliminated short of structural change. The fact that conflict and change are contained should not obscure the persistence of underlying contradictions. As we noted early in the chapter, traditional mediations that have prevented the emergence of full-scale structural conflict have been decaying, leaving rulers more vulnerable to challenge.

As opposed to any time since the New Deal, the recent past has been a time of political and social turmoil. Each of the struggles discussed in the accommodationist outcome implicitly contains the seeds of an opposition outcome. Wildcat strikes place issues of workers' control ahead of higher wages. Insurgencies within unions challenge the locked-in arrangements that tie union leaders to the corporate complex. Radical caucuses within professional associations—American Medical Association, American Economics Association, American Bar Association—challenge patterns of control within the professions and seek to overcome the distance between professional and client. The women's movement, which began as a protest against job discrimination, has developed a more total structural analysis of the subordinate place of women in American capitalism. Similarly, protest against the Vietnam war broadened into a thoroughgoing critique of militarism and the corporate complex abroad. This adds up to evidence both of increasing protest of a particular nature and of an incipient opposition movement.

As varied struggles develop, formerly segmented groups begin to see shared interests. Relatively powerless workers are also powerless consumers. Cumulative inequality is especially great in the case of blacks, chicanos, and American Indians. The dominant have become a more homogeneous group as the corporate sector and the state have fused into the corporate complex. Thus, at both the top and bottom of the social structure interests are coalescing. The likelihood of structural change increases as the gulf between the two camps becomes wider and clearer.

There is an increasing rapidity and ease with which those sharing interests may communicate. The mass media, especially television, make it possible for individuals sharing interests within the same sector to reach each other and a much broader constituency. At the same time, the media break down the isolation of different groups. Chicanos become aware of black struggles, and both became aware of the welfare-rights movement. The media also bring authorities down to vulnerable human size. Through the media's extensive coverage of Watergate, Americans learned that "The President" and his most trusted colleagues were capable of venality, corruption, and criminal conduct.

Changes in the international and economic spheres have sharpened contradictions in the United States. During a brief period following the Second World War, the United States was in a uniquely privileged position in the world. The only major industrial power not to suffer war damage, the United States was also able—through its military, economic, and political advantages—to command a plentiful supply of raw materials on favorable terms. The result was the largest economic boom in world history.

As long as the economy continued to grow, the basic structural cleavage between capital and labor in the United States could be masked. Materially, a larger economic "pie" meant more jobs, better wages, and growing numbers of consumer goods—television sets, washing machines, and automobiles. Ideologically, an expanding economy fostered the belief that all could benefit from economic advances and that economic inequality could be redressed without political struggle.

Beginning in the late 1960s, however, this privileged situation based on international dominance became less secure. Other industrial powers (Western Europe and Japan) narrowed the economic gap separating them from the United States. United States military dominance was challenged both as a result of advances in weaponry by the USSR and by America's unsuccessful attempt to impose its will in Indochina. The era of cheap and abundant commodities—most dramatically, petroleum, but also food, fertilizer, and other raw materials—has come to an end. As a result, inflation and scarcity have developed, manifested most clearly by a slowdown of economic growth and sharply rising prices. The economic "pie" is no longer growing rapidly, and most Americans have found their "slices" getting smaller. There is no longer a plentiful supply of jobs, as both the college graduate and the high-school dropout have been discovering. Even many with good jobs find that wage hikes are more than offset by the rise in the cost of living: when inflation is at the rate of 10 percent annually, a wage gain of 7 percent a year results in a loss of real wages. The dilemma is compounded by the fact that without opportunities for expansion, the tendency is for a capitalist system to stagnate.

Such a situation produces heightened inequalities. Those who are better off are "cushioned" against a decline in living standards; those who are rich can remain oblivious. In 1974, the president of General Motors was granted a $50,000 raise, bringing his yearly income to over $900,000; at the other extreme, during the five-year period from 1969 to 1974, welfare grants in New York City remained constant despite the fact that food and housing costs increased by over 40 percent. Most Americans are somewhere between these extremes—but closer to the welfare recipient than to the president of GM. A school teacher, policeman, or Air Force colonel earn incomes above the median. Yet all have seen a decline in their purchasing power (real wages) in the past five years. Thus, for most Americans, it is no longer true that their standard of living grows year by year.

It is impossible to conceal these economic realities. The period has ended when glib pronouncements can be made about the fabulous success of American capitalism and the inevitability of growing affluence for most Americans. As this realization becomes widespread, the potential for an opposition movement that can unite American wage earners and unemployed against the corporate complex is increased.

Despite the wide-ranging evidence indicating that the opposition outcome is a possibility, it is far from a certainty. The commanding heights of the productive apparatus, the state, the means of physical force (police, army), and institutions of socialization (media, schools, government) remain firmly in the control of the corporate complex. Challenges have not gone unmet. A far-ranging program of repression has already been mounted: police violence, expansion and rationalization of police forces, political trials, harrassment of the media, and surveillance of political opponents and potential revolutionaries. In the White House of the early 1970s, no measure was excluded from consideration—no matter how illegal or unconstitutional. Examples of actions considered or authorized by the president, drawn from transcriptions of the taped presidential conversations Nixon released in 1974 in an unsuccessful attempt to stay in office, included paying "hush money" to Watergate defendants, committing perjury, falsely invoking national security to cover up the investigation, promising executive clemency to defendants in return for their silence, and obstructing criminal investigation of the Watergate affair. While a wave of popular revulsion against official misconduct was set off by the impeachment proceedings against President Nixon, there was little mobilization to achieve substantive democracy. Moreover, indignation concerned the measures taken against established groups, not against those more fully opposed to the status quo.

The repression of opposition movements will not be without support. Many Americans have—or believe they have—a stake in existing arrangements. The position of the United States as the most privileged country in the world continues to provide many Americans with benefits. Many communities are dependent for their livelihood on high military spending. Many workers fear that structural change would threaten the niche they have found for themselves in society: white-collar workers believe it is in their interest to stress what divides them from manual workers; organized labor presses for advantages over small-capital workers and the unemployed. Even those Americans with serious grievances find it hard to favor structural change.

In the absence of a mass movement, there is little to convince workers and consumers that they share common interests and that under a different system they would be better off. Structural change requires a well-organized mass opposition movement that links diverse sectors. But at the earliest appearance of tendencies in such a direction, the dominant employ repressive techniques and the incipient movement is quashed.

THE NECESSITY FOR CHOICE:
A STRATEGY FOR CHANGE

There are critical turning points in history. Most observers agree we are living in such an era. It is common to hear terms like *the crisis of the West, the post-industrial society,* and *the crisis of authority.* Ours is an age of flux; whatever the future holds, it will be very different from the present. As sociologist Daniel Bell has pointed out, the sense is present that "in Western society, we are in the midst of a vast historical change in which old social relations (which are property-bound), existing power structures (centered on narrow elites), and bourgeois culture (based on notions of restraint and delayed gratification) are being rapidly eroded."[4]

Given the fact that we are living at a turning point in history, the question is not whether change will come or whether we should favor present arrangements or new ones but rather what kind of change will come and what we can do to help bring about the particular changes that we favor. For, to choose not to act is also to make a choice—to let history carry you where others choose.

We have delineated the three possible outcomes and have

[4]Daniel Bell, *The Coming of Post-Industrial Society* (New York, 1973), p. 37.

tried to present the evidence for and against the likelihood of each. Clearly, our attitude toward the three is not neutral. Indeed, neutrality is impossible: it means choosing to oppose the opposition outcome since that choice requires active struggle.

Unless one is prepared to defend privilege, inequality, and repression, one is forced to reject the dominant outcome. The real choice, then, is between an accommodationist and an opposition outcome. Between the two, the accommodationist outcome might appear the more sensible, prudent, reasonable, and responsible. It would focus on what appear to be the most pressing and flagrant problems in America—racial discrimination, environmental pollution, poverty, and malfeasance in high places. For each problem, it would offer a reasoned solution. It would attempt to minimize disruption by leaving much unchanged.

We have tried to apply a rigorous and demanding standard in this book, one which requires democratizing areas of human activity (such as production) ignored by the accommodationist perspective. Even if one conceded the goals of substantive democracy or socialism were impossible to attain, it would be a useful exercise to analyze the ways in which American practice falls short of the democratic ideal. An additional reason for using the standard of substantive democracy linked to socialism is to avoid complacency about the United States. The tendency toward self-congratulation, common in the United States, often functions to permit inequalities to persist or even increase. (During the 1970s, for example, income inequalities increased between the rich and poor.) By striving for the democratic ideal, one may at least achieve greater improvements or reduce antidemocratic developments. The absence of such a vision may only make matters worse.

And yet we do not agree that to be realistic requires preferring the accommodationist to the opposition outcome. The accommodationist outcome may not always be the most responsible or effective choice. Politics becomes a never-ending quest for solutions to one problem after another—racial discrimination and poverty in the early 1960s, the Vietnam war later in the decade, and, after that, environmental pollution. Note, however, a distressing fact: none of these questions on the accommodationist agenda was really resolved. As political scientist Michael Parenti has pointed out, despite the accommodationist struggles of the 1960s things are getting worse, not better. As opposed to a decade ago, there are more, not less people living in poverty today, more substandard housing, more environmental pollution and devastation, more deficiencies in our schools, hospitals, and systems of public transportation, more military dictatorships throughout the world feeding on the largesse and power of the Pentagon, more people from Thailand to Brazil to Greece to Chicago suffering the social oppression and political repression of an American-based status quo.[5]

In a similar fashion, New Deal reforms, adopted as the result of mass pressure over the resistance of most business groups, provided government protection for corporate workers, social security benefits, and some measure of economic stability. Yet the ultimate significance of the New Deal era (one of the most fruitful accommodationist reform periods in American history) was to strengthen corporate capitalism and postpone a thorough confrontation of its inequities.

The accommodationist approach misunderstands the basic characteristics of the corporate complex. As we have seen throughout this book, the particular "ills" of American society are closely intertwined with the activities of the corporate complex. The routine operation of the corporate complex generates class inequality, the misuse of resources, and an elaborate military apparatus. However flexible the corporate complex may seem to be in particular areas, its fundamental requisite is the concentration of capital in private hands and a work force that sells its labor for a wage to those in control. This requirement sets the outer limit to accommodationist reform and accounts for the failure of accommodationist struggles. No amount of tinkering can deal with the source of America's problems—the basic cleavage between capital and labor.

Why then does government choose to be bound to the imperatives of corporate capitalism? Granted that government derives its revenues from corporate production. But a society does not have to be organized within a capitalist framework. Production can occur, jobs made available, and living standards secured in a socialist economy. Indeed, as we suggested earlier, a socialist order could minimize costs and democratize benefits. In theory, then, there are no barriers to government acting as the

[5]Michael Parenti, "The Possibilities for Political Change," *Politics and Society* 1 (November 1970): 86.

spokesman for the majority and helping to bring about the opposition outcome.

In practice, however, an opposition outcome can only occur as the result of struggle by a broad-based opposition movement. Yet the integration of the state and corporate capitalism means that government actions are designed to prevent rather than facilitate this result. Socialist thinker and activist Michael Harrington points out, "As long as the system is dominated by private corporations and wealth, that fact will tend in the long run to make all collectivist measures discriminate in favor of the status quo."[6] In earlier chapters we have seen how government programs in housing, transportation, and education provide more benefits for the well-off than the poor. Hence, it is unrealistic to expect state action to remedy injustice in America.

Thus, our analysis leaves us no alternative. Among the three outcomes, the truly responsible choice is the opposition outcome.

The job of the activist only begins with the choice of the socialist outcome. The next step is to translate that choice into action: to develop a strategy that will achieve the goal of socialism effectively and responsibly. André Gorz has suggested a strategy geared to advanced capitalist societies. It revolves around the notion of *structural reform:* the posing of demands that utilize the rhetoric and machinery of procedural democracy to stretch structural limits.[7] An example would be a demand by workers in collective bargaining not simply for higher wages but for control over aspects of production that have been left solely to management, such as the speed of the assembly line, authority over firing, and wage differentials between white-collar and manual workers. This strategy counterposes a logic of need (socialism) to the logic of production for profit (capitalism). It uses the machinery of procedural democracy in order to broaden the sphere of substantive democracy.

Posing structural demands does not mean that they will be met. In fact, the reverse is more likely. Demands will not be conceded as gestures of good will, on the basis of superior intellectual argument, or as a response to the logic of need. Too much is at stake. But it is useful to pose these demands whether or not they are met. If they are not, authorities demonstrate that

[6]Michael Harrington, *Socialism* (New York, 1972), p. 242.
[7]André Gorz, *Strategy for Labor* (New York, 1967), part one.

they are unresponsive to demands rooted in human need and democratic imperatives. Thus they will be less able to rely on symbol manipulation and the dominant ideology to secure control. For those posing the demand, the experience is revealing. It exposes dominant myths (including the myth of consensus), and it reveals the shortcomings of a seemingly equitable order. Thus, as a result of posing the demand, more and more people become aware of the obstacles and steps necessary to overcome resistance to democracy.

The most important tools available to activists are numbers and organization. The posing of structural demands is a means both of creating mass organization and of solidifying it in struggle. Mass organization holds out the possibility of coordinating the small resources available to each member. The result may be that it is "cheaper" for authorities to grant the organization's demands than to resist and suffer the penalties. A long strike called in support of structural demands may reduce a firm's share of the market permanently or force it out of business. Mass sit-ins or boycotts of public schools may be threatened to gain a measure of community control by black parents over ghetto schools.

Should structural demands be granted as a result of these sanctions, the opposition outcome has been moved that much closer. The achievement represents an incremental change in structure that results in a weakening of corporate capitalism, however imperceptible it may seem at the time. There is also an ideological and organizational result. Citizens have learned that the dominant are not invincible, that struggles may succeed. Their sense of collective power grows, just as the confidence of the corporate complex declines. Citizens are better equipped to pose further structural demands even more advanced on the road to socialism. The victory is thus not an end in itself, as it is in the accommodationist alternative, but a means to pose new demands animated by a vision of the socialist outcome that seeks to transform and overcome remaining inequalities.

Until now we have discussed the posing of structural demands and the building of opposition organization in diverse arenas. These struggles are an integral part of the movement for the socialist outcome. But if they stopped at this level, however successful, at best they would represent an advanced form of the accommodationist outcome. The additional quantum leap to structural transformation will be taken only when an effective, broad-based, mass democratic movement emerges to link citizens. This development has never happened in the American past, and the difficulties ahead should not be underestimated. For this reason, we are under no illusion that socialism in America is just around the corner.

Yet if naive optimism about the possibility of socialism in America is unwarranted, so too is despair that socialism is impossible. We have seen that increasing numbers of Americans are beginning to realize the costs of living under corporate capitalism at the very time that political-control techniques are weakening. A mass opposition movement could potentially recruit from a wide variety of groups: workers—both manual and white collar, in both the small-capital and corporate sectors—who face ever-greater difficulties concerning job security, wages, and conditions and control of the work process; blacks and Latin minorities, whose lot has not substantially improved despite accommodationist rhetoric; the poor, for whom government handouts are increasingly meager under inflationary conditions; women, who continue to be cast in demeaning subordinate roles; and students, who will be harder to coopt as corporate capitalism proves unable to generate an adequate number of challenging jobs. Rather than socialism representing a plot of elitist intellectuals to be crammed down the throats of the American people, the potential constituency for a socialist movement includes the immense majority of Americans.

This strategy of structural reform, then, is part of a revolutionary process: it is a patient step-by-step effort to build a new society. It is sensitive to the relation of particular struggles to overall changes in the structure of society. It rejects both a piecemeal view of reality and a simplistic view of structure that sees America being transformed in one fell swoop. Success will mean a democratic socialist America.

Selected Bibliography

The following bibliography indicates some of the most important work in the field. Additional works are cited in footnotes throughout the text.

Books indicated by * are available in paperback.

Chapter 1

*Shlomo Avineri, *The Social and Political Thought of Karl Marx.* Cambridge: Cambridge University Press, 1968.
A clear and influential introduction to the work of Marx that includes discussions of politics and bureaucracy.

*Richard C. Edwards, Michael Reich, and Thomas E. Weisskopf, eds., *The Capitalist System.* Englewood Cliffs, N.J.: Prentice-Hall, 1972.
A comprehensive anthology containing a broad range of essays on the structure of the capitalist system and the functioning of capitalism in the United States.

*Hans Gerth and C. Wright Mills, eds., *From Max Weber.* New York: Oxford University Press, 1958.
A representative selection of the major theoretical essays of the German sociologist Max Weber, including "Class, Status, Party," and "Politics as a Vocation."

*C. Wright Mills, *The Sociological Imagination.* New York: Oxford University Press, 1958.
A provocative critique of the social sciences that connects people's everyday lives with the social structure in which they must live

*Robert Tucker, ed., *The Marx-Engels Reader.* New York: W. W. Norton, 1972.
The best available one volume anthology of the essential writings of Marx and Engels. It also contains a useful interpretive introduction.

Chapter 2

*Robert Dahl, *Who Governs?* New Haven: Yale University Press, 1961.
A study of community power in New Haven, Connecticut, that raises important issues about the relationship between formal democracy and substantive inequalities.

*Gabriel Kolko, *Wealth and Power in America.* New York: Praeger, 1962.
Kolko analyzes the unchanging structure of income distribution in the United States in this century and the implications for American democracy.

*Carole Pateman, *Participation and Democratic Theory.* Cambridge: Cambridge University Press, 1970.
In this analysis of the role of participation in democratic theory, the author emphasizes the work of political theorist Jean Jacques Rousseau.

*Joseph Pechman, *Federal Tax Policy.* New York: W. W. Norton, 1971.
This comprehensive study explains in nontechnical terms the nature of the United States tax system and the effects of taxation on the economy. It stresses that the tax system undergirds the existing unequal distribution of income and wealth.

*Hanna Pitkin, *The Concept of Representation.* Berkeley: University of California Press, 1967.
The most important recent statement by a political theorist on the central role played by the concept of representation in constructing a critical approach to democracy.

*Joseph Schumpeter, *Capitalism, Socialism and Democracy.* New York: Harper & Row, 1962.

490   SELECTED BIBLIOGRAPHY

Economist Joseph Schumpeter defines democracy wholly in procedural terms, an approach we reject in this chapter.

Chapter 3

Richard J. Barber, *The American Corporation: Its Power, Its Money, Its Politics.* New York: E. P. Dutton & Co., 1970.
Barber reviews the functioning of the modern giant corporation.

Thomas S. Burns, *Tales of ITT: An Insider's Report.* Boston: Houghton Mifflin, 1974.
Burns, a former ITT executive, gives an informative account of ITT, one of the nation's ten largest corporations.

*John Kenneth Galbraith, *The New Industrial State.* New York: Signet Books, 1972 (revised edition).
Galbraith's controversial analysis of how corporate requirements have shaped American society and politics.

*———, *Economics and the Public Purpose.* Boston: Houghton Mifflin, 1973.
Galbraith restates his earlier argument, describes how the corporate sector co-exists with and exploits the rest of the economy, and proposes reforms to tame corporate power.

*Morton Mintz and Jerry S. Cohen, *America, Inc.: Who Owns and Operates the United States.* New York: Dell Publishing Co., 1971.
A lively polemic describing corporate power.

*James H. Weaver, ed., *Modern Political Economy: Radical and Orthodox Views on Current Issues.* Boston: Allyn and Bacon, 1973.
Weaver presents conflicting viewpoints on key issues by leading economists.

Chapter 4

Stanley Aronowitz, *False Promises.* New York: McGraw-Hill, 1973.
This study of America's working class emphasizes workers' social history, the importance of trade unions, and working class culture in an attempt to grasp the forces that shape working class consciousness.

*Robert Averitt, *The Dual Economy,* New York: W. W. Norton, 1968.
Averitt argues that American capitalism has two distinct business sectors: a dominant center economy of large capital and a periphery economy of small-capital firms.

*Robert Blauner, *Racial Oppression in America.* New York: Harper & Row, 1972.
The essays in this book develop the perspective that America's racial minorities are colonized minorities, sharing a colonization process and experience with Third World peoples. Blauner points out the differences in the experiences of the ethnic immigrants and blacks and stresses the themes of culture and institutional racism.

Harry Braverman, *Labor and Monopoly Capital.* New York: Monthly Review Press, 1974.
A major analysis both of the changing class structure of the United States and of the character of work in America. More than any other recent book, this study makes clear the bases of workers' discontents.

*Jeremy Brecher, *Strike!* San Francisco: Straight Arrow Books, 1972.
Brecher treats the neglected history of mass strikes in the United States and demonstrates that mass strikes are recurring phenomena.

*James O'Connor, *The Fiscal Crisis of the State.* New York: St. Martin's Press, 1973.

O'Connor analyzes the various sectors of American capitalism, discusses the role of government in managing the economy, and points to basic emerging contradictions in American economic and political development.

Chapter 5

*Barry Blechman *et al.*, *Setting National Priorities: The 1975 Budget.* Washington, D.C.: The Brookings Institution, 1974.
A detailed analysis of federal expenditures. One of an annual series published by Brookings analyzing the federal budget.

*G. William Domhoff, *The Higher Circles: The Governing Class in America.* New York: Vintage Books, 1971.

*———, *Who Rules America?* Englewood Cliffs, N.J.: Prentice-Hall, 1967.
In both books Domhoff describes the American elite and its wealth and power.

Morton Grodzins, *The American System.* Chicago: Rand McNally, 1966.
An influential statement of how cooperation occurs among officials at different levels of government.

*Gabriel Kolko, *The Triumph of Conservatism: A Reinterpretation of American History, 1900–1916.* New York: Quadrangle, 1974.
A classic description of how the growth of the corporate economy was made possible by government protection.

*Theodore Lowi, *The End of Liberalism: Ideology, Policy and the Crisis of Public Authority.* New York: W. W. Norton, 1969.
A critique of the American "interest group liberalism" system of logrolling.

¹Grant McConnell, *Private Power and American Democracy.* New York: Vintage Books, 1970.
A critical analysis of how American government is responsive to narrow private interests.

See also books by J. K. Galbraith in Chapter 3 bibliography and James O'Connor, *The Fiscal Crisis of the State* in Chapter 4 bibliography.

Chapter 6

*Richard J. Barnet, *Roots of War.* New York: Atheneum, 1973.
Barnet argues that the bureaucratic interests of the government lie in expanding control within the United States and abroad.

A. Ernest Fitzgerald, *The High Priests of Waste.* New York: W. W. Norton, 1972.
A fascinating account of how Fitzgerald was fired from a high Pentagon position for exposing cost overruns on the Lockhead C-5A jet transport.

*Michael T. Klare, *War Without End: American Planning for the Next Vietnam.* New York: Vintage Books, 1972.
Klare describes military planning and foreign intervention.

*Seymour Melman. *Our Depleted Society.* New York: Holt, Rinehart & Winston, 1965.

*———, *Pentagon Capitalism: The Political Economy of War.* New York: McGraw-Hill, 1970.

———, *The Permanent War Economy.* Boston: Simon and Schuster, 1974.
In these books Melman argues that the Department of Defense controls a private constituency (whose most notable members are giant military producers) favorable to military production. He traces the damaging effects on the rest of the economy.

Raymond Vernon, *Sovereignty at Bay: The Multinational Spread of U.S. Enterprises.* New York: Basic Books, 1971.
Vernon describes American corporate expansion abroad.

*David Wise, *The Politics of Lying: Government Deception, Secrecy, and Power.* New York: Random House, 1973.
Wise presents numerous examples that illustrate the validity of the book's title.

Chapter 7

*James David Barber, ed., *Choosing the President.* Englewood Cliffs, N.J.: Prentice-Hall, 1974.
Essays on various aspects of presidential selection, including procedures, strategy, symbolic aspects, and recent trends.

George Reedy, *The Twilight of the Presidency.* New York: NAL-World, 1970.
President Johnson's former press secretary describes how isolated from reality the modern president has become.

*Rexford G. Tugwell and Thomas E. Cronin, eds., *The Presidency Reappraised.* New York: Praeger, 1974.
Recent essays challenging the earlier scholarly consensus on the value of a strong president.

Aaron Wildavsky, ed., *The Presidency.* Boston: Little Brown and Co., 1969.
Essays on various aspects of the presidency.

*Carl Woodward and Robert Bernstein, *All the President's Men.* Boston: Simon and Schuster, 1973.
Fascinating account by *Washington Post* reporters of how they helped break the story of high-level involvement and cover-up of the Watergate break-in.

**The Presidential Transcripts.* (various editions, 1974.)
The spontaneous and unrehearsed Watergate drama, as seen through transcriptions of White House tape recordings of presidential conversations.

Chapter 8

*Walter Dean Burnham, *Critical Elections and the Mainsprings of American Politics.* New York: W. W. Norton, 1970.
Burnham traces the decline of the party system through analysis of turnout figures and other methods.

Angus Campbell *et al., The American Voter.* New York: Wiley, 1960.
A classic study of how partisan attachments develop.

*Timothy Crouse, *The Boys on the Bus.* New York: Ballantine Books, 1973.
Crouse gives a colorful account of political journalism, with particular attention to how the press covered the 1972 presidential campaign.

James N. Rosenau, *Citizenship Between Elections: An Inquiry into the Mobilizable American.* New York: Free Press, 1974.
Rosenau compares the characteristics of those citizens who are attentive to political issues and those who are mobilized to participate in politics.

*James Sundquist, *Dynamics of the Party System: Alignment and Realignment of Political Parties in the United States.* Washington, D.C.: The Brookings Institution, 1973.
Sundquist presents a careful review of changing party cleavages in American history.

Sidney Verba and Norman H. Nie, *Participation in America: Political Democracy and Social Equality.* New York: Harper & Row, 1972.

The authors study the linkages among socioeconomic status, political opinions, and political participation.

Chapter 9

Richard Fenno, *Congressmen in Committees.* Boston: Little Brown and Co., 1972. The author looks at House and Senate committees and analyzes the effects various factors have on committee autonomy and influence in legislative deliberations.

*André Gorz, *Socialism and Revolution.* Garden City, N.Y.: Doubleday, 1973. The title essay in this collection of the writings of a French Marxist contains a provocative analysis of the causes of the decline of legislatures in most western liberal democracies.

*Mark Green *et al., Who Runs Congress?* New York: Bantam Books, 1972. A solid muckraking book by the Ralph Nader Congress Project focuses on the themes of campaign financing, the internal control of Congress, congressional culture and norms, and relations between Congress and the executive branch.

Bertram Gross, *The Legislative Struggle.* New York: McGraw-Hill, 1953. Still the most comprehensive treatment of legislative politics available. Included is a solid discussion of the symbiotic relationship between Congress and the regulatory agencies.

*Theodore Lowi and Randall Ripley, eds., *Legislative Politics U.S.A.* Boston. Little Brown and Co., 1973. One of the best anthologies collected for students on Congress. Its essays deal with the nature of representation, external pressures on Congress, and internal determinants of congressional behavior.

Chapter 10

*Henry Abraham, *The Judicial Process.* New York: Oxford University Press, 1968. This introduction to the judicial process contains a first-rate treatment of the Supreme Court and judicial review and has much useful comparative material about European systems of justice.

*Herbert Jacob, *Justice in America.* Boston: Little Brown and Co., 1972. The best accessbile treatment of the justice system as a whole. It is direct, scholarly, and lays bare the shocking conditions under which justice is dispensed.

————, *Urban Justice.* Englewood Cliffs. N.J.: Prentice-Hall, 1973. Focusing on the roles of the police, prosecutors, and interest groups, Jacob analyzes the relationship between civil and criminal justice and urban politics.

*Richard Richardson and Kenneth Vines, *The Politics of Federal Courts.* Boston: Little Brown and Co., 1970. The authors examine the neglected topic of lower federal courts in the United States. They trace the history of the court system, review mechanisms of judicial selection, and examine patterns of decision making.

Lloyd Ohlin, ed., *Prisoners in America.* Englewood Cliffs, N.J.: Prentice-Hall, 1973. This collection of essays indicts our prisons for their degrading, dehumanizing, and criminalizing effects, and proposes programs of prison reform.

*Jerome Skolnick, *Justice Without Trial.* New York: Wiley, 1967. Based in part on his actual participation as a detective, Skolnick, a sociologist, explores the operations of a west coast police department that emphasizes the discretion policemen have on the job and the development of a police working personality.

Chapter 11

David Easton and Jack Dennis, *Children in the Political System*. New York: McGraw-Hill, 1969.
The authors offer an analysis of how children develop positive attitudes toward the political regime.

*Murray Edelman, *Politics as Symbolic Action: Mass Arousal and Quiescence*. Chicago: Markham Publishing Co., 1971.

*————, *The Symbolic Uses of Politics*. Urbana, Ill.: The University of Illinois Press, 1964.
Both books are imaginative analyses of how political symbols influence political behavior.

Richard Hamilton, *Class and Politics in the United States*. New York: Wiley, 1972.
For Hamilton, the real majority is substantially more liberal than are prevailing government policies—a result of the political influence exercised by conservative groups who control key institutions.

Joan Huber and William Form, *Income and Ideology: An Analysis of the American Political Formula*. New York: Free Press, 1974.
The authors compare attitudes toward wealth and equality of different income, racial, and ethnic groups in two cities.

V. O. Key, Jr., *Public Opinion and American Democracy*. New York: Knopf, 1961.
Key delves into the sources of political attitudes.

Marcus G. Raskin, *Being and Doing*. New York: Random House, 1971.
Raskin analyzes how American society stresses performance at the expense of fulfillment.

See also Sidney Verba and Norman H. Nie, *Participation in America: Political Democracy and Social Equality* in Chapter 8 bibliography.

Chapter 12

*David Gordon, ed., *Problems in Political Economy: An Urban Perspective*. Boston: D.C. Heath, 1971.
A collection of essays that examines the basic social problems of cities—including crime, poverty, poor education, unemployment, and inadequate housing—from a radical political economy point of view.

*Eugene Lewis, *The Urban Political System*. Hinsdale, Ill.: The Dryden Press, 1973.
Particularly useful treatments of government and the urban economy as well as the political machine and reform movements.

*Robert Lineberry and Ira Sharkansky, *Urban Politics and Public Policy*. New York: Harper & Row, 1974.
This overview is very good in its discussions of urban taxation and fiscal questions, spending priorities, and the dilemmas of metropolitanization.

*Michael Lipsky, *Protest in City Politics*. Chicago: Rand McNally, 1970.
In his examination of the rent-strike movement in New York City in the early 1960s, Lipsky asks what poor people can expect to gain from protest politics. He examines their strategies and elite counterstrategies aimed at blunting protest.

Theodore Lowi, *At the Pleasure of the Mayor*. New York: Free Press, 1964.
By exploring the changing personal and political characteristics of top appointive officers in New York City, this study of patronage and power traces the shift in the locus of political power from machine to bureaucracy.

*Sam Bass Warner, Jr., *The Urban Wilderness.* New York: Harper & Row, 1972.
A provocative, well-written history of the American city, this book contains much useful material on land-use patterns and includes a well-annotated bibliography.

Chapter 13

J. David Greenstone and Paul Peterson, *Race and Authority in Urban Politics.* New York: Russell Sage Foundation, 1973.
An analysis of Community Action programs in five cities traces the impact of local contexts on the implementation of the War on Poverty. The study illuminates the structures of race and authority that undergird much of American political life.

*Health Policy Advisory Center, *The American Health Empire.* New York: Random House, 1970.
This treatment of health politics emphasizes how health has become big business, how government helps reproduce an inegalitarian health care system, and discusses worker and client struggles.

*Peter Marris and Martin Rein, *Dilemmas of Social Reform.* Chicago: Aldine, 1973.
The authors argue that the barriers to meaningful social reform in the present political economy are enormous. Their study of Community Action programs stresses the conservatism of bureaucracy, rivalries among political and administrative jurisdictions, and the meager resources of the poor.

*Daniel Moynihan, *The Politics of a Guaranteed Income.* New York: Random House, 1973.
A lively case study of President Nixon's Family Assistance Plan. Particularly important is the discussion of the origins of the legislation and its relationship to the urban turmoil of the 1960s.

*Frances Fox Piven and Richard Cloward, *Regulating the Poor.* New York: Pantheon, 1971.
Relief giving, the authors argue, arises from the need to stem political disorder during periods of mass discontent and to enforce low-wage work during periods of economic and political stability. Welfare is thus a system for regulating the poor.

*Gilbert Steiner, *The State of Welfare,* Washington, D.C.: The Brookings Institution, 1972.
A broad survey of welfare-state programs, including public housing, food stamps, veterans' relief, and AFDC.

Chapter 14

*André Gorz. *Socialism and Revolution.* Garden City, N.Y.: Doubleday, 1973.
*———, *Strategy for Labor.* Boston: Beacon Press, 1967.
In both books Gorz sketches a Marxist analysis of the outlines of a socialist society and how to achieve it through structural reforms.

*Michael Harrington, *Socialism.* New York: Bantam Books, 1973.
Harrington gives a history of socialist thought and its application to American society.

*Staughton Lynd and Gar Alperovitz, *Strategy and Program: Two Essays Toward a New American Socialism.* Boston: Beacon Press, 1973.
Two American radicals develop a strategy and program to achieve a socialist America.

*Herbert Marcuse, *An Essay on Liberation.* Boston: Beacon Press, 1969.
A discussion of the requirements and possibilities for human liberation given modern technology.

*Barrington Moore, Jr., *Reflections on the Causes of Human Misery and Upon Certain Proposals to Eliminate Them.* Boston: Beacon Press, 1973.
A challenging study of the obstacles impeding the elimination of human misery; Moore also reviews critically but sympathetically some radical critiques of American politics and foreign policy.

*Marcus Raskin, *Notes on the Old System: To Transform American Politics.* New York: David McKay, 1974.
An analysis of how to achieve structural change in America by a leading social critic.
See also Marcus Raskin, *Being and Doing* in Chapter 11 bibliography.

index